AMERICAN MOVIES: THE FIRST THIRTY YEARS

THE STARS APPEAR

Richard Dyer MacCann

THE SCARECROW PRESS, INC.
Metuchen, New Jersey & London

in association with

IMAGE & IDEA, INC.
Iowa City, Iowa

Other Books by Richard Dyer MacCann:

Hollywood in Transition (1962)
Film and Society (1964)
Film: A Montage of Theories (1966)
The People's Films (1973)
The New Film Index (1975)
    (with Edward S. Perry)
Cinema Examined (1982)
    (with Jack C. Ellis)
The First Tycoons (1987)
The First Film Makers (1989)

In Preparation:

The Comedians
Films of the 1920s
The Eye Is Not Satisfied

Film/Video Works:

Degas: Master of Motion (1960)
How to Build a Freeway (1965)
How to Look at Freeways (1965)
Murder at Best (1981)
The Quiet Channel series (1983)
American Movies: The First 30 Years (1984)
A New York Boy Comes to Iowa (1988)

Library of Congress Cataloging-in-Publication Data

MacCann, Richard Dyer.
    The stars appear / Richard Dyer MacCann.
        p.   cm. — (American movies)
    Includes bibliographical references and index.
    ISBN 0-8108-2527-9. — ISBN 0-8108-2528-7 (pbk.) (alk. paper)
    1. Silent films — United States — History and criticism. 2. Motion
picture actors and actresses — United States — Biography. I. Title. II. Series.
PN1995.75.M32   1992
791.43'0973—dc20   91-42748

THE STARS APPEAR

Mary Pickford in *The New York Hat*

TO
Alistair Cooke
and
Edward Wagenknecht
discerning lovers
of American silent films
who captured in words
the Fairbanks and Pickford
images on the screen

•

Acknowledgments

My thanks . . . to Kevin Brownlow for reading portions of the manuscript and for his cheery letters . . . to David Culbert for reading and commenting on the Introduction . . . to Helen Lemley at Technigraphics in Iowa City for her extraordinary typesetting skills, for somehow making my software agree with her software, and for making me and my frequent changes always seem welcome . . . to Donnarae for warning me when I overwrote and standing by me when I overworked.   –R.D.M.

Acknowledgment is made of the following permissions to use material from copyrighted works:

Excerpts from "An Actor's Art," by Conrad Nagel, in *Introduction to the Photoplay*, copyright 1977 by National Film Society, reprint with commentary by John C. Tibbetts, editor, of 1929 publication by Academy of Motion Picture Arts and Sciences and the University of Southern California. Reprinted by permission of editor.

Excerpts from "Acting Style in Silent Films," by Blake Lucas, reprinted from *Magill's Survey of Cinema: Silent Films*, pages 1-11. By permission of the publisher, Salem Press, Inc. Copyright, 1982, by Frank Magill.

Extract from "Close-Ups," by Norma Talmadge, March 12, 1927, first of three articles of memoirs. Reprinted from *The Saturday Evening Post*, (c) 1927 The Curtis Publishing Co.

"Flesh and the Devil," and "Panthea," by DeWitt Bodeen; "The Great K and A Train Robbery," by Lennox Sanderson Jr.; "Manhandled," by Ronald Bowers; "Stella Maris," by Rob Edelman. Reprinted from *Magill's Survey of Cinema: Silent Films*. By permission of the publisher, Salem Press, Inc. Copyright, 1982, by Frank N. Magill.

Extract from *I Blow My Own Horn*, copyright 1957 by Jesse L. Lasky. Reprinted by permission of Pat Silver-Lasky.

Excerpts from "Theda Bara." Reprinted from *Sex Goddesses of the Silent Screen*, (c) 1973 by Norman Zierold, with permission of Contemporary Books, Inc., Chicago.

"Excuse My Dust," by Eileen Bowser, and "The Coward," by Richard Griffith. Reprinted by permission from *Film Notes*, copyright (c) 1940 The Museum of Modern Art.

Extract from "The Two-Gun Man: William S. Hart," introduction to *The Complete Films of William S. Hart: A Pictorial Record*, copyright 1980 by Diane Kaiser Koszarski. Reprinted by permission of Dover Publications.

"All-American Boy: A Note on Barthelmess"and "Make Money, Spend Passion," from *Stardom*, (1970); "Elinor Glyn and Clara Bow," from *The Celluloid Sacrifice*, reprinted as *Sex in the Movies*, (1967) all copyright (c) Conundrum Ltd. Reprinted by permission of the author.

"True Heart Susie and the Art of Lillian Gish," by James Naremore, from *Quarterly Review of Film Studies*, copyright (c) 1981 Harwood Academic Publishers GmbH.

"Lillian Gish in London, 1983," by Kevin Brownlow, in *American Film*, copyright 1984. Reprinted by permission from BPI Communications Inc.

"Mary Pickford, Douglas Fairbanks, Gloria Swanson, Rudolph Valentino," from *The Film Encyclopedia*, by Ephraim Katz. Copyright (c) by Ephraim Katz and See Hear Productions. Reprinted by permission of Harper & Row, Publishers, Inc.

Excerpts from *Sunshine and Shadow*, copyright by Mary Pickford 1955. Reprinted by permission of Buddy Rogers.

Extract from "America's Sweetheart." From *The Movies in the Age of Innocence*, by Edward Wagenknecht. Copyright (c) 1962 by the University of Oklahoma Press.

Contents

Preface

It is difficult to take seriously a view
of history which ignores personality.[*]

The sorrow of the silent era is the terrible absence of so many of the films—wantonly destroyed or merely forgotten, decayed, or lost after sound pictures began.

A number of outstanding examples have survived, thanks to devoted lovers of the silent screen—the Museum of Modern Art, the American Film Institute, private collectors, and various archives here and abroad. But we cannot say for certain how many there are or which titles are possible to see. Or how available they are in the popular form of today, the videocassette.

Nevertheless, the lack of a broad selection of films makes it even more important to try to reconstruct something of the history of that rich beginning time—to try to recapture the way it was when enterprise, talent, personalities and stories set so many models for the future.

The first thirty years of motion pictures was a major turning-point in American culture. With all its idiosyncrasies, wildness, charm, and freshness, this period still had its seriousness, conscious of being new, yet largely unsure of its goals.

And at the heart of it all were the unpredictable, hardworking, lively, beautiful people who were chosen to appear on the screen. Most of them were there, not for art, but out of dire necessity. When they learned how things worked, they set about reaping wealth from their popularity.

At least three strands of historical inquiry may be found in the following pages.

Probably foremost for professional observers of American life and of motion pictures is an interest in the various images presented on the screen by certain popular stars.

The happiest and most thought-provoking treatment of this subject is Alistair Cooke's characterization of Douglas Fairbanks' screen image—his athleticism, his flattery of the audience, his presumption that most Americans believe in heroes, and especially his implication

---

[*] This is a quotation from page 232 of Appendix A, "Author's Note About Motion Picture History," in the first volume of this series, *The First Tycoons* (1987).

xi

that all that is needed to solve the problems of this or any society is the "arrival of an average healthy man." This is a keenly perceptive comment on the American psyche.

There are other notable examples in this book of "image analysis":

Norman Zierold on Theda Bara
Diane Koszarski on William S. Hart
Alexander Walker on Richard Barthelmess
Edward Wagenknecht on Mary Pickford
Alexander Walker on Clara Bow

But if we want to understand the history of Hollywood in America, we are also drawn to the actual personal attitudes and lives of leading figures in that history, in this case the leading performers. Some memorable insights can be gleaned from autobiographical writings: Mary Pickford remembering the struggle to get started, Gloria Swanson on the tragic choice she made for career rather than home, Esther Ralston's encounter with the libidinous head of a studio, Pola Negri excited to find just the right script for Lubitsch—and for herself.

A more distant stance is offered by professional observations — Conrad Nagel on acting technique, Mae Marsh on the need to draw on more than technique, Norma Talmadge on early cinematography, James Naremore on Lillian Gish as an actress, Joe Franklin on the physical characterizations of Lon Chaney.

Life stories written by outsiders become revealing and emotionally involved when S. George Ullman remembers the last public appearances of his friend and employer Rudolph Valentino, or Harry Brundidge relates Charles Farrell's struggle for success in Hollywood, or Kevin Brownlow tells the sorry chronicle of the downturn of John Gilbert's life.

Some critics doubt the value of such "anecdotal" material, calling it "merely journalistic." But it is hardly possible to see the truth of "how it was" without some kind of richness of background, blending all kinds of human viewpoints, risking the possibility of involvement with those who were loved by audiences.

Leo Braudy, in a piece on "Film Acting" in the *Quarterly Review of Film Studies* (February 1976) has called attention to the usefulness of working with actors' lives—"ghost-written, admirer-written, and even personally written." The real need, he says, is "not to eliminate biography or gossip from our understanding of performers but to discover better ways to use such material." Thus we will not only discover attitudes toward the craft of acting and evidence of "the ways actors and studios wanted themselves to be perceived by their audiences." There is more to be gained:

> Movie stars are at once the highest, or at least most
> visible, assertion of individuality in a mass society and
> the potential locus for the greatest problems of that
> individuality. The sense of completion, the search for
> a personal model, that is so often satisfied by movie
> stars is the extension and distorted mirror of the psychic
> completion we seek for ourselves.

Many Americans looked on early screen stars as their friends. They were men and women who occupied places not only of pleasure but of honor in the American democratic scheme of things. They were heroes and heroines in varying degrees, objects of devotion and approval. At the same time they were broadly representative of the people who were watching them.

In the 1920s, certainly, such personalities seemed to many people more alive and genuine and worthy of emulation than the Presidential leaders of that decade. Acquaintance with these famous and influential people is essential for the student of American history and culture. It would be a curious foreshortening of American civilization to study only the intellectual or political or literary events of the time and leave out the movie stars.

A third strand of historical importance offered here, and emphasized throughout the series of volumes, is the proposition that Hollywood and its successor image industries became the new frontier of the 20th century. Here fame and fortune could be successfully sought, just as they were in the cities and plains beyond the mountain ranges in the 19th century. Success was individual, often lucky, usually the result of hard work.

The American dream at the very least was some sort of get-rich prospect, whether "quick" or steady. It assumed a continent of vast resources and the freedom to exploit them. Those who professed to follow the dream rarely took time to think of it as some political or economic theory but rather as a way of life for the strong and healthy, the natural operation of an individualist ethic.

Such early motion picture entrepreneurs as Adolph Zukor, Marcus Loew, and William Fox were beginning to be conscious imitators of John D. Rockefeller and Andrew Carnegie. The Hamiltonian model of American business enterprise was well adapted for Hollywood in the 1920s. The competitive atmosphere carried over to the arts and crafts, delaying the arrival of unions, collective bargaining, and other late paraphernalia of capitalist societies. The prevailing attitude was one of getting ahead on an individual basis, promoting self and salary as opportunity and advantage allowed.

The implications are (1) that these unconscious pioneers, seeking the new frontier of the Hollywood studios, brought with them conscious and intense demands for financial success and (2) that having been inducted into the routines of the new world of images, those expectations and experiences of material success were also reflected in many of the movie stories they made about America.

This last inference is one that would benefit from further research. We may be able to say easily enough that the pattern of privation and absence of at least one parent fits all the leading cases–Lillian Gish, Mary Pickford, Douglas Fairbanks, Gloria Swanson, Rudolph Valentino–plus an extraordinary number of others: Miriam Cooper, Blanche Sweet, Norma and Constance Talmadge, Marguerite Clark, Mary Miles Minter, Betty Compson, Clara Bow, Charles Ray, Antonio Moreno, John Gilbert, Ronald Colman, and so on. But what kinds of economic struggles and emotional crises may have occurred in a number of their films because of these personal memories–and whether these stars actually had a hand in choosing any of these stories–these are auteur-oriented problems of causation suited for exploration by historians in some future study of a thousand films. Dependable documentation will be rare, and we may still be left with common-sense guesses. On the other hand, there may be enough knowledge about the pictures on American themes to tell a coherent story.

The documents used here are mostly self-told stories (or stories "as told to" interviewers). There are no adequate dollar figures assignable to the poverty and privation of the job seekers, and there is little documentation for their salaried wealth later on. Nevertheless, memoirs are primary sources, more coherent than trade papers or payrolls. And *Photoplay* interviews can be a lot more informative about essential humanistic factors than corporate reports. Therefore one of the modest intentions of this book is to put together some cumulative sense of what it was like to be an aspiring actor in the silent era, to report the drives of individualism which seemed to result in fame and fortune.

Success was not rationed out only to a few. It was given to many. Where there had been nothing before, there grew up a new industry. Where there had been no dreams at all of picture-making, there began to appear a lot of fast learners: photographers, actors, writers, directors, editors, technicians, producers, and business executives.

The American dream of distributing wealth to be gained from open land became a fact of life in the 19th century. In the 20th century the dream of distributing wealth from rolls of pictures on celluloid was becoming a new fact of life with unpredictable cultural consequences.

In years to come, the emphasis on self-help, on getting ahead, would be tempered by a sense of community. In the 1930s especially, depression and war would begin to pull Hollywood into the 20th century in spite of the industry's natural commitment to 19th century frontier values. There began to be a new concern for the many people in the American scheme of things who didn't "make it." But for the first thirty years of the American motion picture industry, the grand prospect of arrival at the top with fame and fortune in hand was practical and pleasing. It was not a myth. It was happening all the time.

As Herbert Howe wrote in a *Photoplay* article called "Returning to Hollywood," in May of 1925:

> Money unquestionably is the greatest incentive in the world.
> That incentive no longer grips Chaplin, Fairbanks, Miss
> Pickford, and the Talmadges. They are all multi-millionaires.

Two lesser themes are hinted at in the author's introductions but inadequately developed.

One is that the 1920s preeminently called upon women as star performers. This is hard to quantify, although there do appear on the surface to be more of them in the starring ranks.   William K. Everson, in a provocative and persuasive short chapter, "The Mid 1920s: The New Dominance of the Female Star" (*American Silent Film,* 1978) suggests that the best stories, the strongest roles, and the dominant strength within the stories belonged to female stars, especially in those stories having contemporary themes.

This tendency might be said to have begun earlier than the 1920s with D.W. Griffith's preference for women actors and women's stories and his early promotion of the talents of the Gish sisters. It surely continued with the industry preeminence of Mary Pickford, and her appearance in a very large number of extremely popular films. It also drew strength from the many cases described in this book of real life necessity: the absent father, the pressures of poverty and privation, the nurturing mother. On the other hand there was the openness of the acting profession at the turn of the century and beyond, compared with the limited nature of other opportunities for women: theater and film, unlike the old Greek tradition, required women in women's roles, providing interesting challenges and pay according to popular response. Of course the temper of the postwar period loosened the definitions of proper behavior, attitudes toward marriage, and personality. As a natural result, such themes turned up in the movies and provided strong situations for women performers.

Certain landmark films that placed women at the center of the story tend to support Everson's thesis— *Way Down East, Miss Lulu Bett, Dancing Mothers, The Wind, A Woman of Paris, The Marriage Circle, Flesh and the Devil.*

He further insists that "the male exotics were relatively few," (Fairbanks, Valentino, Gilbert) and that they rarely played Americans. "Dependability, linked with a certain dullness, were the most typical qualities in the male heroes of the twenties" (Milton Sills, Thomas Meighan, Lewis Stone, Conrad Nagel). "Weakness" of roles and individual players is certainly impossible to quantify. Perhaps it has its emblematic real life situation in the domination of Valentino by his wife Natacha Rambova, and the resulting unfortunate casting of the youth made famous as the "sheik" in the roles of the foppish *Monsieur Beaucaire* and the bejewelled *Young Rajah.* Everson also declares that Gloria Swanson "was always stronger than her men."

A second lesser theme deserves further working out by future commentators on the silent screen. In the introduction to the chapter on "Mary and Doug," the author has suggested that one of the appeals—perhaps the basic appeal—of both Pickford and Fairbanks was the constant tendency to represent and recapture the joys of childhood. The lively little girl and the athletic schoolboy, both of them rescuing us from our petty conservatisms and Victorian parenting, were to a very great extent filling the screen experience with childlike and adolescent themes. They made audiences feel superior and secure, perhaps, and entertained them in an atmosphere, however fantasized, which was consistent, funny, and acceptable as American.

It would be more problematic to propose within the movies of Gloria Swanson and Rudolph Valentino a predominance of childlike and adolescent themes. This nevertheless could be the basis for a fruitful argument. Such an analysis might include reference to the tendency of each of them to undertake occasional physical stunts, resulting in light comedy situations. Of course the game of "dressing up" is apparent in many of their films.

The influence upon all these dramatic performers of the presence of Charlie Chaplin should not be forgotten. (In *Manhandled* Gloria does an imitation of him. Mary is often involved in slapstick incidents.) Together with Buster Keaton, who is forever the adolescent seeking to prove himself and gain the hand of the uncommitted young lady, and Harold Lloyd, who is the get-ahead adolescent danger comedian *par excellence,* Chaplin led the comics of the 1920s in providing plots in which poor young characters make their way in spite of odds—or fail. When we bring in the baby-talk of Langdon,

Laurel, and Hardy, the picture is complete. Silent comedy is a world of children.

If the silent era was a time in which women increasingly got the best parts in high drama, perhaps the teens and twenties also provided roles in comedy-dramas for both women and men that were exhilarating adventures into the realm of childhood and young romance.

There has been up to now no book quite like this. The author hopes it may carry for the reader a kind of submersion in the life and work of the time—a time of spontaneity, originality, and excitement—plus an acquaintance with many memorable people and a few of their best films. It is offered in the special faith that a future generation of film students will turn to history to discover that movies were not made by unseen impersonal forces.

According to Adela Rogers St. Johns (*Love, Laughter, and Tears*, 1978) Bebe Daniels was the "most all-around popular girl who has ever been in Hollywood." One day she was driving to San Diego in a convertible roadster with her mother and Jack Dempsey, the heavyweight boxing champion. She was arrested in Orange County for speeding.

When it became known that she was to spend ten days in jail, Abe Lyman's orchestra left the Cocoanut Grove and went to Santa Ana to serenade her. Dempsey took up residence in a hotel nearby to make sure she was properly treated. The judge welcomed her with a bouquet of flowers. Restaurants vied to provide her with meals. Furniture companies decorated her cell. So many fans and friends and suitors came by that the jailer kept a guest book and took visiting cards.

It may be true that Bebe asked him to tell certain visitors: I'm out.

DeWitt Bodeen reports (*From Hollywood*, 1976) that Paramount, vexed with the Arbuckle scandal, and finding that the newspapers and fan magazines considered this a lively and innocent escapade, made a 1921 movie based upon it called *The Speed Girl*.

To the world of Hollywood, and the wider world beyond, this was an episode of high comedy and delight. Of course it says something about stars and about America. But what exactly it says is hard to explain rationally. It is doubtful that it can be fitted into any overall theory of motion picture history. It is simply one of the best of all stories that can be told about Hollywood.

Movie star as girl next door:
James Kirkwood, actor-director,
and Mary Miles Minter, silent film actress

Introduction

Acting Out the American Dream

From childhood I've had the fear of poverty.
— Betty Compson.[1]

Insecurity was a great gift. — Lillian Gish.[2]

The movies are the last great Klondike.
— Gary Cooper.[3]

The young American may often be endowed with energy, enthusiasm, persistence, and hope, but with no tangible assets to offer — no wealth, no education, no skills. Where can such a willing worker turn for a way to make a living, a way to get ahead?

In the 19th century, the land was still new. Frontier towns and farms offered a future to all who were willing to bend their backs and invest their lives. Strong or weak, easygoing or ambitious, Americans and immigrants came west. In an era notable for individual freedom, many men and women earned wealth and power on the land. Then, as the century waned, factories drew millions of isolated souls, from farms and from overseas, into a dark inhuman industrial life which threatened to blot out the American dream for all but the privileged and propertied few.

1 DeWitt Bodeen, "Betty Compson," *From Hollywood* (1976), p. 243.
2 Lillian Gish, *The Movies, Mr. Griffith, and Me* (1969), p. 6.
3 Harry T. Brundidge, "Gary Cooper," *Twinkle, Twinkle, Movie Star!* (1930), p. 22.

In the 20th century another frontier drew men and women westward. The bright new world of movies promised fame and fortune to anyone with good looks and natural talents — anyone with that mysterious combination of simplicity and superior charm that wins public popularity. Hollywood seemed to ask no special skills. Personality alone might be enough.

Such auguries were somewhat misleading. Here, as on the farm, long hours of willing labor had a lot to do with getting ahead. Yet there was always the possibility of luck: the great hope of sudden success never wavered. This was because overnight fame did happen, again and again. Of course it happened sometimes for women who were pliant and willing to yield to extra-curricular activities — also known as the "casting couch." But it also happened, most often, to young men and women who burned with ambition, worked to learn the ropes, and persisted beyond all reason in demanding a chance to show their talent — seeking a foothold, a step upward, a still better role, a break into stardom.

The successful ones — the ones who became rich and famous — were winners by competition, as must be the case in any unregulated capitalist enterprise. They were prominent examples of get-ahead individualism in the land of the free, the home of the brave.

For those who were the long-lasting top stars of the American silent drama — Lillian Gish, Mary Pickford, Douglas Fairbanks, Gloria Swanson, Rudolph Valentino — individual paths to fame varied, and the images they offered on the screen were different. But these five performers were very much alike in their middle-class backgrounds, their willingness to work, their determination to get ahead, their acceptance of 19th century values in the 20th century.

In every case, severe economic hardships made careers problematic and urgent. In every case the father either died or abandoned his wife while the future star was young, leaving the mother as head of the family. Although artistry became important to all five, the primary drive to succeed in movies was not self-expression. It was necessity.

At the age of five, Lillian Gish became an important breadwinner in her family. Her father, unsatisfied and unsuccessful as the owner of a candy store, had left the family in Baltimore and gone to New York. Her mother tried to join him there, but found herself alone, making a poor living as demonstrator in a department store. She then turned to the theater, where she made $15 a week. Lillian was entrusted to an actress friend in a touring company that needed a child performer. She was paid $10 a week. Seven of those dollars went to her mother.

In her autobiography, Lillian Gish recalls some of the rigors of life on the road. There was often a long wait for the train after a one-night performance. In the depot, she would lie down on men's overcoats placed for her on top of the telegraph desk, or she might slip under the arm rests (two feet apart) on a waiting room bench. When she got too big for that, she bedded down on newspapers on the floor.[4]

Did waiting, riding, sleeping in the dreary depot or dusty coach help actors stand up to both the long runs and the failures? Would they shrug off more easily in coming years the rigors of location work for motion pictures? It might be so. At any rate the healthy, spunky, ambitious ones stuck it out. Such challenges, plus something in her own indomitable make-up, helped Lillian Gish to be, in the words of Molly Haskell, "delicate as a figurine but durable as an ox."[5]

The Gish fame was parallel to that of D.W. Griffith. From 1912, when Mary Pickford introduced her to Griffith, till 1921, when she left him to go on her own, her salary increased and became (in her words) "quite high." She then contracted with Inspiration Pictures for $1250 a week and a percentage of profits, and when she moved to Metro-Goldwyn-Mayer in 1925 was offered $800,000 for two years and six pictures.[6] She was still acting in theater and films up to 1988, when she was in her 90s.

Mary Pickford, too, never forgot the years of trying to sleep on the day-coaches, which "always smelled of coal dust." For a long time afterward she "couldn't bear the color crimson" which reminded her of the heavy red upholstery in the trains. The miseries of 3:00 a.m. calls to reach the next small town theater were part of what drove her to say: "I've got to make good by the time I'm twenty."[7]

4 Gish, pp. 7, 15.
5 Molly Haskell, *From Reverence to Rape: The Treatment of Women in the Movies* 1974, p. 76.
6 Bosley Crowther gives this figure in his history of M-G-M, *The Lion's Share* (1957), p. 107. Gish remembers it in her autobiography as "I believe, a million dollars," p. 274.
7 Mary Pickford, *Sunshine and Shadow* (1955), pp. 93, 157.

Her father, a steamship purser, had been fatally injured in an accident on deck. Her mother, a widow in Toronto with three children, a house, and no prospects, had rented out a room to a mature couple. The man was a stage manager, and Mrs. Smith allowed him to hire five-year-old Gladys to speak a few lines in a play. From then on the little family worked in the theater. "Nineteen weeks of one-night stands for *The Fatal Wedding*," she recalled, "never sleeping twice in the same bed!"

One day when the family fortunes were low, her mother asked her to try for a job in the lowly "flickers." Gladys — who had now been named Mary Pickford by the theatrical producer, David Belasco — was depressed by the thought, but was willing to try. She checked in at Biograph. D.W. Griffith found her bright-eyed, feisty, and somewhat grasping. When he offered her five dollars a day, she asked for twice that, and got it. Griffith took the company to California the following winter. Brother Jack went along for five dollars a day "falling off horses and out of windows as a double." With that, and her forty dollars a week and fourteen for expenses, they brought home to New York "an unbelievable hoard of $1200." They presented it to Mother in $50 bills. She thought it was stage money.

This was "the beginning of affluence for the Pickford family."[8] After a while Mary left Griffith for Laemmle, then went back to Griffith, then made 34 feature films for Adolph Zukor and Famous Players-Lasky, starting at $500 a week. By 1916 (age 23) she was making $10,000 a week plus bonuses, which totaled over a million for two years' work. The little girl with the golden curls had become "America's Sweetheart." She was also "the industry's most valuable asset."[9]

The Pickford millions have often been paralleled with Chaplin's. Their competitive ratings were well known in the trade. But the rise to fame of Douglas Fairbanks was exhilarating in its own way and perhaps more self-aware as a success story. In fact, Mary recalled years later that Douglas, when he "doodled" on a scratch pad at the phone, would often write the word "SUCCESS" over and over again.[10]

Douglas' life began in relative security, but like Lillian and Mary, at the age of five he was abruptly deprived of it. His father,

8   Pickford, p. 130.
9   Benjamin Hampton, *A History of the Movies* (1931), p. 190.
10   Pickford, p. 223.

a lawyer and mining speculator in Denver, took off for the east, leaving the mother and three sons. Like Mary Pickford's mother, she elected to let out rooms. And it was the acting successes of young Douglas in Denver that induced her to try a trip to New York with him in 1899.

Going east worked out well in the long run, but the first few years were discouraging. By 1910,Fairbanks was a popular star in highly athletic roles in Broadway comedies. In 1915 Harry Aitken tempted him with an offer to make movies for his new Triangle corporation. Hesitating, Fairbanks wondered if he might be supervised by D.W. Griffith. This was agreed to, and the offer increased to $2000 a week for ten weeks.[11] Before long, he chose to be on his own in Hollywood. With his brother Robert's help, and at Mary Pickford's suggestion, he moved from comedies to costume pictures. The final leap was co-ownership, with Mary, Charlie Chaplin, and D.W. Griffith, of United Artists Corporation.

Success was no myth for Douglas Fairbanks. By the time he chose to play *Robin Hood,* (1922) he could snap his fingers and have built for him the biggest set since *Intolerance.* The set was no myth and neither were the millions that came in at the boxoffice. Therefore when he wrote several "self-help" books for his fans, he was perfectly serious in encouraging his readers to "run and jump and laugh" and expect every obstacle to fall before them.

Gloria Swanson also began with some middle class advantages. Her father was a captain in the army, and she was treated to tours of duty in Key West and Puerto Rico. But when he was transferred to Manila, her mother did not go along: she went only as far as Los Angeles. Gloria, who had heard her parents "argue over money for years," was informed that the marriage was at an end: "Your father's biggest problem is that he can't face problems." At fifteen, Gloria had to go to work.

She had paid a visit with her Aunt Inga to the Essanay movie studios while she was living in Chicago. They immediately asked her to be in some scenes and when she left for the coast, they gave her a letter of introduction to Mack Sennett. He put her in comedies, a notch above the usual slapstick. A chance encounter with Jack Conway led to six pictures at Triangle and after that six more with Cecil B. DeMille.[12]

11 Booton Herndon, *Mary Pickford and Douglas Fairbanks* (1977), p. 63.
12 Gloria Swanson, *Swanson on Swanson,* (1980), pp. 45, 47, 83, 98.

Swanson discovered that her pictures were being "held over" for additional weeks in the theaters. She was not a natural bargainer, like Pickford, but her second husband — and in fact, DeMille himself — urged her to begin making demands at Famous Players. By 1925 she was earning $7000 a week.[13] Encouraged by her employers to appear in public always at the very height of fashion, she saw to it that her clothing bills were news in the fan magazines. It was said she might not be the first woman to make a million in Hollywood, but she was the first to spend it.

Rudolph Valentino was also a willing spender. He had little to start with. His father was a small-town veterinarian in southern Italy who had once quit the army to join the circus. The boy was eleven years old when his father died. He failed military school, finished a course in agriculture, then went off to Paris, losing most of his allowance at gaming tables. Back home, he faced a family conference: his uncle and widowed mother would settle $4000 on him if he would go to America.

He arrived in December 1913. Again he spent or gambled most of his money with casual acquaintances. He found a job as a landscape gardener, but an episode with a motorcycle put him out on the street. By his own account, his situation grew more and more desperate. Although he looked for work every day, he found himself sleeping in closets and in Central Park. Finally a headwaiter he had tipped in the past offered to hire him as dancer-escort for wealthy women.[14]

One of his friends had taught him to tango, and that was literally the key to his future. He became a member of a dance team in night clubs at $50 a week, then a starving bit player in San Francisco theater and Hollywood films. Moving up to speaking roles as villains, he was noticed by June Mathis and cast as Julio in *The Four Horsemen of the Apocalypse* (1921). This paid him $350 a week and led to a contract at Famous Players-Lasky which soon reached $1000. After a break with the studio during 1923, when he toured the country as a dancer with his wife Natacha

---

13 Swanson. p. 159.
14 Rudolph Valentino, "My Life Story," Chapter II, *Photoplay*, March 1923, p. 112. Ghost-written by Herbert Howe, staff writer for the magazine, during the time Valentino was on suspension at Famous Players, these remarkable and largely believable memoirs ran for three issues, February through April. Note that Valentino had with him a hundred times as much as Adolph Zukor had in 1888.

Rambova, he came back for a salary of $7500. His last two pictures before his sudden death were with United Artists at $10,000.

Lillian Gish	at age 5	father abandoned family
Mary Pickford	at age 5	father killed in accident
Douglas Fairbanks	at age 5	father abandoned family
Gloria Swanson	at age 15	father divorced
Rudolph Valentino	at age 11	father died

In later years, these five stars of the silent film each had special confirmation of their extraordinary popular and financial success by the unmistakable evidence of crowd response.

In 1920, Mary Pickford and Douglas Fairbanks chose as their honeymoon a trip to Europe, and they found that they were virtual prisoners in their London hotel because of the massing of their fans in the streets.

In 1925, when Gloria Swanson came back from Paris to New York and Los Angeles for premiere showings of her newest film, she discovered that thousands of other people wanted to see her arrive.

When Rudolph Valentino made his last trip to Chicago and New York in 1926 to publicize what was to be his final movie, he was greeted in both places by an enormous surge of crowd adoration.

In 1926, after completing *The Scarlet Letter* at M-G-M, Lillian Gish took the five-day train trip across the country to go to London to be with her mother.

> The newspapers carried the story of Mother's illness and my journey to her side. Wherever the train stopped, hundreds of people were waiting on the platform. At first I wondered why they were there, and the conductor told us they had all come to see me and express their sympathy and their prayers for her recovery...Never before or since have I felt such warmth from so many.[15]

For Lillian Gish, whose life was a miracle of discipline and dedication, it was possible to say, "insecurity was a great gift," and in her autobiography even thank her father for leaving her with that grim inheritance. She saw it as a lesson: "You learn to

15 Gish, p. 287.

do for yourself and not to count on the other fellow to do it for you."[16]

There has never been anyone in American films quite like Lillian Gish. Yet a surprising number of young women in the early history of Hollywood were able to meet challenges in the same spirit — coming from the lowest levels of income, often lacking one or both parents, yet seeking and finding the success they longed for.

Miriam Cooper was one of five children in the first five years of her mother's marriage. Thereupon her father left for Europe and didn't come back. Grandmother Cooper helped out till she died, but then the little family had to move to the tenements of "Little Italy" where the dreamy dark-haired future movie star was scared and miserable. Miriam echoed Lillian Gish's thought in her autobiography. "I loved Papa and wished he had stayed. But then, if he had, I doubt if I would have been desperate enough to even think of going into pictures."

One day Cooper walked into the Biograph building at 11 East 14th. She did extra work for Griffith right away, went with the Kalem company to Florida for the winter, then rejoined Biograph for a trip to California. She played — at $65 a week — important roles in both *The Birth of a Nation* and *Intolerance* . "None of us had fathers," she noted, "I learned later that this was the kind of girl Mr. Griffith liked — young, beautiful, and supporting her mother."[17]

Blanche Sweet, one of the earliest Griffith performers, was on stage from the age of 18 months. Her mother, deserted by her husband, had died at the age of nineteen; she had been a professional dancer. "Little Blanche" thereafter was dependent on her grandmother, who found jobs for the child in the theater thanks to her daughter's friends. Among her surviving Griffith films are the two-reel *The Lonedale Operator* and the four-reel *Judith of Bethulia*, (1914).

For Famous-Players-Lasky, Sweet had the advantage of being directed in three pictures apiece by William C. deMille and Marshall Neilan, but she told DeWitt Bodeen, "I seem to have always been fighting to make pictures I never got to do."[18] After 1930, she worked in radio and theater, all the way to the 1980s.

16 Gish, p. 6.
17 Miriam Cooper, *Dark Lady of the Silents*, (1973), pp. 14, 33.
18 Bodeen, "Blanche Sweet," *More From Hollywood*, pp. 239, 249.

The three Talmadge sisters had one of the more indomitable mothers in Hollywood history. Faced with the unexpected unemployment and repeated disappearances of her handsome spouse, "Peg" Talmadge began a career of taking in laundry, teaching painting to housewives, renting out the hall bedroom, and selling cosmetics door-to-door. Convinced in due course of the saleability of the inherited beauty offered by her teen-age daughters, she worked her way into the management structure of the Vitagraph company, which was only blocks away in Brooklyn, and at 13 Norma was going to work instead of to school. Seven years later, Norma's marriage (1917-1926) to Joseph Schenck , who gave up his association in the theater business with Marcus Loew in order to manage her pictures, assured her of the "trust fund" that Mama Talmadge had long had in mind. When Norma and Constance retired from the screen in 1929-30 they were so independent that hardly anyone knew how many millions they were worth.[19]

Annual *Exhibitors Herald* Boxoffice Poll

1915	Mary Pickford	William S. Hart
1916	Mary Pickford	William S. Hart
1917	Anita Stewart	Douglas Fairbanks
1918	Mary Pickford	Douglas Fairbanks
1919	Mary Pickford	Wallace Reid
1920	Marguerite Clark	Wallace Reid
1921	Mary Pickford	Douglas Fairbanks
1922	Mary Pickford	Douglas Fairbanks
1923	Norma Talmadge	Thomas Meighan
1924	Norma Talmadge	Rudolph Valentino
1925	Norma Talmadge	Rudolph Valentino
1926	Colleen Moore	Tom Mix
1927	Colleen Moore	Tom Mix
1928	Clara Bow	Lon Chaney
1929	Clara Bow	Lon Chaney

[As judged by 2500 theater owners, these were the female and male motion picture stars which brought in the most money each year.]

The men who reached stardom in the silent era do not appear to have been subject to privations in early life so frequently as the

19 Anita Loos, *The Talmadge Girls,* (1978), p. 12, 18-20.

women. We know less about their lives since they did not —
except for the comedians — write autobiographies, nor were they
so likely to be written about by columnists or fan magazines. We
can only assume that they were not so often lacking in parental
guidance or financial support as the women. Nor were they so
restricted to theater and film as main opportunities to make a living. In general, entry into movies was easier for men, once they
decided on it, and it would seem that they did not strive so hard
or rise so high in public favor. There were in fact fewer "romantic
leads" among men available for casting in any given year: the
decade of the 1920s was notable for women stars.

Valentino seemed to have more difficulty than most in reaching stardom, but once he was accepted by the public, the way
was easily open for other "Latin lovers" — Ramon Novarro, Gilbert Roland, Antonio Moreno. Even William S. Hart, though
somewhat deprived in early life (his father was a janitor and traveling laborer), managed to achieve Shakespearean roles at 19 in
New York and didn't get around to asking his friend Tom Ince
for movie work until he was 44. Charles Ray was 21 when his father, a railroad man, died: he got money for dramatic school from
an older sister and turned up at Inceville just in time to become
accepted there in 1912, starring in *The Coward* in 1915. William
Powell got his loan for the American Academy of Dramatic Arts
from a wealthy aunt, and after some "starvation" times, began to
get the smooth villain roles that set him up for a later career in
sound comedies.

Thomas Meighan, born in 1879, was already a mature stage
performer when he moved easily into films in 1913 as a popular
leading character. Wallace Reid had little difficulty catching onto
the motion picture business: his father was a successful playwright and a scenario writer for the Selig company, and the son
played the game of work-up there until 1910 as actor, writer, and
director. Tom Mix, a school dropout and son of a poor lumberman, was "making it" as a rider in wild west shows when the
Selig company came around and asked him to be in the movies
— a career that lasted from 1910 to 1934.[20]

Robert Harron was a clerk at Biograph when Griffith tapped
him for a series of young romantic leading roles. Richard

20 Bodeen, "Charles Ray," *More From Hollywood*, pp. 213-235. Also
Brundidge, "William Powell," p. 241. Bodeen, "Wallace Reid," *From
Hollywood*, pp. 93-115. See Appendix A for more life stories.

Barthelmess was about to embark on the study of business administration when Nazimova, a friend of his mother's, requested his services for a play; soon after he became D.W. Griffith's most notable male star.

Even if the men had less trouble finding work and getting ahead than the women, they often — in the showbusiness tradition — found it hard going at first. It was not unusual for them to have to go through a purgatory of delay and desperation before fortune smiled on them.

Antonio Moreno was born in Spain. His father died soon after he was born, and he worked nights in a bakery while going to school. In his teen years, he was a construction worker. Coming to New York, he worked in a factory, read gas meters, became attracted to the theater, and in 1912 discovered that he "photographed well." He had many leading roles at Mutual, Vitagraph, Paramount, and M-G-M. Despite his accent he worked in film for 44 years and appeared opposite most of the top stars of the silent era.[21]

Ronald Colman was at one time the victim of studio publicity claiming he was a scholarly chap with noble British parentage. His father actually was an obscure shopkeeper who died when he was sixteen. He got a job as an accountant with a shipping company and worked up in five years to $12 a week. Wounded in World War I, he tried showbusiness, where men were scarce, and with a small loan came to New York. There he was hungry more than once until 1922, when he began a long career as Hollywood's favorite upper-class "man of distinction."[22]

Gary Cooper was the son of a Montana state supreme court judge who also owned a ranch, and he had the advantage of some education in England and at Grinnell College. But hard times hit the cattle ranch and he went home to help out. Unsuccessful as a newspaper cartoonist, he determined to find two old Montana friends now working as extras in the movies. He had his months of trial on his own in Los Angeles in 1925, trying to sell advertising space and then portrait photography door to door. He later told interviewers he got down to "one lone dime," but he finally found his friends and they got him a job riding a

21 Bodeen, "Antonio Moreno," More From Hollywood, (1977) pp. 150, 152
22 Brundidge, "Ronald Colman," pp. 169-75.

horse. He was on his way to becoming one of the ideal images of Americanism on the screen.[23]

Of course it was not necessary to be poor in order to find a place on the silver screen. There were a number of stars who came from backgrounds of comfort or wealth. Established stage families like the Costellos and the Barrymores were attracted by the bigger, steadier salaries, and anybody who broke into the star ranks on Broadway was likely to be enticed into the movies at different times by Adolph Zukor, Harry Aitken, and Samuel Goldwyn. Yet the upper class types didn't seem to stay on the screen very long, and this was only partly because stage performers found it hard to adapt to motion picture technique.

Elsie Ferguson, whose father was a prominent New York lawyer, joined the chorus of *The Belle of New York* "more through childlike curiosity than anything else," and by 1916 she was playing Portia. Zukor, because she was a famous stage star, offered her $5000 a week for 18 pictures. She became known as "the aristocrat of the screen."[24]

Pauline Frederick's father was a railroad conductor. He disapproved of her singing in a vaudeville act "on a dare," and eventually disowned her. Meanwhile, her mother divorced him, took Pauline to New York, and before long, in the legendary way, she was replacing the star in what became a popular musical. By 1915, she got an offer from Zukor ($2000 rising to $4000 in two years) and later, while working for Goldwyn, became famous as an interpreter of *Madame X.*[25]

Zukor hoped these and other "Famous Players in Famous Plays" would draw admiring patrons. But all the time Mary Pickford and other less professional players were drawing much bigger audiences. Elsie Ferguson went back to the theater in the mid-twenties. Dorothy Dalton and Alice Brady held $5000 contracts, too expensive by 1923, and Brady was asked to work off her salary in the less costly environment of a stage play.[26]

For every Elsie Ferguson or Dolores Costello or Geraldine Farrar there were many more like Mae Marsh, whose father "died in the San Francisco earthquake, leaving her mother with six chil-

23 Larry Swindell, *The Last Hero: A Biography of Gary Cooper* (1980) pp. 51-60.
24 Bodeen, "Elsie Ferguson," *More From Hollywood,* pp. 14-23.
25 Bodeen, "Pauline Frederick," *More From Hollywood,* pp. 28-40.
26 "What Do They Earn Today?" *Photoplay,* September 1923, p. 44.

dren,"[27] Marguerite Clark, an orphan guided by her older sister into showbusiness, Corinne Griffith, whose father "suffered severe business reverses" so that she had to "get out and earn a living,"[28] and Norma Shearer, whose father lost all he had and "the family home was sold." These all became first rank popular stars, Marsh appearing on screen from 1911 to 1925, Clark from 1914 to 1921,Griffith from 1916 to 1932, Shearer from 1920 to 1942.

Norma Shearer is a marginal case, to be sure. She retained her inbred stylishness through all the years of bit parts and modeling until she was noticed, hired, and eventually married by Irving Thalberg, vice president of M-G-M. Still, her emphatic echo of Lillian Gish, delivered to an interviewer, ran like this: "A lack of money, an absolute need of it, is, in my opinion, a great advantage with which to start life."[29]

The moral seems to be that starting at the top was not perceived by audiences as the American way. Those who came from poor beginnings were far more likely to be beloved of the public. The stories of the lives of stars — and their struggles to get ahead — were well known to their fans. To some extent the fans themselves were involved in those struggles, working for their favorites in fan clubs, bombarding the movie magazines with questions, proposing appropriate roles. The stars that moved up in the boxoffice returns — the ones that got mobbed in personal appearances — were the ones who had started poor and risen to fame and fortune without forgetting their origins. Putting on airs was not the way to popularity. Participating in this democratic interplay was part of the understood function of fan magazines and columnists: they reminded the audience of the commonplace backgrounds of their stars and thus made them feel a close common bond with them.

American public preference is unpredictable, variable, and wide-ranging, to be sure. The popular nude athleticism (1914 to 1924) of a swimmer like Annette Kellerman contrasts with the love many people felt for the ethereal Lillian Gish. The terrifying Theda Bara vampire phenomenon had little to do with the acceptance of the gracious opera singer, Geraldine Farrar. John Barry-

27 Miriam Cooper, p. 48.
28 Hal C. Herman, "Corinne Griffith," *How I Broke Into the Movies* (1928) p. 77.
29 Brundidge, "Norma Shearer," pp. 236, 237.

more was accepted as a famous figure just as Charles Ray was accepted as a "country boy" type.

But it is probably fair to say that the top stars of the American screen have not been, by and large, vamps, athletes, veterans of Broadway, or rich dilettantes who broke into films for a lark. Craig Biddle, Jr., of the wealthy Philadelphia Biddles, came out to Hollywood in 1923 to try to break in. All he managed to do was to sell a brief by-line article in *Photoplay* about how hard it was to be an extra.[30] Even Marion Davies, imposed upon M-G-M and the public by her rich godfather, William Randolph Hearst, was understood not to be any kind of a princess, real or fake, but rather a humble girl plucked from the chorus line and presented with an easy chance to succeed.

Americans don't make their screen friends into elevated beings — into "royalty." This is an easy conceit, a shrugging theory held against American fans by some European critics. The claim of such outsiders is that the audience in the United States is no different from European peasants, needing to give loyalty to somebody beyond their reach — to royalty made up of movie stars. But the American people have never bowed and scraped to anybody since 1776. They were naturally fascinated for a while when Gloria Swanson or Douglas Fairbanks or Mae Murray married a titled foreigner. But that meant the beginning of the end of the love affair with the fans. Popularity is not the same as royalty.

Certainly there have been the mysterious ones. But Greta Garbo, like Pola Negri and other imported beauties, never was "top boxoffice"in the U.S.: the greater part of her audience was overseas. And the tragic sex-electric juveniles like Clara Bow and Marilyn Monroe, although reared in poverty, were very special cases. Most of the movie idols who lasted a long time were like Florence Lawrence or Mae Marsh or Mary Pickford — or in later years, Betty Grable and Doris Day.

The American people have always wanted stars like themselves to love. The really big boxoffice stars, while they certainly range from the boy and girl next door to more sophisticated types, have usually represented the common traits of an ideal democratic society: moral strength, a tilt toward generosity and social responsibility, and more than a trace of self-deprecation and humor. The performers who were most likely to have these

---

30 Craig Biddle, "The Millionaire Extra Man's Story," *Photoplay* June 1923, pp. 31,106.

qualities were those who had made their way on their own, took their chances, worked hard, and never forgot either their struggle for fame nor the public that rewarded them with success.

The personalities who worked their way to the top were also likely to be attracted to story ideas reflecting their experiences and their aspirations. If life has been a constant search for security and a place to settle down, as it was for William S. Hart, objects and journeys and encounters on the screen will tend to be linked with that search — for food, home, a little property, a ranch or a bag of gold. Seekers for romance may also gain wealth.

At the very least, there was in many American silent films about American themes a recurring acute awareness of class distinctions — in costumes, decor, power relations, personal discourtesies, and other dramatic ways. In *Way Down East* and many other films of the 20s, the rich folks live in houses with two-story windows and drapes; ordinary folk live in cramped rooms and farmhouses. The European concept of these class divisions leads through bitter conflict to a tragic end. The American way is to try to bridge the gap — the sort of thing that was happening all the time in Hollywood.

Marjorie Rosen, who consulted the *American Film Institute Catalog* on 1920s film themes, found plenty of recurring plots suggesting upward mobility for women, in such roles as

> dime store clerks . . . housemaids . . . chambermaids . . . factory workers . . . governesses, housekeepers, nurses, cooks, dishwashers, hatcheck girls, and stenographers — all represented in formula flicks where the grimy waif, transformed into a cheeky beauty, wins (a) the rich boss or (b) the poor, handsome hero with the bright future.[31]

In his report on the joint career and films of Harold Lockwood and May Allison (1915-17), DeWitt Bodeen remarks that in some of these romances "Lockwood was rich and Allison poor *(The Secretary of Frivolous Affairs)*; in others *(The Secret Wire)* she was a millionaire's daughter and he a hardworking young laborer."[32] In *Madame Sans-Gene*, Gloria Swanson plays a laundress elevated by Napoleon to the nobility: as a gauche diamond-in-the-rough she manages to be ladylike at a reception, but turns on her ene-

---

31 Marjorie Rosen, *Popcorn Venus: Women, Movies, and the American Dream* (1973), p. 81 (paperback).
32 Bodeen, *From Hollywood*, p. 74.

mies to remind them that they, too, were nobodies before the Revolution.[33]

Gloria Swanson was fascinated by rich men and women, and became very wealthy herself. But her upper-class roles, especially for Cecil DeMille, often brought her through some kind of humiliation or learning process, whereas under Allan Dwan she was just as likely to be at the bottom as at the top of the social scale, and the plot might even make it possible for her to be both in the same movie.

One of the best examples is *Fine Manners*, which begins in the street on New Year's Eve. She shouts hello through the window of a car occupied by a very well dressed young man, and before we know it they are getting to know one another and proceeding to get married. This jars the man's family considerably. He agrees to have her learn all the things she should know as a member of society while he goes away on a trip to South America. The aunt delegated to accomplish this fearsome task has rather more success than we might expect, and when the husband comes back he finds his new wife insufferably smug in deportment and attitude. He begs her to recover the untrammeled qualities of the happy little hoyden he married. Gloria is confused at this outcome, but happy. Alone in her room, she turns a couple of joyous handsprings.[34]

As much as any other moment in silent pictures, this scene typifies the intentions of movie-makers and performers when they tried to express their own lives and those of other ambitious Americans — lives of struggle, success, and release into self-confidence. Turning a handspring is an unequivocal statement of freedom and a clear rejection of stuffiness. In *Fine Manners* it is a claim that both poverty and riches are respectable — that it's not unusual to have had it both ways.

33 Ronald Bowers, " *Madame Sans-Gene, " Magill's Survey of Cinema: Silent Films* (1982)
34 Directed by Richard Rosson, 1926.

Chapter 1

Performing for the Silent Screen

"We didn't need dialogue. We had faces."
— *Norma Desmond in* Sunset Boulevard.

Acting involves more than trying to be another person. It reflects the actor's consciousness not only of the history and personal drive of the character being played but also of every other character in the drama. It requires imagining a whole range of events and attitudes that intersect in a scene, and then making visible a selection of moves and expressions among a great many possible choices.

This work of imagining and revealing cannot be done alone. It cannot even be done in simple collaboration with other actors. It must be shaped in rehearsals in accordance with the vision of a director. This is often traumatic, involving a clash of concepts and feelings. The work also has to be realized in a subconscious collaboration with the expectations of a participating audience — the audience of this one performance and the cumulative audience of the actor's whole career. Of course the performance is also the end-point of a chain of efforts beginning with words and ideas: a writer's struggle is finally re-lived by an actor.

In order to express through their bodies the concepts of writer and director, actors may find they are shouted at, made sport of, and wooed like lovers into positions and moods that seem uncomfortable, degrading, even dangerous. They are trapped in rehearsals expressing emotional extremes over and over. If they are working in film, they are brought into close-ups in which eyes and emotions must be precisely controlled. Why shouldn't they be temperamental? They are soft, eager, troubled puppets of the wills of others, these human beings, and when they are so often used as punching-bags, they may double up and cry, explode and shriek, throw things, or grasp as soon as they leave the scene the ever-comforting bottle.

They are asked to be puppets and then, after the day is over, to be natural, to be themselves. How can they know what it is to be themselves? At home and abroad, offstage, stars are expected to be gracious to their fans and handle easily the role of public eminence. So they work to find in life, as well as onscreen, an image the public wants and will continue to want. Then they discover they are trapped in this image. They grow into and become the image, almost without realizing it. Sometimes this is a kind of protection for them. More often it is a confusion. They find they are suffering the high and low expectations of all who watch them act this peculiarly public mixture of pretense and uncertainty about themselves.

It is no easy matter to be oneself, on or off the screen. Idols of silent and sound movies have usually been most secure with their audience when they performed within recognizable patterns of personality, with stories and situations not too different from those they have been used to. Keeping a consistent image then requires mainly working out, for each movie, minor fresh twists of style.

"Typage," as the Soviet silent film director, V.I. Pudovkin, called it, was logical from the beginning. In America and elsewhere in the years before sound, the director of short films naturally called for actors who would express as obviously as possible, in face and body, the style of life, personality, and emotional range proposed for the character by the story. Anything but casting for type would have been considered a waste of time, and pictures were made fast in those days.

This closeness between part and player could only be reenforced by the gradual development of screen technique as demonstrated in the films of D.W. Griffith. The camera drew closer to the actors and began to capture every nuance of gesture and attitude. These were the actors' own movements and expressions, far more than they were those of the characters. With the arrival of the close shot and extreme close-up, the camera seemed to see inside the very soul of the performer, and the emotion of the character could not easily be separated from the real self of the actor, trying to reproduce that emotion. Certainly for movie-goers this separation was difficult to make. For many viewers, each film was simply another episode in the life of the familiar friend they saw up on the screen. If there was much divergence from the personality traits they knew and loved—no matter if such "acting" might impress critics as "art"—the loyal fan would write letters.

This did not keep the conscientious actor from developing techniques and attitudes intended to reveal depths of personality. Griffith's earliest films met demands by Biograph to get as much action into one or two reels as possible. But he was soon encouraged by responses to his experiments in acting style: Frank Woods approved his quieter scenes offering "deliberation and repose." As he left more and more of her own preparation to Lillian Gish, their collaboration resulted in silent film acting which reached out to the audience and stirred deeper emotions. She was also willing to startle everyone with intense and frantic whirling fear, as she did in the closet in *Broken Blossoms* when her crazed father is trying to break in and kill her.

Close students of the Griffith style in writing "titles" for the screen may observe that in the earliest days especially he was not much given to dialogue. There was more likely to be a general description of the character's mood and situation, leaving the performer to act out the consequences through movement and facial expression. Later it became more common in Hollywood for title writers to provide dialogue lines, cut into the middle of a character's action and reaction, and of course Griffith used that technique as well.

Such limitations of silence did tend to present characters as simplified and stylized, compared to the later years of sound movies. Perhaps they impressed their audiences as a little larger than life, or, as some observers have proposed, they seemed less realistic—more distant—than characters would later seem with the additional distinctiveness of spoken dialogue. None of these logical factors, however, kept silent film viewers from taking their stars into their hearts when they felt like it. And this same affection for silent stars can be felt today.

When projection speeds are properly controlled and not made to conform to the iron demands of 24 frames a second in our sound era, when music is provided that is suitable for the story, and when audiences try to adjust to a sense of a different time, silent movies can provide for anyone with a degree of discernment and taste quite satisfying dramatic experiences. The actors had faces. In the tragically small percentage of films which have survived, we can still see the struggle of the actor to transmit to us the struggle of the writer to speak.

HERBERT HOWE
On Screen and Off

A reporter's interview with a performer may sometimes deal simply with the plot and message of the actor's current film, or with the challenge the role presents. But the conversation is also likely to veer off into questions of identity. Is this role one that is "close" to the actor's experience? Is it close to other, earlier roles? Will it please the public by presenting personal style in familiar situations, so that the performer will seem like "an old friend"?

Herbert Howe, one of the top writers for Photoplay magazine, makes clear in this article ("They Can't Fool the Public," June 1922) that he doesn't believe movie stars should strive for versatility, so prized in the theater. Personality is what makes a successful film actor, and the personality that is most successful over the years is the one which is warm and rather consistent in character. He lists a few favorites, and leaves anonymous those who have got too "big" for their audiences.

Movies are an intimate business, Howe is saying, and we all know this instinctively. This is partly due to technology: the camera is often so close it seems to inspect the deepest feelings of the actor. Therefore the job of the fan magazine writer is frankly to try to find out and to show what the "real personality" of the actor is. There can be no effective separation between that and the image on the screen.

. . . There used to be a lively discussion as to whether a player should be chosen for his acting ability or because he looked the part. Actors from the stage snorted at the idea of "types" and contended that a good actor could give life to any part.

Therein do the stage and screen differ. The stage is chiefly vocal; the screen entirely visual, save for subtitles which must be in harmony with expression. On the stage a player may characterize by his voice and create the necessary optic illusion as to his appearance by the use of make-up and lights. Distance lends enchantment, and there is considerable distance between the man behind the footlights and the man in the orchestra chair.

On the screen a player must characterize entirely by facial and bodily appearances. . . .

No less an authority than David Wark Griffith declares absolutely that the camera goes straight to the heart and that the eye of the director must be keen if it is to see what the spectators out front are going to see when the player faces them.

You may not know that you are judging a person's character when you see his face on the screen. You only know vaguely — subconsciously — that you like or dislike that person. You have often said, no doubt, that a certain star is a good actor but that there is something about him that you do not like. Instinctively your eye has recorded an impression which your mind has not taken the time or effort to analyze and formulate.

The regular motion picture public is infallible in its election of stellar favorites.

Such is my conviction after several years' close contact with famous stars. I have known players of all ranks and, with a few exceptions to prove the rule, I've found that those who are the most attractive on screen are the most attractive off.

The policy of *Photoplay* since its inception has been to mirror the personality of players as truthfully as it is humanly possible. An interviewer must neither gloss nor besmirch. He must take an absolutely impersonal position, just as a portrait artist does before his subject. There is no one since the year of our Lord of whom it might be said, here is a perfect creature. Therefore, with humanity toward all and malice toward none the writer endeavors to portray character with all accuracy within his power. Because of this standard there have been occasions during my five years of interviewing for this publication when I found it impossible to do an assignment. Perhaps the subject seemed to me so devoid of merit that I could find no high lights to relieve the shadows, and rather than paint an unpleasant character I refrained entirely. Or, perhaps, — and it does happen now and then, — I felt such an intense admiration and respect for a person that if I told my true impression I would be accused of being laudatory if not downright fulsome.

Publicity is a tremendous force in developing the value of a star, but it must have material with which to work. Only a very small part of the public can be fooled all the time. Fortunes have been expended in publicity and in lavish productions to force a player into favor — but to no avail. You can stuff a ballot box but you can't stuff a boxoffice. Here is one democratic institution where the public will prevails.

Producers have lost fortunes in gambling upon stellar potentialities. Oftentimes they have picked actresses of beauty and average ability who appeared to be good bets but who failed to receive public endorsement. Why? They lacked *character*. They hadn't that something within which gives individuality and holds interest. Physically they might be as beautiful as Mary Pickford or Lillian Gish; they might even have as much acting ability as those stars had a few years ago; but they haven't that most precious of assets which both Miss Pickford and Miss Gish possess — lovable character.

Occasionally I have been perplexed upon meeting a star who on the screen is distinguished for certain likable traits, but who off screen seems to be of entirely different character. But upon coming to know such a one more intimately I have found that the real is shown to the camera while the artificial is worn at home. In a word, he is himself on the screen; off-screen he is an actor.

Sometimes, too, certain traits of a player's nature may be so emphasized on the screen that you almost overlook other qualities.

This was an error I made in regard to Mabel Normand. I thought of her as a roistering hoyden, pert and cocky, but not subtly charming. Perhaps I had not devoted very much attention to her because she was not one of my favorites. Then I met Miss Normand. Expecting little to entice me, I found much. Through knowing her off screen I have become an intense admirer of her on the screen. Of all the models in the Hollywood ateliers Miss Normand's seems to me the most captivating. That is because she has the qualities which I like — spontaneity, loyalty, tolerance, generosity, a brilliant mind and a lightning wit.

Another alert personality is Norma Talmadge: a warm and genuine one which the camera treats with consideration. She is a creature of moods; that is why she is able to express young girlhood in one picture and mature and dignified womanhood in the next. Her actual self — which her family and friends know — is warm-hearted, generous, impulsive, mischievous, unassuming. In fact, there is no celebrity who has so little veneer as Norma, excepting Mabel Normand. The proof that she is herself very much like her screen personality is that her work has matured with her, becoming more finished and less fiery with the seasons.

Viola Dana plays herself on the screen. She is the eternal flapper, the expression of flippant Young America. Her sister, Shirley Mason, is more serious, more boyish than her celluloid shadow. There is an unexpected sprightliness in the real Ruby de Remer, whose film performances would lead one to expect an aloof dignity. Gloria Swanson is actually a petite, reserved person; there is nothing in the least demilleish about her. The close observer of the screen can easily detect this. Marion Davies, Priscilla Dean, Constance Talmadge, Betty Compson — all express after office hours the same qualities which their screen work reveals, in greater or lesser degrees.

Down in our hearts we all have a tremendous regard for certain virtues. Some of us prefer a sense of humor to all else; others demand sincerity first. Each has certain pet virtues, and the star who appears to have these becomes a favorite. Thus you adore Mary Pickford because you see in her face the reflection of sweet womanliness and consideration for others. Or you may worship Lillian Gish for her fragile loveliness and spirituelle. Or Mabel Normand for her droll impudence, her quick wit and her air of *bonhomie.*

If you like them for these qualities you will not be disappointed upon meeting them. On the contrary you will find their charm enhanced with personal contact.

But the mistake which an idol-worshipper too often makes is in attributing *all* the virtues to his favorite. He likes a star for certain very human qualities and ends by expecting that star to be a divinity without a blemish.

Stars sometimes undergo a change of character. Very few mortals can remain adamant to flattery. And I find — alas, alack! — that 'tis the male of the movie species who is the more susceptible. A matinee idol quite often listens to sycophantic droolings until he becomes persuaded that he really is a superman and that the earth is operated solely because he is on it. But about the time he has reached such a conviction he experiences an awful crash and has to pick himself up from the debris, brush off a little vanity and seek a job in vaudeville. Was the public mistaken about him all along? Probably not. At the outset he doubtlessly was a likable fellow with certain claims to merit, but success turned his head and he changed completely. Noting the change, the public simply declared a referendum and gently, but definitely, booted him off the pedestal.

I have heard numerous votaries remark that a certain idol of the present is manifesting undue conceit. These, you may be sure are the first rumors of that idol's impending doom.

The reason Wallace Reid has endured so long with both men and women is his frank geniality and his devil-may-care air. He doesn't appear to take himself very seriously. Unless you know actors you cannot appreciate what a relief it is to find one who does not brood over himself and his future.

Thomas Meighan has gained a tremendous following in the last year. Here, again is absolute proof of the public's perspicacity. Thomas is the regular, sane, all-round man that everyone — particularly men — like to see come out on top.

Antonio Moreno, despite his fiery Spanish temperament, is another one who despises conceit. He once bawled out a fellow actor who was manifesting airs. "Why should we be conceited?" he shouted. "If it weren't for the movies we'd be making about fifty a week."

CONRAD NAGEL
An Actor's Art

When the Academy of Motion Picture Arts and Sciences agreed to provide speakers for the University of Southern California's first film course in 1929, one of the opportunities offered was to counter some of the "erroneous publicity" about the wayward ways of the acting profession. The unjustified persecution of Fatty Arbuckle (acquitted of manslaughter in a rape case in 1921) was still remembered.

Searching the roster of top stars, they managed to find articulateness, dignity, and intelligence in the person of tall, handsome Milton Sills, who had played many a trustworthy character on the screen. When he was unable at the last moment to appear, they found a second such paragon: Conrad Nagel, an icon of decorous maturity who fulfilled the task very well and also gave some generous comments on the artistic achievements of certain top stars—Ray, Swanson, Negri, Garbo, Gaynor.

His interest was in crediting them with technical skills, hard work, and a sense of training – qualities he would associate with successful theater performers. Thus Janet Gaynor was a "rare" exception. James Naremore might agree. Mae Marsh did not.

Nagel was an Iowan who had played in midwestern stock companies and found his way to Broadway and Hollywood, where he worked for both Cecil and William deMille. His busy career extended from 1919 to 1959, and he was one of the founders and president of the Academy.

The 1929 talks were published in mimeographed form by the Academy and USC. They were reprinted more handsomely in 1977 by the National Film Society, publisher of American Classic Screen, *then based in Shawnee Mission, Kansas. The book has an introduction and extensive notes by the editor, John C. Tibbetts, associate professor, University of Kansas, and lecturer, University of Missouri at Kansas City. Both versions are entitled Introduction to the* Photoplay. *Our selections are from pages 189-190, 194-196, 201.*

The actor in the theatre has one great advantage over the actor in the studio. He appears personally before his audience and the inspiration received from two or three thousand people on the other side of the footlights provides a great incentive. Many times actors have played when seriously ill, in great pain, or while suffering a great sorrow and yet have given fine performances because of the stimulus they receive from stepping in front of a theatre full of people. If the actor on the stage makes a mistake, it is gone in a second and he can make the audience forget it by excellent acting; the mistake is gone with that performance and only a theatre full of people witnessed it. The motion picture actor must be absolutely perfect in everything he does because he can only do it once and what he does is seen by many millions of people throughout the world. It only increases the responsibility of a screen actor to give the best that he has at all times.

The general public seems to have the idea that working in motion pictures is fairly easy, and believe the wildly exaggerated stories which tell of stars and film actors and actresses spending most of their time at parties and going around at all hours of the night. Anyone slightly familiar with studio work knows that working before powerful lights eight, ten, and twelve hours a day makes it even more necessary to keep fit, in condition and even to train much as an athlete has to train. Such endless nonsense has been published about film players and so much erroneous publicity given out that it has been suggested to me that I give you a few actual facts and figures this afternoon.

The impression seems to exist outside the industry, of course, that anyone who is connected with motion pictures automatically is earning a big salary. As a matter of fact, there are approximately thirty thousand men and women who earn their living in motion pictures. These people are not employed all the time, but there are thirty thousand dependent on motion pictures for their livelihood. Of these thirty thousand are 677 who have definite contracts calling for work for periods from three months to five years. In all branches of the industry, consisting of directors, actors, writers, producers, and technicians, there are only 439 big names; there are less than one hundred players who receive what we might term "big money." The stories of big salaries — four and five thousand dollars a week and even more — are greatly exaggerated. Artists drawing these salaries can be counted on the fingers of two hands.

Five or six years ago most of the actors living in Hollywood were employed regularly and were able to make a good living.

Hollywood came to be known as the promised land as far as the professional actor was concerned, so from all over the world, actors and actresses, young and old, flocked to California. Beginning three or four years ago, the over-supply of players became a serious situation. A very careful survey was made a year or two ago by a group of actors and the facts they gathered are very interesting. In this community there are at present approximately forty-five hundred actors and actresses who are entitled to play screen credit parts. This, of course, includes players who play small parts or even bits but are entitled to have their names on the program. Only once or twice a year are the studios operating at full capacity at what might be termed the peak of production. At the peak of production, there are six hundred parts available for these forty-five hundred players.

The condition among the extras is far worse than it is among the actors. A few years ago there were some sixty thousand registered at the various studios. The different firms joined in forming a Central Casting Bureau and now all of their extras come through this office. By this means the number of extras was greatly decreased until today there are listed some fourteen thousand experienced extras of all types. Out of the Central Casting Bureau office goes each day, approximately, calls for between seven and eight hundred extras. . . .

Success in any line of endeavor whatever is based on craftsmanship, and craftsmanship is achieved only at the price of much toil and effort and time. The player with natural gifts, who also applies himself to the learning of the technical tools of his trade and how to use them, will maintain his position indefinitely. If a star is merely a novelty, the public will soon tire of him because novelty soon wears off. The proof of that statement is contained in the fact that most of the great figures of the screen today, most of the big stars who are still at the height of their popularity, have been on the screen since motion pictures began — Mary Pickford, Douglas Fairbanks, Charlie Chaplin, Gloria Swanson, Harold Lloyd, Norma Talmadge, John Gilbert, Corinne Griffith, Emil Jannings, Lon Chaney, and so on through a long list, all having enjoyed their popularity since pictures began.

Why is it then that some players shoot up to the stars and then die out? Why is it that others maintain their popularity over a long period of years? What rule is there that we can supply to ourselves if we are interested in becoming a motion picture player? The secret of the long record of success enjoyed by the stars I have just mentioned is contained in the fact that every one of them has a complete and sound basis of knowledge of the technique or of the tools of their trade. In addition to natural endowments, such as beauty, charm, colorful personality, or unusual appeal, each one is an expert technician; each one of them has learned the age-old secret, which can be a motto for any human being, that trifles make perfection and perfection is no trifle.

The screen player in the old days of motion pictures had to create an entirely new technique for himself; the technique of the stage artist has been built up by many generations of actors. The screen being an entirely new medium in artistic expression, the screen players had to devise and create an entirely new method of getting over to the audience their thoughts and ideas. Much of the action that took place on the silent screen was against the natural instinct of the expressive artist and against the natural action of the character because of the mechanical limitations of the silent screen.

The basis of all acting is contained in one line of Hamlet's speech to the players, when he says, "Suit the action to the word, and the word to the action." That, of course, is easily done on the stage, but in the silent motion picture it could not be done, due to the fact that during the time the actor is speaking the film is cut and a printed title is inserted. Therefore, it is easy to be seen that the player couldn't suit the action to the word or the word to the action. Any action the player wished to use must necessarily precede or follow his speaking, otherwise it would be cut out when the title was inserted.

One of the greatest pantomimic artists of the silent drama was Charles Ray. He had natural gifts of pantomimic expression such as no other actor possessed. In many discussions with actors, and such directors as Lubitsch and Niblo, there was always unanimous agreement that Charles Ray was the outstanding pantomimic artist of the silent screen. With a minimum of gestures and facial expression Charles Ray could tell volumes. In the old silent pictures, he has often held an audience with a single closeup running five or six hundred feet. Charles Ray gave what many consider his finest performance in his picture, *The Girl I Loved,* based on Riley's poem, "An Old Sweetheart of Mine." Those who were fortunate enough to see it will never forget it. Time and time again Ray had to let the audience know, in this particular picture, what he was thinking without letting the other character in the scene with him know. . .

It has always seemed to me that among the actresses, the outstanding artist is Gloria Swanson. She was one of the first really great artists of the silent screen, has maintained her position for many years, and in her first talking picture has now made one of the great successes in this new medium. She is richly endowed with emotion, has a fine technique, and a great gift for characterization. She has never given a performance without establishing some innovation, some new trick of technique, a different way of getting across to the audience just what she wanted them to know. The next time you see Miss Swanson in any of her pictures, withdraw yourself from the interest you have in the story and merely observe it closely as a student, and you will discover the tremendous knowledge of impersonation and the art of acting she always shows. Miss Swanson has played practically every type of character — she has played in comedy, tragedy, farce, and even slapstick, and has been successful in them all because of the fact that she has a thorough technique and a comprehensive knowledge of all branches of the motion picture art. Ample evidence of Miss Swanson's great intelligence and complete understanding of her art is given in her first talking picture. Not only does she adapt herself to an entirely new medium of expression but she exhibits talents that only her closest friends suspected. She is truly a great artist.

Another great player of the silent screen is Pola Negri. Miss Negri is gifted more emotionally than technically; she can play nothing but herself, but as a personality she is vitally interesting. She is a true artist but lacks the ability to characterize, to get out of herself.

Another of the great artists of the silent screen is Greta Garbo. Far from being just a "personality" actress or an interesting type, Miss Garbo is one of the finest actresses before the public today. She has just completed her first talking picture, and I am sure that her fine mentality and her true knowledge of the art of acting will enable her to make the transition with great success...

One of the rare things that we encounter either in the theatre or on the screen is what may be termed the inspired performance. A typical example of the inspired performance was that given by Janet Gaynor in *Seventh Heaven*. Miss Gaynor at that time had very little technical knowledge of the screen, yet she stepped into one of the biggest parts of the year and moved not only the entire world but the actors and actresses in motion pictures with her beautiful performance. Such an occurrence happens rarely. It was a part that suited Miss Gaynor perfectly, and as she was a perfect photographic subject with an extremely fascinating and attractive photographic personality she naturally did what it would take most people years and years to accomplish. We encounter people who can sit down at a piano and play a tune, and yet they cannot read a note of music. People sometimes have a natural ability to draw and can make fine sketches without knowing any of the rules of painting. So, occasionally we have in pictures and in the theatre such an inspired performance as Janet Gaynor's was in *Seventh Heaven*. By hard work Miss Gaynor has acquired a knowledge of her craft and, along with many of the other screen artists, has adapted herself to the talking pictures and will maintain her position in the new art as she did in the old.

MAE MARSH
Screen Acting

In a pocket-size book with this title, published by the Photo-Star Company in 1921, Mae Marsh recorded some of her experiences as a star in D.W. Griffith productions and for Samuel Goldwyn after 1919. (Our selection includes pages 40-41, 81, 76, 79-80.) Memorable for her role as the young wife in the modern episode of Intolerance, *she was also the Little Sister in* The Birth of a Nation *and returned to work for Griffith in* The White Rose *(1923). While calling attention to the importance of hard work and good health if one is to be a performer in silent pictures, she also reveals the spirit of good will and love for the medium which often prevailed in the earliest days. And she confirms the viewpoints of Herbert Howe and Blake Lucas: genuineness of emotion, not technical skill, is what works on the screen.*

. . . it is not only because good health radiates from the screen that it is important. In point of nervous and muscular strain, and the often long studio hours that are necessary when production has begun, good health is essential.

To illustrate: While we were filming "Polly of The Circus" in Fort Lee one morning I reported at the studio at nine o'clock. We were working on some interior scenes that were vital to the success of the story. My director at that time was Mr. Charles Horan. Mr. Vernon Steele was playing the male lead.

That day we became so engrossed in playing some rather delicate scenes that before we knew it — or at least before I could realize it — it was six o'clock, and we weren't half done.

"What do you say to continuing?" asked Mr. Horan.

"Good; we're right in the spirit of it," I replied.

We had a bite to eat and worked on until midnight. In spite of our hard and earnest efforts there were several scenes with which we were dissatisfied.

"Well," said Mr. Horan ruefully. "Tomorrow will be another day."

As he spoke it dawned upon me how one of the scenes on which we felt we had failed could be done with probable success.

"Why tomorrow?" I replied. "Let's make a night of it if necessary. We simply have to get that scene."

Mr. Horan grinned. That had been his wish. But he had feared breaking the camel's back.

We worked until four o'clock that morning. Things went swimmingly. It was broad daylight when I ferried across the Hudson but if I was very tired I was equally happy.

Several times during "Polly of the Circus" we had experiences which, in the number of hours put in, were similar to that which I have related. But in the end it was worth while. We had a picture.

At that time I was feeling in the best of health but, even so, the long hours had been a severe drain upon my none too great vitality. For anyone lacking strength and vitality such hours would have been impossible.

It is not my intention to write a booklet on health. But all of us should be very careful of our most precious possession. I know of so many young girls in motion pictures who have let their health get away from them. And some of the cases are so pitiful...

My candidate, then, will have strength and vitality and, equally important, he or she will cling to both, whatever social sacrifices may have to be made to preserve them...

Good screen acting consists of the ability to accurately portray a state of mind.

That sounds simple, yet how often upon the screen have you seen an important part played in a manner that made you, yourself, feel that you were passing through the experiences being unfolded in the plot. I imagine not often.

If a part is under-played or, worse, overplayed — for there is nothing so depressing as a screen actress run amuck in a flood of sundry emotions — it exerts a definite influence upon you, the audience.

You begin to lose sympathy with the character itself. You are interested or irritated by the mannerisms — often hardly less than gymnastics — of the actor or actress. You never identify such an actor or actress with the part they are playing for the very good reason that they are not playing the part. They are playing their idea of acting at a part. . .

While we were playing "Intolerance," one cycle of which is still being released as "The Mother and the Law," I had to do a scene where, in the big city's slums, my father dies.

The night before I did this scene I went to the theater — something, by the way, I seldom do when working — to see Marjorie Rambeau in "Kindling."

To my surprise and gratification she had to do a scene in this play that was somewhat similar to the one that I was scheduled to play in "Intolerance." It made a deep impression upon me.

As a consequence, the next day before the camera in the scene depicting my sorrow and misery at the death of my father, I began to cry with the memory of Marjorie Rambeau's part uppermost in my mind. I thought, however, that it had been done quite well and was anxious to see it on the screen.

I was in for very much of a surprise. A few of us gathered in the projection room and the camera began humming. I saw myself enter with a fair semblance of misery. But there was something about it that was not convincing.

Mr. Griffith, who was closely studying the action, finally turned in his seat and said:

"I don't know what you were thinking about when you did that, but it is evident that it was not about the death of your father."

"That is true," I said. I did not admit what I was thinking about.

We began immediately upon the scene again. This time I thought of the death of my own father and the big tragedy to our little home, then in Texas. I could recall the deep sorrow of my mother, my sisters, my brother and myself.

This scene is said to be one of the most effective in "The Mother and the Law."

The beginner may learn from that that it never pays to imitate anyone else's interpretation of any emotion. Each of us when we are pleased, injured, or affected in any way have our own way of showing our feelings. This is one thing that is our very own.

When before the camera, therefore, we must remember that when we feel great sorrow the audience wants to see our own sorrow and not an imitation of Miss Blanche Sweet's or Mme. Nazimova's. We must feel our own part and take heed of my favorite screen maxim, which is that thoughts do register.

It is true that we have good and bad days before the camera. There are times when to feel and to act are the easiest things imaginable and other occasions when it seems impossible to catch the spirit that we know is necessary. In this we are more fortunate than our brothers upon the spoken stage, for we can do it over again.

It is also very often true that even when we are entirely in the spirit of our part, and believe we have done a good day's work, that there will be some mechanical defect in the scenes taken which makes it necessary to do them over, possibly when we feel least like so doing.

In this event it is a good thing to remember that it doesn't pay to cry over spilt milk. We must learn to take the bitter with the sweet. Fortunately the mechanics of picture taking are constantly improving.

The hardest dramatic work I ever did was in the courtroom scenes in "Intolerance." We retook these scenes on four different occasions. Each time I gave to the limit of my vitality and ability. I put everything into my portrayal that was in me. It certainly paid. Parts of each of the four takes — some of them done at two weeks' intervals — were assembled to make up those scenes which you, as the audience, finally beheld upon the screen.

Therefore when first going before a camera it is well to resolve to put as much into one's performance as possible. We cannot too greatly concentrate upon our parts. If we do not feel them we can be very sure they will not convince our audiences.

Mae Marsh in *Intolerance*

BLAKE LUCAS
Acting Style in Silent Films

Among the introductory essays for the three-volume set of Magill's
Survey of Cinema: Silent Films *(Salem Press, 1982, pages 1-11), may be
found this thoughtful examination of the film actor's professional skills. It
will repay close study for critics and performers alike. "The natural cinema
actor," Lucas says, "understands the camera but behaves as if it is not
there." Unlike the technically-oriented actor in the theater, "the reality of
that individual, composed equally of the conviction he or she brings to the
characterization and fidelity to the inner self, will result in an effective
performance." This is true for all screen acting, but especially true for the
silent era.*

*Lucas refers to a number of the stars who are given special attention in
this book. While they all had their own particular star styles, at the same
time the best of them (like Gloria Swanson) were wise enough to modify
those styles in relation to the leadership of particular directors. Lucas notes
also that the successful ones "generally play roles within a relatively narrow
range" but have an ability "to project persuasively an image in cinema."
Mary Pickford's heroines, for instance, "are artistically shaped reflections of
her real self."*

Lucas quotes the line from Sunset Boulevard *as most of us remember it.
Norma Desmond actually says, however, "We had faces!"*

In the 1950 film *Sunset Boulevard*, Gloria Swanson, a former
star of the silent era, plays Norma Desmond, an almost forgotten
star of the silent era. Unlike Swanson, however, Desmond has
been driven into a fantasy world as a result of her exile from the
world of motion-picture make-believe. When Joe Gillis (William
Holden), the cynical screenwriter "hero" of the film, recognizes
her and acknowledges that she was a big star, she responds, "I
am big. It's the pictures that got small." Billy Wilder, director and
co-scenarist of *Sunset Boulevard*, probably intended this line to get
the laugh it invariably provokes, but only a few scenes later,
Norma's posturing abruptly ceases to be derided. Showing a
print of one of her films — actually one of Swanson's, *Queen
Kelly* (1928), directed by Erich Von Stroheim who himself
appears in *Sunset Boulevard* as a has-been director — Desmond
stands in the projector beam announcing dramatically, "We had
faces then!" It is an eloquent moment, at the same time
establishing Norma Desmond as the character in the film most
deserving of the audience's sympathetic respect and evoking the
lost world of which Swanson herself was a queen. The end of the
silent era had broken many careers, sometimes cruelly and

unfairly, especially those of actors and actresses. Playing in silent films required great skill, as the actors and actresses had to make a leap of imagination to project their own nonmute personalities persuasively in order to obtain the audience's suspension of disbelief.

The screen star of mythical stature was a later development of the silent years. The first film actors came from the theater. Cinema was considered coarse popular entertainment, and the actors felt they were doing something that was beneath them, so they often worked uncredited or under assumed names. In the second decade of the twentieth century, stars were born, the most important of whom was Mary Pickford, and careful cultivation of their screen images became a tradition. The basic tension between serious thespian and screen personality which resulted has continued throughout the history of the cinema, with the result that theatrical performances on film often receive immediate acclaim, although historically it has been demonstrated that they do not wear as well over the years as less flamboyant playing. Silent film acting is often thought of as exaggerated and lacking in subtlety, but this is an oversimplification which does not deal with performance in the various ways in which it is utilized in individual films. Patterns of effective screen acting are clearly established in the silent cinema and have changed very little. Lillian Gish, one of the most revered actresses in cinema history, gave most of her great performances in silent films.

The key to film acting is a simple one and has never changed. The actor or actress must understand the presence of the camera and play in relationship to it. The camera will, of its own accord, register the genuineness of the individual and the subtlest expression of emotion, especially in close-up. In the theater, a complementary medium in many respects, the severity of the camera's gaze is absent. Playing for effect is required on the stage. The actor or actress who drifts quietly into the scenery will make little or no impression. In cinema, an individual who is called upon to do nothing more than stand there can be very moving, even if there is no dialogue and the scene is emotionally neutral. The reality of that individual, composed equally of the conviction he or she brings to the characterization and fidelity to the inner self, will result in an effective performance. Theater requires *acting* in a sense that cinema often does not, and that is why some of the best performers of cinema have often been undervalued by those who measure cinematic acting by the standards of live drama. In cinema, much of the best acting is intuitive and not the result of polished technique. Veteran film actors and actresses will often learn from experience how to exploit their intuitive skills with unusual effectiveness and that becomes their technique. Motion-picture acting requires as much professionalism and ability as other cinematic crafts, and the willingness not to savor histrionic impressiveness with a theatrical fervor is crucial. Ironically, the theatrical actor tends to seem more aware of the camera and to play to it than the natural cinema actor who understands the camera but behaves as if it is not there.

A valuable comparison would be between Buster Keaton and Emil Jannings. Both were major stars of the silent era and were universally admired. Of course, their roles required different styles. Keaton was a comedian and Jannings was a dramatic actor. Keaton obtained laughs from what was sometimes regarded as the immobility of his face but what was in fact a manifestation of stoicism in the face of an absurd universe. The contrast between outrageous comic events and Keaton's relative calm gave his films their distinctive tone. Keaton was also a director, and his playing style was perfected in relation to his directorial style. Jannings, on the other hand, was an obviously expressive actor. Extreme emotions were displayed in his performances, and his characterizations were often charged with pathos, as in *The Last Laugh* (1925) and *The Last Command* (1928). In 1929, Jannings won the first Academy Award for Best Actor for *The Last Command* and *The Way of All Flesh* at about the time that Keaton was beginning to encounter serious career problems. Although Keaton had been appreciated for doing what he did well, Jannings was more deeply respected as an actor in the traditional sense. It was believed that Jannings' powerful emoting brought to life the most profound aspects of the human experience.

Today, however, these two actors look quite different. Keaton is perceived as being not at all inexpressive; rather, he is extremely subtle. He did not need to overwhelm the frames of a film with emotional displays because the grace with which he moved and the barely perceptible changes of mood which his face reflected were captured perfectly by the attentiveness of a well-placed camera. Jannings, on the other hand, seems to overplay and to make a studied bid for the audience's pity. The anguish he projects from the first frames is so overwhelming that it rapidly becomes tiresome. In *The Cameraman* (1928), Keaton has a dramatic moment during the film's climax when he sinks to his knees on a beach as the girl he loves walks away with another man whom she mistakenly believes performed the heroic rescue for which the Keaton character was responsible. A monkey has made a film of the event, prompting the happy ending which follows and permitting the audience to see the long shot of the despairing Keaton twice. Keaton performs this scene with a simple eloquence that arguably makes it a more poignant moment than any achieved by Jannings.

The dramatic skill of a Jannings is not in question. The problem with his playing is that he himself seems to be more theatrical than the characters he plays. An actor may be effectively theatrical if it is the nature of the character and if it is inherent in the actor's offscreen personality. John Barrymore is a good example of this type. In *Don Juan* (1926), the actor plays a legendary rogue with a flamboyant personality. The personality is that of both Barrymore and Don Juan, and the actor's performance is therefore precisely suited to the role. This is also true, in an even more obvious way, when Barrymore plays an actor in *Dinner at Eight* (1933) or an egomaniacal producer in *Twentieth Century* (1935), sound films in which the Barrymore *persona* is consistent with that of his silent films. Throughout the history of the cinema, there have always been roles which required this kind of flamboyance and plenty of actors and actresses ready to provide it. Painful screen acting only occurs when there is a Jannings-type disparity between bravura emoting and the actual needs of the role.

The extent to which silent films are *not* customarily overplayed deserves stress because of some unfortunate misconceptions about the actuality of silent films in their pristine form. The sad truth is that silent films are usually projected at the wrong speed (although a growing awareness of the damage this does to the experience of the film has started to lead to more conscientious presentations). Sound films are correctly projected at twenty-four frames a second, and when silent films made to be projected at about two-thirds that rate are subjected to this treatment, the result is exaggerated movement and gesture. Nuances are lost in the artificial speeding up of the actor's performance. It cannot be stressed too strongly that even slapstick comedy was never meant to be seen this way. The physical grace and comic timing of silent comedians such as Charles Chaplin and Keaton are best appreciated and most entertaining when the elaborate routines are viewed as they were actually performed. Although pantomime is one aspect of silent-screen acting, it is a form of pantomime radically different from the traditional kind. In cinema, actors and actresses do not pretend that they have no voices. They appear to speak, and intertitles convey the most important lines of dialogue and tell the audience what it needs to know about the plot exposition. Strong emotions are registered by carriage and facial expression; but in the hands of a sensitive director, the player does not need to be unnatural. Thoughtful camera angles and judiciously selected close-ups will enhance the emotional value of these important moments. Wild gesticulations and facial contortions represent an unimaginative response to the limitation of silence, which is most happily regarded as a discipline to spur the imaginations of director and performer.

In every respect, D.W. Griffith is most responsible for the evolution and refinement of cinematic acting style. Interestingly, Griffith's early ambitions had been to write for and act in the theater. This did not prevent him from understanding that cinema required a different form of dramatic expression. The actors and actresses he utilized learned how to play in relation to the camera, and those who did so most ably earned Griffith's reciprocal loyalty and were given roles of increasing depth and complexity. Griffith began to take great care with close-ups and discovered a range of emotion on the human face which became more the province of the cinema than of the theater. The extent to which the emotional intensity of close-ups provoked the audience's sympathetic identification with the performer was one factor in the emergence of film stars.

Regardless of the nature of the film or the part being played by a star, the public would be lured by something they believed to be real in the star's personality; and, that aspect of the star's personality was usually seized upon and became the basis of the star's enduring popularity. It is sometimes argued that this has nothing to do with acting. Whether by design or personal limitation, stars generally play roles within a relatively narrow range. A really skilled actor, it is contended, would not be so easily typed. On the contrary, the ability to project persuasively an image in cinema is a gift. There is always an imprecise point at which the actor and the role merge, and the actor whose personality is taken to be absolutely real gracefully obscures this point. Mary Pickford, who began her career in some of Griffith's earliest films, beautifully illustrates this and remains one of the best examples to this day. She became "America's Sweetheart" playing winsome and good-hearted young ladies throughout the silent period. No one is quite so consistently endearing in life as Pickford is in these films, but she invariably gives the illusion that these heroines are artistically shaped reflections of her real self.

Griffith's benevolent mediation resulted in a rich gallery of acting styles, and Pickford is actually not one of the actresses most associated with him.

Although male actors are important in his films, as exemplified in various phases of his career by the recurring presence of Henry B. Walthall, Robert Harron, and Richard Barthelmess — each one in his own way a sensitive prototype of the often chivalrous and sometimes fallible Griffith male — women tend to display the most extraordinary acting range in the films of this master. For Griffith, the twentieth century woman was caught between the puritanical repressions of the Victorian age and the ambiguous liberation of the twentieth century. Through various actresses, he explored a world of differing feminine responses to the challenges of this difficult change and its accompanying confusions. Mae Marsh represented the greatest innocence in *The Birth of a Nation* (1915) and *Intolerance* (1916). In the former, she played Lillian Gish's younger sister, so terrified by the awkward but harmless advances of a black man that she jumps to her death. In the latter, she played The Little Dear One, heroine of the modern story. Audiences invariably laugh at her first appearance; she is so naive and carefree. During the course of this long film, however, Marsh's remarkable performance does justice to an exceptionally demanding role. The Little Dear One credibly changes from a girl to a woman. As misfortune overcomes her, her eyes lose their sparkle and her gait becomes less spontaneous. Griffith's neglected *The White Rose* (1923) further attests to Marsh's abilities. In that film, she plays a well-bred young woman who gives way to sexual temptation and judges herself too harshly for it. The bewilderment of an unsophisticated character only half able to accept her natural longings is poignantly conveyed.

Other Griffith heroines have more free will and are played by other actresses. In the Babylonian sequence of *Intolerance*, Constance Talmadge gives a spirited performance as The Mountain Girl, whose independence and aggressiveness are at first treated humorously and then heroically. Talmadge wins the audience's heart by cleverly combining masculine and feminine attributes. The Mountain Girl is at once daringly resolute and charmingly brash, and it is a tragic surprise when a character treated and played in this manner is not spared a tragic end. Earlier Griffith heroines were later replaced by Carol Dempster, who tended to portray more knowing and modern types of women with captivating energy but less emotional resonance. By contrast to Marsh, Talmadge, Dempster, and other actresses, including Lillian and Dorothy Gish, the performances of Miriam Cooper in *The Birth of a Nation* and *Intolerance* are marked by the apparent absence of dazzling virtuosity. A dark-haired beauty of a type not commonly associated with Griffith, Cooper's haunting presence and understated approach — especially as The Friendless One, the most complex character in *Intolerance* — have worn unusually well with the passage of time. It is unfortunate that her numerous subsequent films for director Raoul Walsh, whom she married, are lost, as they would probably confirm her significance as one of the most modern silent actresses, a worthy precursor to Louise Brooks.

The greatest Griffith actress, however — and the one who undeniably excelled also in works by other directors — is Lillian Gish. The tragedy of the virginal and submissive woman, mistaken in her presumption that the ways of the world actually honor these negligible virtues, is conveyed with knowing subtlety by Gish. In such films as *Broken Blossoms* and *True Heart Susie* (both 1919) and *Way Down East* (1920), Gish's performances continually suggest that inside the heroines, so violently tossed about on the currents of melodrama, there are mature and reasoning women who could determine their own fates if they had the courage to do so. These heroines are caught between acceptance of the often unjust standards and values of an earlier time and an awareness of alternatives. In this context, Gish's performance in *Way Down East*, a film much admired by contemporary feminists, is one of the most timeless incarnations associated with any actress. Gish plays Anna Moore, a beautiful young woman tricked into a mock marriage by an insincere playboy (Lowell Sherman). Deserted, she has a baby who dies; and subsequently she tries to conceal her past in order to work and live on the farm of a dismayingly puritanical family. There she falls in love with the son (Richard Barthelmess), a sensitive young man remarkably free of his family's prejudices. Anna becomes the victim of a guilt she unjustly imposes on herself, but at the same time the cruelty of events has not really spoiled her essential nature, and she intuitively knows that she deserves more than a life of subservience and fear. This inner conflict results in a very credible climax when her past catches up with her. Torn by conflicting values, she runs out in a snowstorm and throws herself on an ice floe drifting toward a treacherous waterfall, a perfect metaphor for the numbing frigidity which would solve all of her problems by consigning her to an emotional and spiritual death. The hero, who has never wanted her to be less than a warm and responsive woman, saves her.

The film is propelled much less by outward events than by the inner changes of Anna Moore, and Gish has the gift for externalizing this interior drama. Her performance evokes a continuous transfiguration which does not support the character's apparent lack of rebellion. Gish has the physical attributes and skill to convey softness, delicacy, and vulnerability readily; but she also suggests an implicit strength. The artistry of Gish is therefore crucial to Griffith's intentions. The meaning of the film does not need to be stated overtly in a sermonizing manner because his interpretation is expressed by the actress rather than by the surface plot.

The lesson of Gish is reflected in the acting of others in the silent era. The popularity of cinema seemed to demand an allegiance to melodramatic conventions, and the sincerity and intelligence which distinguished the acting styles most attuned to softening the narrative contrivances are crucial to the continuing freshness of the classic films of the era. Greta Garbo and John Gilbert, teamed in a number of love stories such as *Love* (1927) and *Flesh and the Devil* (1927), remain a credible couple whose screen romances are articulated with enough behavioral detail to have an intense ring of truth. *Sunrise* (1927), directed by F.W. Murnau, is distinguished by a touch of expressionism in the playing of George O'Brien and Janet Gaynor, who are both essentially natural performers. The result is not a distortion of the acting personalities of O'Brien and Gaynor but a rewarding deepening and intensification of those personalities. They inhabit the roles of a man and wife beset by a severe marital crisis with a genuineness of feeling which makes Murnau's stylized approach to the characters infinitely richer than would be the case with more mannered players.

Ronald Colman, an actor known for his beautiful voice in sound films, already possessed much of his elegant style in silent films. The admirable restraint of which silent actors were often capable is beautifully expressed by Colman in a scene from Ernst Lubitsch's *Lady Windermere's Fan* (1925). The character Colman plays is sitting on the other side of an immense room from the heroine. He walks across the room to her and calmly tells her that he is in love with her. Not encouraged by the passivity of her response, he then returns to his original place on the other side of the room. The entire scene is played in long shot and Lubitsch characteristically permits no overt display of emotion.

Nevertheless, Colman makes the character's melancholy an element of the scene by the way he walks. Additionally, the gallantry of the character and the reticence with which he declares his love are conveyed not by a change of expression on Colman's face but by the consistent manifestation of a quiet yearning in his eyes which the character seems to be cleverly suppressing.

Some styles of acting were geared either to the highly idiosyncratic demands of a director or to the actualities of the period. A good example of the latter is the acting of Clara Bow, the "It" girl, a lovely and very underappreciated actress who mingled sweetness and sexiness in a manner very becoming to the Jazz Age of the 1920's. A good example of the former is the work of George Bancroft, Evelyn Brent, Clive Brook, William Powell, and Betty Compson in the films of Josef von Sternberg: *Underworld* (1927), *The Last Command*, and *The Docks of New York* (1928). The attempted suppression of emotion typical of Sternberg characters required an acting language in which physical gestures and mask-like countenances would permit the characters' deepest feelings to emerge seemingly against their will, and the players mentioned demonstrated remarkable understanding of this difficult acting style. . .

Some actors created their own style independently of fashions or directors. One of the supreme examples is William S. Hart, perhaps the greatest Western star of the silent years. Hart not only fashioned a manner of playing which involves an interesting synthesis of taciturn calm and emotional anguish but also conceived a distinctive characterization of a good badman which was emulated by other Western stars. The validity of Hart's playing style and his believability as a westerner are confirmed by the work of sound actors associated with the same genre. Both Randolph Scott and Gary Cooper have been said to resemble him and often play characters conceived along the same lines. The Hart hero always has a violent past and is morally ambiguous at the outset, but he is redeemed by love and his finer instincts. As Westerns even in this period had a mythical or legendary aspect, the hero does not have to die in the process and can be seen at the fadeout shyly adapting to a new way of life much to the delight of the gentle heroine. An outstanding example of the Hart style is *The Return of Draw Egan* (1917) in which the heroine is played by the lovely Margery Wilson, who was Brown Eyes in the French sequence of *Intolerance*. Hart, who directed *The Return of Draw Egan* among others, often entrusted the guidance of his vehicles to others, notably Thomas H. Ince and Lambert Hillyer, but the Hart characterization never varied in precision and assurance. . . .

Another distinctive style of playing was achieved at about the same time by Louise Brooks in G.W. Pabst's *Pandora's Box* (1929) and *The Diary of a Lost Girl* (1929). Brooks was an American actress of a reasonably conventional naturalistic style working for a German expressionist director in these two films. Wisely, Pabst does not rob Brooks of her reality, but the psychological sophistication underlying the roles and the expressionistic ambience of the *mise-en-scene* permit Brooks to shatter cinematic prototypes and to imbue naturalistic playing with a sense of mystery and fatalism. Brooks's characterizations in these two films are arguably freer of sentiment than those of any other actress of the silent era. The notably modern severity of her playing gives her a mesmerizing aura. Her seductive beauty is at the same time provocative and forbidding. *Femmes fatales* have been recurring figures in the cinema, notably in *film noir*, but the silent version of the archetype created by the Brooks-Pabst collaboration has never been sufficiently assimilated to render the original less remarkable.

The disparate acting styles nurtured in very different kinds of films throughout the silent era make it difficult to generalize about notions of screen performance in these early years. Silent films were necessarily and fortuitously adventurous in approach and the complacent attitudes which would eventually begin to rob cinema of its vitality, at least with regard to the mainstream commercial film, were many years away.

There are a few timeless lessons about screen acting to be learned from even a brief consideration of performances that have worn well, such as those of Louise Brooks, Lillian Gish, and William S. Hart. One is that humility and genuineness count for more than showy displays of facile dramatics and clever acting tricks. The Jannings-Keaton comparison previously evoked remains valid in terms of sound-film actors. Marlon Brando, who brought an impressive sensitivity and compelling presence to some of his early roles, notably those directed by Elia Kazan, has become, in the opinion of many critics, one of the worst actors in the history of cinema, whose mannered, self-indulgent portrayals fail totally to serve the films in which he appears. On the other hand, Robert Mitchum, although he often has been cast in roles sadly unworthy of him and has been as critically neglected as Brando has been overpraised, is coming to be recognized as one of the best actors in cinema. He has a remarkable sense of the camera's power to perceive the subtlest registrations of emotion, and his performances are modulated accordingly. He has a sense of the part he is playing and its place in the design of the film rather than a flair for what will make him look like a brilliant actor. Not surprisingly, he survived his bad films and periodically appeared in outstanding ones, in which his self-effacing skill is invaluable because it serves the films rather than drawing attention to itself. Since the silent era, the cinema has thrived on the gifts of actors and actresses who understood that they were one element of the *mise-en-scene* and the narrative dynamics of a film and has suffered at the hands of egocentric players narrowly preoccupied with the presumed brilliance of their hopefully dominant interpretations.

The second and even more instructive lesson, which is related to the first, to be learned from the performances which adorn the silent cinema is that actors and actresses, if they are professionally astute, will modify their styles in relation to individual directors while retaining their essential identities. This is well illustrated by returning to Gloria Swanson, whose career in the silent era was a model of intelligent submission to the requirements of different directors and contrasting projects. At her peak, Swanson was able to seek parts which would show her to best advantage and to this end produced several of her best films. At the same time, she permitted herself to be guided by the prevailing sensibility of the director; as a result, she never appears foolish or out of place. In Cecil B. De Mille's *The Affairs of Anatol* (1921), she is appropriately elegant and superficial; in Allan Dwan's *Manhandled* (1924), she is more natural and playful; in Erich Von Stroheim's *Queen Kelly* (1928), she is gravely romantic; and in Raoul Walsh's *Sadie Thompson* (1928), she is a lusty and knowing lady with deep reserves of warmth and generosity. Swanson's resurrection as Norma Desmond in *Sunset Boulevard* is unlike her characterizations in any of those silent films. She incarnates a forgotten star, proudly remembering vanished days of genuine glory and understandably ardent in her passionate attachment to those days. It is sometimes foolishly assumed that Desmond is the character most like Swanson herself, especially by those who revel in what they mistakenly believe to be the grotesque camp pathos of the characterization. It is much more likely, however, that the actress was once again bringing all her skill and self-knowledge to a role which summoned a more private aspect of her personality than had been customary in her more glamorous days. . . .

Chapter 2

Early Luminaries

Personalities plus a good story were all that we needed in pictures. —*Adolph Zukor.*[1]

The 1908 combination of ten producers in the Motion Picture Patents Company, led by Thomas Edison, controlled almost all of the movie business for about four years. By 1915, U.S. antitrust prosecution broke up the trust and its distribution arm, the General Film Company, but in the meantime various independent firms had proved they could make and sell motion pictures on their own. They managed to get hold of film stock, cameras, and projection equipment—and they even hired actors away from the trust companies.

This was the second wave of American film production history, led in the first instance by Carl Laemmle, founder in 1909 of the Independent Motion Picture Company, known as "IMP." This company's successor in 1912 was Universal (still in existence today), and by 1912 a good many others were active in circumventing the trust — Fox, American, Keystone, Mutual (which would soon win D.W. Griffith away from Biograph). They were joined in the same year by Adolph Zukor and his Famous Players.

Laemmle was eventually hit by 289 lawsuits, but he was so irate over the fees and controls imposed by the trust that he launched

---

1   Joseph P. Kennedy, The Story of the Films (1927) p. 64.

advertising campaigns in the trade papers, attacking the Edison policies and announcing his own pictures. Those pictures were feature-length instead of the trust-approved fifteen-minute shorts. And more and more they began to be aglow with the names of specific star personalities.

This was a dangerous thing to do. It was specifically forbidden by the trust in contracts with its own members. But it also led down a road everyone recognized as fraught with financial perils. Some of the great stars of the theater were able to command high salaries because their names brought big audiences. If the movie business began offering credit to particular personalities, they would begin to demand more money according to their popularity.

At the same time, there was a very good chance that advertising star names would please the public and bring in greater profits than before. Already there were letters flooding in even to Vitagraph, Biograph, and other trust-bound companies, asking for the names of certain players. Such letters, of course, could not be answered.[2] Audiences in the nickelodeon theaters of the time had to find their own names: one favorite was given the title of "the Biograph girl."

Laemmle was able in 1910 to tempt "the Biograph girl" away from her production company and announce to the world that she had now become the "Imp girl" — and perhaps more important for history, that her name was Florence Lawrence. He did this in a particularly flamboyant way. He and his valiant publicity man, Robert Cochrane, planted a story in the St. Louis newspapers that Florence Lawrence had been killed by a streetcar. Soon afterward, they denounced this in an advertisement in the Moving Picture World as a lie circulated by enemies of IMP. All of this hullaballoo naturally doubled the attention they got for signing their new "Imp girl."

Whether or not this heavy-handed publicity gag deserves its hallowed place in motion picture history, it has pretty much been established as the first public announcement of the existence of a movie star. As a performer, Florence Lawrence did not last long, but

2   Especially by Biograph, which was most adamant against such revelations. But see Gorham Kindem *The Business of Motion Pictures* (1982) p. 81, for 1910 publicity in *North American* magazine about Florence Turner at Vitagraph. This was in May, a month after the Laemmle episode. See also Richard de Cordova, *Picture Personalities: The Emergence of the Star System in America*, (1990) based on UCLA thesis, 1986.

as "the first star," she is likely to last forever. And she was the first of a long list of people who moved from the trust companies to the ranks of the independents, gaining fortune and fame overnight.

In time it became clear to the top executives in the movie business that the popular stars were actually a kind of insurance. Once established, their presence determined the probable boxoffice of their pictures. With the right talent combinations over a year's time, a company could almost predict its balance sheet.

Thus began the permanent game of trying to explain what makes a star a star. Is it beauty of face or figure? Is it acting talent? Is it force of personality? Is it some unexplainable uniqueness expressed in the eyes? Nobody will ever be sure. Predicting the popularity of a new star before the picture comes out is no way for a sensible person to spend valuable time.

After a picture with a new star boosts the boxoffice, then there are certain ways of trying to measure the public acceptance of a screen personality: (1) number of letters received at the studio (2) number of dollars for particular movies received at the boxoffice (3) judgments by theater owners as to the importance of the star in bringing in those dollars (4) size of crowds that can be made to gather for personal appearances (5) contract salaries or payments per picture offered by producers. All of these supposedly statistical judgments of course are inflatable at will.

Photoplay magazine ran a story in September 1923 claiming to inform readers about the relative dollar values of a good many leading performers. The editors did not, however, indicate any of the sources for this information. They might have had access in some cases to company records, via executives or publicity offices. They might have simply asked the stars themselves. Or they might have made well-informed guesses based on interviews in the recent past plus news releases. None of these sources could be unfailingly exact.

All such figures have been untrustworthy throughout the history of the movie business, for various reasons of inefficiency, misrepresentation, and self-interest. From the point of view of the producing company alone, there might be conflicting views about letting the salaries of stars be known at all. Some producers might agree to such publicity — and exaggerate it — in order to impress the customers. Others would argue that this could reap bigger contract demands by other actors.

Where possible, biographical material in this book has included crumbs of financial information, as gleaned from memoirs and magazine articles. Such shaky sources may well be improved in future by new discoveries — old corporate accounts, for example, that have been saved from shredding and made available in odd lots at film archives and university libraries. It may be that actors' salaries will one day be spread on the historical record, year by year. But a complete picture is unlikely, and even if possible, would not tell us everything.

Statistics, like anecdotes, tend to be deceiving. They spread a general fog over what historians may seek as "causation." Why certain persons were given better salaries may be lost in the psychology of executives who sought advantages either in the marketplace or in the bedroom.

The most dependable clue to change in movie trends is the long line at the boxoffice that continues for weeks. Once that happens, it is easy to predict the reappearance of the star soon afterward in a similar characterization and a similar story, with just enough variation to give the advertising staff something to write about. Thereafter, as night follows day, any alert star will ascend in salary and power — or seek employment at some other studio.

There is nothing very mysterious about this process, except for the fact that swings of public taste always are mysterious. So-called "genres" have been created and controlled by boxoffice response ever since *The Great Train Robbery* and Theda Bara. The western lasted into the 1970s. The vamp vogue lasted through 40 pictures, concentrated in four years, and has not really reappeared in the same form again. Mary Pickford, just as severely typed, lasted from 1909 to 1933.

There is always some unpredictability, however, in the decision-making process that initiates change. New departures, however slight, in a studio schedule, may result in surprises at the boxoffice. William Fox wanted to try out a script called *A Fool There Was*, and Frank Powell found the star for it. Jesse Lasky wanted to try out an opera star in Hollywood and found scripts for her. Such small gestures toward innovation may come from any person in the creative chain of events and may have far-reaching effects.

NORMA TALMADGE
Close-Ups

If more of her pictures had survived, Norma Talmadge might now be a candidate for rediscovery as a major silent star. There has been some disagreement about the depth of her acting talent, and her two sound pictures put her out of the movie business. But from her debut at Vitagraph at the age of 14, she became that studio's most famous star, and while she was married to producer Joseph Schenck (1916-27) her pictures released by First National and United Artists were enormously popular. Writers for fan magazines describe her as versatile on screen and completely without airs off-screen. She could handle comedy parts, but mostly suffered in melodramas, and Adela Rogers St. Johns, in an admiring article in Photoplay, *likened her to a beautiful polished vase. Her salary for a time was $7500 a week, and at First National in the early twenties she delivered eight pictures for $1,280,000, the same kind of deal made by Charlie Chaplin.*

Here she offers us a nostalgic look at the methods of film making in the earliest days, with all kinds of revealing details. Our extract is from the first of three autobiographical articles in the Saturday Evening Post, March 12, 1927.

Our particular picture was *The Four-Footed Pest* and dealt with the adventures of a filly that was always getting people into hot water. My bit was to be kissing a young man, whose name I forget, on a street corner, under a black cloth that was thrown over a camera, until the horse came along and lifted the cloth with her teeth. Only the back of my head was revealed, with my arms around the youth's neck. Then we had to run away. That was a sad humiliation for me — to be in the movies at last and not show my face! When I told the family that night how the business was almost entirely with my arms and feet, Natalie, in true sisterly fashion, remarked, "Since you didn't have to use your head, old dear, you will probably be a great success." But to me there was very little joke attached to that initial appearance. I was in constant terror every time we rehearsed, lest the horse, when lifting the focusing cloth between her teeth, might take my hair along with it and do a scalping act that was not in the scenario.

We finished the whole picture in half a day! The great majority of pictures then were told in only one reel, consisting of a thousand feet, with nine hundred feet of story and titles, the remainder for winding, advertising trailer, and so on. Often little comedies were done in split reels, or five hundred feet. It was quite the usual routine to complete an entire production in from one to three days. Sometimes the story was written only the night before. How amusing this seems to me now, when we devote several weeks to mere cutting and titling, and in my own company, average from eight weeks to six months on a single production!

Constance played one of a group of girls on the sidewalk who crowded around the camera to watch the antics of the horse. She wore her own clothes, but I was given a young girl's dress to replace my borrowed finery.

Florence Turner's mother had charge of the wardrobe department, which consisted of one long room with many poles stretched across, from which hung row after row of coats, dresses, and period gowns. Often a little group of players who were waiting around to be called would assist in the making or mending of costumes. They even helped paint the scenery, and, as personal maids were unheard-of, everybody took a turn at buttoning everybody else's clothes, assisted with each other's makeups, and dressed each other's hair.

Even Florence Turner, herself one of the most important players, lent a hand at everything. She had charge of the supers' salaries and doled out their money every evening. Also, she helped her mother with the wardrobe department.

Maurice Costello had caused the greatest upheaval at the Vitagraph by being the first actor to join the company with the express stipulation that he was never to wear a hammer in his belt and assist the carpenters, nor would he touch a paint brush.

He had come from the speaking stage, and informed A.E. Smith, one of the executives, that he was an actor, not a handy man. But even Costello dressed in a room with seven or eight others. As for me, that first day I dressed in a long room with a sort of wooden counter built against the wall as a dressing table, with a square mirror above it. We sat on stools, as at a lunch counter, and borrowed each other's powder and cold cream.

Harry Mayo, the casting man, had asked me if I knew how to make up.

"Yes, indeed," I answered, but as a matter of fact I knew nothing about it. I watched the girls on either side of me and copied everything they did with the most elaborate care. I might have spared myself all these pains had I known they were not going to use my face. It wasn't necessary for Baby to make up, as she was just a quick flash in the crowd. At the end of the day I received two dollars and fifty cents for my services and Constance was given two dollars. But more precious to me than any amount of money was the sweet smile from Miss Turner as she handed us our envelopes.

"When shall I come again?" I asked at the desk on my way out.

"When you're sent for," was the taciturn reply. "We have your address on file and will notify you by mail."

The next day Baby and I again returned to school, but I, for one, gained very little knowledge. Across the pages of my history book stepped brave knights in doublet and hose, and beautiful ladies in trailing gowns with diadems in their hair were gesticulating before a camera. During the English period the books we studied began to dramatize themselves in my mind as motion pictures. Algebra became utterly hateful because I could find no way of relating it to my brief acting experience. I had flunked in nearly all my classes because my mind was on one thing only. When would that letter come from the studio?

A week of watching and waiting for the postman went by. Every day I hurried home and dashed down the hall to the old-fashioned hat rack where Peg used to place the mail, but, alas, there was no envelope with Vitagraph Company in the upper left-hand corner.

The second week passed and I was beginning to give up hope, when about the middle of the third week a loud whistle heralded a letter carrier, who, leaving his bicycle at the gate, trotted up the walk with a special-delivery letter in his hand. It bore the typewritten address:

Miss Norma Talmadge
Fenimore St.
Brooklyn, N.Y.

My hand shook so with excitement that I could hardly open the letter, and even while I was enjoying the gorgeous thrill of suspense, Peg calmly snatched it from my fingers, and with unbelievably steady hands tore it open — as if a special delivery addressed to a fourteen-year-old girl were an everyday occurrence. All my hopes were realized, for it was a brief form letter to report for work at nine o'clock the following morning and ask for Mr. Charles Kent.

Peg accompanied me, and on arriving at the studio, imagine my joy when they told me I was to play in a Florence Turner picture! It was called *The Dixie Mother*.

Miss Turner was the Southern mother of seven sons and I was their little sister. The story told of the last call to arms, which meant that the youngest son, inclined to cowardice and afraid to go to war, must answer. In less than fifty feet the mother had to make the son, played by Carlyle Blackwell, understand his duty to his country and march him off to join his father and brothers at the front.

Though no word was received concerning the older boys, yet news came that the youngest son had been killed, whereupon the mother, having forced her last boy to answer duty's call, became insane. Meantime there had been a love affair going on between me, a daughter of the South, and a Northern soldier, whose parents heartily disapproved. But my father, played by Charles Kent, who was also the director, arrived home on leave just in time absolutely to forbid my having any communication with a Northern family.

Nevertheless, young love had its way and I eloped with the Northerner, returning to my family after the war with a child — symbolizing the union of the North and South — the child's appearance bringing about the recovery of the mother's sanity. As a grand finale the Union flag fluttered in the breeze. Never will I forget how inexpressibly thrilled I was when Miss Turner took me in her arms and hugged me close, sobbing out her forgiveness. Thus, I, who had longed to kneel at her feet, was actually in flesh-and-blood embrace with my idol.

This first picture is typical of how much story and action was crowded into nine hundred feet in 1910.

We rehearsed each scene over and over again, because footage was the all-important thing, and we had to know exactly where to stand, how many steps to take to the right, and on just what signal to start our business so as not to waste a scrap of film. We even made our entrances and exits on counts. There was a board placed exactly nine feet from the camera and a space chalk-marked on the floor about fifteen feet wide. Whether there were two or ten persons in a scene, all of them had to be within that radius of the camera; otherwise they were out of the picture entirely. The camera, of course, was stationary and only one camera was used. To have had different cameras at varied angles, such as we have today, would have been an expense unheard-of, and devices for moving the camera for long shots, medium shots, and three-foot close-ups had not yet been invented. . . .

Norma Talmadge in *Panthea*

DEWITT BODEEN
Panthea

From the valuable collection of new reviews Magill's Survey of
Cinema: Silent Films, *(Englewood Cliffs, N.J., Salem Press, 1982, pp.
847-849) we have selected one of the films no longer in existence. DeWitt
Bodeen has used various sources and his own memory to give us a careful
report on this film and on the career of Norma Talmadge.*

Released: 1917
Production: Lewis J. Selznick
Direction: Allan Dwan
Screenplay: Mildred Considine; based on the play of the same name
by Monckton Hoffe
Cinematography: Roy F. Overbaugh
Length: 5 reels
Principal characters:

Panthea Romoff	*Norma Talmadge*
Gerald Mordaunt	*Earle Foxe*
Baron de Duisitor	*L. Rogers Lytton*
Prefect of Police	*George Fawcett*
Secret Agent	*Murdock MacQuarrie*

During the shooting of *Panthea* for Lewis J. Selznick, Norma
Talmadge married producer Joseph Schenck. It was perhaps the
wisest move she ever made, for Schenck was deeply in love with her,
and, under his sponsorship, she became the top dramatic actress in
Hollywood, as well as one of the richest. She purchased some of the
choicest property in Los Angeles, including a large apartment house
still in existence on Wilshire Blvd. called the Talmadge; and, with her
sister Constance, she also owned her own studio in West
Hollywood. Furthermore, any story property that she wanted to
produce for herself, Schenck usually bought.

Talmadge, Schenck, and Allan Dwan joined forces to produce
Panthea, and after she completed her Selznick contract, Talmadge
formed the Norma Talmadge Production Company, with Schenck
supervising the films that she made. *Panthea*, a 1913 play by
Monckton Hoffe, showed in London and then on Broadway, with
Mme. Olga Petrova as its star.

In the film, Talmadge plays a Russian pianist named Panthea
Romoff, a graduate of the Moscow conservatory, who is suspected of
revolutionary sympathies. While attending one of Panthea's
concerts, the Baron de Duisitor (L. Rogers Lytton) conspires with the
Moscow Prefect of Police (George Fawcett) to have her home raided,

after which she was to be brought up before him on charges of nihilism and advocating the overthrow of social institutions. The Baron would then secure her release and thus make her indebted to him. Circumstances, however, conspire against them. Panthea's brother actually is a nihilist and is holding a meeting in the house when the police come to arrest Panthea. The brother manages to escape, but a soldier is killed in the process. The Baron curses fate, especially when Panthea escapes her prison and sails for England. Her ship is wrecked off the English coast, and Panthea, unconscious, is rescued and brought to the nearby Mordaunt estate to recover. Young Gerald Mordaunt (Earle Foxe), heir to the estate, immediately falls in love with her. Their mutual love of music is a special bond, and Gerald confesses that he lives to have one of his original operas produced. They marry and move to Paris, where they live in happiness for a year. Panthea herself takes her husband's opera around to producers, but she cannot generate any interest in his work.

Then she again encounters Baron de Duisitor, and he agrees to produce her husband's opera, provided that she becomes his mistress. The opera is a great success, and the Baron arranges to have her arrested as soon as he seduces her. The Baron, however, has a heart attack and dies when the international police, headed by the Moscow prefect, come to arrest her. Panthea must go back to Russia, possibly to be condemned to Siberia, but Gerald insists that he will go with her. At the end of the story, he has already started the diplomatic corps working on evidence that will free her entirely so that they can both eventually return to London.

If Talmadge's career had begun to blossom with a promising start at Vitagraph, where she is said to have made over a hundred short features, and later with a short term at Triangle, it finally burst into full bloom with *Panthea*, her first film for Selznick. She gained a real following with subsequent vehicles such as *Poppy* (1917), released six months after *Panthea; The Forbidden City* (1918), in which she played a dual role; and *The Safety Curtain* (1918), in which she was a much-abused waif. She changed releasing companies to Associated First National in 1920, and the ensuing decade marked the bulk of her great successes. Eugene O'Brien had been her leading man in ten of the features that she made in the 1917-1918 period, and since it was openly acknowledged that O'Brien was a homosexual, Schenck did not mind how torrid their love scenes were. He was, in fact, very happy when O'Brien could give up his short-lived starring career and return to being leading man again for his wife in a second series that included *Secrets* (1924) and *Graustark* (1925).

The Schencks nevertheless drifted apart, although he still managed her career and brought her to United Artists in 1927 with *The Dove*. When she played Marguerite Gauthier in 1927 in a beautiful modern production of *Camille*, based as much on the novel as it was on the play, she chose Gilbert Roland to be her Armand. They were a handsome couple, and Lionel Barrymore even coached Roland for the role in a Los Angeles stage production of *Camille* starring Jane Cowl. By this time, Roland and Talmadge were lovers, and it was, oddly enough, for the time, well known and fully accepted in the Hollywood community. She was a well-liked, generous woman and even gave Roland so many marvelous close-ups in *Camille* that at least one local critic remarked that perhaps the title of the piece should be *Armand*. Roland was her leading man four times, in *Camille*, *The Dove* (1928), *The Woman Disputed* (1928), and her first talking film, *New York Nights* (1929), a gangster melodrama.

Realizing that sound pictures were going to change the industry forever, Talmadge feared for her career since she had no stage training which was a liability in the early sound period, and both she and her sister Constance had very identifiable Brooklyn accents. Leslie Carter was hired to coach her in *Dubarry, Woman of Passion* (1930). Carter had created that role for David Belasco on stage, but she could do nothing for Talmadge, who thereupon retired, divorced Schenck, and soon afterward, married George Jessel. They did a vaudeville act together, for which Jessel coached her. They did not last long as a team, and when they divorced, Talmadge married San Francisco physician, Dr. Carvel James. They lived most of the time in San Francisco, or in Florida, where she also owned a home. She was a very rich woman when she died in 1957.

The films she made, starting with *Panthea*, were wonderfully romantic, and this type of drama was clearly her forte. She suffered gloriously on the screen, and most of her vehicles were styled around at least one tearful scene. *Panthea* was perfect for her; it even included a scene in which she was to "give all" in order to let her husband live in a dream world. Among her most memorable films are *Smilin' Through* (1922), *Within the Law* (1923), and *The Lady* (1925); and it is because of her that these films remain unforgettable today.

JESSE L. LASKY
Geraldine Farrar in the Movies

As head of the west coast studio for Famous Players-Lasky (later known as Paramount Pictures) Jesse Lasky was the first of a historic list of such top producers — Irving Thalberg, Harry Cohn, Jack Warner, Darryl Zanuck, and their successors in network television. Lasky was evidently a knowing and relatively gentle example of the type, a man who had started out in music and vaudeville and found himself, somewhat to his surprise, on the west coast as a partner of Cecil B. DeMille and Sam Goldwyn in the moving picture business. His story is told more fully in the first volume of this series, The First Tycoons.

In this selection from his autobiography, I Blow My Own Horn, *(pages 116-118) he remembers hiring one of history's greatest opera singers to bring her star value to the movies. She was an uncommonly "good sport" and endeared herself to cast and crew alike, in spite of having to undergo rugged costume and location challenges. A performance of* Carmen *not sung? Yes, and not even heard. But this was a major episode in what would be an accelerating trend toward star personalities in movies.*

To bring attention to our offerings and help overcome prejudice against films in general, we had hired Harry Reichenbach to handle publicity for *The Squaw Man* and subsequent pictures. He had already shown a flair that was to make him the undisputed king of sensational hoaxes, by sparking the crusade that made *September Morn* the most famous painting of the day. He simply hired a crowd of ragamuffins to ogle a reproduction of the nude in a Fifth Avenue art-store window, and then phoned the New York Society for Suppression of Vice that the picture was corrupting youth. During the ensuing battle of the press the picture was exhibited on a nationwide tour and made a fortune for its promoters. We thought that, if Reichenbach could breathe that much life into a still picture, he should certainly be very valuable in exploiting moving pictures. But the frustrating task of trying to publicize our pictures without being allowed to mention the names of their noteworthy stars almost drove Reichenbach crazy. It was like writing up one of Mrs. Cornelius Vanderbilt's society balls and omitting the name of the hostess.

This impasse had to be broken some way, and the problem was much on my mind when Morris Gest, son-in-law of David Belasco and a well-known impresario himself, asked me at luncheon to go along with him to a matinee of *Madame Butterfly*. Geraldine Farrar was making her farewell appearance of the season at the Metropolitan Opera House under Gest's management.

There were no seats left, and we stood in the rear.

Farrar was currently the greatest dramatic soprano in grand opera and a fine actress. I have never seen such adulation as when the final curtain came down. She had a devoted following of young student fans as ardently demonstrative as Frank Sinatra's bobby-soxers in later years. Her idol-worshipers were called "Gerry-flappers." I got a sudden idea and told Gest I wanted to meet her.

Backstage I came quickly to the point. "Miss Farrar," I said, "I don't know whether you have ever seen a motion picture, but my company makes them, and I'd like to persuade you to do the story of Carmen for us. (I knew it was her favorite role.) We have no trouble securing famous plays and engaging their stars," I continued, "but they're always afraid acting in a movie will hurt their stage prestige. I could see by the ovation you got today that your prestige is such that whatever you do, your public will accept it as right."

"You think I could turn the tide?" she asked cordially, intrigued by the compliment.

"I'm sure other stars would follow your lead," I said, "and I can see that you'd photograph beautifully. If you consent, I'm prepared to offer you — in addition to whatever salary we agree on — a number of other inducements . . ." I ad-libbed as many as I could think of — our best director, an orchestra on the set to play music whenever she liked, a private railroad car to take her and her family to Hollywood, a house completely furnished and staffed with servants for her stay, a car and chauffeur at her complete disposal, a private dressing room for her comfort at the studio, which I promised to have built right next to the stage and equipped with a grand piano for her practicing. . . .

Perhaps Geraldine Farrar's decision to accept my offer was influenced by the fact that she had recently overtaxed her voice to the point of despairing she might ever sing again, and the chance to give her throat a rest in silent pictures couldn't have come at a more opportune time. Be that as it may, she proved the most charming, gracious actress I ever brought to Hollywood, and was completely devoid of temperament, contrary to the tradition of prima donnas. If the script called for her to be in mud up to her waist, or with clothing, skin, and hair fire-proofed and cotton saturated with ammonia in her nostrils and mouth for burning at the stake scenes, she didn't demur for an instant.

The Farrar expedition to the wilds of Hollywood was heralded in banner headlines across the continent. Accompanying her in the private car were her parents (her father was Sid Farrar, a famous National League baseball player), her personal press agent, and her manager, Morris Gest, with his wife, Reina. Our New York publicity men saw them off with great fanfare, while I rushed ahead to the Coast to make sure the diva would be ushered in like a visiting queen. The Santa Fe platform and depot were carpeted from her private car to the waiting limousine. School children lined both sides of her path, strewing it with roses. The mayor and other dignitaries formed a welcoming committee and a reception was to be held in Hollywood.

Since she was the first personality in motion-picture history to receive what has since become known as "the full treatment," every detail of it was front-page news.

I rode with Miss Farrar to the two-story house we had rented for her stay. Every room was banked with flowers. I introduced her to the maid, cook, and butler we had provided. As I started back to the studio, I mentioned that DeMille was looking forward to meeting her the next day, after she was rested from her long trip, as he was anxious to talk over her role in *Carmen.*

"Give me a few minutes to change," she said with a smile, "and I'll go with you now."

I think perhaps she couldn't wait until the next day to view her bungalow dressing room, a luxury bestowed on most stars now but unheard of then. Built next to the open-air stage, as I had promised, it contained a tastefully furnished living room, dressing room, and bathroom. I left her in Cecil's office, deeply engrossed with him over wardrobe details.

The next morning as soon as I came in the studio, Cecil said, "I want to show you something you'll never forget." He led me out through the orchard toward the stage. Work had come to a dead standstill. Everyone on our payroll — the cast, carpenters, grips, cowboys, and office staff — was standing bareheaded in a transfixed circle around Miss Farrar's bungalow. The door was open and she was at the grand piano joyously singing an aria from *Madame Butterfly.* The radio had not yet been invented, and those people — many of whom had never before heard an opera singer — were hearing the greatest.

Although she was dignified in billing as *Miss* Geraldine Farrar (stage artists of the first rank were accorded a "Miss" or "Mr." to distinguish them from those who were primarily film actors like Mary Pickford and Wallace Reid), she was "Gerry" to all of us after a brief acquaintance.

Carmen turned out to be the biggest money-maker we had up to that time. And it took the curse off movie work for stage personalities. Reichenbach was no longer pledged to secrecy about what famous actors from the theatre had been seen in a Lasky picture. He would come right out and name them in bold type. In fact matinee idols of Broadway began to look to Hollywood with envious eyes and to demand "the full treatment" with plenty of interviews and newspaper build-up when they entrained for a studio commitment.

After *Carmen*, Farrar worked straight through two more pictures, *Temptation* and *Maria Rosa*. In the latter we teamed her with Lou Tellegen, who had created his same role on the stage and before that had been Sarah Bernhardt's leading man on the stage and in her picture *Queen Elizabeth*. He looked like a Greek god and fascinated the singer from the moment I introduced them. Some months later in New York she invited Bessie and me to an intimate dinner at which she announced their engagement.

A year or so later she interspersed her concert engagements with three more movies. Cecil directed all six of the pictures she made for us. One of them, I note by the list of one thousand pictures made under my supervision between 1913 and 1932, was called *The Woman God Forgot*. I'm afraid I've also forgotten the woman God forgot, but I clearly recall Gerry as Joan of Arc in *Joan the Woman*.

NORMAN ZIEROLD
Theda Bara

> *William Fox found a different kind of headliner in Theodosia Goodman, a stagestruck young woman from Cleveland. She played a "death-dealing, smouldering-eyed screen vampire" in more than forty films within four years. Her career was an early example of publicity-made profiteering and it was followed by female "vamps" with widely varying approaches: Garbo, Harlow, Monroe and others. Zierold's cheerful report on some of these characters, Sex Goddesses of the Silent Screen (Chicago, Regnery Co., 1973) naturally puts Theda Bara first. We have tried to extract the most salient portions: pages 5-11, 13-15, 25-27, 41-43.*

For more than three years, in a proliferating series of meetings across the land, outraged women had put the burgeoning film medium on trial, just as a half century later their grandchildren were to debate the baneful influence of television on their homes. With a war raging in Europe they found time to worry about violence and gore and Wild West escapades at the neighborhood theater. But most of all they worried about Theda Bara, the Vampire, the Wickedest Woman in the World, as the Fox organization gleefully billed her.

St. Augustine had said there was little merit to resisting temptation unless you had experienced it. The multitudes who went to see the Vampire were confirmed, if unknowing, Augustinians. Most of them were also unaware that the object of their co-mingled hate and love was the first full-scale product of filmdom's newly founded publicity mills. The prefabrication, the hoax, was of such magnitude that even today the name of Theda Bara is symbolic of fatal feminine charm.

Godfather to the legend was William Fox, a former cloth sponger turned penny arcade proprietor and film exhibitor. In 1913 Fox decided to turn producer. His first film, *Life's Shop Window*, was made on Staten Island at a cost of $4,500. Somewhat more went into *A Fool There Was*, the outdoor scenes for which were filmed in Florida. Because the leading woman was an unknown, the advance publicity concentrated on the male star, Edward Jose, who had played on stage opposite Sarah Bernhardt. When the film was released, in January, 1915, Jose was praised for his performance, but the uproar over the interpretation of the female lead reached hysterical proportions. The fantastic fame and infamy of Theda Bara were literally created overnight.

"As the Vampire, Theda Bara gives the woman not one redeeming feature, her only appeal being purely animal," wrote the *New York Morning Telegraph*. "She is imperious, a fury, a perfect volcano of conflicting emotions. The only real pleasure she gets out of life seems to be in inflicting pain and anguish upon foe and friend alike. It is quite the most revolting but fascinating character that has appeared upon the screen for some time. Magnificent gowns — and an occasional lack of them — add greatly to the forcefulness of Miss Bara's work."

"Miss Bara misses no chance for sensuous appeal in her portrayal of the Vampire," wrote the *New York Dramatic Mirror*. "She is a horribly fascinating woman, vicious to the core, and cruel. When she says, 'Kiss me, my fool,' the fool is generally ready to obey and enjoy a prolonged moment, irrespective of the less enjoyable ones to follow...."

While history had provided numerous prototypes for the vampire, it was a nineteenth-century painting by Sir Edward Burne-Jones that was the immediate ancestor. In a remarkable portrait the Victorian master had tried to show the soul, or lack of soul, in the face of a woman who takes all and gives nothing in return, who squeezes everything out of a man and leaves a desiccated rind. The work had inspired Rudyard Kipling to write an unflattering poem about the female of the species called "The Vampire," which began with the lines:

A fool there was and he made his prayer —
(Even as you and I)
To a rag and a bone and a hank of hair —
(We called her the woman who did not care)
But the fool he called her his lady fair —
(Even as you and I)

In 1909 Porter Emerson Browne knocked out a melodrama that took its title from the first line of Kipling's poem. With Robert Hilliard playing the fool and Katharine Kaelred his tormentor, it enjoyed a ready success on the legitimate stage before its transfer to the screen. . . .

Early in the film the audience learned of a youth who commits suicide because the Vampire deserts him in favor of John Schuyler, the pathetic "hero" of *A Fool There Was*. The affair with Schuyler, a married man, starts on an ocean liner and continues abroad under the romantic skies of Italy. Alternating with languorous tableaux and scenes of unleashed passion are sequences showing this latest fool's wife and child at home in America: pathos and even comic relief are supplied by his little girl. Completely dominated by the wanton woman, Schuyler returns her to New York, where his physical and moral degeneration continues despite the efforts of friends to drag him out of the quicksand of the Vampire's lips. As Kipling's poem put it,

So some of him lived but the most of him died . . .

The Fox organization was not fully prepared for the breathtaking leap of their new star's popularity. Since no vehicle was immediately available for her talents, she was cast in a film based on Tolstoy's *The Kreutzer Sonata*, which starred the much-admired dramatic actress Nance O'Neil. The Bara role had her playing a beautiful and ruthlessly passionate girl who without scruples breaks the heart of her sister Miriam so that she may possess Miriam's husband, a brilliant violinist.

Never again was Theda Bara to share star billing with a woman. With *The Clemenceau Case*, still early in 1915, she settled into a mold that was to hug her well-rounded form for endless reels. Based on a play by the younger Dumas, author of *Camille*, the film was directed by Herbert Brenon: stage actor William Shay was cast as Pierre Clemenceau and Stuart Holmes as his best friend, Ritz Constantin. As the beautiful but wicked Iza, Theda Bara was out to avenge wrongs supposedly done to her sex by men. Following a long train of victims were Pierre, whom she lured into marriage, and Ritz Constantin. The final scene of the film was so characteristic that it deserves elaboration.

In her luxurious and exotic boudoir the restless Iza tries to find distraction. For a few moments she toys with a giant king python but tires of it and puts it aside, easing herself languidly onto an ottoman lounge. Here she awaits the coming of Pierre, who, unbeknownst to her, has learned of her affair with his friend Ritz. When Pierre arrives, Iza throws her arms about his neck and drags him down beside her. As their lips meet, they hear the sound of a key in the locked door. Ritz Constantin dashes in, looks wildly about, and with a savage oath rushes at Iza — who laughs cruelly at his distraction. Suddenly her beautiful face becomes horribly contorted, and her lips let out a fearful scream. In the moment of their clinging embrace Pierre has seized a jeweled dagger from the wall close to his hand and has plunged the blade deep into her heart. His own life has been ruined, but he still has the courage to save his friend from a similar fate. The vampire is dead in her lair. As her limp body falls back on the blood-splattered draperies, Pierre goes calmly over to the telephone. "Sergeant, send up your man. I have just killed my wife," says the film's melodramatic final caption.

Death was a suitable punishment for Iza Clemenceau, but filmgoers knew that Theda Bara lived, that her menace was likely to grow. William Fox knew it too, and he made sure that it grew at the fastest possible pace, on screen and off. He fabricated a vampire symbol that took its hold on the public and helped to characterize an era.

Among his major assets in these endeavors were the immense physical appeal of his star and her lively, pliant mentality. By her fans Theda Bara was considered strangely, sensually, exotically, perversely beautiful. Large black hypnotic eyes were her most salient feature. Makeup men set them in heavy Kohl-like frames within a rounded dead-white face. Dark lustrous hair was at times left to trail in great waves over bare shoulders, at others contained within black spit curls, and on still other occasions was tucked behind elaborate headgear that ran the gamut from peacock feathers to jeweled crowns. Hoop earrings became a Bara trademark, as did bronze spangles, the leopard-skin couch, the tiger-skin rug, and the long gold cigarette holder.

The Vampire's generously voluptuous frame seldom moved to an ordinary rhythm. Rather it glided, slinked, undulated, its lush curves displayed in diaphanous gowns or filmy shawls. Low necks and soft slithery satins were much in evidence. A veil or two and a few festoons of synthetic pearls were often ample costume for the bosomy, sultry-eyed Theda. A sinister droop to the left eye and a cruel expression of the mouth appeared when the vampire was about to strike.

No woman so calculatingly seductive, so alluringly cruel, so wonderfully wicked could possibly be of American origin. Theda Bara was a love pirate, a sex bitch. She could be French perhaps, or Oriental, but certainly not American. Even before the cameras had started rolling for *A Fool There Was*, William Fox realized that the female lead could certainly not be named Theodosia Goodman. Twenty-five-year-old Theodosia had herself pondered the matter and came forth with a new name. Theda was a contraction of her first name and Bara was the family name of her maternal grandfather, who was Swiss. . . .

In point of fact, Mlle. Goodman had made her first stage performance in the suburbs of Cincinnati in 1898. At the age of seven she recited "The Dirty-Faced Brat," a maudlin piece about a starving boy who goes out to shovel snow in the bitter cold to earn money for food. The exhibition took place in a neighbor's barn to which her brother had lured a youthful audience with promises of lemonade and cookies and threats of reprisal for nonattendance.

After a relatively normal childhood, including public school, a year with a tutor, and a term at a girls' college, eighteen-year-old Theodosia — called "Teddy" and "Theda" by her friends — made up her mind to become an actress, although her studies had emphasized music. Reluctantly her father paid her way to New York, where she moved into a small hotel near Washington Square. Failing to land a Broadway role, she accepted a small part in a road company at $25 a week. When the company manager threatened to cut that meager sum to $18, the disillusioned young actress returned to Washington Square. The Great White Way still paid her no mind. . . .

Director Frank Powell of Fox Pictures became acquainted with Theda and asked her to watch him direct. When he offered her the female lead in *A Fool There Was*, the worn-out girl swallowed her pride and accepted with stoic distaste.

If *A Fool There Was* gave a clear-cut definition of Theda Bara as a death-dealing, smouldering-eyed screen vampire, a home-wrecker to end all home-wreckers, William Fox, his man Goldfarp, and the lackeys poured out to the press a word portrait of Theda Bara that was easily as exaggerated and outlandish as her screen portrayals. For the next four years, Theodosia Goodman was the accomplice, the beneficiary, and to a considerable extent, the victim of this high-powered exploitation.

The Clemenceau Case had made everyone's work easy, arousing both institutions and individuals. "Were the National Board of Censorship possessed of any judgement whatsoever, this is the kind of a picture it should place the ban of its disapproval upon," wrote one critic, so upset that he ended his sentence with a preposition. Many local boards did issue edicts of disapproval. A female correspondent, one of an incipient avalanche, wrote bitterly to Theda: "It is such women as you who break up happy homes." From Theda came a reply: "I am working for my living, dear friend, and if I were the kind of woman you seem to think I am, I wouldn't have to." Protests were in vain. The screen Theda made her viewers hate her, and the hatred reached beyond the screen. . . .

It was the face of the Vampire that a young man in the Midwest saw one evening as he returned home and looked at his mother-in-law. Without further ado, he proceeded to do her in, and he was promptly charged with murder. The Fox organization was not displeased when the defendant's lawyer asked that a print of *The Clemenceau Case* be made available for jurors in the case. The defendant had seen the film immediately before committing the felony; it was his lawyer's contention that it had affected his mind, leading him to imitate Pierre Clemenceau in an effort to end his own domestic troubles. The defense plea was not sustained, but one more stroke of the brush was added to the picture of Theda Bara as a destroyer.

Artists of stature were enlisted by Fox to fill out the portrait. Charles Dana Gibson depicted Mlle. Bara as "Sin." "Never have I had a model who impressed me as deeply as Miss Bara," the dutiful Gibson said. Famous magazine illustrator James Montgomery Flagg hewed more closely to the line. "Mlle. Bara is unique," he said. "I do not believe there is another woman like her." He called his picture *The Vampire*, and in it the model was seen in a greenish light, with snake-like coils of hair hanging about a dead-white face in which two burning and passionate eyes glowed with a subdued flame. . . .

Theda Bara's final film in 1915 was entitled *The Serpent,* and in it she writhed and glided and lured and fascinated to her heart's content.

Seldom had even an old-fashioned melodrama carried a plot putting so severe a strain on credulity. Theda Bara fans did not seem to mind. She had made eleven pictures in one year, and "Hell's Handmaiden" was now receiving over 200 letters a day. Effusive poems accompanied many; 1,329 contained offers of marriage. A Sing Sing convict entered into weekly correspondence, in which he said that he was writing a screen play for his idol. Unsolicited scenarios arrived from plumbers, college boys, ministers, and shop girls at the rate of thirty a week. Gifts within the year added up to 1,186 pounds, plus a hundred pounds of candy each month, all donated to hospitals or orphanages. Twelve months earlier no one knew whether Bara was the name of a new toothpaste or a rare malady, but by the end of the year 162 babies had been named after Theda, a number that easily outdistanced those honoring Colonel Theodore Roosevelt, the runner-up.

"Box office receipts from Coney Island to the Golden Gate prove that the public wants her to be a vampire," wrote columnist Archie Bell. "But how long can she keep on the same track?" For the moment, there seemed little cause for apprehension. The *New York Times* made a statistical study of what it called "the flaming comet of the cinema firmament." Of each of Theda's eleven pictures there were forty prints, all constantly in use. In the larger playhouses, three performances a day were the rule, while in the far more numerous smaller theaters, performances were continuous, up to six a day. If the average attendance was tabulated at 200 persons and the average daily performances at five, 400,000 people a day were seeing Theda Bara films. Since these estimates were conservative, a half million was a more likely figure. In a week the Vampire's face thus flashed on the retinas of more than three million fans in a movie-mad world. In the year the staggering figures of 182 million witnessed her celluloid charms.

At the end of 1915 the leading deaf-and-dumb institute in New York voted Theda Bara the most expressive actress on the screen, and a motion picture popularity contest listed the country's favorite female stars in this order: (1) Clara Kimball Young; (2) Anita Stewart; (3) Virginia Norden; (4) Mary Pickford; (5) Theda Bara; (6) Pearl White; (7) Beverly Bayne; (8) Edith Storey; (9) Alice Joyce; (10) Florence LaBadie.

Theda had much to be grateful for, but she also had her worries. The women who were frightened of Theda in turn frightened her. To her mind, they completely misunderstood her, failed to grasp what she increasingly viewed as her unique professional mission. "Why do people hate me so?" she asked mournfully. "I try to show the world how attractive sin may be, how very beautiful, so that one must be always on the lookout and know evil even in disguise. I am a moral teacher then. But what is my reward? I am detested. . . ."

Support for Theda's position, albeit with a twist, came from Victor O. Freeburg, Professor of Photoplay at Columbia University. One of the first academics to bear a title relating to the new film industry, Freeburg announced that the screen vampire had a healthy influence on her audiences. "Most girls are good, but good girls do not want to see other good girls upon the screen," he said. "There's no interest, no fascination in that for them. Miss Bara shows something different, vastly different from the life they know. Most moving picture audiences want enjoyment by contrast.   Few are either daring enough or desirous enough of leading a vampire existence, but through the medium of Theda Bara they can do her deeds and live her life. Their emotions are enriched by just that much. . . ."

The continued assault on her "art" and the condemnation of Vampire roles kept Theda searching for alternatives, but with little success. "Whenever I try to be a nice, good little thing, you all stay away from my pictures," she chided her fans. Nevertheless, in mid-1919 she persuaded Fox to cast her as the sweet little colleen of rhyme and story in *Kathleen Mavourneen*. Torn cotton dresses replaced the shimmering gowns of the vampire, and golden Mary Pickford curls framed the famous Bara eyes. "This is the best role I've ever had," Theda glowed. "There isn't the slightest trace of the Vampire in *Kathleen*."

No one wanted Theda Bara to be natural. Fox refused to renew her contract. No other firm offer came her way. Rumor had it that she was going to form her own company, that she was dickering with Paramount, that she was talking to foreign filmmakers. Whatever was about to happen, Theda let it be known that she would have to be exploited as a symbol of purity; her purpose to spread happiness. Reluctantly she vamped once more to fill out her contract for Fox in *Lure of Ambition*, released in November 1919. And then she vamped no more for the screen. The film career of one of Hollywood's most magnetic stars ended with the same dramatic speed with which it had begun, though at the time no one was aware of its being over.

Theda Bara

EILEEN BOWSER
Excuse My Dust

There was no one quite like Wallace Reid in the silent era. Tall and lean like Gary Cooper, a daring race driver like Paul Newman, lover of books and the arts like Cary Grant, he was an accomplished painter, singer, and dancer, and could play almost any instrument. His mother and father were descended from prominent people in the original American colonies and worked together on the stage. They separated while he was very young, and his mother tried to divert his interest from theater, without success. During his early years in film at Universal he wrote and directed many of his own two-reelers.

Jesse Lasky, who signed him after his appearance as the blacksmith in The Birth of a Nation, *called him "the most magnetic, charming, personable, handsome young man I've ever met." James Quirk, publisher of* Photoplay, *declared "there wasn't an ounce of personal conceit in him." It was Reid's remarkable generosity that kept him working to save the survivors of a wrecked train carrying cast and crew to a movie location in the Sierras, even though he was injured himself. To counteract the pain from an injured spine, he was given morphine and thus enabled to finish playing his role. His later attempt to break the grip of the drug killed him, and he is remembered now in most history books only because this was one of the Hollywood scandals of 1921-23.*

Eileen Bowser, curator for the Department of Film at the Museum of Modern Art in New York City, wrote this review for a book called Film Notes *published in 1969 by the Museum as a guide to the films they then had available for distribution. It not only gives us a glimpse of one of the surviving Reid films about racing cars but also places it in some historical perspective.*

1920   Produced by Paramount-Artcraft   Directed by Sam Wood Screenplay by Will M. Ritchey, based on a   Saturday Evening Post story, "The Bear Trap," by Byron Morgan Photographed by Alfred Gilks   60 minutes Cast: Toodles Walden *Wallace Reid*   J.D. Ward *Theodore Roberts* President Mutchler *Tully Marshall*   Dorothy Walden *Ann Little* Darby *Guy Oliver*   Henderson *Otto Brower* Griggs *James Gordon*   Ritz *Walter Long*   Oldham *Jack Herbert* Police Magistrate *Fred Huntley*

". . . a fine, upstanding young American man — a kind of animated Arrow collar advertisement — not an innocent like Charles Ray, but gallant, well-behaved . . . and certainly not oversexed." So Edward Wagenknecht remembers Wallace Reid in *The Movies in the Age of Innocence*. The clean-cut Reid shocked his fans when he died at the age of thirty, in 1923, his health ruined by drug addiction.

Reid's career follows the rise of the star system. After an active early career with Vitagraph, Imp, and Universal, he graduated to leading roles under D.W. Griffith when the latter was production head at Mutual and Fine Arts-Triangle. Reid appeared in the small though memorable part of the blacksmith in *The Birth of a Nation*. Famous Players-Lasky acquired him as a romantic leading man, giving him, for example, important roles playing opposite Geraldine Farrar in *Carmen* (1915), *Joan the Woman* (1916), and *The Woman God Forgot* (1917). He became a full-fledged matinee idol, and Paramount (as Famous Players-Lasky was soon to be known) began to present him in light comedy vehicles designed to show off his talents, which largely consisted of his handsome face, his good humor, his carefree, offhand acting style, and his ability to represent the "regular fellow," the ideal American. He portrayed a character type similar to that of Douglas Fairbanks in his earlier comedies, and Reid's films employed wisecracking dialogue titles like those Anita Loos wrote for Fairbanks.

During his last few years, Reid was for the most part cast in program pictures, modest productions with a formula of romance and excitement, designed for an audience that came to see the star more than the story. In the spring of 1919 he had a great success in *The Roaring Road*, in which he played the driver of a racing car (a sport for which he had a passion in private life, a frustrated passion because the studio would not permit its high-priced property to risk accident in real racing). Speeding cars became Reid's trademark as he followed *The Roaring Road* with *Double-Speed, Excuse My Dust, What's Your Hurry?*, and *Too Much Speed*. By 1922, reviewers thought it cause for comment when Reid appeared in a couple of films without an auto story.

Excuse My Dust is a sequel to *The Roaring Road* and the same actors repeat their roles: Wallace Reid as Toodles Walden, champion racing driver, married to the boss's daughter (Ann Little), and working as salesman for his father-in-law's (Theodore Roberts) auto business. The fact that it is a sequel explains the opening titles, intended to remind audiences of the earlier story: "It will be remembered that when Toodles Walden, champion of *The Roaring Road*, broke the auto record from Los Angeles to San Francisco he also won a wife." Walter Long, perennial villain, is the unscrupulous racing driver of the competition. The story, drawn from a series by Byron Morgan in the *Saturday Evening Post* that supplied the plots of several of Reid's auto stories, concerns the tumultuous competition of the early automobile industry and reflects contemporary attitudes about big business and success.

The story is flimsy and motivation slight; however, the raison d'être of the film is the appearance of Wallace Reid in a series of thrilling episodes, and accordingly, the entire final reel of this short feature consists of the race between Los Angeles and San Francisco. There are spills and thrills — and even a race on a railroad bridge between a car and an approaching train. Even in its most exciting moments, however, the film lacks the skilled cutting that would have avoided confusion and increased suspense. Today, the film is of special interest to antique-automobile buffs. There is a nostalgic charm about a period when "doing fifty" was enough to say "Excuse my dust!"

DIANE KAISER KOSZARSKI
The Two-Gun Man: William S. Hart

His face evoked "both the wild wolf and the Puritan forefather," but he "incarnated Western virtues," together with a certain dry humor and melancholy, making him a potent mediator between the wilderness and civilization. Diane Koszarski thus sums up the cinema image of Bill Hart, who placed such a singular stamp on the American western during the ten years he devoted to screen acting and directing (1914-1925). She suggests a parallel with Clint Eastwood's gloomy moral stance. In the plots he picked for himself, Hart might well be on the wrong side of the law, but it was often the influence of a woman which changed him.

He had a hard time expressing tenderness. "His male fortitude is so strong that the Hart character must often suffer terrible wounds to weaken him before he can achieve some communion with the heroine." In such passages does Ms. Koszarski develop one of the most impressive auteur studies in the critical literature of American film: The Complete Films of William S. Hart: A Pictorial Record *(N.Y., Dover, 1980). Our selection is from pages ix, xv-xviii of her introduction.*

More about Hart and his relationship as director to his executive producer, Thomas Ince, can be found in the second volume of this series, including a few pages from his autobiography, My Life East and West.

The proliferation of film-producing units on the West Coast, one consequence of the monopolistic Patents War among film manufacturers back East, stimulated the progress of Westerns. The essence of the cowboy hero had already been limned in the work of Gilbert M. "Broncho Billy" Anderson for Essanay and by Tom Mix for Selig Polyscope; Thomas H. Ince and D.W. Griffith were soon producing romantic tales about Indians and vaqueros in the tradition of James Fenimore Cooper and Helen Hunt Jackson. In 1914 another interpreter of Western roles traveled to California: William Surrey Hart. He would show himself more effective than any of his movie predecessors in communicating the potent new vision of the West as a mirror of treasured American values. He was not the first cowboy hero of the movies, or the most realistic; he was, rather, the paramount interpreter of the West as an Anglo-Saxon heritage, the theme first sounded by Turner, Roosevelt, Remington and Wister.

Bill Hart was a stage actor turned filmmaker in his forty-ninth year. He had a knack for his new craft, and was fortunate to work for one of the industry's ablest young producers, Tom Ince. From 1914 until the mid-twenties, he starred in a series of widely popular two-reel and feature-length Westerns. Audiences found Hart's "two-gun man" protagonist a serious characterization, and the most authentic embodiment yet of frontier virtues in the movies. America during the period of the Great War hungered for moral passion; Hart delivered it on screen. His work, especially in the teens, strengthened the dramatic value of the Western as a film genre, and at its zenith his stardom was equal to that of Chaplin, Pickford or Fairbanks.

In addition to playing the lead role, Hart directed his own films or worked closely with a trusted colleague as director. He embraced with a whole heart the responsibilities of authorship, eager to portray his gospel of Western values; but his "truth of the West" was in fact a very subjective vision, highly colored by his family's history and his own personal disposition. Yet as Hart was a frontier-bred man of the Victorian age and a cultural peer of the Westerner he portrayed, his dramatic fictions (replete with his inner convictions and self-delusions) are authentic artifacts of the West. Modern sensibilities may quail before the ready, righteous violence, the racism and sexism so casually presented, the unambiguous delineations central to fundamentalist melodrama. But one must also find refreshment in his sincere vision of a frontier tamed to the service of families, a natural order sympathetic to man's presence and the benevolent progress of a civilization lived both East and West under the eye of a judging but merciful Deity....

Hart took his work in Westerns most seriously because they were ideal vehicles for the expression of his personal art. The broad basis for their fixed appeal was concisely outlined in a studio house-paper article entitled "Hart's Westerns Money Getters for Exhibitors":

> Three special features of early Western life make it especially adaptable to photoplay purposes; it is animated, with plenty of room

for running horses, splashing water and lots of gunplay; it is picturesque, with its prairie schooners, rough shacks, cowboys, Indians, and so on; and it shows life in the small community, where human nature reacting on itself at close quarters develops strongly individual characters. [*Triangle*, March 25, 1916]

Against this background the cowboy protagonist emerges as a mythologically potent mediator between Wilderness and Civilization. Hart brought to the melodramatic commonplace of the "Good-Badman" role unprecedented personal charisma. His physical presence incarnated Western virtues: he was tall and lean (6′2″, 180 pounds), he wore the rumpled, bulky costume of the cowhand or prospector or faro dealer with authority and grace, he could ride and shoot pretty well. His face was a most extraordinary icon: its hard planes evoke both the wild wolf and the Puritan forefather. It was a face made for expressing the dark emotions: Hart gave portrayals of cold, murderous hatred and unbridled fury that retain their power half a century later. Melancholy and a certain dryly understated humor with sardonic peaks also became him and are equally timeless.

Hart suffered his greatest creative problems in the expression of tender emotions. He prized their importance as a director and as a storyteller; as an actor he was limited physically and emotionally in their portrayal, relying more heavily on classic gestures and mise-en-scène from the stage in these instances. Though he was natural and convincing with children, his imagination was heavily constrained in scenes with his leading ladies; they are usually embraced in romantic climaxes more like a favorite pet than like an attractive young woman; Hart was an austere screen lover. Though reviewers of the period praised his thoughtful handling of emotional scenes of sentiment and their understated craftsmanship, today his devices often seem mechanical and inexpressive. Hart quelled too many strong feelings with blinked tears and repressed gulps, vowed vengeance too often with a quivering clenched fist. His face failed him in the active expression of such interesting emotions: the more "soulful" his eyes, the more he resembled a yearning collie dog. His most effective solution in these cases is a stoical and passive countenance, its sculptural planes offering a Calvinist enigma to be illuminated by montage rather than facial gestures. It was a solution he disregarded, especially later in his career, when so much in his films was dependent on the personality of the star. Even his faults as an actor are familiar masculine, Anglo-Saxon limitations: he could depict violence and anger with fine imaginative force, while the more vulnerable states of passion, grief, joy are protected and limited by conventionalized expressions. In 1918 the noted French actor Charles Dullin complimented Hart:

> He is never on his guard against the blow he will receive, and plays as though absolutely ignorant of what will happen to him. He knows how to contain himself, and to burst forth at the right moment, and this outburst is superb, because it is profoundly human. [*New France*, December 2, 1918]

The "Good-Badman" characterization gave way even during his work for NYMPCo to more modulated gamblers, workingmen, even sheriffs; but Hart on screen always remained a rough-hewn sort, apt to eat his peas with a knife, familiar with violence but with a strong sense of honor that could be activated for the defense of the heroine and the civilized community she represented. His mark as an auteur lay in his consistent choice of a particular boomtown milieu, in stories suffused with his own personal sense of the family, and in a craftsman's care for the plausible gesture and the motivating circumstances that redeemed the most melodramatic story lines.

His films offer a great variety of physical locales on the frontier: Northern woods and Barbary Coast waterfronts; Alaskan mining camps and Midwestern riverboat landings, the Great American Desert crossed by wagon tracks, anonymous adobe bordertowns. Hart returned continually, however, to a critical moment in the development of the frontier, when the raw, teeming Western boomtown is challenged by a growing cluster of "decent folk." The wide-open town's enormous saloons, dance halls and palaces of chance stand in picturesque and economical antithesis to the newcomer's notions of temperance and chastity. Here hard and hardworking men seek amusement; and they are well supplied by the complaisant "hostesses," card sharks and busy bartenders; here the devil inevitably makes work for idling hands. This is the natural habitat of the two-gun man, on whichever side of the law he may be cast. A few of the early films link the "Good-Badman" more strongly to the saloon milieu by providing a romantic relationship with one of its "soiled doves"; whether this proved too seamy for family audiences or went against Hart's own imaginative disposition, the later stories do emphasize the bottle, a game of cards or a shooting contest as the preferred form of recreation.

Hart's two-gun man was very much the loner in these films. His characteristic "honest" occupation was as a prospector (the quintessential hermit) rather than the infrequent cowhand (a group worker). For reliable companionship he depended as much on his horse as on any human being. Some stories provide him with a partner; and the theme of friendship, teasing, humorous and easy, is quite charmingly illustrated in *The Square Deal Man*, *Truthful Tulliver* or *Tumbleweeds*, but such camaraderie is rare. More often his partner betrays him, as in *Selfish Yates* or *The Toll Gate*. Later films often took particular pains to designate the Hart character as a leader of men, reflecting perhaps the actor's growing sense of himself as a director and star with a public. But as Hart was indifferent to the interplay of men in groups as a subject, his band soon breaks up or recedes into the background, as in *The Narrow Trail*, so that the main character may confront the essential problem of each tale on his own.

For Hart this problem was posed again and again in terms of family: fragmented families, families left broken and defenseless by the absence of a significant male figure, their strong protector. Apart from instances when he himself played the role, there are only two plausible father images in all Hart's work: J. Barney Sherry's role in *The Bargain* and that of the aged Walter Whitman in *John Petticoats*. If present at all, fathers are deeply flawed: the drunkard in *The Man from Nowhere*, the thoughtless magnate in *Between Men*. Brothers also are usually liabilities: in *Shark Monroe*, a drunk and pander; in *Hell's Hinges*, a moral weakling; in *O'Malley of the Mounted*, an honorable lad but young and forceless. But if fathers are absent, elderly mothers have great power in Hart's films. Their approval is sought, even to the point of courting death, as in *Blue Blazes Rawden*. The criminal matriarch in *The Cradle of Courage* is a piquant opposite, posing great problems for Hart as her straight-minded son.

Hart's heroine is rarely a lone figure; she comes as an orphan with younger siblings, a maiden with an aged mother, a widow with small children; occasionally as the wife of a zealous (and asexual) preacher: the sister and daughter of inadequate men. Hart's two-gun man offers his protection, and the family is made complete. His male fortitude is so strong that the Hart character must often suffer terrible wounds to weaken him before he can achieve some communion with the heroine, as in *A Knight of the Trails* or *Wolf Lowry*. Conversely, in *Bad Buck of Santa Ynez* or *The Disciple*, the strong man is forced by the illness of a child to give or seek help previously begrudged (and surely there is some memory of his sister Lotta's death in these classic Victorian invocations of innocence and mortality).

The many adumbrations of rape in Hart's films are further expressions of this male fortitude, rather than outbursts of romantic passion. Revenge is his motive in *The Toll Gate*, simple possession in *The Tiger Man* and *The Testing Block*. Physical desire is elided, and sublimated, into conversion experiences. His heroines, whether maidens or young matrons, are chaste in spirit, and therefore in physical demeanor, as an expression of their loyalty to a higher order. For all the characteristic Victorian reverence showered on women, or rather a certain image of them, Hart was not interested in delineating their personalities (as was a contemporaneous fellow director, D.W. Griffith). Their character, their chastity, are a given quality; by their faith in heavenly commandments they are able to hold faith in the spark of worth and goodness that may yet abide in this unregenerate brute of a two-gun man. They are personifications of his conscience, his human soul. Their very presence is a lever for change, and so provides a catalyst for plot construction.

ALEXANDER WALKER
All-American Boy:
A Note on Barthelmess

A leading man of the stalwart type associated later with William Holden or Dana Andrews, Barthelmess was, as Walker suggests, a more rural and adolescent character. This was in keeping with the general youthfulness of silent screen personalities, especially those chosen for stardom by D.W. Griffith. His first film role was the gift of Alla Nazimova, who had been tutored in the English language by his mother. After War Brides *(1916) he chose acting instead of business.*

In Way Down East *(1920) we are rooting for him to speak his love for Lillian Gish, and in* Tol'able David *(1921) we are waiting for him to strike back at the villains. In both cases the story and direction give him easy access to our approval, but he accomplishes this in an appealing way. One wonders why better parts were not written for him in this era when male stars were so few and women so dominant. He continued to be active in sound films, but often as the heavy. He retired from motion pictures when he joined the navy in 1942.*

Our selection is from Stardom *(N.Y., Stein & Day, 1970, pages 82-85) by the film critic of the* London Evening Standard.

The close personal and working relationship which D.W. Griffith maintained with his young actresses has tended to squeeze his young actors to the side of the picture. But Richard Barthelmess deserves attention. He is not only a good case of someone who began at the height of his power, at full imaginative stretch as an actor, and continued at a somewhat lower but still significant level as a star; but he set a pattern in American heroes which persisted, with different stars, in different films, until well into the 1930s and even the 1940s. It is open to doubt if he was an artist of much original inspiration, but he had a gift for taking direction in a way that made it look as if he was. Through his performances some of the best acting in silent films has survived — and hence some of the best direction.

If Lillian Gish is the unforgettable sensation of *Broken Blossoms*, Barthelmess is its unexpected revelation. Over fifty years later his lonely Chinaman, cut off from home by the Limehouse fogs, is as modern an image of isolation as one could fear to meet in a refugee camp. It is so mesmerising that one could suspect the actor has been mesmerised: one watches him as one watches a person who has temporarily been dissociated from his conscious control of his body and made to perform functions and assume states not usually within his competence or sympathies. There may be some truth in this impression, too, for Griffith was a mesmerising presence. Moreover he began rehearsals for *Broken Blossoms* without anyone definitely cast for the part of the Chinaman who befriends Gish's little waif; and a veteran actor called George Fawcett stood in temporarily. Barthelmess is said to have watched closely as Fawcett elaborated the part under Griffith's instruction; and when he was finally cast, this is how he played it, too. Performances "created" by a group in this way are rare in Hollywood cinema: but they are the end result of much of Stanislavsky's teaching and the affection of Russian film directors for Griffith's cinema might very well be extended to the way his best players embodied, however innocently, the principles of their own Soviet stage master.

Broken Blossoms was filmed, complete, in eighteen days. Such concentration has kept everyone in it at full emotional stretch, but Barthelmess has benefited particularly. He might have gone on hunger strike for those eighteen days, his Chinaman has such an unearthly sense of self-containment: the semi-mystical sense associated with confinement and deprivation. It recalls Gandhi and indeed is close to the Mahatma in the way the impassive features are the visible passport to a pacifist temperament. The film opens in the Orient as a statuesque Barthelmess receives the blessing of a Buddhist before his journey; and Griffith's close-ups lay great stress on the quiet face and eyelids that look too heavy to be kept open. His face takes on the fixed lines of a brass rubbing against the softer focused London mists enveloping it. The character's gentleness has to be expressed by gestures that have the digital economy of a conversation between the deaf and dumb, which in turn helps the spiritual configuration so that when Barthelmess intervenes in a sailors' brawl and holds up an admonishing finger, it is with the restraint of a saint.

The Limehouse scenes show the director's creative liaison with the player even more strikingly where Barthelmess hunches himself up against the alien cold with one foot planted against a wall in a posture suggesting an act of martyrdom with the victim's limb contracted in a spasm of suffering. (A similarly illuminating touch occurs when the Chinaman shoots the brutal step-father and Donald Crisp's dying rictus jerks him into the weaving, ducking posture of the pugilist he once was.) Barthelmess's scenes with Lillian Gish have a poetic reticence — the Oriental's glances of love and compassion are angular ones, like stolen looks. It is a wonderful conception of a character — its inner and outer renderings unite to enrich its significance and compel belief.

But stardom has to be created in the image of the actor — presumed or real. It rarely collects round the image of the character, unless this is one repeated from picture to picture, like Karloff's monster, in which case the character eventually takes over. Barthelmess had sunk his own characteristics untraceably into the Chinaman and, in spite of a variety of parts as a half-breed Mexican, a drunken beach bum and a roving sailor, he had to wait for the hugely popular *Way Down East* to bring out the characteristics henceforth associated with him — the good-hearted, uncomplicated, rural American boy whose story combined a tenderly awkward profession of love with the gallant rescue of Lillian Gish from the drifting ice floes.

He quit Griffith and acting on the logic of a film that had brought him stardom in a wholly American image, and in an indigenously American setting, he set up his own production company, with Henry King to direct him, and made *Tol'able David* (1921). The film was an immense success. Incorporating an affection for a rural America that was still a reality to many and a nostalgic memory to most, it proved the vast, continuing film audience for simpler heroes than the Valentino type who was then in fashion. *Tol'able David's* very lack of fashion, like the cut of country clothes, was part of his durability: he was built to last. Perhaps the spread of the motor-car and the tarred road ironically assisted the film's widespread appeal by bringing the farming communities out to see it at the small-town cinemas.

From then on, Barthelmess was David, the grassroots boy with a cast-iron conscience, a love for his mother and a sense of duty as clearly spelled out as any lesson in McGuffey's Reader. Mother worship was a potent feature of *Tol'able David's* popularity (just as it was an additional quantity in the appeal of the first really popular talkie, *The Jazz Singer*, six years later). It is the simple story of a farm boy trying to prove himself a man and having to save the mail wagon from being robbed after a terrific do-or-die fight before he gets more than a "tol'able, David, jest tol'able" measure of approval from his fond but firm parent. Barthelmess catches very skillfully the gawky uncertainties of American adolescence — he was 25 at the time — but what makes his performance disturbingly memorable is the amount of worrying that the boy does. David just has to be a success in his mother's eyes. Barthelmess's own physique assists the impression powerfully, for his shortish neck keeps David continually bowed down as if by the load on his conscience. The superhuman fight at the end is the timely release of the super ego in action.

JAMES NAREMORE
True Heart Susie
and the Art of Lillian Gish

Agreeing with Blake Lucas that Lillian Gish had inner reserves of strength and endurance, contrasting with her delicate appearance, and that Griffith's use of personalities had a "documentary" realism, Naremore is more concerned to emphasize the art of acting — the ways in which Gish as actress and as Susie within the story of True Heart Susie *(1919) is creating a character who is manipulative and sexually driven underneath the innocence and propriety we see at first.*

Neither critical reviewers nor academic analysts are usually up to the task of dealing with the skill of the performer in a film. This is one of the rare attempts to deal even with the description of what happens on the screen. Naremore is well enough informed historically, too, to remark that Griffith left much of the development of body and eye movements to the actress, and in the case of Gish, who had worked with him so long, he deferred to her ideas almost entirely. Thus if the movie medium calls for naturalness, Naremore says silent film challenged the star also to express "poetic" nuances of meaning in pantomime.

Professor Naremore is director of film studies at Indiana University. He contributed this article to the Quarterly Review of Film Studies, Winter 1981, *of which we have used pages 93-100. He has since written a book on* Acting in the Cinema *(1988) with a more extensive chapter on this film. More about D.W. Griffith and his working relationship with Lillian Gish can be found in the second volume of this series,* The First Film Makers.

. . . Throughout the history of the medium, acting has been regarded less as an art than as an event that the camera records or the director manipulates. Thus the Russians in the twenties subordinated

mime to montage; the Italian neorealists, operating under a different
aesthetic, turned to nonprofessional players; and in Hollywood there
is a long-standing belief that actors are simply types, spectacular
presences who know how to be "themselves" in front of a camera.
"Just know your lines and don't bump into the furniture," Spencer
Tracy is supposed to have said, and most non-comic movie acting
has been founded on a roughly equivalent minimalism.

In silent pictures the conception of acting was somewhat different. The
absence of sound meant that the players were artists by definition, "poets"
who suggested through pantomime more than they actually stated.
Furthermore, as Charles Affron has indicated in his admirable book,
Star Acting, Lillian Gish had a certain bravura quality about her, and
audiences must have gone to her movies because at some level they
enjoyed watching her rather mannerist representation of emotion.
Even so, the dominant theory of movie acting in Hollywood silent
films was articulated in terms of realism. "We are forced to develop a
new technique of acting before the camera," Griffith wrote. "People
who come to me from the theatre use the quick broad gestures and
movements which they have employed upon the stage. I am trying
to develop realism in pictures by teaching the value of deliberation
and repose."[1] The star system contributed to this artless conception
of acting because it made some of the links between actors and roles
seem inevitable. If actors were aesthetic objects, they appeared to be
objects of a special kind, more like landscapes or "found" art than
conscious workmen; their "personalities" were assumed to have a
documentary reality more important than the fictions they played.
Thus Edward Wagenknecht, an English professor who in 1927 wrote
the first extended critical interpretation of Lillian Gish's art,
remarked that "she always claims the right to make her roles over to
suit Lillian Gish." He praised her for expressing "her own point of
view, a distinctive something which is Lillian Gish and nobody else
on earth." "The part and the actress are one," he wrote. "In a very
deep and very true sense, she is the profoundest kind of actress: that
is to say she does not 'act' at all; she is."[2]

It is interesting to note that *True Heart Susie* seems to lend support
to such ideas because it contains a virtual sermon on the theme of
Art versus Nature. "Is real life interesting?" Griffith asks in the first
title card. "Every incident in this story is taken from real life." As the
story develops, it becomes a sort of parable about craft and
deception in conflict with simple, artless goodness. Susie, the
true-hearted country girl, is contrasted at every point with Bettina
(Clarine Seymour), the scheming milliner from Chicago who
deceives men with her paint and powder. When Susie tries to imitate
her rival by daubing her face with cornstarch (a homelier,

presumably more "honest" substance which is the only thing she can afford), her puritanical aunt berates her: "Do you think you can improve on the *Lord's* work?" Throughout the film, Art is connected with the city, with "Sporty" Malone's flashy clothes and painted car, with the Charleston and the loose sex of Bettina's crowd. Meanwhile Nature is represented by the groves of trees where William and Susie have their early courtship, by the animals that gather around Susie in her moments of solitude, by her spontaneous little dances and her single-minded love for William. Bettina spends her time in front of a mirror, fashioning an image of herself, but Susie is shown hoeing the fields. The equation seems exact: if Art is as deceptive as Bettina, then Nature or "reality" is as true and good as Susie.

But Griffith's parable doesn't work out so neatly. Just as his own nostalgia is compromised by the fact that movies are an art of machines, so his fictional character is not so naive or artless as the title cards keep insisting. In fact, Susie is in one sense as much a schemer and deceiver as Bettina. She determines early in the film that she will change William from a clod-kicking bumpkin into a man educated by the wide world. ("I *must* marry a smart man.") She sells her farm animals in order to pay for William's college and then keeps the source of the money a secret from him. From the first we see that she is more clever than William, and that she is a passive manipulator of his life. Unable, because she is a woman, to become a Horatio Alger, she determines to help create one and marry him. And although she is less sophisticated than Bettina, she seems no less sexually and romantically driven, ready at any moment to dress up for William. In fact, Bettina is her sister, perhaps her *doppelgänger*, as Susie inadvertently acknowledges in the scene where she is overcome with pity and holds her ailing rival in her arms. The real difference between the two is that Susie is wiser and more self-sufficient, and her craftiness is benign. William becomes her work of art.[3]

Likewise, Lillian Gish is far from being a distinctive "natural" personality which Griffith simply uses in appropriate fictional contexts. True, she had certain physical characteristics that well suited her for Griffith's typically Victorian fantasies of delicate, idealized girls tormented by brutish males. Never an extraordinarily beautiful or striking woman, she had a china doll's complexion and an ability to look young which she retains even today. It is interesting, however, how much even her physical appearance was the product of design. Her features seem petite and regular, the perfect incarnation of WASP beauty, but she has said that she never laughed in her early films because her mouth, which is so tiny on the screen, was oversized in relation to her eyes. She is usually described as "frail," but her frailty is an illusion, like Chaplin's. She is small but strong, as anyone can see from her erect carriage, which in some contexts makes her look prim. She had an iron constitution, a highly conditioned and flexible body, a cheerful and attractive face, and an extraordinary capacity for delicate gestures. Out of this raw material, plus her intelligence and apparently Spartan devotion to her job, she made herself into a complex character type and an expressive instrument with more range than critics have usually recognized.

Gish specialized in child women with a strong maternal streak — a description which already suggests some of the oppositions she was able to contain. But even in her most cloyingly sweet roles she was able to seduce the audience and redeem the movie, sometimes doing it with such skill that her art wasn't apparent. Thus Charles Affron, who nicely illustrates her inventiveness in other contexts, finds her "adorable" in *True Heart Susie*, and then goes on to describe the film as a "personal" and "original" Griffith work in which Gish is "never asked to be anything more than cutesy-pie." He claims her performance is "simplistic" and "shackled by sweetness."[4] The trouble with this conclusion is that if the film works — and virtually everyone seems to agree that it does — it must do so largely because of Gish, who contributed to its most compelling imagery, and who completes what one might call the "writing out" of the plot through action. In fact she is asked to do a great deal in the course of the film. She has to convey Susie's growth from innocence to experience, and she has to provide a vitality that will countervail self-sacrificing goodness. At every moment she has to suggest a certain duality in the character, making us feel cleverness beneath youth, strength beneath fragility, humor beneath spirituality, and sexual warmth beneath propriety. To do all this, she has to call upon a variety of performance skills and a number of possible "selves." Gish's contribution in this regard is largely the result of mimetic talents she had developed in turn-of-the-century theater. But Griffith also needed her special gifts as a mannequin. He was influenced by the general style of late Victorian painting, nearly all of which was narrative in its inspiration and photographic in its detail. He therefore needed models who could fit the popular conventions, and Gish became not only his Little Nell but his Elizabeth Sidall and his Jane Burden. She seems to have been eager and skillful at turning herself into a pictorial representation and an object of desire; she selected her own clothes with fastidious care, she persuaded Griffith to hire Sartov because of his ability to light her hair, and she was able to pose for some of Griffith's virtually still, "painterly" imagery without appearing as rigid as a figure in a *tableau vivant*. *Susie* is full of these images, largely because the central character spends so much time "waiting" for her man. It is worth considering some of them, to illustrate how even in this relatively simple function Gish appears in a number of different guises.

At one point, for example, she is Susie the rural maid, patting her cow on the neck and kissing it farewell; the dumb animal nuzzles her, its broad, hair face in vivid contrast to her own, which is childlike, pigtailed, sad, and very pretty beneath a flat little hat. Later, preparing herself to be a "fitting mate for her hero," she is posed like a young Lincoln as she reads books by firelight, her hair gathered in a bun and a look of eager studiousness on her face. Still later, in a shot titled "Susie's Diary," we see her in her room at night, the hair down to its full, Pre-Raphaelite length, like an illustration for a ninetyish, pseudo-Arthurian romance. Wearing a loose dressing gown, she is seated on a stool at the right of the frame, her knees toward us and her upper body twisted slightly to the right as she leans forward on a desk to write — an unnatural position which creates a languid, graceful line and contributes to the sublimated, voyeuristic eroticism of the image. An unmotivated keylight falls from the upper left, making her skin glow white, and backlighting halos her fine hair, which spills in ringlets down her cheeks; her lashes are lowered to the paper, her slender hand holds a pencil, and her features are relaxed and aristocratically serene. By contrast, toward the end of the film she is depicted as a "single-track heart," and is seated more naturally at the same desk, her hair gathered in a spinsterish bun and romantically backlit; two white, furry kittens are perched on her shoulders, making her look like an angelic *Venus im Peltz*.

In shots like these Gish is virtually a piece of statuary, but in the more dynamic portions of the film she was called upon to employ a wide vocabulary of movement. The demand upon her in this regard would have been great in any film, but Griffith's rehearsal methods gave the leading players an especially important function in what I have already described as the "writing" of his films. He seldom used a script, preferring to start with a vague outline and develop the story by positioning the actors on a bare stage. Sometimes he demonstrated all the parts himself, but by 1919 Gish had become so sensitive to his methods that she was left virtually alone in working out the details of her behavior and appearance. Nearly all her activity in *Susie* consists of variations and sudden departures from a simple, graphic set of movements: she holds her head straight and high, squarely topped by a series of flat, narrow-brimmed hats, and keeps her arms stiff at her sides, so that when she walks her upper body seems disassociated from her legs. In the first part of the film the posture and walk are comically stylized, and in context with the rest of the action they help suggest various things about Susie: her naive innocence, her puritanism, her directness, her single-minded devotion to a man, her almost soldierly courage, her sense of duty, and her "unaffected" country truthfulness. Her movements make an amusing contrast to Bettina's swively hips and butterfly gestures, especially in the scene where the two women are brought together at the ice cream social in the local church; and although Gish modulates her behavior slightly as the character grows older and gains dignity, she always foreshadows the best work of the silent comedians. Her doggedness as she paces along behind her lover is much like Keaton; her slump-shouldered movement away from Bettina's flirtations with William is pure Chaplin; and her innocent, level-headed gaze whenever she enters or exits a scene resembles no one so much as Harry Langdon.

Susie's wide-eyed face and fairly rigid upper body become a character "tag" and a recurrent joke (at one point, delighted to discover that Bettina is showing interest in another man, she skips across the floor of her room and spins in a joyful circle without moving her arms and head), but they also establish a pattern which can be broken in interesting ways. Because her posture suggests idealism, determination, and restraint bred into her by an aunt who tells her, "Deport yourself," her moments of letting go have a special force, like emotions breaking through repression. Sometimes they also reveal new aspects to the character, as if a mask had been dropped briefly.

One of the best examples of this latter effect is in Gish's brilliant pantomime during the comic sequence when Susie and William walk through a lovely, almost expressionist bower of trees on their way home from school. Susie is in an adoring trance, walking about one step behind William but occasionally brushing his arm. Each time he moves, she follows. He pauses, turns, and paces toward the camera with her right behind. Awkwardly pretending that his mind is on something besides the girl at his side, he turns again and walks toward the trees; she wheels and turns with him, patiently waiting for his attention but not demanding it. Griffith cuts to a closer view as they come to a stop before a tree, showing them from the waist up, looking at each other in a 50-50 composition. Susie stares straight up at William from beneath her flat bonnet, her eyes no longer adoring nor quite so innocent; in fact the look has a great deal of frankly knowing sexual desire behind it, so that it tempts William and flusters him at the same time. He bends slightly to her; suddenly she leans forward on tiptoe most of the way toward his face, closing her eyes in a comic gesture of passivity. At the crucial moment he hesitates, backs off, and turns his head toward the tree so that his back is to the camera. For just an instant Gish makes a gesture that almost breaks the surface of the fiction; she turns her own face away from William for the first time, showing it to the camera but not quite looking into the lens. She registers frustration and sad disappointment, but she also seems to comment on William, taking the audience into Susie's confidence as if she were a roguish character in a farce. "I can't believe this," she seems to say; almost immediately her expression turns back into the sad look of a little girl, but not before it has told us that she is more clever and self-aware than we had thought.

Gish also changes the basic pattern of her behavior when she expresses hysteria or inconsolable grief. Her pantomime when she receives William's first letter from college is silly (she wrote that she had a "constant argument" with Griffith because he wanted her to play little girls as if they had "St. Vitus's dance."[5]), but her moments of pain are among the most effective in the film. At one point, wearing the flat hat and a frilly, beribboned dress that makes her look as old-fashioned as ever, she prepares for an "overwhelming assault" on William by virtually marching to his house; she arrives only to find him embracing Bettina, and she instantly shrinks back against a door to hide herself, holding a small black fan like a shield in front of her body. As she leaves the scene, she is hunched over and hobbling slightly, shaking with ironic laughter and tears. Later in the film her spunky, straightbacked posture will give way completely: after the wedding ceremony between William and Bettina, she waves goodbye to the married couple, backs away into the garden behind her house, walks slowly and weak-kneed towards a fence, holds it briefly for support, and then suddenly collapses to the ground, her body curling into a fetal position. It is one of many occasions in Gish's career when she is subjected to overwhelming torment, but here there are no bullies, no ice floes, no blasts of wind or ravages of disease, only the force of the character's emotions and a sudden loosening of stiff muscles.

But Gish's truly privileged moments involve her face alone. I am speaking here not only of the relatively crowded, middle-distance shots which she usually dominates by her position in the frame and the animation of her features, but also of the several occasions when she is given large, lengthy closeups. In these shots, where she is virtually unaided by costume or an expressive mise-en-scene, she reduces theatrical pantomime to its most microscopic and naturalistic form, giving us a near river of emotions, stringing her movements together so gracefully and inventively that we hardly notice how various they are. Because she is using facial signs rather than speech, her "soliloquies" are relatively ambiguous, but they are nonetheless eloquent, and they are impressive examples of a specialized art.

NOTES

1 Quoted by Gish in *The Movies, Mr. Griffith, and Me* (Englewood Cliffs, N.J.: Prentice-Hall, 1969), p. 66. Gish also recalls that one of Griffith's favorite mottos was "Expression without distortion," although his comments on acting are usually quite contradictory. Mack Sennett once claimed that when he tried acting for Griffith he was congratulated by the director for simply standing in front of the camera. Notice that there is also a kind of "natural" relation between the actor and the role in some Griffith films. For example, when Susie carries on imaginary conversations with her dead mother, the picture she looks at shows the infant Lillian Gish herself, cradled in her mother's arms. When William later tells Susie that men flirt with "painted and powdered women" but marry the "plain and simple ones," the joke is partly on Robert Harron, who often said the same thing when he was courting Dorothy Gish.

For helpful suggestions about research for this paper, I am indebted to my colleague, Harry M. Geduld.

2 *The Movies in the Age of Innocence* (Norman: University of Oklahoma Press, 1962), pp. 249-50. Wagenknecht's enraptured mystification of Gish is understandable, given her charm, and is no different from countless other essays about actors. It is interesting that Hollywood, which inadvertently created this notion, sometimes tried to create counter-illusions that would dispel it selectively. Hence the typical fan magazine story that showed an actor like Edward G. Robinson at home among his paintings and children, a happy bourgeois rather than a Little Caesar. Dorothy Gish once joked about how her sister was confused with her screen persona: "The popular conception of Lillian as soft and dreamy makes me think a little of the 'gag' used too often in the comic strips. A hat lies upon the sidewalk; some person kicks it enthusiastically and finds to his astonishment and pain that there is hidden inside it a brick." (*The Movies, Mr. Griffith, and Me*, p. 92). She admits that she has no idea what her sister is "really like," and mentions Pirandello to explain the mystery of acting.

3 The film seems only partly aware of these ironies. A much more sophisticated movie than the titles suggest, it nevertheless gives us an illogical happy ending that turns Susie from a mature woman back into the girlish "innocent" we saw in the opening. In a particularly coy scene, William proposes at Susie's window, and the film closes with a nostalgic image of the couple as *children* walking down a country road.

4 *Star Acting: Gish, Garbo, Davis* (New York: E.P. Dutton, 1977), pp. 46-47.

5 *The Movies, Mr. Griffith, and Me*, p. 99.

KEVIN BROWNLOW
Lillian Gish in London, 1983

In 1893, the same year Edison got a patent for the kinetograph, Lillian Gish was born. She later put off her birth date by three years. (The American Film Institute tracked down the birth certificate when giving her a Life Achievement Award.) She was still acting in a movie in 1988, at 95, and her appearance at the showings of The Wind *and* Broken Blossoms, *described below, took place when she was 90.*

Music was always an important part of silent movie presentations in the theaters, and the "Thames Silents," produced in London as an annual series of money-making events by Brownlow and David Gill, proudly offered themselves as new-old experiences with old art-works and new music. The crowds that turned out to see Lillian Gish indicated something about the agelessness not only of Lillian but of these movies.

Brownlow is the author of an extraordinary book of interviews and history, The Parade's Gone By, *(1968) celebrating the silent film. His report on Gish in London is the last section (pages 26-27) of an article, "Lillian Gish," which appeared in* American Film, *March 1984.*

It is hard for most filmgoers these days to see silent films. But in London last year, we staged a tribute to Lillian Gish as part of the "Thames Silents" film program. "Thames Silents" is an outgrowth of the "Hollywood" television series that David Gill and I produced a few years ago for Thames Television.

David Gill and Composer Carl Davis were determined to present a silent film in a West End theater with a live orchestra, just as it would have been shown in the twenties. In November 1980, they presented Abel Gance's *Napoleon,* and its success led to "Thames Silents" becoming an annual event. In 1981 they showed King Vidor's *The Crowd* and in 1982 Clarence Brown's *Flesh and the Devil,* with Garbo and Gilbert, and later that year Vidor's *Show People,* with Marion Davies — all with new scores by Carl Davis (Each film is being prepared for television. MGM/UA will distribute the MGM productions on video.)

Last year's event was highly appropriate, for no one has championed the cause of silent film with orchestral accompaniment more energetically than Lillian Gish. We were very anxious that she should make a personal appearance at the event, but, aware of her hectic schedule, we were doubtful whether she would have the energy to travel to London. We underestimated her. Above all, Lillian Gish is a trouper. She said she would come, and come she did.

There was a ripple of anticipation at the airport when her plane arrived. An off-duty immigration officer asked who we were waiting for, and when he heard the name, he produced a camera from his shoulder bag and joined us by the railings. Our spirits soared when we caught our first glimpse of that exquisite face. Miss Gish may technically be an old woman, but she is still astonishingly beautiful.

We broke the news to her and her manager, James Frasher, that a newspaper strike had wiped out our publicity, and that now everything depended on her. "We'll do a lot of radio," she said, "That'll help."

Given one day in which to rest, she then plunged into a schedule that exhausted everyone but her. When she arrived for a lecture at the National Film Theatre, she was mobbed. Cameramen, professional and amateur, crowded round, and it was all James Frasher could do to get her to the reception room. The theater was packed and she delighted the audience with her enthusiastic recall and her humor.

"Is there any part you wished you'd played?" asked a member of the audience.

"A vamp," she replied. "Oh, I'd love to have played a vamp. Seventy-five percent of your work is done for you. When you play those innocent little virgins, that's when you have to work hard. They're all right for five minutes, but after that you have to work to hold the interest. I always called them 'ga-ga babies.'"

During the next few days, she embarked on a nonstop series of interviews for radio, television, and the newspapers, which gradually returned from the strike. She was interviewed by Carol Thatcher, the prime minister's daughter, for the *Daily Telegraph* and by John Gielgud, an old friend, who talked with her about the theater for the *Guardian*. Ticket sales showed a marked improvement.

The films, *Broken Blossoms* and *The Wind*, were shown in a West End theater called the Dominion, built in 1929. Chaplin premiered *City Lights* there. The twenties decor is still intact, and, more important, there's still a pit for the orchestra.

I was very pessimistic about the size of the audience; I recalled seeing *The Wind* many years ago at the National Film Theatre with seven people. But our tribute averaged more than a thousand people at each of the four performances. As anyone who has tried to program silent films will agree, that is an astonishing turnout.

It was also gratifying to see Lillian Gish's name in huge letters on a marquee again, and to see the crowds gathering before each show with autograph books. The first night, *Broken Blossoms* was attended by some of the most famous names in the English theater, not only John Gielgud, but also Emlyn Williams, who played Richard Barthelmess's part in the remake of *Broken Blossoms*. Silent star Bessie Love came to see her old friend; they had both been in *Intolerance*. They posed for pictures with Dame Anna Neagle, whose husband Herbert Wilcox directed Dorothy Gish in the silent era.

Lillian Gish introduced the film and supplied some of the background. She also explained the importance of the music. Carl Davis had arranged the original Louis Gottschalk score of 1919 (the Gish character's theme, "White Blossom," was composed by D.W. Griffith himself). The audience watched the beautiful tinted print with rapt attention. The occasion was unmarred by those titters that so often wreck showings of silent films. One could feel the emotion, and the applause afterward was tremendous. "I have been going to the cinema for fifty years," said one man, "but this was my greatest evening."

I hope he was there the following evening, for it was even more impressive. In her introduction, Lillian Gish left no doubt that *The Wind* was physically the most uncomfortable picture she had ever made — even worse than *Way Down East*. "I can stand cold," she explained, "but not heat." The exteriors were photographed in the Mojave Desert, near Bakersfield, where it was seldom under 120 degrees. "I remember having to fix my makeup and I went to the car and I left part of the skin of my hand on the door handle. It was like picking up a red-hot poker. To create the windstorm, they used eight airplane engines blowing sand, smoke, and sawdust at me."

MGM/UA allowed us to provide a new score for *The Wind* (which will also replace the 1928 Movietone recording in the television version). Carl Davis and arrangers Colin and David Matthews created a storm sequence of earsplitting volume. As one critic said, it was as though they had brought the hurricane into the theater. The effect of the film and the music pulverized the audience. Lillian Gish said it was the most exciting presentation of *The Wind* she had seen in years. Some people compared the experience to seeing *Napoleon*, and several found it even more powerful. The critic of the *Daily Telegraph* compared Gish to Sarah Bernhardt and that of the *Guardian* thought the director of *The Wind*, Victor Seastrom, was now on a level with D.W. Griffith.

Lillian Gish received a standing ovation, and days later people were still talking of her astonishing performance in the film. "It was the film event of the year," said George Perry of the *Sunday Times*. . . .

We said farewell to Miss Gish at her hotel while she was busy packing. Her hair was down, and I have seldom seen her look so beautiful. All of us connected with the event were exhausted, but Lillian Gish was as full of vitality as ever. "When I get back to New York," she joked, "I shall go to bed and I won't get up until 1984. When you think of me, think of me horizontal."

When we think of her, we will think of her striding onto the stage of the Dominion to receive the acclamation of an audience that, thanks to her, has rediscovered its faith in the cinema.

Chapter 3

Mary and Doug

Some minds naturally feel confident. These are the lucky ones...Success comes to them as easily as rolling off the proverbial log. They come sweeping along, conquering, sure of themselves, confident, aspiring, true to their inner selves, ready for work... —Douglas Fairbanks[1]

"The most popular couple the world has ever known." This is the subtitle for Booton Herndon's dual biography, *Mary Pickford and Douglas Fairbanks* (1977). It seems a fair enough description. No prince or President has ever experienced the excited crowd worship given to these two motion picture stars, so representative of the ordinary American's self-image. Jack and Jackie Kennedy were given similar attentions — more like movie stars than President and wife. Clark Gable and Carole Lombard, like Mary and Doug, were famous before they were a couple. But these public companionships were tragically brief. The Pickford-Fairbanks marriage took place in 1920 and lasted till 1936.

Their honeymoon was a trip to Europe, and they thought of it as some kind of test for their popularity. After all, divorce was not yet, as it is today, a familiar, even acceptable, status. Both were Catholic and each of them had put off a partner in favor of each other. They feared their careers might not stand the strain of criticism, and the

1   *Laugh and Live,* (1917), p. 44.

boxoffice would suffer. But the trip — from New York to London to Holland and Italy and France — turned into a kind of democratic jubilee.

Their popularity was so palpable it was frightening. The crowds at the dock would have kept them from getting to the London train, and at Waterloo station in London would have kept them from reaching their hotel, if policemen had not managed to surround them. Nothing like this had ever occurred in England before, and it was not comprehended even the following day: the annual Theatrical Garden Party was invaded by hundreds of people and the Ritz dining room was rushed by fans. When they fled to a country mansion, the crowds arrived in the morning.

Yet this was a confirmation of their status in the world, and they reveled in it. There was real terror in Mary's eyes in a photograph taken at the time of the tumultuous garden party: she is being lifted onto Doug's shoulder to avoid being clutched by worshipful hands. But when they got to Germany, where American films had not been shown during the war, they were not recognized. In answer to Doug's question, she said: "Let's go some place where we are known!"[2]

Both of them had worked hard for fame. Herndon suggests that for each of them fame was a necessary replacement for the rejection each had suffered at the age of five: Mary's father died in an accident, and Doug's father had abandoned his family. Each of them had become the mainstay of the family finances by reaching out to a wide public in theater and film, offering love and expecting love in return. It was a relationship which had to be constantly renewed.

Mary's early day fears about herself — searching for jobs in New York, dreaming of empty theaters and failing plays, nightmares of forgetting her lines — were carried forward in her days of accelerating fame and fortune.[3] She could not afford to slip backward in public popularity. She took meticulous care of her skin and hair, worked out certain exercises that suited her and a diet which meant she habitually left the table hungry, read and reread scripts, studied every aspect of the production process, negotiated each contract as if it were the last.[4]

2   Booton Herndon, *Mary Pickford and Douglas Fairbanks,*, (1977) pp. 3-6. Mary Pickford, *Sunshine and Shadow*, (1955) pp. 209-215.
3   Pickford, pp. 69-70.
4   Herndon, pp. 124-5.

When she encountered Douglas Fairbanks and their relationship began to be a serious one, she was just beyond the zenith of her career and was beginning to have trouble finding stories. She was especially troubled about the public demand for her to stay with childlike roles. Owen Moore, whom she had married while she was still working for Griffith, had turned out to be an abusive, ego-centered alcoholic. Douglas' wife, on the other hand, was not part of the show business world and seemed aloof from his emotional problems. One of those problems was his fast-rising popularity with critics and public alike.

They first met at a party in the New York state countryside. A group of guests were crossing a brook and Mary hesitated. Douglas swept her up in his arms and carried her across. She was ready to be dazzled, and in coming years he would continue to play that part. He presented a new experience for her, sincerely and perceptively praising her as an actress and in turn asking her confidence and support when his mother died. For him, she was simply the most famous woman in the world, and he discovered that he really liked her enormously.[5]

They were thrown together on many public occasions: selling Liberty Bonds in wartime, setting up the United Artists Corporation in 1919. And after many romantic secret meetings, she finally yielded to the same kind of ultimatum Owen Moore had given her: Fairbanks telephoned and declared he would go away and never see her again unless she agreed that very night to divorce Owen and marry him. She did not want to lose him. She paid off Owen Moore, who then agreed not to contest the divorce.

Despite Adolph Zukor's doubts and warnings, the public demonstrated that the twenties indeed represented a new era in moral behavior. Although many people deplored the marriage as a sign of breakdown in values, their devoted fans saw it as a marvelous culmination of romantic dreams. Critics of American culture shrugged and said it proved Americans yearned for royalty: the princess of the screen had encountered the healthy, athletic prince. At any rate, it appeared that Mary Pickford and Douglas Fairbanks were beyond and above condemnation, and they were expected to live happily ever after.

This was not to be. There were at least five years of the closest companionship and obvious joys. Douglas managed to accept his wife's closeness to her family—Mother and Lottie and Jack, who had

5   Pickford, pp. 197-200.

struggled so long together to reach security and wealth. Mary, for her part, accepted her husband's need to have cronies around him to approve his physical stunts and practical jokes, his need to play everything for publicity, living out the movie stories (like *His Picture in the Papers*) which were based in part on his life. She understood that he was really Robin Hood and Zorro, and herself suggested that he undertake those costumed roles once the comedy genre had been played out. She even accepted his inexplicable jealous demand that she always sit next to him when invited to dinner and never dance with anyone else—not even with the Duke of York.

But she could not, in the end, outwait his restlessness. Their separation and divorce were almost as long drawn out as their courtship, and there were moments when everything could have been patched up. But the tyranny of expectations the silver screen imposes—the demands for youth, for variety, for constant surpassing of everything that has gone before—these were especially hard on the ebullient and aging Douglas Fairbanks. He married an English showgirl who had previously married a noble title. Mary married Buddy Rogers, who co-starred with her in one of her last and happiest vehicles, *My Best Girl*. Doug died in 1939. Mary survived him by forty years.

Twenty-two years after her last movie, Mary Pickford gave us her autobiography, *Sunshine and Shadow*. Much of the focus was on her early years of struggle to earn the family's livelihood—years which set the pattern for her unremitting practical sense and close attention to salary and bonuses during the contracts with Griffith, Laemmle, and Zukor. The days of privation were proudly professional, but they meant (as her own brother once ruefully remarked) that she had had no real childhood. She stored away in thought whatever she could recall from watching other youngsters and put those impressions on the screen when she was playing child roles in her twenties. At the same time, the early deprivations also enabled her to share and understand the experiences of most Americans in her audience.

She was unable to have children of her own because of an accident that happened while she was making her third film for Zukor in 1913: she was supposed to carry a girl to safety from a burning building and the strain caused serious internal injuries. (In later years, with Buddy Rogers, she adopted two children.) During the shooting of *The Foundling* in Central Park in 1916, she watched a group of children sledding in the snow—an experience she had never had. She finally went over to them and begged to borrow a sled, a ride which cost her ten cents. She was twenty-three.[6]

As for Fairbanks, his happiest five-year-old memory was a jump (or a fall?) off a roof. When he came to, he found himself in his mother's arms, the center of attention, and (by his own account) for the first time he laughed out loud. For the rest of his life, his practical jokes and personal stunts were not so much extrovert exhibitionism as demands for attention, an adolescent fixation which never left him. His smiling charm and readiness to take charge in entertaining others were qualities that were attractive to a guest for an evening and exhilarating on the screen. But he was pretty exhausting as a constant companion.[7]

"Lost childhood" is a conscious or unconscious mental picture everyone shares. The child looks forward to growing up. The adult longs to go back at least to the happy times of childhood, even of adolescence— perhaps with a few changes in the script. Mary and Doug fulfilled that common yearning. Mary Pickford's screen persona was most often that of a little girl. In pictures like *Rebecca of Sunnybrook Farm* and *The Poor Little Rich Girl*, she was the lively youngster who shows the older folks how to live, how to be nicer and happier. Douglas Fairbanks' persona was most often an exuberant schoolboy rescuing us from the long faces or the dangerous tyrannies of the old folks.

This was probably the secret of their success, and the success of many of their contemporaries on the silent screen. They were young, as the country was still young, and the exhilaration of conquest was written on their films. Much the same qualities of enthusiasm and drive, the same expectations of good luck, were expressed in the films of Gloria Swanson and Rudolph Valentino and many of the others who found their livelihood on the Holly-wood frontier.

---

6   Herndon, p. 131.
7   See Herndon pp. 13-20, for theories that Douglas as a third child was (a) unwanted by his mother (b) a case of narcissism rooted in insecurity. He is supposed to have said in later years that during his youthful pranks he was always physically afraid. This has led others to suggest that he expected to buy something with his risks.

EPHRAIM KATZ
Mary Pickford

*From that extraordinary and dependable motion picture reference work,
The Film Encyclopedia, (N.Y., Crowell/Harper and Row, 1979, pages
912-913) here is a compact biography of "America's Sweetheart." In the list
of her films, one key date is 1912, her hundredth and last short film for D.W.
Griffith: The New York Hat.*

*In 1965, when she was 73, she paid a visit to the Paris Cinematheque
where her pictures were being shown in a month-long retrospective. The
welcome she received may have encouraged her to think more positively
about her work and later to give the earliest films to the Library of Congress
in Washington. There, in one of the newest buildings of the Library
complex, a small theater is named after her and shows monthly a variety of
silent and sound films from the extensive U.S. collection.*

Pickford, Mary. Actress, *b.* Gladys Smith, Apr. 8, 1893, Toronto. *d.*
1979. When she was five, her father, a laborer, was killed in a
job-related accident and she found herself prematurely burdened
with the dual role of mother's helper to sister Lottie, three, and
brother Jack, two, and breadwinner. Billed as "Baby Gladys," she
toured with various road companies, and within several years had
gained enough experience and confidence to feel she was ready for
Broadway. At 14 she stormed into David Belasco's office and
charmed him into giving her a starring role in his play "The Warrens
of Virginia." It was he who rechristened her Mary Pickford. In 1909,
at 16, she used a similar combination of childlike charm and
feminine wile to win over D.W. Griffith at Biograph and begin a
unique film career that made her the most popular star in screen
history.

Like all other Biograph personalities, she was not identified by
name, because it was feared that publicity might cause stars to
demand higher wages; but she had a trademark, a head of golden
curls, and once played a character identified in the film's continuity
titles as "Little Mary." Within several months she proved to be so
popular that exhibitors were advertising her as "The Girl with the
Golden Hair" or simply "Little Mary." When she was lured away
from Biograph in 1910 by Carl Laemmle's IMP, that company
proudly pronounced in its ads: "Little Mary is an Imp now."

An astute businesswoman, Miss Pickford moved from company
to company, driving a hard bargain for higher wages and greater
control over her vehicles. She started at $40 a week at Biograph in
1909. In 1910 she was earning $175 a week at IMP; in 1911, $275 at
Majestic. She then returned briefly to Biograph, and in 1912 she went

to work for Adolph Zukor's Famous Players Company at $500 a week. Her salary was doubled periodically, and in mid-1916 she signed an astounding contract with Zukor calling for $10,000 weekly and a $300,000 bonus, plus the formation of an affiliate, The Mary Pickford Company, a studio devoted exclusively to the making of her films, and also a share in the profits of the studio. But even that proved not enough. In the following year she signed with First National for $350,000 a picture.

Mary Pickford's appeal was international. A born charmer with a radiant, dimpled, child-woman beauty and a spirited and spontaneous screen personality, she captivated audiences' emotions with a natural ease. For many years she remained the nation's biggest box-office draw. During her long career she played a variety of parts but was best loved and remembered in her typical role as a sweet, innocent, lovable little girl, for which she was dubbed "America's Sweetheart" (she was known as "The World's Sweetheart" abroad). From time to time she tried to rebel against her standardized screen portrayals but found herself giving in to public pressure and returning to sweet-innocent-little-thing roles. As late as 1920, at the age of 27, she played a girl of 12 in *Pollyanna*.

From an early point in her career, Miss Pickford exercised veto power over her films and was given a choice of script, director, and co-stars. As a result, her vehicles usually boasted high production values and most were immensely profitable. In 1919 she entered a partnership with three other formidable luminaries of the business — Charlie Chaplin, D.W. Griffith, and Douglas Fairbanks — to form the United Artists Corporation. The following year she married Fairbanks, her second husband (she had married the first, actor Owen Moore, in 1911 and divorced him in 1919 after he became an incurable alcoholic). The marriage to Fairbanks, although not a happy one, had the public aura of a dream come true. To star-struck millions, the couple represented Hollywood royalty at its loftiest and their legendary home, Pickfair (a combination of their last names), a fairy tale castle.

Mary kept on playing her stock Cinderella parts, her popularity diminishing but little with the ensuing years. Finally, in 1928, in a daring rebellious rage, she had her famous blond curls shorn and acquired the then-contemporary shingled hair style. (Some of the locks now repose in museums in Los Angeles and San Diego.) In 1929 she made her first talkie, *Coquette*, wearing her new hair style and playing a modern swinger role.She won an Academy Award for her performance, but the film and her new personality did not click with audiences. Her next vehicle, a much-publicized screen adaptation of Shakespeare's *The Taming of the Shrew* (famous for the credit line "additional dialogue by Sam Taylor"), co-starring Fairbanks, was a catastrophe that virtually ended her career. After appearing in two other disheartening failures, she retired from the screen in 1933. In the mid-30s she made frequent broadcasts on network radio and published several books, including her memoirs, *Sunshine and Shadow* (1955). Having divorced Fairbanks in 1936 she married former co-star Charles "Buddy" Rogers in 1937. In 1936 she was named first vice president of United Artists and the following year she established the Mary Pickford Cosmetics Company. In 1953 she and Chaplin, the sole survivors of the partnership, sold United Artists. Miss Pickford, who in the early 30s bought out many of her early silent films with the intention of having them burned at her death, had a change of heart and in 1970 donated 50 of more than 130 of her Biograph-period films to the American Film Institute. She received a special Academy Award in 1975, in recognition of her contribution to the American film. A compilation film biography of her career, *America's Sweetheart: The Mary Pickford Story*, was released in 1978. Mary's younger sister, Lottie Pickford (*b.* Lottie Smith, 1895, Toronto. *d.* 1936), and her brother Jack Pickford, also had careers in films.

Films include: *The Violin Maker of Cremona, The Lonely Villa, Her First Biscuits, Two Memories, The Way of May, Sweet and Twenty, 1776 or The Hessian Renegades, The Gibson Goddess, The Slave, Getting Even, In Old Kentucky, The Little Darling, His Wife's Visitor, The Little Teacher (also co-sc.), The Restoration, To Save Her Soul 1909; The Englishman and the Girl, As It Is in Life, An Affair of Hearts, Ramona, The Kid, A Rich Revenge, In the Season of Buds, May and December (also sc.), A Son's Return, The Call to Arms, A Child's Impulse, Love Among the Roses, What the Daisy Said, The Indian Runner's Romance, Wilful Peggy, The Sorrows of the Unfaithful, The Arcadian Maid, The Masher, The Awakening, A Lucky Toothache, Simple Charity, The Song of the Wildwood Flute, Sunshine Sue, Their First Misunderstanding, A Plain Song, A Summer Tragedy, White Roses 1910; The Italian Barber, All on Account of the Milk, The Dream, Maid or Man, The Woman From Mellon's, Artful Kate, When the Cat's Away, A Manly Man, Her Darkest Hour, In Old Madrid, The Fisher-Maid, A Decree of Destiny, Three Sisters, For Her Brother's Sake, Science, In the Sultan's Garden, The Aggressor, Behind the Stockade, The Courting of Mary, Little Red Riding Hood 1911; The Mender of Nets, Fate's Interception, Won by a Fish, The Old Actor, A Lodging for the Night, A Beast at Bay, Home Folks, Lena and the Geese (also sc.), The Narrow Road, A Pueblo Legend, With the Enemy's Help, The Inner Circle, So Near Yet So Far, The One She Loved, Friends, The Informer, My Baby, The New York Hat 1912; A Good Little Devil, The Unwelcome Guest, In a Bishop's Carriage, Caprice 1913; Hearts Adrift (also sc.), Tess of the Storm Country, The Eagle's Mate, Such a Little Queen, Behind the Scenes 1914; Cinderella, Mistress Nell, Fanchon the Cricket, The Dawn of a Tomorrow, Little Pal, Rags, A Girl of Yesterday (also sc.), Esmeralda, Madame Butterfly 1915; Poor Little Peppina, The Foundling, The Eternal Grind, Hulda From*

Holland, *Less Than the Dust* 1916; *The Pride of the Clan, The Poor Little Rich Girl, A Romance of the Redwoods, The Little American, Rebecca of Sunnybrook Farm, The Little Princess* 1917; *Stella Maris, Amarilly of Clothes Line Alley, M'liss, How Could You Jean?, Johanna Enlists* 1918; *Captain Kidd Jr., Daddy Long Legs, The Hoodlum, Heart o' the Hills* 1919; *Pollyanna, Suds* 1920; *The Love Light* (also prod.), *Little Lord Fauntleroy* (dual role; also prod.), *Through the Back Door* (also prod.) 1921; *Tess of the Storm Country* (remake; also prod.) 1922; *Rosita* (also prod.) 1923; *Dorothy Vernon of Haddon Hall* (also prod.) 1924; *Little Annie Rooney* (also prod.) 1925; *Sparrows* (also prod.) 1926; *My Best Girl* (also prod.), *The Gaucho* 1927; *Coquette, The Taming of the Shrew* (as Katharina) 1929; *Kiki* 1931; *Secrets* 1933.

MARY PICKFORD
Life With Mother

When Mary Pickford's autobiography, Sunshine and Shadow, was published in 1955 by Doubleday, it was reviewed in the New York Times by Deems Taylor, the distinguished music critic who had also edited A Pictorial History of the Movies. He said it was "the story of a shrewd trader with an indomitable will, who slugged it out with the Hollywood moguls in their own bailiwick and retired a millionaire; the story of a sensitive, warm-hearted, and generous woman." Our selections are from various pages from 37 to 130.

From her first day working for D.W. Griffith she asserted her independent judgment of her worth, and there was a frequent running battle between them in the years afterward. Linda Arvidson, as Griffith's wife, was naturally jealous of her, and reports another episode when Mary asked for a promised raise immediately after emerging from a "wet stunt" involving a canoe on the river.

All of this -- and her close attention to contracts later on with Laemmle and Zukor -- is easily understandable in view of the Pickford family's early days of privation in the theater. She learned to love making movies, though, as she discovered when she went back to do a Belasco play: she missed "the exciting jigsaw puzzle of a motion picture in progress."

Mother was still in her middle twenties when she became a widow with three baby children and Grandma Hennessey, an invalid, to support. . . .

In years to come we were to be known as the Four Musketeers — Mother, my sister Lottie, my brother Jack, and myself. When the money began to come in, we had one pocketbook for it, and Mother remained the custodian to the end.

I never had any young companions my age except for my brother and sister. Also as Mother and I grew closer Lottie and Johnny banded together against us. All this matured me very early, I suppose, but it cheated me of any real childhood.

I am grateful this was not so with my brother and sister, and I have treasured a remark Jack made to me one morning in my dressing room during the filming of *Little Lord Fauntleroy*. He was sitting beside me as I was brushing my curls before going on the movie set. I noticed that he was studying me intently in the mirror. Our eyes finally met and he said:

"You poor kid, you've never lived, have you?"

"Certainly I have," I said. "I'm doing exactly what I always wanted to do."

"Well, I don't know. You see, if Chuckie and I were bumped off tomorrow, the world would owe us nothing. We've had a million laughs. You've had everything, yes, but, Mary, you've never really lived. And you don't know how to play." . . .

It wasn't long after Father's death that Mother decided to rent the master bedroom, as there was plenty of space in that large house for the family.

One day a well-dressed man applied for the vacant room. Up to then the room had been occupied only by women. But this man explained that he was married and he was sure Mother would like his wife. The pros and cons of the situation were warmly debated by Mother, Aunt Lizzie, and Grandma. They finally agreed that renting the room under these circumstances would be quite respectable — a decision which was probably the greatest turning point in my life. The man in question was the stage manager of the Cummings Stock Company of Toronto.

One day, about two weeks after the couple were installed, the man asked Mother if he could have a moment with her.

"Mrs. Smith," he began, "you may have read in the papers that I'm producing a play called *The Silver King*."

"I believe I have."

"Well, would you consider letting your two little girls appear in a schoolroom scene?"

Mother was highly indignant.

"I'm sorry," she said, "but I will never allow my innocent babies to associate with actresses who smoke."

"I respect your misgivings, Mrs. Smith," the man said, "but will you do me a favor before you make a decision?"

"It's completely out of the question. The thought of those infants making a spectacle of themselves on a public stage! . . ."

"This is all I ask, Mrs. Smith. Come backstage with us tonight. I assure you that professional people are no different from any others. They are good, bad, and indifferent like the rest of the world. This happens to be a very happy and respectable group of actors and actresses who have been together a long time."

Mother made the daring trip backstage that night and was evidently impressed by the behavior of the people in the company. The result of that tour of inspection was that Lottie and I made our debut in the theater in a play called *The Silver King*.

I played two parts. In the first act I was a villainous little girl who was mean to Cissy Denver, the Silver King's daughter. My opening line on stage was:

"Don't speak to her, girls; her father killed a man!" — a statement accompanied by a smart stamp of the foot, in which I had been very meticulously coached. My sister Lottie's function in the play was just as elaborate, but without words. Hers was the kindly gesture of handing Cissy a stick of peppermint candy and giving her a pat on the back. . . .

The intensive and discouraging job hunt that now began laid the pattern for recurring years of pavement-pounding. No one can have an idea of what this means who has not personally looked for work on the stage. The motley crews of the fly-by-night theatrical companies of those days; the merciless summer heat of New York; the rudeness of the receptionists; the sight of starving actors with their celluloid collars and brave faces; the overly bleached blondes with their inevitable turquoise jewelry and one lingering piece of soiled finery, like a blouse or jabot, and the lip rouge that would begin to wear off as the heat grew and the day lengthened. The picture of Mother, Lottie, Johnny, and me trudging along to these offices will stay with me to my dying day.And later came the terrifying uncertainty of the nightly attendance.

All my life I have dreamed two recurring dreams, both nightmarish with dread. One of them involved an empty theater. To this day I have that dream before any sort of journey or project I may be embarking on. I seem to gauge the scope of the disaster ahead by the endless rows of empty seats. While the dream varies in some details, I am always on the stage when the curtain goes up. And always there is that unpeopled hollow before me, and the certainty that the play is a failure and the company will pack up and go home.

In the other nightmare I am again on the stage. This time I have forgotten my lines. I stand there speechless in the growing horror of my humiliation. I suppose deep down in me I fear being unprepared, unrehearsed, for what tomorrow may bring.

I have never really lost my nervousness of the theater, or of the camera, or of any public appearance, for that matter. I don't remember ever stepping before a camera without a certain anxiety. Often I would have chills and run a temperature for the first three or four days, whether it was a play or a movie. That still happens to me before making a speech. I have always been hounded by this lack of confidence in myself. And I should like to say, emphatically and without exception, that I never liked any one of my pictures in its entirety. Once, in Pasadena, at the preview of one of my pictures and to the amazement of the entire company including myself, I suddenly heard my voice saying out loud, "I wish to apologize for this picture and for my performance. I think they are both inexcusably bad." It seems that as the lights went on, they had called for a speech, I had jumped to my feet, and, like an automaton, I made that impulsive little speech. I was never so filled with remorse, because I had hurt the director and members of the cast.

To go back to my childhood. Mother finally signed us all up with Sullivan, Harris, and Woods for a famous play of the time called *The Fatal Wedding*. Since work was not to begin till the fall, we returned to Toronto to get through the long summer months as best we could with almost no funds. We had a rooster, I remember, which we all came to love as if it were another member of the family. It was kept in the back yard of the house where Mother had rented our rooms in Toronto. We had not eaten a good meal for a long time, and suddenly, one day, as if out of nowhere, chicken appeared on the table. I glanced at the window that opened on the back yard. No one said a word, and no one so much as touched the chicken. When we had finished our dinner, such as it was, my brother Jack flung himself down on the bed and wept bitterly. To add to our woes, Mother came down with an illness that required surgery. It was performed in our rooms — we couldn't afford a hospital. During her operation I rocked myself in abject misery on the pedal of the sewing machine. I was in terror that I would now lose my mother as well as my father. Twenty-four hours later we were on the train for New York. Ordinarily Mother should have spent two weeks in the hospital, followed by a period of convalescence.

How she survived that journey sitting up all night on the train I shall never know. We arrived next morning just in time to report to rehearsal. There was no time for breakfast.

The director of *The Fatal Wedding* was a cruel, pompous individual who delighted in crucifying those under his supervision. He snapped at Mother, "You'll have to do better than that or I'll replace you." Those words lashed me. Mother was able to whisper that none of us had eaten since the day before, that she would do better when she had had a cup of tea.

"I promise I'll be much better at rehearsal this afternoon," she pleaded.

I was the only one of the children to realize fully what Mother was going through at that moment. I knew that she was in pain, weak, tired, and frightened, that the whole uncertain future of the Smith family hung on the outcome of this cruel day. . . .

Nineteen weeks of one-night stands of *The Fatal Wedding*, averaging eight and nine performances a week, including matinees — never sleeping twice in the same bed! What hectic weeks they were for the Widow Smith and her three children. Johnny aged five, Lottie aged seven, and Gladys aged eight. Mother was always washing and packing and sewing. When she could, and the facilities were at hand, she would make clothes for all of us. One of my most cherished memories during those bustling weeks is of Mother sitting up in the middle of the night making new dresses for Lottie and me. Mother was so facile with her hands she even learned to make fur coats for us, buying the skins and stretching them herself.

While we were on the road, often rushing out of the hotel in the wee small hours to catch the next train, Mother had all she could do to keep us awake. One morning she devised a little game. Bringing us all sharply to attention, she announced that we would be a German band, she carrying the main theme, I the "oompah" part, and Johnny and Chuckie filling in as they saw fit. Tired and sleepy as we were, the trick worked. Like rigid little toy soldiers, we marched down the hotel stairs, along the street, and over to the station into the train. But one morning, Johnny, the family sleepyhead, rebelled. It was three o'clock and we had to catch one of those awful milk trains for our next one-night stand.

"We've got to get up, Johnny," said Mother. But Johnny went skittering across the big wide bed and curled up against the wall. "I'm so sleepy, Mama," he said; "I want to stay here. I don't want to go."

That was one of the few times I every saw Mother very close to the breaking point. I knew it tore at her heart to force sleepy-eyed little Johnny to dress and go out into that cold night and onto that musty, uncomfortable train. She sat down and cried, whereupon Lottie and I went after Jack and, in double-quick time, put on his long-ribbed cotton stockings. Seeing Mother cry had sobered us into determined action. But that wasn't the end of it. In the middle of our marching game, with all the imitated brass effects, Johnny revolted again. He planted his foot in the snow and said: "I won't go, Mama. I want to go back home to bed; I'm too sleepy."

Mother coaxed and pleaded and promised him a top, or whatever his heart was set on, if only he would be a sport and make one more effort. To no avail. Johnny stood his ground and said, "I won't go!" Mother was carrying both her suitcase and his, while Lottie and I carried our own. There was a very low iron railing where Johnny had stopped. Mother determinedly dropped the two bags on the sidewalk and walked back the few steps to Johnny. Without a word she picked him up and threw him over that railing into a deep, soft bed of snow. That was the only moment in my life that I actually disliked my mother. I was too young to realize that she was using drastic methods because the situation was drastic. Our livelihood depended on our catching that train; even more important, it meant that the four of us would remain together. Mother stubbornly marched on, Lottie and I, torn between her and Johnny, following disconsolately behind. I turned my head, and to my great relief I saw my brother scramble out of the snow and call out, "Mama, don't leave me!" Lottie and I broke rank and dashed back to Johnny, and when we again caught up with Mother, tears were silently streaming down four faces in the cold early morning air.

For years I couldn't bear the color crimson and the reason was the heavy red upholstery of the day coaches that always smelled of coal dust. Mother would stretch us out on the seats with the iron rests and lie awake herself. The train would slowly fill up as it stopped at all the little villages of the milk route. I would awaken three or four hours later with my feet on top of the radiator and my shoes fairly bursting with the heat. I learned to sleep sitting up, even standing up. In our fondest dreams we never knew the luxury of a Pullman berth. Anything was improvised for a pillow, from a suitcase to a fat roll of newspapers. Our breakfast generally consisted of stale ham sandwiches left over from the day before, and a glass of ice water. Since those days I've heard actors complain about the most trivial inconveniences. On such occasions I wonder even more at the unbelievable courage of Charlotte Pickford Hennessey Smith. . . .

That particular spring after *The Warrens of Virginia* closed our funds got so low that Mother made what seemed to me a very shocking proposal.

"Would you be very much against applying for work at the Biograph Studios, Gladdie?" she said one day.

"Oh no, not that, Mama!"

"Well, now, it's not what I would want for you, either, dear. I thought if you could make enough money we could keep the family together. I'm sure it would make up for the lowering of our standard."

I wanted to argue with her, but I knew better. I agreed.

"I knew you would, dear," said Mother. "It's only to tide us over. They say the pay is good . . . and besides, I'll let you wear your first silk stockings and high-heeled shoes."

Maybe that as much as anything else decided me. The following morning, glorying in my new finery, I decide to walk from where we were living on West Seventeenth Street to Fourteenth Street, take a cross-town trolley, and in paying my fare ask the conductor for a transfer up Broadway. I had no intention of wasting a perfectly good nickel. I alighted in front of the Biograph and Bioscope Studios with the transfer clasped firmly in my hand. I would step into this hated place, I told myself, pay the promised call and get out as fast as I could. I would then use my transfer to reach the legitimate-theater agencies on Broadway, where I was convinced I belonged. I would be able to say to Mother, honestly and truthfully, "I did what you asked me to." In my secret heart I was disappointed in Mother: permitting a Belasco actress, and her own daughter at that, to go into one of those despised, cheap, loathsome motion-picture studios. It was beneath my dignity as an artist, which I most certainly considered myself at the time. Belligerently I marched up the steps of Biograph.

Up to that time the family had always called me Gladys. They had never taken the "Mary" business very seriously. But on that March day of 1909, on East Fourteenth Street in New York, Gladys was sent back to Canada and Mary Pickford was to embark on a great and thrilling career.

As I crossed the marble-floored foyer of the old mansion occupied by the Biograph Studio, a man came through the swinging door opposite me and began to look me over in a manner that was too jaunty and familiar for my taste.

"Are you an actress?" he demanded at once.

"I most certainly am," I retorted.

"What, if any, experience have you had, may I ask?"

"Only ten years in the theater, sir, and two of them with David Belasco," I said icily.

"You're too little and too fat, but I may give you a chance. My name is Griffith. What's yours?"

The name meant nothing to me at all. I thought him a pompous and insufferable creature and I wanted more than ever to escape. Instead I found myself being led through two swinging doors and into the ladies' dressing room. . . .

I was hastily tiptoeing out of the dressing room when Mr. Griffith reappeared. He told me that I was to be given a test, the first, and, I may add, the *only* test that I was ever subjected to at Biograph. It was for *Pippa Passes*, and Mr. Griffith himself put on my make-up.

The result seemed more appropriate for Pancho Villa than for Pippa. A makeshift costume was rounded up in the wardrobe department — a tiny cellar alcove set aside for the Biograph costume rack.

Wearing this grotesque make-up, I was led on the stage and, without any introduction to the cast, given a quick briefing on what I was to do. Then came my second shock of the day: I heard the actors and actresses calling each other by their first names. That I thought improper beyond belief. In the Belasco company, and in the theater in general, I had heard people addressed only by their surnames. I noticed, however, that no one ever addressed the gentleman in the striped suit as anything but "Mr. Griffith."

To add to my worries, I was handed a guitar and told to act as if I were singing and strumming!

During the filming of this scene in which everyone improvised his own lines, a handsome young man, with a melodious Irish voice, stepped forth and nonchalantly said:

"Who's the dame?"

That was going too far. I forgot all all about the guitar, the scene, my grotesque make-up, and Mr. Griffith, and turned the full force of my indignation on this boor.

"How dare you, sir, insult me? I'll have you understand I'm a perfectly respectable young girl, and don't you dare call me a bad name!"

With that Mr. Griffith let out a roar that would have done the M.G.M. lion credit.

"Miss . . . Miss . . . what the devil is your name? But no matter . . . Never, do you hear, never stop in the middle of a scene. Do you know how much film costs per foot? You've ruined it! Start from the beginning!"

In those days "dame" meant to me just one thing — a loose woman. I had just never heard a girl publicly referred to as "a dame." Of course that young Irishman had meant no offense and was simply ad-libbing as they all did in the early movies. Whatever his faults, obscene language in the presence of a lady was not one of them. I should know, because his name was Owen Moore, and he later became my first husband.

Why Mr. Griffith asked me to come back the next day is still a matter of amazement to me. I was positive this was the end of my career in the "flickers." I knew it in my heart. I put ten years in the theater, and I knew whether a performance was good or bad. Mine that day at the Biograph Studio was distinctly bad.

It was well past eight o'clock when I returned to the dressing room and removed my hated make-up. Mr. Griffith was waiting for me outside.

"Will you dine with me?"

"I'm sorry, Mr. Griffith, I've never dined with any boy, let alone a man, and besides I have to leave immediately for Brooklyn. My mother and sister are playing there with Mr. Olcott."

"Will you come back tomorrow? Our pay for everybody is five dollars a day. We pay only by the day."

Already my Scotch blood was coming to the fore.

"I'm a Belasco actress, Mr. Griffith, and I must have ten."

He laughed.

"Agreed! Five dollars for today and ten for tomorrow. But keep it to yourself. No one is paid that much, and there will be a riot if it leaks out."

It had begun to rain earlier and by now it was coming down in buckets. Mr. Griffith kindly accompanied me in the downpour with his umbrella, leaving me at the subway with the words, "Till tomorrow at nine sharp." . . .

The following winter, without the slightest forewarning, the news broke that the company was going to take its first trip to California. In those days it took four nights and five days to go from New York to Los Angeles. When the train was about to pull out, Jack suddenly started to whimper, "I want to go too!"

"Don't be silly, Johnny!" I said, "You haven't any luggage!"

Mother joined in, "Oh, take the poor little fellow!"

"He's a nuisance, and I don't want him," I said.

The train was already in motion as Mother, undaunted by my protests, picked my brother up bodily and, with the cry "Look after your sister, Johnny!" deposited him on the steps of the moving train. . . .

My salary remained forty dollars a week, augmented by a liberal stipend of fourteen dollars for expenses. And it wasn't very long before Jack was working six days a week too, at the standard pay of five dollars a day. The poor little fellow had to fall off horses and out of windows as a double for all the young girls in the company. By spring we had accumulated the unbelievable hoard of $1200. I suddenly could not wait to get back East to see Mother and surprise her with our savings.

In April, 1910, Jack and I arrived in New York only to find that Mother and Lottie had not returned yet from an engagement on the road in *Custer's Last Stand*. I promptly went to the cashier of the Biograph company and asked her to change my hoard into twenty-four, new, crisp fifty-dollar bills. Jack and I then bought Mother a handsome black handbag into which we tucked the bills. The moment Mother stepped into the house we presented her with the bag. She was delighted, but it was agony for us to wait till she opened it. Instead of the astonishment we expected when she looked inside all we saw was a pleasant smile.

"Oh, stage money," she said simply.

Mother had never seen a real fifty-dollar bill in her life, and neither had the rest of us. When Jack and I assured her that this was the real business, she counted the bills in a voice of mounting excitement. No sooner had she finished than that rascally brother of mine pounced on them and began throwing them in the air. Mother started chasing Jack around the room, and Lottie and I joined in the pursuit, till we got all the bills away from him. That was the beginning of affluence for the Pickford family.

EDWARD WAGENKNECHT
America's Sweetheart

Here is a particularly satisfying and helpful description of the image Mary Pickford presented to Americans on the screen. She was the girl next door, of course, not a vamp, not Theda Bara — although in the long run she was almost as stuck in her own image as Theda Bara was in hers. But she was not a sweet young thing, either. She had a range which included lively and feisty reactions to villains and other unlikely characters. In this, she provided an early model for such beloved American screen personalities as Ginger Rogers and Doris Day.

Wagenknecht, author of a number of literary biographies and textbooks, undertook to write a series of essays on silent films at a time when there were relatively few serious books on motion pictures. He called his book The Movies in the Age of Innocence *(University of Oklahoma Press, 1962) and his personal zest in recalling encounters with favorite pictures combines with meticulous scholarship to make this still an enjoyable and informative critical study of the silent era. Our selection is from pages 156 to 161.*

. . . Nobody has ever questioned Miss Pickford's great skill and knowledge in all matters relating to motion-picture technique, but there is a tendency among those who do not know her films well to identify her exclusively with the portrayal of children and young girls

Standing with reluctant feet,
Where the brook and river meet.

If this were true, I should not think it necessary to apologize for it in any terms of abjectness. Most actors specialize in one thing or another; to all intents and purposes, Mr. Chaplin has played only one character, but those who disparage Miss Pickford have not, therefore, thought it necessary to remain blind to his great achievements. If you are going to specialize, it seems to me that children and young girls afford a very good field. I can think of highly regarded actresses who have specialized in prostitutes, and I do not believe that prostitutes are more important than young girls or that they are more varied in their motivations or more difficult to portray. "A woman of moral depravity," said Julia Marlowe, "offers the modern playwright greater scope than a good woman because her life is full of incidents that are dramatic." But, she added, rightly, that "it takes a greater artist to make a good woman interesting than to make a base woman sympathetic and thrilling."

As a matter of fact, however, it was not until after the beginning of the feature era that Miss Pickford became definitely associated with ingénue roles, and it was not until *Poor Little Rich Girl* that she appeared all through a feature film as a child. As we have already seen, the public preference for seeing her in youthful roles became an ever-increasing problem to her as she grew older, and she made a number of attempts to break away. "Through my professional creations," she says, "I became, in a sense, my own baby," and I think there can be no doubt that her cutting her curls (an act which she now questions her right to have performed, and says she would not do again), was an attempt to destroy the persona standing in the way of her future development.[12] Nevertheless, Mary's children and girls were not undifferentiated; of course there was a family relationship between them, but is not this also true of the types favored by certain other actresses? Gwen in *A Poor Little Rich Girl*, for example, is a very different girl from either Rebecca or Pollyanna — more helpless and less resourceful and considerably more wistful. She also gives the impression of being considerably younger. Her movements, her reactions are all those of a *small* child; so too is her fright when she is told by a lazy servant that she cannot be taken to her father's office because the place is full of bears. When she asks another girl, "Are you scared of bears?" she reads the line like a small child, and it is no exaggeration to speak of her "reading" such lines, though the film is silent, and we cannot hear what she says except in the mind's ear. Her tantrums are a small child's tantrums too, entirely lacking the elements of calculation and self-satisfaction of which Rebecca is capable or the sense of compulsion which sometimes possesses Pollyanna.

What I am saying of course is that the composite Pickford character was considerably less simple than she is generally supposed to have been. As I have already said, if she was "America's Sweetheart," she was also America's — and the world's — darling child, sometimes even problem child. But she was also the Madonna in *The Foundling* and again, briefly, in Douglas Fairbanks' production of *The Gaucho* in 1927.

She was, to be sure, in general, "good," and if you do not like good women in art — or if you subscribe to the juvenile and idiotic nonsense that bad women are more "interesting" — then she is not for you; but if you reject her on this ground, I fear you will have to reject most of Shakespeare's heroines with her. What you will have to learn, however, before you can approach her intelligently, is that "good" and "saccharine" are not synonymous terms.[13] I have already spoken of Mary's high jinks. Her repertoire in this kind was as rich and varied as that of the slapstick artists who did nothing else, and sometimes, as when, in *Through the Back Door*, she tied scrubbing brushes on her feet and turned the kitchen into a skating rink, she achieved a ballet-like ecstasy.

In *Rags, Tess of the Storm Country,* and several other films, she was a captivating and innocent young virago, with what you would have called outrageous conduct in anybody else accepted as endearing in her because of the disarming air of innocence that went along with it; and in *Daddy Long Legs* she was a devil toward all who were in authority over her at the orphan asylum but a tower of strength to every abused younger child. In *Rags* she made her first appearance riding on a goat. Overalls-clad, she charged head-on into a gang of boys who were abusing a dog, disciplined her drunken father in a saloon, and compelled him to return the money he had stolen; then she went into a temper tantrum, culminating in free-swinging a chair about her head after one of the habitués of the place had ventured to rumple her hair. In *The Pride of the Clan* she used equally violent methods to get the fisherman into church. In *The Foundling* she fed Mrs. Grimes's birthday cakes to the puppies, and when the dogcatcher tried to seize her own dog, she not only resisted him but unlocked the back of his wagon and set every animal imprisoned in it loose in the streets. She also made a statuette of the cruel Mrs. Grimes and then punished it; probably she did not know that she was practicing witchcraft, but the impulse was there. In *Poor Little Peppina* she and her brother Beppo (Jack Pickford) attacked a servant and kicked him in the shin in order to get in to see the duchess when Peppina needed her help to avoid an unwelcome marriage, and from there went on to more violence, culminating in an escape for Peppina in Beppo's clothes. But perhaps she was more vigorous in

Tess than anywhere else. She jumped on Dan Jordan's back when he tried to put out the squatters' fire, made impudent faces at Elias Graves and did a mocking dance step to tease him, and rushed into a tug of war when the warden was taking a net from a fisherwoman so that she got pulled along the ground on her bottom.

In *Rags*, Mary prepares to entertain an admirer (Marshall Neilan) at a miserable little lunch in her poor hut. She gets everything arranged to her satisfaction, but when she steps out for a moment, her drunken father and his companions come in and wolf the food. Mary, returning, arranges the few remaining scraps on Neilan's plate and greets him with a disarming "I was so hungry I jes' couldn't wait for you." James Card has rightly compared this with the famous scene in *The Gold Rush* in which Chaplin waits for the girl who never comes, and Iris Barry long ago pointed out the Chaplinesque elements in her arrangement of her hat and gloves before she sets out for church in *The New York Hat*. These are no isolated instances, and since Mary was doing this kind of thing before Chaplin came to the movies, there can be no question of indebtedness on her part. Unity Blake's pantomime with John Risca's coat in *Stella Maris*, which culminates when she makes him put his arm about her — perhaps the best thing about Mary's characterization of Unity is that she holds our sympathy for the girl even when she quite fails to keep her "place" — is Chaplin to the life. And *Rebecca* is full of this kind of thing: consider the dancestep movement Rebecca performs backward during her embarrassment while selling soap to Mr. Aladdin, or her recitations at school; consider her battle with the divided door when she arrives at the brick house (so like Keaton's never-ending war with gadgets). In closing the upper half she knocks the bottom half open again, and when she stoops back under to remedy this, the upper half knocks her hat off. Finally, consider the wonderful running and jumping from one piece of oilcloth to another, trying not to step on Aunt Miranda's carpets, culminating in a run down the final strip close to the camera, ending in a dead stop and jerk which brings her hat down over her eyes and inspires her to remark that she is sure she is going to like it here. In *Hulda from Holland* she falls through a skylight onto a young man's bed. In the way of gadgetry again, she has regular Rube Goldberg contraptions on her bed curtains and fishing tackle in *Tess*, and when she arrives in England in *Less Than the Dust*, she makes a floral offering to a suit of armor.

It must not be supposed that even in her feature pictures, made when she had become such a valuable theatrical property that she could do virtually nothing without considering its probable effect upon millions of admirers, did she ever give the impression of having wrapped herself in cotton wool or of not understanding the world she lived in. In *Madame Butterfly* she killed herself for love (not by the traditional hara-kiri method, to be sure, but more genteelly by wading out into the water). In *Hearts Adrift* she cast herself and her child into a volcano. In *Stella Maris* she committed both murder and suicide. She was a girl thief in both *Less Than the Dust* and *In the Bishop's Carriage*. As a messenger boy in *Poor Little Peppina* she choked on a cigar; in *M'liss* she picked up a five-foot snake. In *A Romance of the Redwoods* she saved Elliott Dexter, as a reformed road agent to whom she was not married, but pretending that she was pregnant by him, using doll clothes as garments which she had prepared for the expected baby. The sheriff married them on the spot, and not until after they had got away did he understand that she had tricked him. *The Moving Picture World* thought this situation very daring and speculated on how the public would take it, though stipulating that "it is hardly necessary to add that the acting and personality of Mary Pickford make the situation without actual offence." . . .

NOTES

12 In her autobiography she writes of being overwhelmed by the avalanche of public criticism which followed her act. "You would have thought I had murdered someone, and perhaps I had, but only to give her successor a chance to live." In 1929 bobbed hair was still a moral issue in America; it marked the difference between the old-fashioned "womanly" woman and her "emancipated" successor, between the Victorian maiden and the "flapper." When Mary Pickford, who had been the symbol par excellence of all the cherished old values, cut her hair, it seemed to many as though the citadel had been betrayed from within. When, as late as 1925, Miss Pickford had appealed through *Photoplay* for letters telling her what she should play, the 25,000 people who responded were overwhelmingly in favor of the youthful roles, the gist of the argument being that other actresses could portray emotional maturity but that what Mary was doing could be done by her alone. The stories most frequently asked for were "Cinderella" (which she had already done), *Anne of Green Gables* (which Mary Miles Minter had done), *Alice in Wonderland*, *Heidi*, *The Little Colonel*, and *Sara Crewe* (which she had done as *A Little Princess*).

13 . . . She was in general, an extremely restrained actress. Look at any of her early films — look, especially, if you can find it, at the Imp, *Going Straight* — and you will find Mary getting her effects by understatement while everybody else is acting all over the place. This was the source of her early squabbles with Griffith: "I will not exaggerate, Mr. Griffith. I think it's an insult to the audience." She once told George Pratt of Eastman House, "Mr Griffith always wanted to have me running around trees and pointing at rabbits, and I wouldn't do it."

EDWARD WAGENKNECHT
A Poor Little Rich Girl

In 1980 Anthony Slide and Wagenknecht wrote a book reviewing Fifty Great American Silent Films, 1912-1920 *(N.Y., Dover Publications) from which we have chosen this Pickford film (page 74). It was the success of this picture which convinced her that Adolph Zukor was right in keeping her in little girl roles. She broke the chain somewhat the very next year with* Stella Maris, *and in 1923 tried the rather unlikely gambit of inviting Ernst Lubitsch to direct her. (*Rosita, *she told everyone, was the worst film making experience she ever had.) But not till 1927 did she really break free from the cycle begun again by this film.*

In her 1972 autobiography, Off With Their Heads! *screenwriter Frances Marion reports that the two previous Pickford vehicles had been poorly received because they called on her to be a bit more mature as an East Indian girl (*Less Than the Dust) *and a Scottish lass (*Pride of the Clan). *Frances and Mary were good friends, and during the course of the production they "ganged up on poor serious Mr. Tourneur and either sweet-talked or fast-talked him into letting us include some wild comedy scenes which were not in the play or the script." Then the top executives at Famous Players-Lasky saw the finished picture in a projection room and decided the combination was so "putrid" they should shelve it. Nevertheless, it was released.*

The two unhappy conspirators slipped into the top balcony of the Strand theater on Broadway to watch it with an audience. It turned out to be a tremendous hit. They decided always thereafter to preview a new picture in a theater and let the public decide.

An Artcraft production. Released March 5, 1917. 6 reels.
Director: Maurice Tourneur.
Screenplay: Ralph Spence and Frances Marion (based on the novel and play by Eleanor Gates).
Photography: John van den Broek and Lucien Andriot.
Art Director: Ben Carré.
Assistant Director: M.N. Litson
CAST: Mary Pickford (*Gwendolyn*); Madeline Traverse (*Her Mother*); Charles Wellesley (*Her Father*); Gladys Fairbanks (*Jane, the Nurse*); Frank McGlynn (*The Plumber*); Emile La Croix (*The Organ Grinder*); Marcia Harris (*Miss Royle, the Governess*); Charles Craig (*Thomas, the Footman*); Frank Andrews (*Potter, the Butler*); Herbert Prior (*The Doctor*); George Gernon (*Johnny Blake*); Maxine Hicks (*Susie May Squaggs*).

SYNOPSIS: Gwendolyn has all the luxuries money can buy, but her father is too busy making money and her mother spending it to pay much attention to her, and most of those employed to look after her are unsympathetic. Her parents come to their senses when she goes into delirium and nearly dies after having been given too much sleeping medicine by a nurse who wished to go out. "We have been fighting death itself," says her father when the long night ends, "and have learned what is truly precious. There is enough left for the life we are going to lead."

COMMENTARY: *A Poor Little Rich Girl*, which Viola Dana had done on the stage for Arthur Hopkins as his initial production in 1913 (it was the same year Mary Pickford did *A Good Little Devil* for Belasco), is an exquisite film — funny, touching, and mounted, directed, and photographed with great sensitivity by Maurice Tourneur and his associates, especially in the dream-delirium sequence. The French director had been working in the United States since 1914, but this was only the second of the many films he would make for the Paramount companies (the first had been *The Pride of the Clan*, also with Miss Pickford). In the opinion of this scribe, he was the finest of all early directors except Griffith.

Rich Girl has been chosen here as our second Pickford film not only because of its individual merits but because of the milestone it marked in her career. She had been young in all her feature films, but never so young as here, and unless you wish to exempt the screen version of *A Good Little Devil*, which hardly counted for anything, this was her first extended portrayal of a child. When the time inevitably came that she must make the transition to more mature roles, she would find the tremendous vogue of her portrayals of childhood no unmixed blessing. Meanwhile, however, years of unalloyed delight would intervene which nobody who lived through them could be persuaded to wish away.

Miss Pickford respected Tourneur's gifts, but she once told me she did not think him a good director for her because he did not understand American humor. The mud fight in *Rich Girl* (for so wistful and inhibited a child, Mary's Gwen was capable of a good deal of mischief) was included over his protest; to him mud was simply ugly. The really astonishing thing about the picture, however, is that neither the star nor her employers had any idea of the value of what they had turned out until its smashing success in the theaters made them aware of it. The actress indeed was as much discouraged about her career after completing *Rich Girl* as she ever was in her life. But *Wid's* called it the best thing she had ever done, and *Motography* thought her role in it brought out her "real genius," also praising Tourneur for the perfect atmosphere that he had achieved, while Edward Weitzel lauded Mary for her complete freedom "from the stock tricks of the ordinary child impersonator."

There are suggestions of both allegory and folklore in the dream sequence which brilliantly explores the mind of a child. Gwen has heard the servants call each other Two-Faced Thing, Snake-in-the-Grass, Big Ears, and Silly Ass, and in her dream they are literally that, though the Snake-in-the-Grass is not a real snake, and the Silly Ass she loves. She sees her father as "made of money" and her mother with a social "bee in her bonnet," she travels about "Robin Hood's Barn," and hears the "bears" growl in Wall Street. One scene shows "Where They Burn the Candle at Both Ends," another "The Forest Where The Lights Go When They Are Blown Out." All this, of course, was material much better adapted to the screen than it had been to the stage, and it was very fortunate that it fell into the hands of just the right people to make the most of it.

C.A. LEJEUNE
Mary Pickford

This is an ingenious critical sketch, beginning with a distant air of seeming disapproval, claiming the privileged stance of the motion picture reviewer as a judge of what is new and what is cinematic. Surely Mary Pickford as symbol, as a kind of royal personage, a legend, is not what we demand in the cinema. Yet Ms. Lejeune (who was for many years a leading film critic in London) warms to her task of explaining this phenomenon of showbusiness, and confesses that she comes away from a Pickford movie "ridiculously touched," admiring the optimism in it which is so "sensible, simple, and sympathetic." (Pages 56-57, 60-62, Cinema, London, Alexander Maclehose Co., 1931.)

It is one of the most curious anomalies of the cinema that Mary Pickford, who has never come to grips with real movie, who has never created a part of first-rate importance nor contributed anything by her productions to the pioneer development of cinema technique, should be accepted all the world over as a figurehead of the industry, as the first woman, and with Chaplin the foremost representative, of the motion picture screen.

Those of us who are working constantly in the stuff of the cinema, alert for the newest and the best in every country's output, and careful for the rare true strain of movie thought, may find it difficult to believe in Mary Pickford as a symbol; she comes so seldom into our calculations, touches so distantly on everything we hold vital and clear. The Pickford productions have never created either a director or a player. They have never made an actress of Pauline Frederick's calibre or Jenny Hasselquist's or Bergner's or even Mae Marsh's out of Mary Pickford herself. But they still, after ten or more years, preserve a kind of royal investiture, they are still less entertainments than occasions, and Mary, in an industry that lives on change, goes on and on in possession, inspiring horticulturalists and fashion designers to name their new creations after her, inviting men and women who have never seen a film to pass their verdicts on her; the recognized leader among the movies' own people, the accredited representative of the movies in the public eye.

Mary Pickford's is a curious celebrity; one of the rare instances of a private life controlling and governing a public reputation. By leading consistently a quiet, hard-working and unspectacular life, by playing consistently in decent, simple, unostentatious pictures with a certain wistful emotional note, she has achieved for herself a position unique among stars and producers. Her home life rarely gets into the limelight; public attention is drawn to her only at such times as Hollywood requires some visiting celebrity to be entertained, or some meeting of hysterical film aspirants to be counseled and pacified. But Mary Pickford's good name is one of the modern cinema's foundations; her credit has become the credit of the industry; the recent rumours of her divorce shook two continents; she is at once a myth and a surety, a legend and a pledge. . . .

She sends us away from the picture-house absurdly generous, ridiculously touched, so that we want to stop the first grubby urchin in the street and surprise it with a five-pound note, buy an orphanage, adopt a township of homeless dogs, or sell all we have and give it to the poor. And now, too, memories of our own early days in the cinema, of lost films that delighted us, and recaptured associations from our own lives, confuse the emotional issue. We see Mary Pickford even more remotely, through our own experiences blurred with time. What we like to think we were — what we like to believe we felt and dreamed — the way we imagine we used to see life — all this is implicit in the Pickford films. Children see in Mary themselves plus an enchanting remoteness towards maturity; adults love in her themselves minus sophistication and age.

If we wanted any proof of Mary Pickford's acumen, we should find it in this building-up of a cumulative envelope of emotion round her screen figure — this deliberate use of an appeal that is strengthened by the audience itself through every personal experience and with every receding year. The trust in sentiment is Mary's sagacity of sagacities. It is paradoxically typical of her cold common-sense, her business surety. A less practical woman would never have dared to trust herself so completely to the wistful, the miniature, the pathetic. But Mary, who had no real childhood, who was playing heavy emotional parts to support her family at the age when other girls are still playing with their dolls, learnt to know the cinema and to assess the cinema audience with the uncanny sureness of necessity; she grew from a sage, business-like, determined child to a sage, business-like, determined woman, who could exploit unerringly, and had the courage to exploit, all the emotional frailties in human nature that make for a player's popularity and success.

And it is to this practical, steely, reasoned Mary Pickford, not to the actress, not to the producer, that we can give, and must give, unqualified admiration. She has never shrunk from hard work and plenty of it. She has never denied herself to the audience, never stinted measure, never supplied us with inferior goods. She has had the good sense to see the commercial value of optimism, and to act on that knowledge. All her stuff is essentially clean and decent. There is no ugliness in it, no sly hinting, no display. It is sensible, simple and sympathetic, always working towards some tangible expression of happiness. It is free of sensationalism, just as Mary's private life is free of sensationalism. It is stuff that anyone can be expected to buy, and that no one, as experience has proved, can quite hope to imitate. And it is, above all, stuff that can fitly give its hall-mark to the cinema — that can guarantee a certain positive level of good sense and integrity in the cinema. What Mary Pickford has really done is to establish the modern cinema under the stamp of her own respectability; to offer it a place in circles to which the old movie never penetrated; to give it standing and citizenship all the world over, and to enlarge it, by her own rigorous conservatism, into an age of experiment and enthusiasm in which it will be free to live and grow.

"Mr. Griffith always wanted to have me running around trees and pointing at rabbits, and I wouldn't do it."--Mary Pickford.

ROB EDELMAN
Stella Maris

From that valuable compendium of new reviews edited by Frank N. Magill, Magill's Survey of Cinema: Silent Films, (Englewood Cliffs, N.J., Salem Press, 1982, pages 1053-56), here is a very thoughtful analysis of the story, the acting, and the historical ambiance of Mary Pickford's most ambitious motion picture. We learn something about her other films, her "greatest" year (1917), her director and screenwriter, and the other actors.

Released: 1918
Production: Paramount/Artcraft Films
Direction: Marshall Neilan
Screenplay: Frances Marion; based on the novel of the same name by William J. Locke
Cinematography: Walter Stradling
Length: 6 reels
    Principal characters:

Stella Maris/Unity Blake	*Mary Pickford*
John Risca	*Conway Tearle*
Louisa Risca	*Camille Ankewich (Marcia Manon)*
Lord Blount	*Herbert Standing*
Lady Blount	*Ida Waterman*

Mary Pickford was not merely a star; she was — and is — a legend. For twenty-three years, in fifty-two features, and more than 125 shorts, she was the most popular actress on America's film screens, playing child and adolescent roles into her twenties and even thirties. She may not have been the best actress of her era — she was no Lillian Gish or Mae Marsh — but she was adept at playing both comedy and drama in contemporary and period settings, usually acting the tomboy who still managed to retain her femininity. Pickford was in her prime between 1914 and 1919, when she was in her mid-twenties; in appearance, she was indescribably lovely, no longer a child but not quite a woman. *Stella Maris* — not to be confused with *Stella Dallas* (1925) — is not the most famous Pickford heroine and is not as fondly recalled as Tess (of the Storm Country), Rebecca (of Sunnybrook Farm), Pollyanna, or Little Annie Rooney. The film features, however, two of Pickford's most impressive performances, and may very well be her best film.

Stella Maris parallels the lives of two young girls, one rich and pretty, the other unattractive and miserable. Garbed in her well-known curls and beautiful dresses, "America's Sweetheart" stars first as the title character, a wealthy, sensitive, beautiful, but crippled and bedridden girl. Stella is brought up by her devoted uncle and aunt,

Lord and Lady Blount (Herbert Standing and Ida Waterman), in a happy little dream world. She lives in a castle amidst gardens and rustic walkways, protected from all the sadness and evil in the world by her enforced isolation. Stella thinks that everyone else is exactly like her; a sign above the room in which she is confined reads: "The court of Stella Maris / All unhappiness and world wisdom leave outside / Those without smiles need not enter."

Pickford's other role is Unity Blake, a poor, homely, unloved waif who was the first "ugly" character Pickford portrayed. The film begins with Unity in a dreary orphan asylum beating a carpet. These shots are crosscut with ones of Stella, in her mansion, lying on a large bed, and petting a white rabbit. Stella's best friend is John Risca (Conway Tearle), a journalist who pampers her, protecting her from the harsh realities that exist beyond her immediate environment. Risca is Stella's idol, but she does not know that he is married.

Risca's wife, Louisa (Camille Ankewich), is semi-insane and a drunkard. She goes to the orphanage to select a servant, and she picks Unity, believing that an ugly girl will work harder than others. Unity tries to say good-bye to her fellow orphans, but they are indifferent or jealous of her supposed good luck. One day, Unity's shopping bag is stolen at the market, and, as a result, Louisa beats her with a hot poker. For this act, Louisa is sentenced to three years in prison. Unity is at first placed in Stella's mansion, but because her family feels that Unity may expose Stella to "real life," the orphan then goes to live with Risca and his aunt. When she accidently breaks a vase, Unity cowers and lies. She thinks she will be beaten, but is surprised to realize that she will be forgiven. Unity is hungry for love and affection, and she grows to care for Risca with slavish devotion.

Three years pass, and Stella undergoes an operation for her paralysis. Miraculously, she is cured, but, now, she will be forced to enter the real world — to her shock and consternation. She meets a poor woman and her starving children and reads crime stories in the newspaper. By now, she and Risca are in love but John is still a married man, and his wife is released from jail. Stella visits Unity and tells the girl of her feelings, but Unity too has fallen for Risca. She holds a photo of Stella, peers into a mirror, and covers her face in disappointment. As this occurs, shots of Risca kissing Stella are crosscut in. Stella goes to the journalist's official address and finds the drunken, insanely jealous Louisa, who tells her that he is not free. Stella realizes that Risca does not live in a castle, that he is not really a Prince Charming, and that he had previously lied to protect her. She becomes disillusioned.

Meanwhile, Unity is still hopelessly in love. She speaks to an image of Risca — his jacket on a hanger, with his hat hanging on a hook above — and proposes marriage. Risca, depressed because Stella's faith in human nature has been destroyed, makes out his will and seems ready to kill himself. His aunt tells Unity that he will never be free as long as Louisa lives, so the girl sneaks into Louisa's house and shoots her with a pistol. Later, Unity is found dead next to Louisa's body. Superficially, her motive is revenge; but she leaves Risca a note, telling him that no one else had ever been kind to her, and that she wishes Stella and Risca happiness. They are married, and they both remember the little Cockney orphan who sacrificed her life for them.

Stella Maris is by far the most unusual film in Pickford's career, not so much for her dual role but for her performance as the homely Unity. As the title character, she has her golden curls, pouts, smiles, and cute mannerisms which are typical of the sweet and radiant Pickford America adored. Stella is indeed a typical Pickford role. Audiences, however, were shocked by her casting as Unity. Production of the film began when Adolph Zukor, Paramount's chairman of the board, was away for several weeks. Pickford instigated the making of the film. Zukor would probably never have approved *Stella Maris* and was aghast at seeing her made up as Unity, but the actress had the foresight to play Stella as well.

While Pickford is fine as the title character, she gives a brilliant character performance as Unity. The orphan is the key character in the film, the driving force in the scenario; a weak performance would have added emphasis to the sentimental, melodramatic nature of the plot. Pickford's curls are combed out and slicked down with vaseline; in their place are two braids that hang down her back. She acts with her shoulders hunched, her eyes squinted, her lips tightened, her face dirty and vacant. By means of the effect of twice exposing the film, in several scenes, both Unity and Stella appear together, and it is difficult at times to believe that both characters are being portrayed by the same actress.

As it is, *Stella Maris* is a mawkish film, but not cloyingly so because of Pickford's superior acting. Also, it has beautiful lighting; cinematographer Walter Stradling emphasizes the actress' already luminous face with just the right amount of backlighting. The scenes with Stella and Risca in her garden are particularly lovely. (The film's photography is sometimes erroneously attributed to Charles Rosher, who with Stradling shot Pickford's features during this period.)

The year 1917 was the greatest in Pickford's distinguished career, with one feature released practically every other month. Although released in January, 1918, *Stella Maris* was produced during the previous year. In 1917, Pickford worked with Maurice Tourneur in *The Pride of the Clan* (released in January) and *Poor Little Rich Girl* (March), for Cecil B. De Mille in *A Romance of the Redwoods* (May) and *The Little American* (July), and for Marshall Neilan in *Rebecca of Sunnybrook Farm* (September) and *A Little Princess* (November). There is not a weak film in the group.

Marshall "Mickey" Neilan, who directed *Stella Maris*, is one of the forgotten pioneers of the American cinema. In addition to his 1917 films with Pickford, he also worked with her in *Amarilly of Clothes-line Alley* (1918), *M'liss* (1918), *Daddy Long Legs* (1919), and *Dorothy Vernon of Haddon Hall* (1924); they acted together in *Rags* (1915), *A Girl of Yesterday* (1915), *Madame Butterfly* (1915), and *Daddy Long Legs*. Neilan was a talented, innovative director with a special ability to create and sustain mood, but he was also a playboy, with a fondness for alcohol, and he never seriously applied himself to his work. He could have become one of the great directors; instead, he developed a reputation for unreliability. By the end of the silent era, he was already a has-been. The last two films he directed, *Sing While You're Able* (1937) and *Swing It, Professor* (1937), were "D"-grade musicals for Ambassador Pictures. Years later, Elia Kazan cast him in a character role as a senator in *A Face in the Crowd* (1957). He died a year later in a charity ward.

Pickford is ably supported in *Stella Maris* by Conway Tearle, who is poised and sympathetic as Risca, and Camille Ankewich, appropriately nasty as Louisa. Tearle, half-brother of Godfrey Tearle, was a leading actor in dozens of silents whose career lasted into the 1930's. Ankewich, an obscure silent film actress, changed her name to Marcia Manon just after the release of *Stella Maris* and appeared in about a dozen features through the 1920's.

The film was written by Frances Marion, Hollywood's most in-demand writer of the silent and early talking eras. Marion also wrote the scenarios for many of Pickford's other films, including *Rebecca of Sunnybrook Farm, A Little Princess, Amarilly of Clothes-line Alley, M'liss, Poor Little Rich Girl, How Could You, Jean?* (1918), *Johanna Enlists* (1918), *Captain Kidd* (1919), *Pollyanna,* and *The Love Light* (1921).

Stella Maris received excellent reviews, with critics predictably highlighting Pickford's performance as Unity. Some writers had previously contended that she could not act, and that her only asset was her personality and inherent cuteness. These barbs were impressively refuted by her work in the film. In *Stella Maris*, Pickford proves herself a more than capable actress. The film, however, was a moderate box-office success.

ADOLPH ZUKOR
Mary and Doug

Now we go behind the scenes and listen to the president of the biggest motion picture company in the world (Famous Players-Lasky, releasing through Paramount Pictures) worry about his most profitable and precious star. He consults with Charlotte Pickford, then with Mary. "It is never pleasant to interfere with the lives of others," he insists, but he clearly envisioned nationwide scandalmongering by newspapers and magazines which might begin to break down boxoffice expectations for upcoming pictures. Here are pages 190-193 of Zukor's memoirs (The Public Is Never Wrong, N.Y., G.P. Putnam's Sons, 1953) written with Dale Kramer.

By this time, Fairbanks was also a Paramount/Artcraft producer and star, but Zukor is not so worried about him. The double standard would work in his favor: the roving male would be allowed his adventures. Mary was a different matter, and double divorces in those days were very newsworthy indeed. The suspense went on for three years, and by the time the marriage took place, the two principals were no longer tied to Zukor but had established their own United Artists Corporation, with Chaplin and Griffith. And of course their European honeymoon trip proved that their popularity had not waned.

. . . Mary had been living apart from Owen Moore for some time. Their marriage was over except in name. Doug was married and had a young son, Douglas, Jr. I understood that he was estranged from his wife. Mary, at least, had talked of divorce. But that was not simple.

The queen does not suddenly get divorced — especially if a large body of her subjects does not even know that she is married. Like many a royal lady before her, Mary chafed at her bonds. She was very tired of her eternal litte-girl role on the screen and in public. Here was a vigorous, blooming young lady in her middle twenties, a millionairess two times over by her own efforts, courageous — even willful. Though plenty of "Little Mary" remained, she wanted to be her whole self before the world, as well as to play more mature roles on the screen.

I was convinced that the public, no matter how much we helped, would not accept a quick change from "Little Mary" to a young woman of the world. Mary and I had argued endlessly over making *A Poor Little Rich Girl,* with her protesting that at last she was too old for the role of teen-ager. In the end I won that argument and the picture was a great hit. But its success only proved the strength of the bonds which tied Mary to her public role. She chafed more than ever.

As soon as I heard the rumors about Doug and Mary, I went to see her mother. She was aware of the situation.

"Yes," she said. "Mary is quite fond of Douglas."

In my mind there was a companion thought — how fond of Mary is Doug? It occurred to me that the mere paying of court to the queen might appeal to his romantic nature.

"The smallest breath of scandal can ruin Mary's career," I said. "Fairbanks will survive. After all, nothing really bad is happening, or is going to happen between them. The public will forgive a dashing fellow like Doug. But it has taken Mary to its heart in a different way. As the sweet daughter or sister much more is expected of her. If Mary appears to fail the public's trust, it will punish her."

Charlotte nodded. "I've told Mary so."

Neither of us had forgotten that Mary had disobeyed her mother by eloping with Owen Moore. If Mary was in love with Doug, and he was in love with her, we knew that she would marry him no matter if it smashed her career beyond repair. It is ironical, I suppose, that Mary could not portray on the screen the indomitable woman who was one part of her.

If Mary and Doug were serious about each other, it was up to Charlotte Pickford and me to do our level best to prevent a smashup of Mary's career.

"Well," I said, rising to go, "I'll have to make inquiries as to whether the intentions of the gentleman are honorable."

Mrs. Pickford laughed. "Will you ask him?"

"Oh, no. Doubtless he would turn three or four cartwheels, shinny up the waterspout, leap from the roof to a tree, do a double back-flip to the ground, and I might not hear enough of his answer to satisfy me."

It is never pleasant to interfere with the lives of others. But the sad truth is that movie producers occasionally have to. This can be regarded, I suppose, as a cynical matter of business. We spend hundreds of thousands of dollars in building a star and often millions more are wrapped up in pictures awaiting release. Naturally we think of those things — as well as possible harm to the entire industry.

But a major film producer must concern himself also with the human elements, or he doesn't last long. Many a star, temporarily overwrought, is unable to clearly judge the public's reaction to a given incident. We therefore often talk in a straightforward but sympathetic way to a player about his or her behavior. I am frank in saying that we take character — for example emotional balance — into account before going all out in star building.

Mary and Doug were beginning to see a good deal of each other. When not together, they telephoned. I couldn't hold a conversation with Mary but that Fairbanks interrupted it with a call. They were very discreet, or thought they were. In New York they sometimes donned motorist's linen dusters and goggles and drove about, believing themselves disguised. It was the sort of thing that appealed especially to Doug's romanticism.

My reason for not discussing the subject with Fairbanks was simply that I would not have been convinced by anything he said. Not that he lacked honesty. I simply had no way of being sure of what went on under his exuberant exterior. It occurred to me that he might have convinced himself that he was sure of his feeling for Mary, while deep down he was not at all.

The person to know best was Mary, and finally I tackled the subject with her. We had dinner at a quiet place and I began by mentioning the talk inside the trade.

"The point has been reached," I said, "that some little incident will occur — maybe that automobile will break down and a reporter will happen along and penetrate your disguise. The dam will break. What if, to put the worst face on it, Owen Moore sues for divorce, naming Fairbanks as co-respondent? Or his wife sues him, naming you? Above all are you very, very sure about your feelings?"

Mary's blue eyes were graver than I had ever seen them. "I am sure," she said simply.

I knew that she was. "And Fairbanks?"

Mary nodded. "Equally, I know."

"All right," I said. "That part is settled. Now what about the public?"

Here we disagreed.

"The public will understand," Mary said. "We are in love and we are sincere and the public will not deny us our happiness."

Three long years were to pass before the royal wedding was possible. In-between there were explosions, but they were kept muffled. At one point Owen Moore stated publicly that he intended to proceed legally against Fairbanks, who was the first to get a divorce. But Moore did nothing and said no more. Finally a divorce was arranged by Mary and Moore in Nevada, after which the Nevada attorney general accused them of collusion and fraud. Charges were not pressed and shortly thereafter — in March of 1920 — Mary and Fairbanks were married at last. . . .

EPHRAIM KATZ
Douglas Fairbanks

The Film Encyclopedia *(Crowell/Harpers 1979, page 399) offers us this summary of the Fairbanks life. One item seems doubtful. Booton Herndon doubts if Fairbanks ever spent time studying at Harvard. He might have dropped in on a class or two, and publicity releases then expanded on this over the years. In His Majesty the American, (1977) James Welsh and John Tibbetts have described a great many of his films.*

Fairbanks, Douglas. Actor. *b.* Douglas Elton Ulman, May 23, 1883, Denver, Colo. *d.* 1939. The son of a prominent Jewish lawyer and a Southern belle who were separated when he was five, he was raised by his mother, who reassumed the surname of her first husband, Fairbanks. Douglas made his stage debut at age 12, playing a newsboy with an Italian accent in a locally produced play. He continued appearing in occasional plays while attending the Colorado School of Mines. In 1900 the family moved to New York, where he joined an unsuccessful touring company. After studying briefly at Harvard and traveling to Europe as a steward on a cattle freighter, he worked as a clerk in a hardware store and as an order clerk with a Wall Street firm. In 1902 he made his Broadway debut in *Her Lord and Master*. In 1907, just as he was beginning to make it as a leading man, he left the stage to marry the daughter of an industrialist, Anna Beth Sully, and to work for her family's soap company. But he returned to the theater the following year when his father-in-law lost his fortune. In 1909, Doug's son, Douglas Fairbanks, Jr., was born.

By 1910, Douglas Sr. was an established Broadway star, widely admired for the same qualities that were to make him the silent screen's most beloved hero — cheerful exuberance, moral courage, a devil-may-care attitude, and physical agility, a prototype of the idealized image of the American male. In 1915, Fairbanks was lured to Hollywood by a generous contract with Triangle. He did his early film work under the supervision of D.W. Griffith, who showed no appreciation for Fairbanks' enthusiastic pranks, which often transcended the requirements of the script. But the public took to him immediately and by 1916 he was popular and secure enough to establish his own production company, the Douglas Fairbanks Film Corporation, with an Artcraft-Paramount release. He had complete control of all phases of production and named members of his family to key positions in the company.

During a WW I Liberty Bond tour with Charlie Chaplin and Mary Pickford, Fairbanks fell in love with "America's Sweetheart." Having divorced his first wife, Fairbanks married Pickford in 1920 and after a whirlwind European honeymoon they settled in their Hollywood mansion, Pickfair, which soon became a social Mecca for the titled and the famous. Earlier, in 1919, Doug and Mary had gone into partnership with Chaplin and Griffith, forming United Artists to distribute all their future productions. Both Fairbanks and Pickford reached the peak of their success in the 20s.

Fairbanks was as popular in his early tongue-in-cheek social comedies as he later became in a succession of swashbuckling adventures. And he was still fit and trim in 1929, when his stage-trained voice allowed him to make a smooth transition to sound. But as he clearly advanced in age, receding hair framing his still handsome but tired face, his popularity began to slip. The failure of *The Taming of the Shrew* (1929), the only film in which he co-starred with his wife, did not help the shaky marriage. The two separated in 1933 and in January 1936 they were divorced. In March he married ex-chorus girl Lady Sylvia Ashley (1904-1977) and announced his retirement from acting. In December of 1939 he died in his sleep of a heart attack.

FILMS: *The Lamb, Double Trouble* 1915; *His Picture in the Papers, The Habit of Happiness, The Good Bad Man, Reggie Mixes In, Flirting With Fate, The Mystery of the Leaping Fish* (2-reel short), *The Half Breed, Intolerance* (cameo), *Manhattan Madness, American Aristocracy, The Matrimaniac, The Americano* (1916); *In Again Out Again* (also prod.), *Wild and Woolly* (also prod.), *Down to Earth* (also prod., story), *The Man From Painted Post* (also prod., sc.), *Reaching for the Moon* (also prod.) 1917; *A Modern Musketeer* (also prod.), *Headin' South* (also prod.), *Mr. Fix-It* (also prod.), *Say! Young Fellow* (also prod.), *Bound in Morocco* (also prod.), *He Comes Up Smiling* (also prod.), *Arizona* (also dir., prod., sc.) 1918; *The Knickerbocker Buckaroo* (also prod., story, co-sc.), *His Majesty the American* (also prod., co-sc. under pseudonym Elton Banks), *Till The Clouds Roll By* (also prod., co-story, co-sc.) 1919; *The Mollycoddle* (also prod., co-sc.), *The Mark of Zorro* (as Zorro; also prod., co-sc. under pseudonym Elton Thomas) 1920; *The Nut* (also prod.), *The Three Musketeers* (as D'Artagnan; also prod.) 1921; *Robin Hood* (title role; also prod., sc. under pseudonym Elton Thomas) 1922; *The Thief of Bagdad* (title role; also prod., story under pseudonym Elton Thomas) 1924; *Don Q Son of Zorro* (again as Zorro; also prod.) 1925; *The Black Pirate* (also prod., story under pseudonym Elton Thomas) 1926; *Potselui Mary Pickford/The Kiss of Mary Pickford* (cameo; USSR), *The Gaucho* (also prod., story under pseudonym Elton Thomas) 1927; *The Iron Mask* (again as D'Artagnan; also prod., sc. under pseudonym Elton Thomas), *Show People* (cameo) 1928; *The Taming of the Shrew* (as Petruchio; also prod.) 1929; *Reaching for the*

Moon (remake; also prod.), *Around the World in 80 Minutes* (also prod., co-dir. with Victor Fleming, co-sc. with Robert E. Sherwood) 1931; *Mr. Robinson Crusoe* (also prod.) 1932; *The Private Life of Don Juan* (as Don Juan; UK) 1934.

ALISTAIR COOKE
Douglas Fairbanks:
The Making of a Screen Character

From a brilliant 31-page monograph published by the Museum of Modern Art in 1940, we have tried to extract the most memorable paragraphs. (pages 16, 17, 20-22, 27, 30-31). Alistair Cooke, for many years the British Broadcasting Corporation's American reporter and one of the most knowledgeable observers of the Hollywood scene, presents Fairbanks as popular philosopher, athlete, and showman. He especially wants to call attention to the early comedies, usually neglected by historians, which satirized the teen years of American life and registered "an affection for the American scene tempered with a wink."

Cooke is himself knowing and witty in his British awareness that Doug Fairbanks sets up for his audience, especially in the middle and later pictures, a "beautifully deceptive act of flattery, suggesting that all that is needed to clear up the stagnation of city life, a capture by Moroccan bandits, or a Cabinet crisis in a South American republic, is the arrival of an average healthy man." Such mythical evocation of the American's mission to save the world was not necessarily a democratic vision, since "all but one were high-born saviors of the people." In fact this is a fair statement of the status and personality of President Theodore Roosevelt, the well-remembered political whirlwind of the early 1900s.

Anita Loos wrote and John Emerson directed most of the early comedies, and the stories for Fairbanks were chosen because they were congruent with his personality. Afterward he found himself, in public, acting the way he did in the pictures. Thus, as Cooke explains, it was natural for him to carry Mary down the aisle of a theater on his shoulder. The star image, even for him, became indistinguishable from the personality.

At a difficult time in American history, when the United States was keeping a precarious neutrality in the European war, Douglas Fairbanks appeared to know all the answers and knew them without pretending to be anything more than "an all-around chap, just a regular American" (*The Americano*). The attraction of this flattering transfer of identity to the audience did not have to be obvious to be enjoyed. The movie fan's pleasure in Fairbanks might have been expressed in the simple sentence of a later French critic: "Douglas Fairbanks is a tonic. He laughs and you feel relieved." In this period of his earliest films it was no accident that his best-liked films should have been *His Picture in the Papers, Reggie Mixes In, Manhattan Madness,* and *American Aristocracy.* These were respectively about the American mania for publicity; about a society playboy who was not above finding his girl in a downtown cabaret and fighting a gangster or two to keep her; about a Westerner appalled at the effete manners of the East, and about a Southerner of good family who married into "bean-can" nobility, and was healthily oblivious of any implied snobbery. Here already was the kernel of a public hero close enough, in manner and get-up, to contemporary America to leave his admirers with the feeling that they were manfully facing the times rather than escaping from them. It is important to insist on this transference of flattery from the screen to the audience, for it is a necessary stop in the process of becoming a public hero in almost any field. The Fairbanks screen character was forming at a time when the American and European peoples were badly in need of just such a rousing popular reassurance.

The 1916 movies did not release this hero full-blown but sketched his cartoon: a young vigorous man as uncompromising as his splendid physique, unfazed by tricky problems of taste and class behavior, gallant to women, with an affection for the American scene tempered by a wink. It had already two of the elements of the finished portrait which may be roughly described as popular philosophy and athletics. Fairbanks' decision to form his own company at the end of 1916 filled in the third element — the necessary background of showmanship.

These three elements are visible at different times of his career; his popular philosophy appears mostly between 1917 and 1920, his showmanship when he turned to costume during the twenties.

It is fair enough to say from all the evidence that Fairbanks was either the most sincere reproduction we know of a screen character, or he was the most hard-working actor there has ever been in laboring to create that belief. French newspapermen and critics often went to unnecessary lengths to explain that it was "Charlot" they loved, not the dapper little man with the sad private life who was known as Charles Chaplin. Nobody had to make such a distinction in Fairbanks. When he arrived at the Gare du Nord, it was "Doug" they saw and cheered, and just to prove it, Douglas Fairbanks vaulted the platform barrier. When he appeared at the opening nights of his movies in New York, he anticipated the audience's desire to have him carry Mary, his equally adored wife, down the aisle on his shoulder.

To "keep faith" with the "public" is one of the tedious vulgarities of theatre people going out of their way to attract applause, but Fairbanks literally had an obligation in this respect. By 1920 he was a mentor, a model for growing boys, a homespun philosopher of the generation after Will Rogers. Once the virility of the first Western comedies was impressed on the public mind, he looked no further than the bewildered manners of his own day for more pungent lessons. Sure of his public and its trust in the essential health of his reaction to all affectation, he took a series of good-humored swipes at most of the modish post-war fads, light-heartedly parodying a society that now looks to us comfortably like a period, but which to the people who lived it was as anxious and unpredictable as our own. He laughed at hypochondriacs, in Dr. Jollyem's Long Island sanitarium for rich neurotics (*Down to Earth*); at "bean-can nobility" in the person of Leander Hick, manufacturer of the One Hump Hat-Pin (*American Aristocracy*); Anglophilia (*Mr. Fix-It* and *The Mollycoddle*); success literature (*Reaching for the Moon*); bachelor girls, bobbed hair and patronizing social work (*The Nut*); the Eastern clubman (*Knickerbocker Buckaroo*); quack psychologists (*When the Clouds Roll By*); and by the way, in casual dissolves and pointed subtitles expressed himself unambiguously on the subject of modern dancing, Couéism, ouija boards, night club entertainment, women's clothes and other incidental oddities of the period.

In 1917, a peak was named after Fairbanks in Yosemite National Park. In 1920 Roscoe (Fatty) Arbuckle made a hit with a comedy in which he dreamed he too could be "Doug." By the spring of 1920, Fairbanks was the favorite male film star in nation-wide polls in the United States, in France and in England. He was the ideal twentieth century American, a young man who could be romantic in our clothes and successful with our handicaps. There was only one girl in all the world that "Doug," if he could step off-screen, deserved to marry. She was Mary Pickford, "The World's Sweetheart." On the 28th of March, 1920, this "poetic and audacious" event, as a French writer called it, took place.

The marriage was the logical end of the Fairbanks role as popular philosopher. He could do no more. He who had preached in many a short sentence and many a rocketing leap across the screen that rewards can be won in this world, had won the hand of the girl so fragile and winsome that every man wanted her — for his sister. Douglas Fairbanks and Mary Pickford came to mean more than a couple of married film stars. They were a living proof of America's chronic belief in happy endings....

Many and varied were the dilemmas of "Doug" over a score or more of his pictures, yet there was a regular technical formula for a

Fairbanks triumph. It was the galvanizing of a cheerful young American into a sort of campus whirlwind who extricates himself in a final scherzo of energy to win romantic and material success. For the audience it is a beautifully deceptive act of flattery, suggesting that all that is needed to clear up the stagnation of city life, a capture by Moroccan bandits, or a Cabinet crisis in a South American republic, is the arrival of an average healthy man. What is nowhere suggested, and available only on painful thought to the holder of an insurance policy savings account, is the fact that aside from his impulses, which were those of a popular evangelist, "Doug" was a person of superbly responsive physique and of quite extraordinary grace and initiative.

Nowhere was this more evident than at the crises, in his movies, when he appeared to be cornered. One of the special excitements of watching Fairbanks at bay was the foreknowledge that he was no more earthbound than Superman, his 1940 counterpart. In the most typical films (especially in *A Modern Musketeer*, *Bound in Morocco*, and many times in *The Mark of Zorro*, *The Three Musketeers* and *Robin Hood*) there was a delicious moment when he would fall back before his adversaries, not in retreat but to gain a second in which to reconsider the resources of a room as a machine for escape. Most romantic melodramas have these ominous bridge passages and they are usually resolved in a single conventional plunge to escape — a decisive revolver shot, a flicking off of the lights, the fortuitous collapse of the villain by an unknown hand. Fairbanks would not have been the incomparable "Doug" if he had not provided the most characteristic pleasure of his films in just these crises. And "Doug" could not have held the popular imagination so long if he had lacked the extraordinary physical rhythm and grace of Douglas Fairbanks, a remarkable all-round athlete. . . .

The formation of the United Artists Company as a major distributing organization brought together D.W. Griffith, Charles Chaplin, Mary Pickford and Douglas Fairbanks, stars who were "too expensive for any single company to maintain on a permanent payroll." With the distribution of his films assured and with the probably preconscious urge to romantic nostalgia on a grand scale, Fairbanks started to make costume films. *The Mark of Zorro* was hardly one, but it was a sign of the times. It was modestly produced; a retrospective lesson from the difficult 1850s of California, when oppression was routed and the poor made whole by a daring nobleman in a mask. *The Mark of Zorro* was an immense success, and when Fairbanks looked back to find other historical shells to clothe the spirit of "Doug," there was D'Artagnan. Later there was Robin Hood, the thief of Bagdad, the son of Zorro, the Black Pirate. All but one were high-born saviors of the people. A fascist or royalist government could probably do much mischief with this continuing theme, which was certainly offered in good faith by Fairbanks as a touching formula of magic, an act of grace from on high, which the post-war world badly needed. Young "Doug," the cracker-barrel gymnast, was now a fly-by-night missionary in fancy dress. . . .

Douglas Fairbanks suffers from the advantage, until now, of being written about very little. The literary discovery of the movies, late though it was, found its darling in Charles Chaplin. It was unlikely that esthetes, so gingerly sorting out the odd and curious in this raffish art, should retrace their steps to find, so close to Chaplin's back door, another pet. Indeed the most revealing and reliable references to Fairbanks can be found, not in critical books on the movies (with the exception of one essay of Delluc and a couple of pages of Rotha's history) but in the index of producers' memoirs and in histories like Terry Ramsay's and Hampton's of the movies as a growing industry.

This surely does not amount to neglect of Fairbanks. He will bear intellectual scrutiny as well as any other artist with a talent of his own, but not the loaded curiosity of those who look at movies with their own constructed hierarchy of movie values. He does not have to be rescued, as Chaplin had, from any cult admiration. When he was most famous, the only fervid cult of him was the universal brotherhood of small boys who translated the effect Fairbanks had on his audience into the direct flattery of leaping over fire hydrants and joining a gymnasium.

Through the 1910s and early twenties, the movies were fighting many a scandal and much imprecise suspicion to get themselves accepted as respectable by the middle class of the western world. They bore then a sneaking reputation, something like that of latter-day burlesque. To many an anxious parent at this time, "Doug" stood for the film industry's total respectability. He was not merely inoffensive, which is what the parents were looking for: he was a positive ideal worthy of any small fry's devoted emulation. To the people in the business, notably to Joe Schenck, it occurred rather late that "this fellow knows more about making pictures than all the rest of us put together." To nobody at all did it occur that Fairbanks had solved as early as anybody in the game the problem — which, when the literati have had their say, is the unblinkable problem of a popular art — of mating audience and actor, as truly as a promoter of bear-baiting or baseball, so that a movie seems to be, not a cultural knick-knack handed down from above, but an actual creation of the audience, a copy of their liveliest impulses. This may be, of course, what Mr. Schenck had in mind.

ARTHUR LENNIG
Wild and Woolly
and *The Mollycoddle*

From a redoubtable and learned lover of silent films who is professor at the State University of New York at Albany, we have these nicely descriptive reviews of two early Fairbanks comedies. They originally appeared in a self-published volume called The Silent Voice: A Text *(1969) pages 104-107. We are able to see how satisfied the audience was with stories closely similar. At the same time the formula of rescue by "an average healthy man" might need pretty soon the variety of swashbuckling costumes and more elaborate plotting.* The Mark of Zorro *came along, at Mary Pickford's suggestion, in 1920.*

Wild and Woolly (1917) is the earliest of the films now available which depicts the transformation of the Eastern Dude to the Western hero. The film contains the Ur-myth of many of his subsequent works. It tells the story of Jeff Hillington, a clerk for his father (the railroad king) who dislikes the New York City atmosphere and longs for the Good Old Bad Days Out West. As the picture opens, Doug sits before a camp-fire, eating "grub," his tent in the background. Here is the Outdoorsman, the Cowboy, the Manly American. But as the camera draws back, the tent and the fire are all within his palatial New York rooms. (This opening is copied in the *Mollycoddle*, when Doug is riding a horse — on a merry-go-round.)

Doug dreams of a West "where the blood runs red in one's veins." He champs at the unimaginative pansy life in the East and lets out his frustrations by lassoing the butler, riding furiously on a saddle (no horse) and "roughing it" amidst the walls of his fancy mansion. His father, not quite grown accustomed to his son's Western experiments, still spills his morning coffee at the sound of his son's pistol.

This ersatz life is finally broken by a delegation from Bitter Creek, Arizona, who have come to ask the railroad king for a branch line. The father introduces his son to the men and suggests that the boy go West to examine the prospects. Doug of course thinks that the delegation has just put on store-bought suits for the occasion and that they usually wear Western togs. He is delighted to make the trip. In an attempt to please the boy — and thus to get their railroad line — the men decide to dress up the town to resemble a Western one. Signs are painted, railroad hold-ups are planned, fights on the city streets arranged: in short, the men try to create the mythical West.

When Doug arrives, he immediately takes to the rugged life, the constant struggles, the frequent confrontations between good and evil, the opportunity to prove himself a he-man. Indeed, he shows more prowess than the Arizonians had first imagined and so the bullets are removed from his guns and blanks substituted.

The plot thickens, however, when some genuine villains decide to take advantage of the charade. They really hold up the train and steal money and impel a number of renegade Indians to besiege the town. Doug begins to fight back and it is at this point he is told he has been using blank bullets. The fact, however, that he had been put on does not discourage him much. With the real bullets back in his gun, he quickly proves himself a hero. Trapped in a downstairs room, he jumps on a rafter, kicks through the ceiling boards, enters his room, and gets the rest of his arsenal. And from this point on, he rescues the town and helps round up the villains. As a result, the townspeople are really impressed. He is a far better hero than even those of the Old West.

Psychologically the film cleverly pleases its audience. It says, okay, the West as you conceive it no longer exists — we know that — but yet, you people who imagine you would have been a hero in the old days are not wrong. Indeed, you *would* be a hero, if only you had the chance. Thus the film, which in some ways satirizes the Dude's desire for a mythical West, ends up in some ways reinforcing the myth.

The film does not take itself seriously, as it could easily have done, and indeed even resolves its problems with wit and humor for when Doug was in Bitter Creek, he met and fell in love with Nell (a courtship, by the way, which is happily brief). Where are they to live? As a title says:

For Nell likes the East
And Jeff likes the West
So where are the twain to meet?

The solution is simple. The last scene shows two fancy footmen opening the front doors of a mansion. Nell and Doug walk down the hallway and out the front doors. (Ah, they are in the East!) But no. Who awaits them? A group of horsemen! (They are in the West!) Thus the comforts and style of the East and the derring-do of the West combine and so Nell and Jeff can have their cake and eat it too.

The Mollycoddle (1920) is typical of Fairbanks' early films. The picture begins by showing how his family (the Marshalls) have been a brave and heroic race of men. A coin, which was given by George Washington to Doug's ancestor for his bravery, has been passed down father to son. Various short scenes of his grandfather and father show that they have kept up the family tradition of heroism. But what has happened to the new generation?

The camera reveals Doug impeccably dressed, sporting a monocle, smoking a cigarette from a long holder, and riding vigorously on a horse. But as the iris of the shot opens wider, this modern heir of countless heroes is riding on a merry-go-round at Monte Carlo. He is now a society dandy, weak, shy, and seemingly upper-class, a mollycoddle. As a title says, "A mollycoddle is a body of men entirely surrounded by super civilization." Although Doug appears to be a sissy, he plays his role so charmingly and appears so ingenuous that one still likes him. When the girl asks him whether he has to wear the monocle, he looks at it rather absent-mindedly, and then puts it away in his pocket. He never did need it; it was merely the thing to do.

Shortly after, Doug is tricked into returning to Arizona; his friends have him tied him up in a wicker basket and brought aboard a diamond smuggler's yacht. It is only when he is faced with the villain aboard ship and later on land, that the rugged spirit of his ancestors comes to the fore. It seems as if the Arizona air instills new blood into his veins, for he immediately becomes shrewd, athletic, and well coordinated. And thus from a bumbling, foolish, sissified English type, he becomes a red-blooded American. Yet this transformation, so corny and chauvinistic, comes off delightfully, for it is all done in good humor. Who can forget the scene where he asks an Indian in "Ugh-me-want-um" kind of language and the Indian stares at him with arched eyebrows a second and says, "What the hell are you talking about?" It is Doug's grin at this remark — at the Indian, at the audience, at himself — that saves him from appearing as a superior type white man. Indeed, the joke's on him and he can take the joke.

When Doug, hot in the pursuit of the villain, rides into a fantastically beautiful Arizona valley, the title says that when Doug's father came upon this sight he shouted, "Hurrah for God!" This statement is outrageous, yet it is a tribute to the film that somehow the title succeeds. It captures in three words Doug's own approach to the world.

Just as readers of Mark Twain's *Huckleberry Finn* feel that they too had floated down the river in their youth, so does Fairbanks make his viewers share in a fantasy that somehow seems real. The success of this audience identification depends entirely on the tone of the films and most of this tone is created by Fairbank's own personality — his gestures, smiles, gymnastics. When he performs a feat, he makes it seem effortless; by not taking himself seriously, his extraordinary acrobatics become even more enjoyable.

ROBERT SHERWOOD
The Thief of Bagdad

From January 1921 to December 1928, the man who was to be a Pulitzer prizewinning playwright and Academy Award winning screenwriter (for The Best Years of Our Lives *in 1946) wrote a weekly column called "The Silent Drama." It appeared in the old* Life, *a humor magazine like today's* New Yorker. *This column appeared April 3, 1924, and was reprinted later in Douglas Fairbanks Jr. and Richard Schickel,* The Fairbanks Album *(1975), page 137. Sherwood was particularly fond of the comedians and ranked Fairbanks along with Chaplin, Keaton, and Lloyd, although he was necessarily focusing on the costume pictures which began about the time he started writing.*

Not every critic would praise this picture as superior to the other Fairbanks adventures: it is 140 minutes long and repetitive as fairy tales are likely to be. But it is extraordinarily graceful in action and in production design, and its plot is kept going well enough by Raoul Walsh, who would be known in the sound era as an action director. It is in fact one of the rare movies that deserves to be called unique.

After seeing *The Thief of Bagdad*, I am more competent to understand the motives which inspired the sturdy Britons who have been struggling for years to reach the peak of Mt. Everest. I now know what it means to be able to say, "Well, I've been to the top."

Standing at the point marked by this Arabian Nights' entertainment which Douglas Fairbanks has fashioned, I can look down to the lesser summits of *Robin Hood, Broken Blossoms, Passion* and the rest; several miles below, and barely discernible from this dizzy altitude, lie *Where Is My Wandering Boy To-night? Rags to Riches* and *The Old Nest.*

There may well be higher peaks than that achieved by *The Thief of Bagdad* — but if there are, they have not as yet been charted on any of the existent contour maps.

The Thief of Bagdad is the farthest and most sudden advance that the movie has ever made and, at the same time, it is a return to the form of the earliest presentable films. I remember that the first picture I ever saw was a ferociously fast French comedy, in which one of the characters was dressed by magic. His clothes leaped at him from the closet and fitted themselves about his passive form, his boots scurried across the floor and slid onto his feet, and his shoe laces wiggled into place like twin serpents.

That was, technically, "trick stuff" — and it is now sneered at by the hyper-realists of Hollywood, who refuse to admit that a scene is ever faked.

It is trick stuff of this same sort that makes *The Thief of Bagdad* extraordinarily fascinating. Fairbanks has not been afraid to resort to magic of the most flagrant variety. He has used ropes which, when thrown into the air, will become rigid and scalable, golden apples which will restore life to the dead, idols' eyes of crystal in which the future is revealed, magic carpets which fly through the heavens, winged horses, star-shaped keys to open the Palace of the Moon, and golden chests from which vast armies may be conjured with the flick of a finger. There is also a supply of genii, djinns, talismans and fire-breathing dragons.

Of course this wizardry is possible on the screen; the first French comedy proved that. But Fairbanks has gone far beyond the mere bounds of possibility: he has performed the superhuman feat of making his magic seem probable.

When, in *The Ten Commandments*, Cecil B. DeMille caused the Red Sea to part, every one remarked, "That's a great trick. How did he do it?" There are no such mental interruptions for the spectator in *The Thief of Bagdad*. He watches Fairbanks' phenomenal stunts without stopping to think of them as tricks. He accepts them as facts.

The Thief of Bagdad has a marvelous fairy tale quality — a romantic sweep which lifts the audience and vaporizes it into pink, fluffy clouds. It also has much beauty and much solidity of dramatic construction.

Fairbanks and Raoul Walsh, the director, have devised scenes of overwhelming magnitude and grandeur; but, in doing so, they have not neglected the details. They have built, with incredible magnificence, the City of Bagdad — and they have also built a story which is sound and workable, and which proceeds rhythmically and gracefully at a steadily increasing rate of speed.

Douglas Fairbanks (Drawing by John Tibbetts)

DOUGLAS FAIRBANKS
Energy, Success, and Laughter

"Get out in the air and run like a schoolboy!" Doesn't this sound like a jogger's manifesto today? The individualist drive mechanisms of the 19th century frontier were behind it, of course, and the outdoor bravado of Theodore Roosevelt. But Fairbanks wasn't kidding. He knew that enthusiasm, bodily conditioning, self-confidence, and willingness to spend energy were elements of success in business and in movies. It is fashionable among literary critics to laugh at this kind of earnest pleading, but they usually miss the point that Fairbanks was already laughing at them. He had proved himself a success on the Hollywood frontier and was jogging all the way to the bank. This selection is taken from one of several books Fairbanks wrote (or dictated): Laugh and Live, *(Britton Publishing, 1917, pages 42-47.)*

If the preceding chapters have been carefully read we may readily believe that the successful youth must start with a wholesome, generous viewpoint, a good constitution, and a clean mind. We have had an inkling by this time of what one must do to achieve success in a world where competition is keen. We are beginning to realize that these matters are of vital importance and that we are face to face with a problem.

Energy is the natural outpouring of a healthy body. It must be directed, it must be controlled, the same as any other living force. Not only is it a positive necessity to the winner, but it must grow and become a natural quality. It does not stand after years of abuse. It does not spring up in the night after a long season of neglect and ill-health. All of us possess it in varying ways. That fact ought to convince us that we can get hold of ourselves and build up that which nature has given us, rather than allow it to die away. We all have a certain amount of energy . . . *why shouldn't we all be successes?* We might to a certain extent, but that doesn't mean that we shall all get rich in the money sense of the word.

When we say: "Why shouldn't we all be successes?" we do not mean that everybody in the world must be greedy for money, nor for power and position. It does not mean that we should be selfish and eager to take everything away from the other fellow. On the contrary, it means that, with energy, we shall be successful *according to our brain tendency.*

Going back to our second chapter we find the phrase "taking stock" of ourselves. Done rightly that alone will inspire success. Now if we are a little farther along on the way towards sane living and the *ability to laugh* and we know that after this struggle is over the battle is won we must use the powers that self-analysis gives us — *to fight.* The mere recognition of them is power and we must not let them go to waste.

Energy is like steam — it cannot be generated under the boiling point. In other words, *half-heartedness* never produced it nor made it a practical working tool. We must be energetic in order to augment energy. We must have confidence along with it . . . the more the merrier. The greater the confidence in ourselves the greater the energy which brought it about. Some minds naturally feel confident. These are the lucky ones, the slender few who have grasped life's meaning at the start by *"taking stock"* before they were threatened with defeat. Success comes to them as easily as rolling off the proverbial log. They come sweeping along, conquering, sure of themselves, confident, aspiring, true to their inner selves, ready to work, unafraid of experiences, and *sure of a smile when the clouds are darkest.*

This does not mean that these successes have exceptional ability. If that were the case we would not waste time either in reading or writing about the matter. If we didn't feel that we were potentially able to become successes and possessed the elements of victory in our present make-up not another moment would be spent on the subject. The very simplicity of this use of energy proves to us that it is a quality bubbling forth *in the least of us* and the strongest. It only needs to be put to work and it becomes self-strengthening. *Living in the open air, sleeping out of doors, taking the proper exercise, looking wholesomely upon life, believing in ourselves,* are all parts of the sane existence which leads to success and laughter.

We ought to feel that everything in life possesses elements akin to human feeling. We should not arrogate to ourselves the sole right to rule and reason. And what has this to do with energy? It is only one of the many vistas that open to us when we learn how to laugh and live. And man alive! *If we never learn to laugh we will never learn to live.*

We must not forget that there can be more than one use made of energy. In the same way that electricity might be misused so might energy be placed in the wrong service. We must not waste any time, therefore, in getting this energy of ours worked into enthusiasm . . . *enthusiasm* for our life work, for our fellow man, *for the zest of life.* We must throw ourselves into the battle and carry the standard. We must leap to the front, not waiting for the other fellow to show the way. Spend your enthusiasm freely and be surprised at how it thrives on usage.

Enthusiasm being produced by energy must of a necessity depend largely upon that. Now the point is, how shall we guard and keep fresh this element in ourselves? We know that the body is producing this quality. Like the steam engine we are keeping the fires going by exercise, wholesome thinking and sincerity of purpose. We are the engineers. Our hand is on the throttle. Sharp turns lie ahead but our eyes look forward fearlessly. We glance about us to see that we are in the pink of condition. We know that our mind is functioning properly and that the awakened confidence is already inherent in our natures and stands beside us night and day like the officer upon the bridge of the ship. *Indeed we are on our way!*

Out of energy and enthusiasm comes something else that must not be neglected . . . in fact it must be cultivated and guarded from the very beginning . . . *laughter.* The mere possession of energy and enthusiasm makes us feel like laughing. We want to leap and jump and dance and sing. If we feel like that don't let us be afraid to do it. *Get out in the air and run like a school boy. Jump ditches, vault fences, swing the arms!* Never fail to get next to nature when responsive to the call. Indeed we may woo this call from within ourselves until it comes to be second nature. And when we rise in the morning let us be determined that we will start the day with a hearty laugh anyhow. Laugh because you are alive, laugh with everything. *Let yourself go.* That is the secret — the ability to let one's self go!

If we follow this religiously we will be surprised how successful the day will be. Everything gives way before it.

The castle set for *Robin Hood.*

Chapter 4

Gloria and Rudy

*Ma querida, you do not understand: there is sometimes in a
man's life a bad love and a good love.*
— *Valentino as the bullfighter in* Blood and Sand

"I am not going to write my memoirs," Gloria Swanson told an
interviewer from *Sight and Sound* Magazine in 1969.[1] But she lived
into her 80s and some of the men she knew intimately didn't, so she
changed her mind. *Swanson on Swanson*, one of the best of all star
autobiographies, was on the best-seller list for many months in
1980-1981. This was partly because she told exactly how she had
been grappled with by Wallace Beery in 1916 and Joseph P. Kennedy
in 1927. But the popularity of the book also rested on her lively
personality, wide-ranging curiosity, and varied achievements, along
with a remarkable skill in drawing characters and writing scenes.

Her personal search for love was inevitably a very public process.
Her happiest and least-known affair was with the actor-director
Marshall Neilan, but it eventually became clear that this talented
joker was going to give in to alcohol. Her late discovery of the actor
Herbert Marshall was wonderfully agreeable, but it became clear he
was always going to give in to his then wife, Edna Best. Another
actor, the handsome Rod La Rocque, held her bemused attention for
the weeks they co-starred in *A Society Scandal* in 1924, but he could

---

1   By Rui Nogueira, Spring 1969. The quotation was also the title.

not accept the fact that she "liked to have lots of people" around her, especially bright and impressive men. At other times she sought a sense of security with producer types (Herbert Somborn and Joseph Kennedy) and with a French marquis, her interpreter during the making of *Madame Sans-Gene* in 1925. This was the most successful of her six marriages. Yet it could not compete with the fierce energy of Kennedy, who was in the process of creating the RKO studio and then went on to become a politician, ambassador, and father of a U.S. President.

This extraordinary range of alliances seemed to the public of the 1920s quite in line with Swanson's onscreen life as a star of various DeMille productions named *Don't Change Your Husband, Why Change Your Wife,* and *The Affairs of Anatol* (1919-1921). The heroines of such stories usually ended up learning that amorous adventures outside of wedlock were unsatisfactory, but for the sake of both the drama and the lesson the adventures had to be elaborately presented. Such movies combined with the postwar mood of moral experimentation to make the 1920s a time of changing behavior and a lot more freedom for women.

Clara Bow, Joan Crawford, Colleen Moore, and Louise Brooks were the leading bobbed-hair "flappers" of the screen in the decade after World War I, acting out their freedoms in part by smoking, drinking, and dancing the Charleston. They were modified vamps, perhaps, not menacing or mysterious like Theda Bara and her ilk, but open and, as they said, "fast." A good title writer could provide them with "wisecracks," and sex was obviously on their minds.

Gloria Swanson was flashy and independent, like the flappers, on and off the screen. But she was a star apart—more important than the others, not to be typed. She reports that she led all the boxoffice polls in 1923 and got 10,000 fan letters a week.[2] And it was just at this point that she began to shift from the fabricated arch image of the DeMille films—a wealthy clothes horse whose outlandish costumes took your breath away. After a transitional period with Sam Wood, she moved to New York and worked in several pictures for Allan Dwan, who insisted on casting her frequently as an ordinary girl trying to get ahead. Instead of a woman born into the upper class who manages to hold onto her husband, she became a working girl who manages to hold onto her lower class charm, even though she comes into—or marries—money *(Manhandled, Madame Sans-Gene, Fine Manners,* 1924-1926).

2 *Swanson on Swanson,* p. 197.

Swanson's screen image therefore can't be typed as some kind of opposite to that of Mary Pickford. In fact, she very often played the girl next door—but in the city, not the small town. She certainly had a wider range of roles, and her progressive versatility in deploying her own brisk personality as a silent film actress is commented on by fan magazine writers. Where she was "sullen, opaque... unknowable, awkward" as an extra girl, she later revealed for Adela Rogers St. Johns "a disconcerting perfection of poise...intelligence...warmth."[3] Another *Photoplay* article (written under the by-line of the actor Ben Lyon) described her in February 1925 as "so lovely, so vivid, so clean-cut, and yet with it all, so cool...You never are quite sure which Gloria it is going to be today—the haughty queen or the naughty imp...or the soft and gentle Gloria who is full of questions and of talk." The consistent factor in the Swanson persona, as Adela St. Johns summed it up in her 1978 book, *Love, Laughter and Tears:* "In my dictionary it says Glamour: charm or enchantment; witchcraft; a magic spell; radiant illusion."[4]

Rudolph Valentino was not one of the actors who tempted Gloria into a liaison, even briefly. They were acquainted, she explains, because they both liked to ride horseback in the early morning in Griffith Park, and as professional actors they shared talk about their careers even before Valentino was well known. She was attracted to him only as "someone nice to look at" and with a "delicious accent." And if she did not find in him the passionate or erotic aura he represented on the screen, she did feel it was about time for that new type of leading man. Before Valentino, she later wrote, most silent movie heroes were "rugged, heavy, preferably fair, and a bit on the clumsy side." She welcomed his success in 1921 and thereafter saw less of him. Like so many others, she thought of him simply as a naive, inexperienced boy who needed help and encouragement.[5]

3 "The Confessions of a Modern Woman—as Told by Gloria Swanson," *Photoplay*, February 1922.

4 Ben Lyon, "Vampires I Have Known," February 1925. Adela Rogers St. Johns, *Love, Laughter and Tears*, p. 155. See p. 16 of this book.

5 *Swanson on Swanson*, pp. 171-172, 212. Listed in *Photoplay* in January 1926 by Adela Rogers St. Johns as "Ten Handsome Men of the Screen," the following might by some observers conform to Gloria's negative categories even at that late date: Novarro, Stone, O'Brien, Lyon, Gilbert, Barthelmess, Denny, Barrymore, Colman, Dix. All but Dix and O'Brien started in pictures before 1920. Novarro was groomed by Rex Ingram to replace Valentino at M-G-M.

Dagmar Godowsky, an actress who played a number of "vamp" roles in the 1920s, told an interviewer in 1970:

> Val was shy; he was a shy man. I used to see him a great deal; he'd come to the house and make spaghetti. We danced a lot, and I introduced him to both of his wives. But Rudy was very retiring. He was so decent. . . . I saw him when he was poor, I saw him when he got rich. I think he was one of the nicest, kindest persons—I can't tell you how nice.[6]

The only masculine personality comparable to Swanson's in the silent era was Rudolph Valentino. His hold on the public was different—more erratic, more intense, more magnetic. Certainly his appeal was that of the foreigner—Italian in fact, Arabian sheik in fancy. He also played a gaucho, a bull fighter, the lover of Camille, the desired lover of the empress of Russia, a shanghaied sailor, an Indian rajah.

Elinor Glyn was a British writer of novels and love manuals who was brought to Hollywood by Famous Players-Lasky to advise film makers on the fine points of sexual attractiveness. She was appalled by the lack of appeal of the so-called leading men of the movie capital. In her stories she was not inclined to promote illicit lovemaking, but she definitely felt that triangular situations might scare one or the other love partner into a more defensive, seductive stance. This attitude might very well retrieve a declining marriage. It would certainly intrigue the audience.

Madame Glyn found that Rudolph Valentino constituted a new sort of performer who could do well in the stories she wrote and promoted. It was an Elinor Glyn novel of 1906, directed by Sam Wood, which brought Gloria Swanson for the only time together with Valentino on the screen. *Beyond the Rocks* was a feeble story about an aristocratic but poor English girl just married to an elderly millionaire. Rescued from a fall "beyond the rocks" in the Alps, she naturally falls in turn for her rescuer, the handsome young Lord Bracondale. Her husband later puts himself in harm's way among the brigands of Arabia, sacrificing his desires and his life for her sake. Meanwhile the story permits the two youthful protagonists to fantasize what it would be like to be lovers —in lavish costumes—in various eras in history.

6   Edith Napean, "Vamp of the 20s," *Silent Picture* #7, Summer 1970, p. 19. Similarly Nita Naldi, *Photoplay*, June 1924: "he's a sweet, adorable, charming boy."

Mrs. Glyn announced that Valentino, like Clara Bow, had what she called "It"—a charismatic quality she claimed was more important than sex appeal. She was thought to have taught Rudy the little trick of brushing a woman's palm with his lips rather than kissing the back of her hand in the accepted manner. Other women, however, were more important in Valentino's life. June Mathis, a screenwriter, saw him in bit parts and decided he was right for Julio in *The Four Horsemen of the Apocalypse*, directed by Rex Ingram in 1921 at Metro Pictures. This single role, in which he danced the tango, was enough to make him a star. Famous Players-Lasky stole him away and made him into *The Sheik*. Before long, he was the very symbol of the dominant male, and many American women began to dream of being swept onto a horse and carried away into the desert.

There are two paradoxes here, one in his private life, one having to do with his image on the screen. Dominance was not quite what he offered.

The Sheik, although it involved a good deal of physical lifting and threatening, is actually a story of a man subdued by a woman, not the other way around. He refrains more than once from forcing the British lady's submission: "You hate them so much—my kisses?" He wants her love in the civilized way, the Hollywood way, and with the advice of a friend from Paris he even decides to give her up. The action scenes bring the story to its romantic climax: she is captured, then recaptured, and Ahmed is badly wounded. She knows by then that he is gallant, generous, daring, and worthy of love. One ultimate revelation (jarring and amusing today) is that he isn't even an Arab, but an adopted son from European parents. The machismo reputation of the film is based on certain early scenes which have a jolt of strangeness, a threat of trouble. But ultimately it is like a western in which the tamed hero says, "Yes, ma'am."

By 1926, in *The Son of the Sheik*, Valentino does appear to be ready to force a young girl, but he is stopped by his father. Vengeance is part of his motive here, for he believes she is part of her father's plot to abduct him. In this case, the protagonists are all part of the same violent desert neighborhood: no strong-willed Englishwoman to cope with this time but a fiery local girl. Of course, since he is the son of the sheik who is the son of an English father and a Spanish mother, and the girl is the daughter of a Frenchman, it seems highly questionable whether there is any Arabic hot blood in either of the two pictures except on the part of the ugly villains who move in from time to time to forward the plot. But the sequel (with Valentino playing both father and son) does go farther in meeting the audience's expectation of violent sex. In one scene, too, the captured hero is strung up stripped to the waist and whipped. The 1920s were moving along.

In his real—that is, his Hollywood—life, Rudolph Valentino was a lot less dominant than he was in his pictures. He seems to have been befriended, guided, and dominated by mother-figures. The manager he finally chose as a wife was not nearly as good for him as Gloria Swanson might have been, or June Mathis, or Elinor Glyn. After a brief episode of marriage to a minor actress, Jean Acker (a marriage which seems not to have been consummated), he was taken over by a dancer, set designer, and believer in spiritualism who had chosen the name Natacha Rambova. The daughter of a rich perfume manufacturer, she was in need of someone to order about. It appears that while he idolized her and admired her talents, she cared little about him as a lover.

Finally, her hypnotic presence was so pervasive and her demands so specific and peculiar that Famous Players-Lasky put them on suspension. Valentino decided to tour the country on his own with a dance exhibition (a great success) and when he came back completed two pictures remaining on his contract. Then he signed with United Artists even though they demanded absolutely that Natacha be barred from the studio and from any decisions. It was belated recognition that his career had been seriously hurt by her obsessions. Before long they separated and made preparations for a divorce.[7]

There was some kind of cultural and psychic gap between Valentino's view of himself and the image held of him by his total audience. He was a success story, but somehow out of place on the great American 20th century frontier of showbusiness. Evidently he wanted to be seen as a man's man and also as a great lover. He tried to write and publish poetry and still satisfy the locker-room mentality of so many Americans. He liked working on his car, having a grand house, and taking lavish trips abroad. When he was attacked in a Chicago *Tribune* editorial for promoting effeminacy in American men, he was fit to be tied. He offered to beat up the editorial writer and in fact did an exhibition turn in the ring with an obliging New York sportswriter. What all this quarreling and controversy did to him is impossible to assess: he continued drinking to prove his manliness even after he suspected a dangerous ulcer, refusing medical examination.

A month after the opening of *Son of the Sheik* in New York City, Valentino died. Thirty thousand people tried to view the body at

7   S. George Ullman, *Valentino As I Knew Him*, (1926), pp. 102, 150, 158.

Broadway and 66th Street. On August 23, 1926, the day of the funeral, there were 100,000 in the streets.

The Paramount building on Times Square, Adolph Zukor's monument to the silent drama, was dedicated in 1926. The first of the features with sound, *Don Juan*, appeared on August 6 of that year. It was the beginning of the end of the silent era.

ALEXANDER WALKER
Make Money, Spend Passion

The film critic of the London Evening Standard *suggests that filmgoers, especially in the early 1920s, wanted to believe that their favorites actually lived in the same ways made familiar by the luxurious backgrounds and romantic plots of the films they played in. Since top stars received fabulous salaries (based on their popularity), they found it easy to spend lavishly on clothes, houses, and parties. These were the visible substance of glamor for many fans, and in a kind of round robin such luxuries were written into scripts. Gloria Swanson played the game with zest. Our selection is from Walker's 1970 book* Stardom *(N.Y., Stein & Day) pages 121, 123, 125-128.*

Stars were never again to be so well rewarded, and at the same time so free from restraint, as in the early years of the 1920s. The star system which had created them was in the ascendant, while the studio system which was to curb their power had not yet been fully formed. Hollywood itself was a multiplicity of small units: producer-directors who signed up talent for their pictures, or stars who owned their own studios and produced and distributed their own movies, or stars who freelanced from film to film at escalating prices, or studio heads who paid their stars percentages of a film plus a salary. The variety of deals that were available was not to become possible again till the economic break-up of Hollywood in the mid-1950s. . . .

Nazimova, the Russian star, was probably the highest-paid Hollywood actress of the period: at her height, she was said to be getting $13,000 a week from Metro. Yet even this was overtaken. Gloria Swanson had been getting $3,500 a week from Paramount in 1923, rising to $5,000 in 1925 and then to $6,500 in 1926. At this stage she showed an impatience to produce her own pictures for she had heard that W.S. Hart, the cowboy star, had got $2,225,000 in two years out of nine of his films. Adolph Zukor offered Swanson a raise to $15,000 a week to remain at Paramount. She still demurred. It was increased to the colossal sum of $900,000 for three pictures a year, plus half of the net profits. But convinced that her future lay in production, she formed her own company backed by Joseph P. Kennedy's millions — only to encounter in Erich von Stroheim, the director of her abortive *Queen Kelly* (1928), a man whose talent for extravagant consumption outran her own. . . .

Audiences, as Gloria Swanson said, wanted their stars to be extraordinary creatures — and they were. In keeping with the baroque movie palaces that were rising up, incorporating fantasies in the shape of frescoes from the Arabian Nights or motifs from Babylon, Old Cathay and Seville, the life led by the stars seemed a product of the romantic imagination. Their salaries provided the means for unrestraint in every part of it.

It was only after the Arbuckle scandal, and the widespread adoption of morality clauses in contracts, that notoriety became a heavy liability rather than the asset which Leo Rosten observed it to be in his classic study of the movie colony.[1] Rosten found evidence that the producers even encouraged conspicuous consumption by their stars in the way of cars, clothes, houses and never-ending parties, not only because the ostentatious confidence thus manifested was "good for the industry", but because it was a way of reducing the economic independence of those with vast amounts of money to spend. Stars were encouraged to overspend so as to put themselves in debt. Sometimes their principal creditor was also their agent — and a reputation would be put into receivership unless its owner did as he was told.

Spending also boosted the ego in a world where insecurity induced moods of excessive elation and depression; while in a world of status-conscious artists, spending was one way of defending prestige. Rosten has suggested that it also showed "a striking resemblance to the spending of gamblers or those who obtained money by means which precipitated guilt on themselves. Spending becomes a mechanism by which one part of the personality pays off another."[2] The fantasy element of the films was extended into the favourite after-hours pastime of an enclosed society like Hollywood, which at this time had to amuse itself in absence of a commercial night life. Costume balls were the main way of doing so. Stars who spent their working lives playing roles seemingly could not exist without the same sort of stimulus in their social lives. Perhaps it was a relief to dress up in a role which one was not being forced to play; perhaps it was a way of playing roles which one might not get the chance to play in films. Whatever the reasons, fancy dress was appropriate wear for the fantasy people in need of continual entertainment themselves. Perhaps it was more fun than seeing each other's pictures.

The emphasis on material goods and fun living, which made Hollywood appear such a festive place in the 1920s, was characteristic of the wider American society. The screen both reflected and stimulated the way of life made possible by the tide of post-war prosperity, in which the luxuries of comfortable living were openly pursued, and sex was freely discussed by most and readily practised by some. The way the stars behaved on and off screen made them objects of the wish-fulfillment drives of such a society. As some of the following accounts reveal, life did not stop at aping art — it transfused it, so that it was hard to tell what was fantasy and what was fact. The most characteristic attribute of stardom in the 1920s was the belief, held by millions in a far more passionate way than in any following decade, that the stars were in real life the same exotic creatures that they appeared to be on the screen.

Gloria Swanson was the chief representative of this glamorous illusion. Even the syllables of her name, rich and indolent, exuded the feeling of extravagance. She herself was perfectly prepared to live up to the fiction: money gave her the means, stardom the incentive, publicity the apparatus. And she acquiesced in the creation of her myth, even helped it along by the life she led in her heyday, because "the public didn't want the truth and I shouldn't have bothered giving it to them."[3]

In retrospect at any rate, she has been able to smile a trifle cynically at the sumptuousness of the "private" life she was reported to be enjoying: the $100,000 New York penthouse, the 25-acre estate on the Hudson, the perfumed elevator in her apartment block, the gold-backed mirror that slid aside to reveal a movie screen. . . . Publicity in the 1920s had worked up a head of steam that could present a personality through the strength alone of its owner's material affluence. "What imagination they had," Swanson said forty years later. But it would have been astonishing at the time if the public had not regarded her films as representative of the total environment she inhabited. It was largely due to Cecil B. De Mille that she was projected as a way of life for people to follow with fascination, as well as a personality for them to pay to see in a De Mille film.

At the height of her stardom she was obliged by contract always to appear in public dressed in the height of fashion. Her yearly clothes bill for personal and professional wear was said to exceed that of any other star: fur coats, $25,000; other wraps, $10,000; gowns, $50,000; stockings, $9,000; shoes, $5,000; perfumes, $6,000; lingerie,

$10,000; purses, $5,000; head-dresses, $5,000. True or false — and the likelihood is in favour of the former — the important thing about such publicity is that it was believed.

The aura of fascination that surrounded Swanson was increased by an emphasis on waste. This was summed up well in the studio's description of her as "The second woman to earn a million" — Pickford had been the first — "and the first to spend it." And other figures not strictly financial soon attached themselves to her — the number of times she got married. The acquisition of fresh husbands, though based on a wry self-confessed lack of judgment about men, seemed in her fans' eyes to endow her with a love life that was an extension of her screen life. (These were also the days when stars' marriages, like that of Rod La Rocque to Vilma Banky, began to be studio-managed so as to create a ferment of curiosity which would boost the newlyweds' box-office receipts.)

The third of Swanson's five marriages, to Henri, Marquis de la Falaise de Coudraye, who had been interpreter on her Frenchmade film *Madame Sans-Gene* (1926), gave her the asset of a genuine title in a status-ridden industry . . .

NOTES

1   *Hollywood: The Movie Colony, The Movie Makers*, by Leo C. Rosten (Harcourt, Brace & Co.) [1941].

2   Leo C. Rosten, op.cit., p. 104.

3   Gloria Swanson, quoted by De Witt Bodeen in *Films in Review*, April 1965.

Gloria Swanson (Drawing by John Tibbetts)

EPHRAIM KATZ
Gloria Swanson

Checking in again with the author of the Film Encyclopedia N.Y., Crowell/Harper & Row, 1979, pages 1112-1113, we find a concise biography of the petite brunette who was for many movie-goers "glamour personified." Published the year before Swanson's own memoirs, this account naturally lacks some of the more personal background exposed in that book, especially the circumstances surrounding her return to the U.S. from Paris in 1925 and also the date of her death, 1983. Queen Kelly is now available in the U.S.

(For more biography and analysis of Gloria Swanson's image, see the author's introduction to this chapter and introduction to the book.)

Swanson, Gloria. Actress. Born Gloria Josephine Mae Swenson, on Mar. 27, 1897, in Chicago, of Swedish-Italian descent. The daughter of an Army officer, she attended more than a dozen schools in various locations before resettling in her native city in her early teens. A chance visit to Chicago's Essanay studios in 1913 resulted in her employment as an extra player and in her acquaintance with actor Wallace Beery, whom she married in 1916. That same year they both went to Hollywood, where Beery accepted an offer from Mack Sennett's Keystone company on the condition that his wife also be hired. Contrary to persistent references in various sources, Miss Swanson was never a Sennett "Bathing Beauty" (she says she still can't swim). Neither was she part of the wild slapstick of the Keystone Kops. Rather, she was teamed with Bobby Vernon in a series of romantic comedies. Early in her career she was occasionally billed as Gloria Mae.

When Sennett pulled out of the Triangle organization in 1917 to join Paramount, Miss Swanson followed him, but she soon tired of comedy and returned to Triangle, where she starred in a succession of tearful dramas. In 1919, following Triangle's debacle, she moved over to Cecil B. De Mille's unit at Paramount and rapidly rose to top stardom in a group of slick, suggestive bedroom farces. By the mid-20s she ranked among Hollywood's reigning queens of the silent screen. A born showwoman, she knew full well the value of publicity. Every dress she wore on or off screen was carefully depicted in fashion magazines and every move she made received wide press coverage. Never more so perhaps than in 1925 when, after filming *Madame Sans-Gêne* in France, she returned to Hollywood with a genuine marquis as her third husband and was welcomed by a brass band and, like royalty, driven home in a motorcade. (She had divorced Beery in 1919, then married and divorced and married again.) For many American women she was glamour personified.

Swanson remained with Paramount until 1926, now specializing mostly in drama. The following year, bankrolled by Joseph P. Kennedy, father of the late President, she struck out on her own, producing her own films for release through United Artists. She lost much of her own money as a result of director Erich von Stroheim's extravagance in the production of *Queen Kelly* (1928). She fired Stroheim in mid-production, then tried to salvage the film by sinking even more of her own money into re-editing the footage and tacking on a forced ending. The final product was shown in Europe and South America but has never been released in the US, where it ran into censorship trouble. During the transition period to sound, Miss Swanson proved she could not only talk effectively but even sing. However, her early talkies were mostly unsuccessful and in 1934 she retired from the screen.

She came back for one comedy opposite Adolphe Menjou in 1941, then made a memorable second comeback in 1950, giving an outstanding performance in *Sunset Boulevard*, in the role of a neurotic, faded silent screen star. Ironically, Stroheim played her former director. She was nominated for an Oscar as best actress for her role in that film (she had two earlier nominations, for *The Trespasser* and *Sadie Thompson*). She subsequently appeared in two poor films, one in Italy, then slipped back into semiretirement. She lent her name to a now-defunct cosmetics line and served as an advisor to a dress company, but her public appearances were restricted mostly to occasional guest spots on TV talk shows, in which she promoted the consumption of health foods. In 1971 she made a third comeback, this time on Broadway, as the star of the play 'Butterflies Are Free.' She returned to the screen once more in 1974, playing a key character role in *Airport 1975*. She married for the sixth time in 1976.

Films: Shorts — *At the End of a Perfect Day, The Ambition of the Baron, The Fable of Elvira and Farina and the Meal Ticket, His New Job (bit), Sweedie Goes to College, The Romance of an American Duchess, The Broken Pledge* 1915; *A Dash of Courage, Hearts and Sparks, A Social Cub, The Danger Girl, Love on Skates, Haystacks and Steeples* 1916; *The Nick-of-Time Baby, Teddy at the Throttle, Baseball Madness, Dangers of a Bride, The Sultan's Wife, The Pullman Bride* 1917. Features — *Society for Sale, Her Decision, You Can't Believe Everything, Every Woman's Husband, Shifting Sands, Station Content, Secret Code, Wife or Country* 1918; *Don't Change Your Husband, For Better for Worse, Male and Female* 1919; *Why Change Your Wife? Something to Think About* 1920; *The Great Moment, The Affairs of Anatol, Under the Lash, Don't Tell Everything* 1921; *Her Husband's Trademark, Beyond the Rocks, Her Gilded Cage, The Impossible Mrs. Bellew* 1922; *My American Wife, Hollywood (cameo),*

Prodigal Daughters, Bluebeard's 8th Wife, Zaza 1923; The Humming Bird, A Society Scandal, Manhandled, Her Love Story, Wages of Virtue 1924; Madame Sans-Gêne, The Coast of Folly, Stage Struck 1925; The Untamed Lady, Fine Manners 1926; The Love of Sunya 1927; Sadie Thompson, Queen Kelly 1928; The Trespasser 1929; What a Widow! 1930; Indiscreet, Tonight or Never 1931; Perfect Understanding (UK) 1933; Music in the Air 1934; Father Takes a Wife 1941; Sunset Boulevard 1950; Three for Bedroom C 1952; Mio Figlio Nerone/Nero's Mistress (It./Fr.)1956; Airport 1975 1974.

RONALD BOWERS
Manhandled

   When Gloria Swanson managed to run away to New York City in 1923, she not only found a whole new set of friends and cultural experiences. She was also placing herself in the care of Allan Dwan, one of the unsung wise mentors of the silent screen. In Manhandled *he moved her far away from the languishing rich women she had played for DeMille. She came closer to the lives of shopgirls who—although they certainly went to the movies to see glamor—were pleased to find her in a different mood and milieu. In fact, she was able to have a considerable taste of the world of wealth and fashion yet choose to reject it in favor of a hardworking young inventor on his way up.*
   Note some of the technical credits here. Frank Tuttle became a director, including one film for Swanson (Untamed Lady, 1926). Harold Rosson, brother of the directors Arthur and Richard Rosson, became one of the leading cinematographers in Hollywood history. William LeBaron became a producer and vice-president in charge of production at RKO (1929-1932) and Paramount (1936-1941).
   Bowers' review appears in Frank N. Magill, Magill's Survey of Cinema: Silent Films, *(1982) pages 699-701.*

Released: 1924
Production: Allan Dwan for Famous Players-Lasky/Paramount
Direction: Allan Dwan
Screenplay: Frank Tuttle; based on the story of the same name by Arthur Stringer
Cinematography: Harold Rosson
Editing: William LeBaron and Julian Johnson
Length: 7 reels/6,998 feet

   Principal characters:
   Tessie McGuire   *Gloria Swanson*
   Jimmy Hogan   *Tom Moore*
   Pinkie Moran   *Lilyan Tashman*
   Robert Brandt   *Ian Keith*

Chip Thorndyke	*Arthur Housman*
Paul Garretson	*Paul McAllister*
Arno Riccardi	*Frank Morgan*
Bippo	*M. Collose*

When *Manhandled* was reviewed in 1924, critics all complimented Gloria Swanson on her remarkable comedic performance and one critic stated that this film pushed Swanson to the top of the small group of expert screen comediennes — small, he said, because there were only two others — and he diplomatically refrained from mentioning any names.

Swanson's portrayal of Tessie McGuire, the Cinderella shopgirl in *Manhandled*, surprised many who had simply regarded her as a glamour queen, for in this lively little romp, charmingly reminiscent of an O. Henry short story with its real-life characters and situations and its natural, unfilmlike pathos, Swanson emerged a delightful comedienne, displaying abilities at both light-hearted slapstick and mimicry.

Manhandled was the third of eight films Swanson made with director Allan Dwan and all were made in New York at Paramount's Astoria Studios on Long Island: *Zaza* (1923), *A Society Scandal* (1924), *Her Love Story* (1924), *Wages of Virtue* (1925), *The Coast of Folly* (1925), *Stage Struck* (1925), and *What a Widow!* (1930).

The original idea for *Manhandled* came from Sidney R. Kent, general sales manager of Famous Players-Lasky/Paramount, who had Arthur Stringer write the story which appeared in the *Saturday Evening Post* before Frank Tuttle adapted the screenplay. As with all Dwan's films, the script was but a basis from which he worked, for he always allowed his actors to improvise material which accounted for a great deal of the naturalism in his pictures.

Dwan opens the film with an impressive 360-degree shot of the panoramic New York City skyline which sets the scene for his Cinderella tale of feisty little Tessie McGuire (Gloria Swanson).

Tessie is an inveterate gum chewer who lives in a boardinghouse in Brooklyn and works as a salesgirl in the bargain basement of Thorndyke's department store. Tessie's boyfriend is Jimmy Hogan (Tom Moore), a taxicab driver-mechanic who has an automobile invention up his sleeve, and who lives in the same boardinghouse as Tessie.

Dwan shows the social milieu of working-class New Yorkers with great humor and lack of pretense. The two most famous scenes are funny and appealing and just the kind of scenes that could be rehearsed only so far, then had to rely on the spontaneity of the cast. One scene shows Tessie behind her counter at Thorndyke's on the day of a bargain sale. In her frantic efforts to attend to each customer, Tessie finds herself literally backed against the wall and fighting for her life as the heaving crowd of women shoppers grows larger and more demanding.

The second scene is one of the finest in film comedy. Viewers watch Tessie, who stands almost five feet tall, struggle to get through the subway turnstile, then into the crowded train car in the middle of rush hour. Tessie, with her unfashionable working-girl clothes and a felt hat with a cluster of grapes over the left ear, struggles to find an empty space in the car; she finds herself pushed, shoved, elbowed; she drops her handbag, cannot keep her hat on her head, and almost hangs herself when she finds her chin in battle with the arm of a tall strap-hanger.

For these scenes, Dwan had Swanson do the real thing before shooting them. He arranged for her to work in Gimbels disguised in a blonde wig and took her into the subway, pushed her into the crowd and left her to fend for herself. Swanson recalls that it was the first and last time she ever rode a subway.

Tessie has aspirations for a better life, and one evening when Jimmy is too busy with his invention to take her to the cinema — a shopgirl's world of fantasy — she gets angry and goes off to a party with fellow salesgirl Pinkie Moran (Lilyan Tashman). At the party, Tessie embarrasses herself by tripping over a rug, gets up looking disheveled, and trying to make it all look like an act, she grabs a bowler and a cane and does an impersonation of Charlie Chaplin's Little Tramp. The party-goers applaud her antics, and she goes on to impersonate Beatrice Lillie impersonating a Russian countess. She ends up being the life of the party and the center of attention of all the men, especially Chip Thorndyke (Arthur Housman), the novelist son of the store owner; Robert Brandt (Ian Keith), a sculptor; and Arno Riccardi (Frank Morgan), the owner of a Fifth Avenue dress salon.

Tessie inspires the novelist, but he wants to compromise her; then she quits her job and goes to work as a model for the sculptor, who also wants to compromise her. She dons a turban which makes her look like Nazimova and adds her Beatrice Lillie Russian-countess accent and goes to work in the dress shop, where she encounters yet another compromising situation. Tessie's new way of life makes Jimmy jealous, and at one point, he burns his finger with a match and warns her that those who play with fire get burned.

Finally, Tessie tires of the specious party crowd and returns home to find that Jimmy is sorry for being jealous of her trying to better herself and they reconcile, after which he tells her he has sold his invention and is now a millionaire. Cinderella comes full circle.

Swanson's clever mimicry of Chaplin and Lillie was another example of Dwan letting his actors "go." At the party scene, Dwan told his actors to whoop it up as if they were at a real party, and Swanson says she simply grabbed a hat and cane and did her impersonation of the Little Tramp. Dwan liked it so much he kept it in. Twenty-six years later she would successfully repeat the imitation in the stunning *Sunset Boulevard* (1950).

Manhandled opened at the Rivoli Theater in New York City on July 28, 1924, and grossed $29,771 during its first week. Critics praised Swanson's newfound comedic abilities and her versatility, and they lauded Dwan for his flair for the natural. He was able to contrast the New York tenement life with that of high society with verve and flair. The picture's "message" was not lost amidst all this frivolity. Critics said the film was daring in its realistic presentation of what dirty dogs men are in the big city and what a tough time a girl has in trying to get along without "paying, paying, paying."

Simultaneously with the premiere of *Manhandled*, the New York *Bulletin* ran the story in a cartoon series format, with the story by Stringer and caricatures of the stars by John Decker. It was entitled: *Manhandled: A Movie Serial Featuring Gloria Swanson.*

This film was a popular and pivotal one in Swanson's career for it offered her public a new image, something she insisted upon during this phase of her career and something she was powerful enough to demand. She had debuted at Essanay in 1915 in Chicago and gone on to appear in Mack Sennett's slapstick comedies. Then with her six pictures in association with Cecil B. De Mille beginning in 1919, she became world famous as a sophisticated glamour queen. She knew the importance of change, and her comedies with Dwan were a calculated risk which paid off. She did not stop changing but went on to fine dramatic performances such as *Sadie Thompson* (1928).

The reasons for her self-imposed "retirement" in 1934 are not quite clear, although Dwan maintained it was partly because she allowed herself to be surrounded by sycophants. She made the comeback of all comebacks by portraying the deluded Norma Desmond in *Sunset Boulevard* and today her name remains synonymous with that of the Hollywood Film Star.

GLORIA SWANSON
Happy and Wretched

This is the first chapter of Gloria Swanson's autobiography, Swanson on Swanson. *Its frank revelations, along with later descriptions of her six marriages and several liaisons, helped to make it a best seller for many months after Random House published it in 1980. But any objective reader of star memoirs must surely put it among the ten best such books in the history of Hollywood. Although she credits several people with some assistance, her personal voice and labors are apparent. Read it for an extensive view of the period and for a cumulative awareness of the brilliant, fallible functioning of a star personality.*

PARIS — Universal service — January 28, 1925

(By-line) Basil Woon

Gloria Swanson, thousand-dollar-a-day film actress, is now Marquise de la Falaise. She was married today in the almost romantic secrecy of the Passy Town Hall. Only nine persons were there. They, including your correspondent, did not know what was afoot until an hour before the ceremony.

I'm going to start with the moment in my life when I thought I had never been happier, because until that moment, I hadn't ever assessed the events that had come before it, and once it was over, I could never view my life or my career in the same way again.

That blissful morning in Passy in 1925 when I married my gorgeous marquis lifted me to the very pinnacle of joy, but at the same time it led me to the edge of the most terrifying abyss that I had ever known. One moment I had everything I had ever wanted, the next I was more wretched than I had ever been before; and in the days that followed, the more I blamed my misery on the fame and success I had achieved in pictures, the more famous and successful I seemed destined to become.

I was then twenty-five and the most popular female celebrity in the world, with the possible exception of my friend Mary Pickford. Headlines in North and South America and Europe usually referred to me by my first name only. I had starred in more than thirty successful films, six in a row directed by Cecil B. De Mille, and my leading men had included all the great heartthrobs from Wallace Reid to Rudolph Valentino. Not only was I the first American star to have filmed a major picture abroad, but I was also the first celebrity in pictures to be marrying a titled European. All over the world, fans were rejoicing because Cinderella had married the prince.

My salary at Paramount — $7,000 a week — was common knowledge, and columnists were already betting that when my contract was up in a year, Jesse Lasky would have to offer me at least a million a year to keep me. Moreover, Doug Fairbanks had unofficially invited me to join United Artists as an independent producer as soon as my contract terminated, promising that I could make much more with UA than I could ever make with Paramount or any other studio on a salaried contract. Oh, I was the golden girl, and everyone said so.

What the press and fans didn't know that January morning was that I was pregnant. Not even my dear, sweet Henri knew that, and I didn't have the heart to tell him, for well connected though he was, he had no money, and I couldn't let him take the responsibility for a decision I would have to make alone. What I knew was that if I had Henri's child in seven months, my career would be finished. The industry and the public would both reject me as a morally unsound character, unfit to represent them. In 1925, the Hays Office with its rigid censorship ruled Hollywood with an iron fist. Therefore, I took a single close friend into my confidence and with his help arranged to have a secret abortion the day after my marriage. The very idea horrified me, but I was convinced that I had no choice. I consoled myself with the fact that Henri and I were young and could therefore have other children. I already had two, a girl of my own and an adopted boy. Surely, I told myself —peremptorily so that I wouldn't argue back — I could have more. With that I stifled my fears and doubts and kept the dreaded appointment.

If the operation had gone as smoothly as I was assured it would, I would have continued my life as usual later that same day and gone on living normally for years to come, with twinges of guilt, of course, but probably never with any full realization of my proper feelings about what I had done. However, the doctor bungled the simple operation, and the next day I was unconscious with fever. Then for weeks I lay between life and death in a Paris hospital, having nightmares about the child I had killed, wishing I were dead myself.

Ironically, all the while I was struggling with my soul in anguish, too weak to talk, my public was growing more ardent. Day after day the newspapers published my temperature, and millions of fans held their breath. They didn't know the cause of my illness, only that I was mortally ill; and when I recovered, they loved me more than ever — more even, for the moment, than they loved Mary Pickford. Suddenly I was not only Cinderella who had married the prince, but also Lazarus who had risen from the dead.

Through me Paramount was receiving millions of dollars' worth of free publicity. In a steady stream of cablegrams Mr. Lasky and Mr.

Zukor begged me to speed up my convalescence and sail with my marquis to America in time for the New York premiere of *Madame Sans-Gêne*, the film I had just made in Paris. Then, they said, they would transport us across the country for the Hollywood premiere, and then back again to New York, where I would start my next picture as soon as I felt up to it.

I wanted to refuse them. I wanted to hold them responsible for my misery and blame them for controlling lives like mine that didn't really belong to them, and for making me destroy my baby. But I am a very pragmatic person. I could not, after all, back up and undo what I had done, so I cabled Mr. Lasky that I would attend both premieres. I sent my children on ahead with their governess and a few trusted friends, and Henri and I sailed on the *Paris* the third week in March.

From the moment we got off the boat in New York, adoring crowds nearly smothered us wherever we went. On the pier and again in the lobby of the Ritz Hotel, reporters and photographers trapped us for interviews while fans behind barricades cheered in the street. When we entered our suite, which was banked with flowers, both phones were ringing, and they never stopped. The Ritz switchboard was so swamped with incoming calls asking us to go here, go there, be photographed, be interviewed, that it was several hours before I could get through to my house in Croton-on-Hudson and speak to my daughter, little Gloria, and my baby Joseph. Valets, butlers, and maids were in and out of the suite every minute. They carried a constant stream of reports to the newspaper people down the hall: what food we ordered, what color Henri's pajamas were, what I was going to wear to the banquet in our honor the following night at the new Park Lane Hotel and to the Broadway premiere of *Madame Sans-Gêne*.

Our second day in the city, Mr. Lasky had arranged a special parade to Astoria, Long Island, to the studio where I'd been making all my pictures since 1923, when I'd escaped from Hollywood. The streets of Astoria were decked with signs and banners of welcome. Children in costume strewed flowers. Jesse Lasky and Adolph Zukor were both on hand, and there were speeches and ceremonies to welcome me back to my dressing room.

The night of the premiere of *Madame Sans-Gêne* at the Rivoli Theatre, the police had to route all traffic around the block. Crowds filled the street in front of the theater, and from a block away, as we crawled closer in our limousine, we could see my name, in gigantic letters ten feet high spelled out with hundreds of light bulbs, over the entire façade of the building. We couldn't get anywhere near the curb. A flying wedge of policemen got to the car and stood guard as

Henri got out. The crowd surged when they saw me, so the police made a circle around us and slowly walked us to the lobby. There they advised us to leave early by a side door, which we did, minutes after the picture started. After that we stayed in the hotel suite most of the time, and friends had to come there to see us.

I couldn't wait for the peace and quiet of the private car we had been promised on the train to California. When we got to the station, however, I was told that Paramount had rented the whole train. The rest of the cars were full of studio executives, exhibitors, and theater owners. My maid was the only other woman aboard.

I was worn out and edgy. The doctors in France had told me to take it easy, but I had not relaxed in New York for a minute of the six days we had been there, so Henri guarded the door to our car like a lion. He let in only very special pals, like Allan Dwan the director, Dick Halliday from the public relations department at Paramount, and René Hubert, my costumer. The instant the train moved, I went into my drawing room to rest. All I wanted was a massage that would last until Pittsburgh and then a long sleep free of telephones from Pittsburgh to Chicago.

Henri wakened me gently an hour later. When I opened my eyes, the conductor and the whole hierarchy of Paramount top executives were before me, begging me to stick my head out the rear platform door. Hundreds of people were waiting to see me.

I said I was covered with mineral oil and this wasn't a regular stop. "Yes, Miss Swanson, we know, but all these children have been let out of school to come down and see you, and if they don't, they'll be very disappointed." I was furious that schoolchildren had got involved in this carnival, but it was too late now. I yanked on a robe and stuck my head out of the window. Hundreds of children were lined up along the tracks, shouting my name. I waved to them and told them they should be in school.

"We wanna see your haircut," they were screeching. When I was ill with fever in Paris, the nurses had cut off most of my hair. It was still sheared off in back like a man's. When the reporters had written about it, many of them mistakenly thought it was the latest Paris style. Naturally, therefore, the children wanted to see it. So I showed them the back of my head, told them how it had happened, and begged them to leave their own beautiful hair alone. They couldn't hear me.

"We wanna see the prince," they were chanting.

I threw on a coat and took Henri by the hand. We walked out on the rear platform and tried to smile while they screamed happily and jumped up and down. Then the whistle blew and the train began moving away from the sea of tiny faces.

"Is it going to be like this from here to California?" Henri asked.

Allan Dwan nodded his answer. "If Gloria were thirty-five instead of twenty-five, she could run for President," he said. "There's no one else like her."

I felt like the half-dead whale that P.T. Barnum had once shipped from Canada to New York on a flatcar, which people had lined the tracks to see.

"Once we get past Chicago and into the Great Plains, you'll have a chance to rest up," the conductor promised. Until then there would be whistle-stops all along the way. According to advance news reports, crowds were gathering all the way to Albuquerque. Sometimes these included official delegations; other times they were just mobs of curious fans. Henri astonished them all, whether they were mayors, cowboys, or Indians, with his dignity, friendliness, and charm. France had never had a better ambassador.

In the forward cars of the train, studio executives and exhibitors were busy playing poker and trying to figure out how to exploit the Swanson gold mine to the fullest. Theater owners called me the mortgage lifter because for the past five years, in a run of twenty pictures beginning with *Male and Female*, all they had to do was put my name on the marquee and watch the money roll in. It didn't matter very much whether the pictures I played in were good, bad, or so-so. People went to all of them. They thought of me as part of their families. They liked to visit me regularly; see if I had changed since the last picture. Nobody knew how long it would last, but while it did, I was worth millions of dollars a year to the studio and the exhibitors, and all the men on that train, therefore, wanted my signature on a new Paramount contract as soon as my present one ran out. All this hoopla and publicity and private train were their way of wooing me.

Henri and I were on the back platform as the train slipped slowly into the Los Angeles station. Two bands were playing, and we could see troops of policemen on horseback, Sid Grauman's theater usherettes on white ponies, a red carpet ten yards wide, and a huge platform decorated with flowers and bunting and signs of welcome. The faces on that platform were like the Last Judgment — everyone I'd worked with or known in Hollywood. Mary Pickford, Douglas Fairbanks, Charlie Chaplin, Joe Schenck, Norma Talmadge, and D.W. Griffith were there in a very conspicuous bloc. They were after me to join them in their company, United Artists, and they wanted the Famous Players-Lasky-Paramount contingent to get the message. If Paramount wanted to keep me in the family, UA was saying, a million dollars a year would not be enough to ensure it. Paramount had most certainly got the message and had rounded up its most famous faces too and brought them down for the welcome — most notably, Mr. De Mille and Rudy Valentino.

In addition to these two competing delegations were the mayor, the city officials, and all the rest of filmdom, it seemed: Mickey Neilan, Lightning Hopper, Clarence Badger, Al Parker, Frank Borzage, Sam Wood, Jack Conway, Francis X. Bushman, Elliott Dexter, Lew Cody, Tommy Meighan, Jack Holt, Bebe Daniels, Lila Lee, Monte Blue, William S. Hart, Hoot Gibson, Sally Eilers, Milton Sills, Richard and Maude Wayne, Teddy Sampson, Ford Sterling, Chester Conklin, Charley Chase, Mack Sennett, Ricardo Cortez, Rod La Rocque, Lilyan Tashman, Ben Lyon — everybody. Everybody but Wallace Reid, who was dead of drug addiction, and Wallace Beery, my first husband, who had once told me he prayed I would be a failure so I would come back to him.

I hadn't set foot in California since 1923. To all of Hollywood gathered at the station that day, I was, in addition to being Cinderella married to the prince and Lazarus risen, the prodigal returned in triumph. They waved and called their approval.

We were carried to the platform. I was terrified I would have to say something because I knew I would burst into tears. Poor Henri was so bewildered that he later told me he was absolutely numb. We had never kissed so many people in our lives. Sid Grauman, the mastermind of Hollywood ballyhoo, had choreographed everything. After the speeches, rows upon rows of people lining the endless red carpet tossed flowers as we made the long walk to the open white Rolls-Royce waiting for us in front of the station.

A platoon of motorcycle cops cleared traffic for the parade of limousines. The streets were festooned with banners. When we got to Hollywood, we slowed down at the corner of Sunset and Vine under the biggest banner of all: WELCOME GLORIA. Famous Players-Lasky-Paramount had shut down for the morning, and hundreds of studio employees were in the street throwing flowers into the car. The parade halted while we got out and shook hands with everyone from the secretaries to the hairdressers, especially Hattie, the little black woman who had ironed my hair the first morning I went to work for Mr. De Mille.

The parade continued up Sunset Boulevard to my house in Beverly Hills. Inside, there was hardly time to show Henri where to hang his hat before the rush began to unpack, bathe, and get dressed for the West Coast premiere of *Madame Sans-Gêne* at Sid Grauman's Million Dollar Theatre in downtown Los Angeles.

It had opened its doors in 1919 with the world premiere of *Male and Female*. Then its entire audience had gasped when I walked out of the Santa Cruz surf in a shipwreck scene with my shredded satin evening dress soaked and clinging to my skin. Now they were gathering to gasp at me again tonight.

I was twenty pounds thinner than I had been in 1919, and I was wearing a gown of clinging silver lamé. Henri looked elegant in his white tie and tails. I made him wear his Croix de Guerre ribbon across his chest and his other decoration in his lapel. Even my mother had given in to the present storm of excitement. She arrived at the house all dressed up, willing to break her rule and go along to the first premiere she'd ever attended in her life.

We caused a tremendous traffic jam near the tunnel on Third Street. The motorcycle cops told us the streets were filled with people for ten blocks in every direction. There was no way around them. They would have to ease us inch by inch through the mob, which was cheering in unison like a football crowd. The car wouldn't budge. Finally the police cleared a path and I got out of the car. The police went ahead of me, and Mother and Henri followed behind. The din was unbelievable.

There were barricades in front of the theater, and the lobby was completely empty, except for a troop of ushers, who were obviously waiting for me.

"Has the picture started?" I asked.

"Yes, Miss Swanson. Right this way, please."

"Just a minute," I said, and turned to wait for Mother and Henri.

More ushers with flashlights hurried the three of us through the dark inner lobby to the main aisle door. As they held it open and we entered, the blackened theater burst into a blaze of light. The orchestra struck up "Home, Sweet Home," I could hear the gasp of a thousand people catching their breath, and then the audience gave out a tremendous roar. Amazed and bewildered, I grabbed Henri's hand.

People were standing and yelling like Indians. Women were throwing orchids in the aisle. I couldn't move. The ushers escorted us to our seats down in front. As soon as we came into view of the people in the balcony, they too began pelting me with orchids and gardenias. Everyone was singing "Home, Sweet Home." Among all the familiar faces I picked out the English actor Ernest Torrence, noticeable in a wheelchair; Mickey Neilan, my wild Irish love; and Mary Pickford and Doug Fairbanks. I turned around and threw kisses. They seated Henri between Mrs. De Mille and my mother. I was seated between Cecil B. De Mille and Mack Sennett, who was drying his eyes. The audience continued to whoop and roar until I got up again and threw more kisses. Mr. Lasky came out on the stage and tried to make a speech, but they wouldn't stop cheering and yelling until the lights dimmed and the picture came on.

A few minutes later the head usher came down the aisle and knelt at our feet to tell me the police couldn't handle the crowd anymore. They were bringing our car around to the alley and wanted us to leave immediately through the orchestra pit and backstage. Mr. De Mille said, "They're right. Hollywood has paid you a tribute tonight, young fellow, that has never been equaled. Every star, every director, every president of every film company in town is here. Everybody wants you to survive. Young fellow, it's time for you to go home to bed."

So Henri and Mother and I sneaked out in the darkness to the alley, where the car was waiting, and the police escorted us on our slow drive home. It was our first quiet moment in days, the first time I could really think. Mother finally said, "Glory, you're so quiet. This should be the happiest night of your life." My mother and I could always look out the same window without ever seeing the same thing.

I shook my head. "No, Mother," I said, "It's the saddest. I'm just twenty-six. Where do I go from here?" I suddenly felt empty and sick and bitter and exhausted and desolate. Henri took my hand. I'm sure he knew what I was thinking. I was thinking that every victory is also a defeat. Nobody gets anything for nothing.

I was thinking of the price I had paid two months ago to be able to walk down that orchid-strewn aisle tonight. I was wondering what all those glamorous and important people would have thought if I had stood up and shushed them and spelled out that price for them; if I had told them that in order not to break my contract or create a scandal, I had had to sneak to a French surgeon like a criminal and sacrifice a child I was carrying.

Would they have forgiven me, all those glamorous people? Would they have thought I had paid sufficiently by nearly dying of blood poisoning in a Paris hospital? I honestly didn't care. I knew only too well that most of them had sad and awful secrets of their own, so their hypothetical forgiveness meant nothing to me. The only thing that mattered was whether I would ever be able to forgive myself.

Even if Sid Grauman built me an Arch of Triumph in California as colossal as the one in Paris, it would always have a tomb under it, the tomb of an unborn baby who had picked Henri and me for parents and who was now dead.

EPHRAIM KATZ
Rudolph Valentino

Biographical material on Valentino is so poor that one must turn to his own brief, early story (Photoplay, February, March, April 1923) *for something approaching objectivity. He didn't mention, of course, the brushes with the law referred to in Katz'* Encyclopedia of Film *(N.Y., Crowell/Harper & Row, 1979, pp. 1181-1182) reprinted here. Nor did he go into any of his own sexual experiences, desires, or preferences, as other more gossipy writers have tried to do. If he was bisexual, or even celibate, we have no evidence.*

His image in history as a dominant male lover is not really confirmed by the plots of the films, nor by his personal life. (See author's introduction to this chapter and introduction to the book.) Katz has summarized his appeal as well as anyone: he "moved gracefully and gazed at his heroines with a mixture of passion and melancholy."

Valentino, Rudolph (also **Rodolph**). Actor. *b.* Rodolfo Alfonzo Raffaele Pierre Philibert Guglielmi, May 6, 1895, Castellaneta, Italy, *d.* 1926. The son of an army veterinarian, he was sent to a military academy at 13 but failed to qualify as officer material. When his application to enter a naval academy was turned down, he settled for agricultural studies. In 1912 he traveled to Paris in search of another vocation but instead found himself begging for coins on street corners. Late in 1913 he arrived in New York, certain of a bright future in the land of opportunity. He found room and board among Italian immigrants in Brooklyn and began the American phase of his life as a landscape gardener. He promptly lost his job and resorted to a succession of odd jobs, including dishwashing and table waiting. He got into trouble with the law and was booked by the New York police on a number of occasions on suspicions of petty theft and blackmail.

Drawn by the glitter of the Broadway district, Valentino became a taxi dancer and eventually began exhibiting his skills with various partners in dance halls and nightclubs. He broke into the big time when he replaced Clifton Webb as the partner of Bonnie Glass, a popular dancer of the period. He later changed partners but not his bad luck. He was again arrested and spent several days in the Tombs, a notorious detention center. After being released, thanks to the intervention of Nazimova, he left New York in the cast of a musical that folded in Ogden, Utah. He continued on his own to San Francisco, where he resumed his career as a dancer. Finally, in 1917, he arrived in Hollywood.

Valentino made the rounds of the casting offices and was soon landing extra and bit parts in films, mostly in the roles of an exotic dancer or a greasy villain. Gradually, his roles improved, but he was still a minor player by 1920. Around this time he married an actress named Jean Acker, but she locked him out of a hotel bridal suite on their wedding night and the marriage was never consummated. Valentino's big break came in 1921 when screenwriter June Mathis, an influential figure at Metro, insisted that he be given the lead in *The Four Horsemen of the Apocalypse*. The film was a tremendous box-office hit and Valentino was catapulted into instant stardom. Within a couple of years he was a national phenomenon, a male star of unprecedented sensual appeal to women.

Darkly handsome and solidly built yet lithe, Valentino moved gracefully and gazed at his heroines with a mixture of passion and melancholy that sent chills down female spines. To the American woman he represented a symbol of mysterious, forbidden eroticism, a vicarious fulfillment of dreams of illicit love and inhibited passions. But male audiences found his acting ludicrous, his manner foppish, and his screen character effeminate. Nevertheless, the Valentino craze reached new heights with *The Sheik* (1921), at Paramount. During the film's exhibition women fainted in the aisles and Arab motifs began to infiltrate fashions and interior design.

Valentino scored sensationally at the box office with *Blood and Sand* (1922) and *Monsieur Beaucaire* (1924), and in 1923 his small volume of mushy poetry, *Day Dreams*, sold hundreds of thousands of copies, but his career was beginning to take a downbeat turn. In contrast to his strong male image on the screen, Valentino played the weaker-sex role in relation to the women in his life. His ambitious second wife, actress (one film, *When Love Grows Cold*, in 1925) and set designer Natacha Rambova (b. Winifred Shaunessy, Jan. 19, 1897; d. 1969), took charge of his career and misguided it pitiably. Under her guidance, the Valentino screen image became more and more effeminate. Her constant interference strained his relationship with studio executives to the point that her absence from the set became a condition to his further employment. To add to his troubles, he was arrested on a charge of bigamy for having married Rambova before the dissolution of his first marriage became final. Just when he seemed to be recovering his popularity with two successful United Artists productions, *The Eagle*(1925) and *The Son of the Sheik* (1926), Valentino was blasted in a strongly worded editorial in the Chicago *Tribune*, headlined "Pink Powder Puff." Lamented the writer: "When will we be rid of all these effeminate youths, pomaded, powdered, bejeweled and bedizened, in the image of Rudy — that painted pansy?"

A few months later he was taken to a New York hospital with a perforated ulcer. His sudden death, on August 23, 1926, at the age of 31, brought on a wave of mass hysteria among female fans. Thousands of women lined the streets during his funeral, causing a near riot. Rumors began spreading that he had been poisoned by a discarded mistress, and a Valentino cult sprang up that had sinister necrophilic overtones. Years after his death, Valentino fan clubs around the country were as active in glorifying their hero as they had been during the peak of his career. Every year on the anniversary of his death, a mysterious woman in black has been seen laying a wreath of flowers on his grave, adding a sense of drama to the life and death of a screen legend. Several Valentino biographies have since been published, including one by Rambova. A brief biography of Valentino, "Adagio Dancer," was included in John Dos Passos' famous trilogy *U.S.A.* (1936). Anthony Dexter portrayed the star in a film biography in 1951 and Rudolf Nureyev in another in 1977. In 1978 a section of Irving Boulevard in Hollywood was renamed Rudolph Valentino Street.

Films: *Alimony, A Society Sensation, All Night 1918; The Delicious Little Devil, A Rogue's Romance, The Home Breaker, Virtuous Sinners, The Big Little Person, Out of Luck, Eyes of Youth 1919; The Married Virgin/Frivolous Wives, An Adventuress, The Cheater, Passion's Playground, Once to Every Woman, Stolen Moments, The Wonderful Chance 1920; The Four Horsemen of the Apocalypse, Uncharted Seas, The Conquering Power, Camille* (as Armand Duval), *The Sheik 1921; Moran of the Lady Letty, Beyond the Rocks, The Isle of Love* (revised version of *An Adventuress,* padding Valentino's small 1920 role with out-takes), *Blood and Sand, The Young Rajah 1922; Monsieur Beaucaire* (title role), *A Sainted Devil 1924; Cobra, The Eagle 1925; The Son of the Sheik 1926.*

SCOTT O'DELL
The Four Horsemen of the Apocalypse

The Palmer Institute of Authorship in Hollywood was a commercial establishment which offered advice and training to amateurs wishing to become successful screenwriters. One of its publications, prepared by O'Dell in 1924, was called Representative Photoplays Analyzed *and our selection is from pages 457-459. It is an efficient synopsis of the story plus an analysis which reflects both dramatic and religious values characteristic of the time. Julio was played by Valentino.*

Problem Drama

(Metro production; all-star cast; from the novel of the same name by Vicente Blasco Ibanez; continuity by June Mathis; directed by Rex Ingram.)

Synopsis

While in no sense a prologue, the opening scenes prepare the way for the intensely tragic drama which is enacted later in Paris and on the Marne.

Madariaga, the Centaur, is an enormously rich old cattle herder of Argentina. His two daughters marry; one, a Frenchman by the name of Marcelo Desnoyers; the other, a German, Karl Von Hartrott. The latter has three lusty sons, whereas the Desnoyers have no children. Madariaga hates the German and his sons and is loath to leave them his vast estate; consequently he is overjoyed when at last a boy, Julio is born to the Desnoyers. Until the very hour of his death, the old Centaur lavishes all his affection upon Julio and, as soon as the latter is old enough to accompany him, takes him on wild debauches in the towns.

When Madariaga dies the estate is divided. The Von Hartrotts go to Germany to live; the Desnoyers, to Paris. Here Julio's father sets up an expensive establishment, buys a castle on the Marne, and becomes a collector of antiques. Julio, true to his grandfather's training, enters upon a gay life and opens a studio where he paints pictures and entertains his friends and his models.

One of his guests is Marguerite Laurier, the young and attractive wife of Monsieur Laurier. Julio falls desperately in love with her and Marguerite returns his passion. Her husband discovers what is going on and drives his wife from home. Then comes the outbreak of the World War. Laurier at once joins his regiment, but soon loses his eyesight because of a wound. Julio continues his painting and his gay life, and even the sight of Marguerite putting on the garb of a Red Cross nurse does not arouse him; but, when he encounters her tending a blind soldier, whom he recognizes as her husband, he hears the thrilling call of war. Enlisting at last, he is sent to the front. Father and mother know that he has answered the call of duty.

Meanwhile Desnoyers, learning of the German advance toward Paris, visits his estate on the Marne to save it from destruction, only to be captured by the Germans and to have his castle turned into the headquarters of the commanding officer, upon whose staff is one of the Von Hartrotts. Desnoyers suffers various indignities, but is finally released when the tide of war is turned.

Marguerite determines to stay by the side of her blind husband who has forgiven her.

At last Julio and his eldest cousin, having both been sent on dangerous missions, meet at night as they crawl forward through the slime of No Man's Land. A star-shell bursts and lights the heavens with the brilliancy of day. They recognize each other but the game of war must be played to the bitter end. Simultaneously they fire at close range and both fall dead, side by side.

Later Julio's father and mother come to see the last resting place of their beloved boy. Here they are met by a stranger who leads them to the grave. "You knew him?" they ask. "I knew them all," answers the stranger, pointing to the thousands of crosses which stand, a mute reminder of war's devastation. The symbolism is unmistakable — it is the Christ, looking with infinite compassion upon the children of Earth.

Analysis

As compelling, sincere, beautiful, as Ibanez' literary classic, this screen classic stands out — a splendid exponent of the cinematic art. It is a powerful story, powerfully delineated. Its action runs the whole gamut of human emotions — from bitterest tragedy to lightest satire and most fantastic humor.

The story's dramatic quality makes itself felt early — in the initial situations of the plot, where the seeds of hatred and potential conflict are sown between the two sons-in-law of Madariaga. Steadily throughout the action, this dramatic force increases in momentum until it culminates in the soul-stirring encounter of the two youths —

son of the German, and son of the Frenchman — on the field of battle. This racial antagonism, which is developed in a sound, psychological way, is what gives the story its epic import.

This theme is the upward struggle of humanity, vivified and made concrete through the symbolism employed throughout the play. The four horsemen, enemies of mankind — Pestilence, Famine, War, and Death — on their giant chargers, trample over the trivial concerns of mortals, strewing disaster and destruction in their wake. The idealism of a suffering world is symbolized in the character of the quiet stranger who "knew them all." It is he who speaks of peace and brotherly love: the Christ who sorrows with his children.

The Four Horsemen is a screen play that deserves study and restudy. The structure is not weakened by the lapse of time, for it would be impossible to show the onward sweep of a world cataclysm more briefly, and, at the same time, as convincingly. The dramatic construction is good; the plot progresses logically to a logical termination. The characterizations cannot be improved upon. The characters, while typifying certain racial tendencies, are distinct individuals, with personalities of their own. Such material as the infidelity of the heroine, Marguerite, might be condemned because of censorship regulations, in a story less powerful than this. Here the sin of the lovers is purified through suffering and idealistic sacrifice. The boy turns bravely to face death, the girl as bravely to face duty. The ending is tragic and rightly so; it is an ending that grows out of the story itself. The terrible devastation is unforgettable. But there is hope — and optimism too — in the wistful, loving face of "The Stranger."

ADOLPH ZUKOR
The Valentino Cult

Here we have the somewhat derisive view of the president of Famous Players-Lasky (and its distributing company, Paramount Pictures). Jesse Lasky had signed Valentino after the Metro company did not seem to comprehend his popular impact in The Four Horsemen. *Collaborating on Zukor's autobiography,* The Public Is Never Wrong *(N.Y., G.P. Putnam's Sons, 1953), Dale Kramer manages to give us a fairly coherent version of the story line of* The Sheik, *followed by some remarks about the influence of that film on young people and the difficulties young Rudy had dealing with Paramount, press, public, and his wife. (Pages 206-211,213-220.)*

Lasky, despite his undoubted gifts for diplomacy, couldn't find a way to deal with Natacha Rambova's demands, as filtered through a loyal and somewhat wayward, sometimes angry husband. An early example of studio suspension, the Valentino case was shocking to the public, and when his manager worked up a series of public appearances, the response was tumultuous. After this demonstration of his continuing popularity Valentino was allowed to come back and complete his contract with two pictures (Monsieur Beaucaire; The Sainted Devil) *which were great successes at the boxoffice.*

Although the tone softens at the end, the businessman who had worked so well with Mary Pickford and Gloria Swanson still finds Rudy a puzzle. He would have been equally puzzled by the measured comments of Audrey Kupferberg about The Sheik *in 1982: "the sincerity of Valentino's performance makes this a most powerful and erotic adventure. It is psychological drama played with no pretenses...Its theme entered popular culture and helped to expand women's awareness of themselves as sexual human beings." (Page 968,* Magill's Survey of Cinema: Silent Films).

Late in 1921 our advertising copywriters took off their gloves, spit on their hands, and hammered out some remarkable advice to the public.

SEE:

— the auction of beautiful girls to the lords of Algerian harems.

— the barbaric gambling fete in the glittering Casino of Biskra.

— the heroine, disguised, invade the Bedouins' secret slave rites.

— Sheik Ahmed raid her caravan and carry her off to his tent.

— her stampede his Arabian horses and dash away to freedom.

— her captured by bandit tribesmen and enslaved by their chief in his stronghold.

— the fierce battle of Ahmed's clans to rescue the girl from his foes.

— the Sheik's vengeance, the storm in the desert, a proud woman's heart surrendered.

— matchless scenes of gorgeous color, and wild free life, and love. In the year's supreme screen thrill —

By this time all readers over forty, and doubtless most of those under, will have guessed the rest. The picture was, of course, *The Sheik*, with Rudolph Valentino.

Top billing went not to Valentino but to the leading lady, Agnes Ayres. Valentino was twenty-six years old and had been in Hollywood for several years, dancing as a professional partner and sometimes playing bit movie parts, chiefly as a villain. Recently he had gained attention as a tango-dancing Argentine in *The Four Horsemen of the Apocalypse*, made by another company. When we hired him for *The Sheik* we expected that he would perform satisfactorily, but little more. We certainly did not expect him to convulse the nation. Valentino was as strange a man as I ever met. Before going into his personality, however, it would seem worthwhile, taking into account what happened afterward, to review *The Sheik*.

The story was taken from a novel of the same title by Edith M. Hull, an Englishwoman. After publication abroad the book had become a sensational best seller in America. We paid fifty thousand dollars for the screen rights, a very large sum for the time, with the idea that the novel's popularity would assure the picture's success.

The story gets under way with Diana Mayo (Agnes Ayres), a haughty English girl visiting in Biskra, remarking that marriage is captivity. Since Diana is a willful, adventurous girl who dislikes the restraining hand of her cautious brother, one knows that trouble is brewing the moment she spots Sheik Ahmed Ben Hassan (Valentino) and their eyes meet. The distance between them is roughly 150 feet, yet she quails, to use understatement, visibly. One might have thought he had hit her on the head with a thrown rock. There was nothing subtle about film emotion in those days.

Learning that non-Arabs are forbidden at the fete the Sheik is holding in the Biskra casino that night, Diana disguises herself as a slave girl and wins admission. The Sheik discovers her identity as she is about to be auctioned off along with other slaves. He allows her to escape, but later that night appears under her window, singing:

> "I'm the Sheik of Araby
> Your love belongs to me.
> At night when you're asleep
> Into your tent I creep."

Valentino moved his lips hardly at all when he sang. As a matter of fact, his acting was largely confined to protruding his large, almost occult, eyes until vast areas of white were visible, drawing back the lips of his wide, sensuous mouth to bare his gleaming teeth, and flaring his nostrils.

But to get on with the film story. Next day the Sheik attacks Diana's caravan and packs her off to his desert oasis camp. Though he regards her as his bride, she fends off his advances. Yet it is soon apparent that she is falling in love with him. After a week of virtual slavery Diana begins to like it at the camp.

Then she learns that Raoul de Saint Hubert, a French author and friend of the Sheik, is coming to visit. Ashamed to be found in her slavelike condition by a fellow European, Diana stampedes her guard's horse while riding in the desert and makes a dash for freedom. Her horse breaks a leg and she staggers across the sand toward a distant caravan.

This is the caravan of the dread bandit Omair (played by Walter Long, a noted heavy). Omair makes her a captive for plainly evil reasons. But soon the Sheik, having been informed of Diana's escape by the stampeded guard, attacks the caravan and rescues her.

The French author (Adolph Menjou, wearing a bushier mustache than was his custom in later years) rebukes the Sheik for what seems to him a selfish attitude toward the girl. Next day while Diana and the Frenchman are riding in the desert, Omair swoops down, wounds the author, and carries the girl off to his stronghold.

The Sheik gathers his horsemen and rides to the rescue.

Meanwhile at the stronghold, Omair pursues the "white gazelle," as he calls Diana, around and around a room in his harem house. One of the bandit's wives, fed up with him, had advised Diana to commit suicide rather than become the brute's victim. But Diana, having faith in the Sheik, fights gamely on.

The Sheik and his horsemen assault the stronghold's walls. Once inside, the Sheik bests Omair in a hand-to-hand struggle. But at the moment of victory a huge slave hits him a terrible blow on the head.

For some days he lies at death's door.

Now the Frenchman tells Diana the true story of the Sheik. He is no Arab at all, but of English and Spanish descent. When a baby he was abandoned in the desert. An old sheik found him, reared him, had him educated in France, and eventually left him in command of the tribe.

And so the story draws to a happy ending. The Sheik recovers and the two lovers set off for civilization and marriage.

The public, especially the women, mobbed the theaters, and it was not very long before the psychologists were busying themselves with explanations. The simplest, I gathered, was that a surprisingly large number of American women wanted a mounted sheik to carry them into the desert. Doubtless for only a short stay, as in the case of Diana, after which they would be returned to civilization in style.

Adult males were inclined to regard *The Sheik* with some levity. But the youths began to model themselves on Valentino, especially after he had appeared in *Blood and Sand* for us. In the latter picture, playing a Spanish bullfighter, he affected sideburns, sleek hair, and widebottomed trousers. Soon thousands of boys and young men had cultivated sideburns, allowed their hair to grow long, plastered it down, and were wearing bell-bottomed pants. Lads in this getup were called "sheiks." Thus two of Valentino's roles were combined to get a young modern sheik.

An audience today viewing *The Sheik* laughs at the melodramatic story, the exaggerated gestures, and Valentino's wild-eyed stares and heaving panting while demonstrating his affection for Diana. Yet some of the impact of his personality remains. He created an atmosphere of otherworldliness. And with reason, for there was much of it about him.

Valentino was born Rodolph Guglielmi in the village of Castellaneta in southern Italy of a French mother and an Italian father. When eighteen he went to Paris and a year later migrated to New York City. It is known that he worked as a landscape gardener, a dishwasher, and a paid dancing partner, or gigolo. After a couple of years he secured occasional vaudeville work as a partner of female dancers of more reputation than his own.

Improvident by nature, with expensive tastes, Valentino lived from day to day as best he could. All his life he was in debt, from $1 to $100,000, according to his status. Being fully convinced that a supernatural "power" watched over him, he did not worry.

Mortal men found this power of Valentino's hard to deal with. We raised his salary far above the terms of his contract. That seemingly only whetted the power's appetite. It became downright unreasonable after *Blood and Sand*, with the lads of America imitating Valentino and women organizing worshipful cults. . . . One day I was privileged to see a Valentino exhibition such as I had been hearing about. He was arguing with an assistant director — what about I did not know, and did not inquire. His face grew pale with fury, his eyes protruded in a wilder stare than any he had managed on the screen, and his whole body commenced to quiver. He was obviously in, or near, a state of hysteria. I departed as quietly as I had come.

The situation grew worse instead of better, and finally Valentino departed from the studios, making it plain that he had no intention of returning. We secured an injunction preventing him from appearing on the screen for anybody else. This did not bother him very much. He went on a lucrative dancing tour and was able to borrow all the money he needed.

Valentino was married but the relationship had not lasted long although it was still in technical force. Now he was in love with a beautiful girl named Winifred O'Shaughnessy. Her mother had married Richard Hudnut, cosmetics manufacturer, and Winifred sometimes used his surname. She preferred, however, to be known as Natacha Rambova, a name of her own choosing. She was art director for Alla Nazimova, the celebrated Russian actress who was one of our stars. Like Valentino, Natacha believed herself to be guided by a supernatural power.

They were married before Valentino's divorce decree was final, and he was arrested in Los Angeles for bigamy. He got out of that by convincing authorities that the marriage had never been consummated, and the ceremony was repeated as soon as legal obstacles were cleared away.

Natacha Rambova appeared, as Valentino's business agent wrote later, "cold, mysterious, Oriental." She affected Oriental garb and manners. Yet she had served Alla Nazimova competently, was familiar with picturemaking, and we felt she would be a good influence on Valentino. At any rate she brought him back to us.

Now, as it turned out, we had two Powers to deal with. She was the stronger personality of the two, or else her power secured domination over his. It was our custom to give stars a good deal of contractual leeway in their material. Natacha began to insert herself into the smallest details and he backed her in everything. His new pictures, *Monsieur Beaucaire* and *The Sainted Devil*, were less successful than those which had gone before.

The Valentino cults continued to blossom, but his publicity was not always good. Newspapers poked fun at the sleek hair and powdered faces of the "sheiks." The situation was not helped when it became known that Valentino wore a slave bracelet. Many people believed it to be a publicity stunt. But the fact was that Natacha Rambova had given it to him. Any suggestion that he discard it sent him into a rage.

A book he published, titled *Day Dreams*, caused raised eyebrows. Both he and his Natacha believed in automatic writing and it seems that the real author was his power, or the combined powers, working through him. An item titled "Your Kiss" is a good sample.

> Your Kiss,
> A flame
>   Of Passion's fire,
> The sensitive Seal

Of Love
In the desire,
  The fragrance
    Of your Caress;
Alas
  At times
    I find
      Exquisite bitterness
In
Your kiss.

We did not care to renew Valentino's contract, particularly since he and his wife wanted even more control over his pictures. He made arrangements with a new company, founded for the purpose, and work was begun on a film titled variously *The Scarlet Power* and *The Hooded Falcon*, dealing with the Moors in early Spain. Author of the story was Natacha Rambova.

After the two had spent eighty thousand dollars traveling in Europe for background material and exotic props, the story was put aside. Another, *Cobra*, was substituted with Natacha in full charge. It did poorly and the venture with the new company was at an end.

Joseph Schenck was now handling the business affairs of United Artists, and he took a chance with Valentino — being careful to draw the papers in a manner keeping decisions out of the hands of either Valentino or Natacha. Valentino accepted the terms, though reluctantly. Not long afterward the couple separated and Natacha sued for divorce.

United Artists filmed *The Son of the Sheik*, which, as it turned out, was the celebrated lover's final picture.

Valentino's publicity became increasingly less favorable. He called his Hollywood home The Falcon's Lair, which opened him to some ridicule. The fun poked at the "sheiks" increased as the title of his new picture became known. Valentino himself grew more irritable.

He was in Chicago when the Chicago *Tribune* carried an editorial headed "The Pink Powder Puffs." One of the editorial writers, it seems, had visited the men's rest room of a popular dance emporium and there noted a coin device containing face powder. Many of the young men carried their own powder puffs, and they could hold it under the machine and by inserting a coin get a sprinkle of powder. The editorial, taking this situation as its theme, viewed the younger male generation with alarm. Most of the blame was placed on "Rudy, the beautiful gardener's boy," and sorrow was expressed that he had not been drowned long ago. In an earlier editorial the *Tribune* had made fun of his slave bracelet.

Valentino's "face paled, his eyes blazed, and his muscles stiffened" when he saw it — according to the later account of his business manager. Seizing a pen, Valentino addressed an open letter "To the Man (?) Who Wrote the Editorial Headed 'The Pink Powder Puffs.'" He handed it to a rival newspaper.

"I call you a contemptible coward," Valentino had flung at the editorial writer, inviting him to come out from behind his anonymity for either a boxing or wrestling contest. After expressing hope that "I will have an opportunity to demonstrate to you that the wrist under the slave bracelet may snap a real fist into your sagging jaw," he closed with "Utter Contempt."

That was in August, 1926. Valentino came on to New York, and I was surprised to receive a telephone call from him inviting me to lunch.

"It is only that I would like to see you," Valentino said. "No business."

I would have agreed in any circumstance, but I was sure that he was telling the truth about not coming with a business proposition, since he was well set with United Artists.

"Certainly," I answered. "Where?"

"The Colony."

I had already guessed his choice, since The Colony was probably New York's most expensive restaurant. He liked the best. We set the time.

Valentino and I had barely reached The Colony when it became apparent that every woman in the place having the slightest acquaintance with me felt an irresistible urge to rush to my table with greetings. Though overwhelmed, I remained in sufficient command of my senses to observe the amenities by introducing each to Valentino.

He was thirty-one at this time, apparently in the best of physical condition, and, in this atmosphere at least, was relaxed. I do not know whether his divorce decree was yet final, but Natacha Rambova was in Paris. Recently Valentino's name had been linked with that of Pola Negri, one of our major stars.

"I only wanted to tell you," Valentino said after things had quieted down, "that I'm sorry about the trouble I made — my strike against the studio and all that. I was wrong and now I want to get it off my conscience by saying so."

I shrugged. "It's water over the dam. In this business if we can't disagree, sometimes violently, and then forget about it we'll never get anywhere. You're young. Many good years are ahead of you."

And so we dropped that line of talk. Valentino truly loved artistic things. He spoke of his ambition, when the time of his romantic roles was over, to direct pictures. I had the feeling that here was a young man to whom fame — and of a rather odd sort — had come too rapidly upon the heels of lean years, and he hadn't known the best way to deal with it.

"Telephone me any time," I said as we parted, "and we'll do this again. I enjoyed myself." And I had.

A day or two later I picked up a newspaper with headlines that Valentino had been stricken with appendicitis. At first it was believed that he was in no danger. But he took a turn for the worse. Joseph Schenck and his wife Norma Talmadge came to our home to wait out the crisis. Schenck was bringing encouraging reports from the hospital, when suddenly there was a relapse.

Valentino died half an hour past noon on August 23, 1926. It was a week to the minute since our meeting for lunch.

I, for one, was stunned by the hysteria which followed Valentino's death. In London a female dancer committed suicide. In New York a woman shot herself on a heap of Valentino's photographs.

A call came through to me from Hollywood. "Pola Negri is overwrought, and she's heading to New York for the funeral."

"Put a nurse and a publicity man on the train," I said, "and ask Pola to guard her statements to the press."

After Pola's arrival, my wife and I called at her hotel to offer condolences. Though very much upset, she intended to remain in seclusion as much as possible.

Valentino's body was laid in state at Campbell's Funeral Home at Broadway and Sixty-sixth Street, with the announcement that the public would be allowed to view it. Immediately a crowd of thirty thousand, mostly women, gathered.

Rioting — described as the worst in the city's history — began as police tried to form orderly lines. Windows were smashed. A dozen mounted policemen charged into the crowd time and time again. After one retreat of the crowd, twenty-eight women's shoes were gathered up. Women then rubbed soap on the pavement to make the horses slip.

The funeral home was now barred to the public — those who got in had nearly wrecked the place by snatching souvenirs — but next day another crowd gathered when news spread that Pola Negri was coming to mourn. She was spirited in through a side door. Word soon came out that she had collapsed at the bier, which she had, and for some reason it excited the crowd.

On the day of the funeral 100,000 persons, again mainly women, lined the street in the neighborhood of the church in which it was being held. I was an honorary pallbearer, along with Marcus Loew, Joseph Schenck, Douglas Fairbanks, and others from the industry.

Natacha Rambova was not present, being still abroad. But Valentino's first wife, actress Jean Acker, collapsed, and Pola Negri, heavily veiled, was for many moments on the point of swooning once more.

As the funeral procession left the church, the throngs fell silent except for subdued weeping of many of the women. The body was sent to Los Angeles for burial. The Valentino cult, I am told, is still in existence. At any rate, enough women visit his grave every year to have provided the gravekeeper with enough material for a book about them.

ARTHUR LENNIG
The Son of the Sheik

> *Dr. Lennig, professor of film history and film production at the State University of New York at Albany, has come to the conclusion that Rudolph Valentino's place in the silent era has been poorly judged by the film analysts and the drama critics alike. Whether his last film can be said to be "passionate, but not physically so" may possibly be questioned, but as a "normal affair between fourteen-year-olds" we may find his viewpoint persuasive today. This is an unpublished piece, not included in his 1969 book* The Silent Voice: A Text.

Although *The Son of the Sheik* deals with torture, lying, betrayal, passion, rape, revenge, and murder, it absorbs these harsh terms like a flimsy cloud absorbing a giant mountaintop. The film is beyond the reality of stones, trees, and crevices. It has created its own myth, its own world, and in this ether it naively tells its story. It is immeasurably aided by a musical score, appended in the 1930's, of almost supernal innocence and simplicity and, if you wish, corniness. The love theme, stemming from Tschaikovsky's Fifth Symphony (first movement), and "Turbulent sequences," devised by more contemporary practitioners, contribute to this world of the never-never land. The small orchestra wheezing away, the occasional sound effects, the heroine's exotic dance (all swirls and veils) to the music of Anitra's dance in *Peer Gynt*, all blend together to form a delicacy like an oriental honey cake, fantastically sweet but irresistibly delightful.

Although *The Sheik* had been a success — far more than most of Valentino's ensuing films — there was a question whether a sequel could possibly be accepted by the public. After all, the "arab" picture and the concept of the romantic sheik had been imitated and also satirized since 1921. Yet there was a hope — even within the short period of five years — that there would be some nostalgic interest in seeing him continue his portrayal of the Arab lover. And indeed, there was. When the film was released in August, 1926, a few weeks before his sudden death, it proved to be his most delightful film, one that has been consistently revived throughout the years.

Briefly, the film tells the story of Ahmed (the son of the sheik) who meets a dancing girl, Vilma Banky, and falls in love with her. Every night he rides across the sands to meet her. While embracing her, his gun holster gets in the way, so she asks him to remove it. As they passionately, though still innocently, commune, the evil members of her troupe steal the weapon and attack him. He is captured, tortured, and held for ransom. The major villain, played by Montagu Love, is magnificently evil as he perpetually narrows his eyes to a close-lidded sneer. Wanting the girl for himself, he tells the prince that she, Yasmin, has inveigled other men as well, and has betrayed him. Ahmed escapes shortly after, and swears to have vengeance on the girl. Later, when her troupe enters another town, she discovers him standing on a balcony, and with gestures of love, throws him a flower. He turns his head in disdain and crushes the proffered flower. That night she performs her exotic dance in a cafe. After smoking a cigarette, which with Valentino always seems to smoulder, he captures her and rides off in the desert to his tent where he threatens to have his revenge on her. She pleads mercy from the imminent rape.

A dull flush crept over his sunburnt face, and starting to his feet, he began to pace up and down as he had paced the adjoining room an hour ago.

Up and down, down and up, his face set, his heart pounding, he strode from end to end of the narrow room.

What stayed him? What lingering scruple hindered the accomplishment of his firm purpose?

Love was dead — but desire remained. Desire that sent the hot blood racing madly through his veins, that, gathering strength momentarily, was like a raging fire consuming him. Passion wrung, the color faded slowly from his cheeks and he grew strangely pale under the deep tan.

His smouldering eyes ranged the room with almost a look of anguish in them. . .

She had lied to him — why should he spare her?

She had betrayed him — why should he not punish her?

He felt no pity for her helplessness. What gentleness had been in his composition was burnt out of him, gone with the love that had died so swiftly.

Moreover, he had sworn and by Allah, he would keep his oath! What scruple to stay him! What had she done to deserve his mercy? She was his — to do with as he would!

The hold he had kept over himself snapped suddenly. Tortured by the physical longing that all at once became unbearable, conscious only of the overwhelming need that was driving him, he went swiftly, with fiercely beating heart and throbbing pulses. But on the threshold of the innermost room he paused, with outstretched hand, his face tormented.

Then, with a smothered oath, he dashed the curtains aside violently.
The Sons of the Sheik, pp. 138-139.

Such is the prose of the novel. The film captures this very mood, but Valentino lends a touch of sensitivity to the Sheik, making him gentle even in his sexually agressive moments. Certainly he is the most likeable of all rapists on the American screen.

Meanwhile, his father, also played by Valentino, and quite convincingly too, is irate at his son's absence and goes to his tent. He orders his son to obey. Their battle of wills is realized in matching their strength on an iron bar. The father bends it, and the son straightens it out again. Finally Ahmed agrees to his father's advice and sends the girl back to her people. Again the villains in the troupe force her to entertain in the cafe. Valentino enters, a fight erupts (his sword against ten others!), but he is helped by his father. The villain abducts the girl. Valentino breaks away, jumps on his horse, and rides in pursuit. The two horses race neck to neck; Valentino leaps at the villain and after a struggle, kills him. A moment later, he takes Yasmin in his arms and together they ride off on a single horse and he kisses her hand.

The Son of the Sheik, taking place in the monied mirage of Hollywood sand dunes, is not a great Film, but a great Movie. Perhaps to the cool and cynical people of today, the film is ridiculous. And, indeed, it is. But it has something, and this something could be described as romanticism. The film is passionate, but not physically so. It has a delicacy beyond that of the novel. The film is as sexual as a normal affair between fourteen-year-olds. The kisses are passionate but discreet. The hands do not wander, but clasp each other. Indeed, the film has captured that same beauty and corniness of postcards from the twenties showing two lovers. The viewer must forget his Kraft-Ebing and his Kinsey report and other statistics concerning sexual response to enjoy the movie. It is one of the most passionate and romantic love stories of the silent era.

The direction is brisk, the shots move swiftly, and attention never wavers. There are no *longeurs*. Many shots are done in close-up for added intensity and both lovers are attractive and enjoyable to watch. Valentino's charm, though appearing a bit wooden in his other films, radiates here magnificently. Whether one can believe his conjectural biographies or not, certainly Valentino seems as if he were more interested in the preliminaries of love, of worshipping his partner's body and soul, than mere fornication. In this sense, he is different from today's so-called romantic leads. If Valentino promised elaborations, they were motivated by more than merely a curious urge to experiment; they were to fulfill love, to capture in any possible physical way what he was feeling mentally.

And when, in the last scene of the film, he pursues the villain and Yasmin turns to see her lover riding furiously on his white horse across the rolling sands, he becomes the realization of any imaginative girl's dream. He is the personification of the lover. That such a rescue scene and such a transcendant fade-out of the lovers riding on horseback across the horizon into the faint rays of the moon will never happen in real life is a pity. *The Son of the Sheik*, for all its commercial intent, simplicity and unpretentiousness, lives as a personification of our youthful visions.

A Typical Letter to *Photoplay* Magazine
November 1923
(during Valentino's suspension at Paramount).

Ramon Novarro is a splendid actor and he is exceedingly handsome, but he will never take the place of our beloved Rodolph. Ruddy's world of admiring fans are waiting with open arms to receive him back when he comes.

—Rubye L. Rutledge
Selma, Alabama

H.L. MENCKEN
Valentino

In the last month of his life, Rudy turned to his familiar father image, Adolph Zukor, for some kind of reconciliation—or perhaps, as Zukor saw it, admission of a mistake. But he also turned to a famous reporter and critic of American life, the editor of the American Mercury. *Mencken saw his problem as partly a gap between cultures. But he also recognized, after a while, a special case of the dilemma of the consuming desire for approval confronted with the unpleasantness of rejection and ridicule. Simply "a highly respectable young man, which is the sort that never metamorphoses into an artist," he would never have found his fame to be satisfying, no matter how hard he tried to make something distinguished out of it.*

This is one of the most remarkable encounters ever recorded between a Hollywood "personality" and a brilliant observer of American civilization. It is from Mencken's collected writings, Prejudices: Sixth Series *(N.Y., Alfred Knopf Inc., 1927) pages 290-311. An aspiring writer or critic might wish to note how a rich vocabulary helps to achieve not only a delicate discrimination among ideas but also a certain generosity of tone.*

By one of the chances that relieve the dullness of life and make it instructive, I had the honor of dining with this celebrated gentleman in New York, a week or so before his fatal illness. I had never met him before, nor seen him on the screen; the meeting was at his instance, and, when it was proposed, vaguely puzzled me. But soon its purpose became clear enough. Valentino was in trouble, and wanted advice. More, he wanted advice from an elder and disinterested man, wholly removed from the movies and all their works. Something that I had written, falling under his eye, had given him the notion that I was a judicious fellow. So he requested one of his colleagues, a lady of the films, to ask me to dinner at her hotel.

The night being infernally warm, we stripped off our coats, and came to terms at once. I recall that he wore suspenders of extraordinary width and thickness — suspenders almost strong enough to hold up the pantaloons of Chief Justice Taft. On so slim a young man they seemed somehow absurd, especially on a hot summer night. We perspired horribly for an hour, mopping our faces with our handkerchiefs, the table napkins, the corners of the table-cloth, and a couple of towels brought in by the humane waiter. Then there came a thunder-storm, and we began to breathe. The hostess, a woman as tactful as she is charming, disappeared mysteriously and left us to commune.

The trouble that was agitating Valentino turned out to be very simple. The ribald New York papers were full of it, and that was what was agitating him. Some time before, out in Chicago, a wandering reporter had discovered, in the men's wash-room of a gaudy hotel, a slot-machine selling talcum-powder. That, of course, was not unusual, but the color of the talcum-powder was. It was pink. The news made the town giggle for a day, and inspired an editorial writer on the eminent Chicago *Tribune* to compose a hot weather editorial. In it he protested humorously against the effeminization of the American man, and laid it light-heartedly to the influence of Valentino and his sheik movies. Well, it so happened that Valentino, passing through Chicago that day on his way east from the Coast, ran full tilt into the editorial, and into a gang of reporters who wanted to know what he had to say about it. What he had to say was full of fire. Throwing off his 100% Americanism and reverting to the *mores* of his fatherland, he challenged the editorial writer to a duel, and, when no answer came, to a fist fight. His masculine honor, it appeared, had been outraged. To the hint that he was less than he, even to the extent of one half of one per cent, there could be no answer save a bath of blood.

Unluckily, all this took place in the United States, where the word honor, save when it is applied to the structural integrity of women has only a comic significance. One hears of the honor of politicians, of bankers, of lawyers, even of the honor of the United States itself. Everyone naturally laughs. So New York laughed at Valentino. More, it ascribed his high dudgeon to mere publicity-seeking: he seemed a vulgar movie ham seeking space. The poor fellow, thus doubly beset, rose to dudgeons higher still. His Italian mind was simply unequal to the situation. So he sought counsel from the neutral, aloof and aged. Unluckily, I could only name the disease, and confess frankly that there was no remedy — none, that is, known to any therapeutics within my ken. He should have passed over the gibe of the Chicago journalist, I suggested, with a lofty snort — perhaps, better still, with a counter gibe. He should have kept away from the reporters in New York. But now, alas, the mischief was done. He was both insulted and ridiculous, but there was nothing to do about it. I advised him to let the dreadful farce roll along to exhaustion. He protested that it was infamous. Infamous? Nothing, I argued, is infamous that is not true. A man still has his inner integrity. Can he still look into the shaving-glass of a morning? Then his is still on his two legs in this world, and ready even for the Devil. We sweated a great deal, discussing these lofty matters. We seemed to get nowhere.

Suddenly it dawned upon me — I was too dull or it was too hot for me to see it sooner — that what we were talking about was really not what we were talking about at all. I began to observe Valentino more closely. A curiously naïve and boyish young fellow, certainly not much beyond thirty, and with a disarming air of inexperience. To my eye, at least, not handsome, but nevertheless rather attractive. There was an obvious fineness in him; even his clothes were not precisely those of this horrible trade. He began talking of his home, his people, his early youth. His words were simple and yet somehow very eloquent. I could still see the mime before me, but now and then, briefly and darkly, there was a flash of something else. That something else, I concluded, was what is commonly called, for want of a better name, a gentleman. In brief, Valentino's agony was the agony of a man of relatively civilized feelings thrown into a situation of intolerable vulgarity, destructive alike to his peace and to his dignity — nay, into a whole series of such situations. It was not that trifling Chicago episode that was riding him; it was the whole grotesque futility of his life. Had he achieved, out of nothing, a vast and dizzy success? Then that success was hollow as well as vast — a colossal and preposterous nothing. Was he acclaimed by yelling multitudes? Then every time the multitudes yelled he felt himself blushing inside. The old story of Diego Valdez once more, but with a new poignancy in it. Valdez, at all events, was High Admiral of Spain. But Valentino, with his touch of fineness in him — he had his commonness, too, but there was that touch of fineness — Valentino was only the hero of the rabble. Imbeciles surrounded him in a dense herd. He was pursued by women — but what women! (Consider the sordid comedy of his two marriages — the brummagem, star-spangled passion that invaded his very death-bed!) The thing, at the start, must have only bewildered him. But in those last days, unless I am a worse psychologist than even the professors of psychology, it was revolting him. Worse, it was making him afraid.

I incline to think that the inscrutable gods, in taking him off so soon and at a moment of fiery revolt, were very kind to him. Living, he would have tried inevitably to change his fame — if such it is to be called — into something closer to his heart's desire. That is to say, he would have gone the way of many another actor — the way of increasing pretension, of solemn artiness, of hollow hocus-pocus, deceptive only to himself. I believe he would have failed, for there was little sign of the genuine artist in him. He was essentially a highly respectable young man, which is the sort that never metamorphoses into an artist. But suppose he had succeeded? Then his tragedy, I believe, would have only become the more acrid and intolerable. For he would have discovered, after vast heavings and yearnings, that what he had come to was indistinguishable from what he had left. Was the fame of Beethoven any more caressing and splendid than the fame of Valentino? To you and me, of course, the question seems to answer itself. But what of Beethoven? He was heard upon the subject, *viva voce*, while he lived, and his answer survives, in all the freshness of its profane eloquence, in his music. Beethoven, too, knew what it meant to be applauded. Walking with Goethe, he heard something that was not unlike the murmur that reached Valentino through his hospital window. Beethoven walked away briskly. Valentino turned his face to the wall.

Here, after all, is the chiefest joke of the gods: that man must remain alone and lonely in this world, even with crowds surging about him. Does he crave approbation, with a sort of furious, instinctive lust? Then it is only to discover, when it comes, that it is somehow disconcerting — that its springs and motives offer an affront to his dignity. But do I sentimentalize the perhaps transparent story of a simple mummer? Then substitute Coolidge, or Mussolini, or any other poor devil that you can think of. Substitute Shakespeare, or Lincoln, or Goethe, or Beethoven, as I have. Sentimental or not, I confess that the predicament of poor Valentino touched me. It provided grist for my mill, but I couldn't quite enjoy it. Here was a young man who was living daily the dream of millions of other young men. Here was one who was catnip to women. Here was one who had wealth and fame. And here was one who was very unhappy.

Rudolph Valentino and Natacha Rambova

S. GEORGE ULLMAN
Valentino As I Knew Him

Because Natacha Rambova "was a very beautiful girl, with a marvelous complexion," and Rudolph Valentino was having a disagreement with Famous Players-Lasky, George Ullman approached the young couple with a business proposition in 1922. They were to tour the country, presenting an evening of dance, and at some point Rudy would make a little speech—a commercial—praising the qualities of a certain "beauty clay" supposedly used by Natacha. This was a great success. The very first show was in Omaha during a blizzard, yet the auditorium was packed and hundreds had to be turned away. Soon after that, Valentino asked Ullman to be his business manager.

Despite grave doubts ("I had a family, whereas Valentino was $50,000 in debt") Ullman eventually agreed to do it. In four years he would be trying to write a sorrowful memorial for his friend and employer. His book is the most sincere and informative record we have of Valentino's last years. While he frequently deplores Valentino's overconfident spending and clearly blames Natacha for her cold ambition, his attitude toward both of them as he argues out their differences is full of respect, sympathy, and admiration—qualities which often result in valid history. On pages 205-208 of Valentino as I Knew Him *(N.Y., Macy-Masius, 1926) he attempts to describe one of Rudy's last public appearances.*

When we went down to Atlantic City we motored, leaving New York at noon and arriving at five o'clock. We were halted on the outskirts by an escort consisting of the Acting Mayor, ten motorcycle policemen, and hundreds of fans in automobiles, which fell in behind our car, and made quite a triumphal procession.

Valentino's appearance had been well advertised. An enormous crowd greeted him at the Ritz-Carlton. Here he found his old friend Gus Edwards, who was then running one of his famous revues at the hotel, and who begged Rudy to come down as his guest, as soon as he had finished making his appearance at the Virginia Theater, where the picture was to open.

In spite of the heat, Rudy promised.

Our attempt to get from the Ritz-Carlton to the Virginia was the most riotous thing I ever experienced. The crowds were suffocating, the largest and most insistent we had ever seen. The ten policemen who attempted to clear a path so that we could get to the waiting car were of no avail whatsoever. They were simply in the way.

When finally we plowed our way to the automobile and got in, both of us had to settle our disordered clothing. The car crawled at a snail's pace, being blocked before and at each side by the crowds of men and women who leaped upon the running boards and thrust their hands in at the open windows. Rudy shook hands with as many as he could reach, quite pleased with these expressions of interest.

When we reached the theater some fifteen minutes later, we had the same trouble in gaining the entrance. As we entered, we could hear the shouts of the audience attempting to silence the announcer, who was vainly endeavoring to quiet their impatience by telling them that Valentino was on the way.

Very quietly Rudy walked on the stage and tapped the announcer on the shoulder. The latter turned with a start.

The great audience was so instantly silenced that you could have heard a pin drop. Then a roar of welcoming applause burst forth which lasted at least three minutes.

It gives me the greatest satisfaction to recall that picture of Rudolph Valentino, as he stood before that vast audience, radiant with health and happiness, smiling boyishly at the sincerity of his welcome. If I had known that death stalked so near, I could not have wished for him any greater joy than came to him during his last five public appearances at the showing of *The Son of the Sheik*. It proved to me, beyond any doubt, that Valentino was indeed the outstanding idol of the screen.

Again he made one of his delightful impromptu speeches, thanking the audience for its appreciation of his efforts and impressing them and me anew with his charm and dignity. At the risk of being considered a bore I repeat that, had Valentino been making a request for contributions for a worthy philanthropy, it is my opinion that he could have turned people's pockets wrong side out.

Thence we made our way through the crowds to the broadcasting station on the Steel Pier. While we were waiting for Rudy's scheduled time for going on the air, the crowd surged around, climbing on each other's shoulders and almost breaking the windows in their attempt to see the star.

If the fan letters which poured in to the station after this speech of Rudy's are any criterion, he must have been as much of a success on the air as ever he was on the screen.

Back at the hotel later, Rudy kept his promise of going to Gus Edwards' Revue. Just as we were entering I saw him rush up to a man, seize him by both hands and pour forth a torrent of voluble Italian, to which the other responded with equal excitement.

I asked what the trouble was, fearing the worst, but Rudy reassured me saying that he was not quarreling. That this was a man whom he had asked for a job as bus boy at the Ritz-Carlton in New

York when he first came to America, but was refused because the man thought he would be no good. Gus Edwards seized upon Rudy and introduced him to the audience. He said that, having heard of the bout with Buck O'Neil, he took pleasure in thus publicly presenting him with a pair of boxing gloves. He complimented Rudy upon his fistic ability, of which he had seen examples, and suggested that Rudy use these gloves on the Chicago editor.

Later in the evening, Edwards asked Valentino if he would dance the tango with the professional dancer in his revue. At first Rudy demurred, but finally consented, and danced the tango that he made famous in *The Four Horsemen*.

This was the last time Valentino ever danced the tango.

RODOLFO DI VALENTINA
Playing a New Style Heavy
in
Joe Maxwell's First Feature
" THE MARRIED VIRGIN "
Address: 7369 Sunset Boulevard
HOLLYWOOD, CAL.

(1918 Motion Picture Studio Directory)

Chapter 5

Some Sad and Happy Endings

For years, after leaving Hollywood, I thought the movies ruined my life, but now I'm not so sure. I made a lot of money, and it not only took me out of poverty, but enabled me to help others.

— *Miriam Cooper*[1]

Can a movie star's life have a happy ending? What would it be like? A sudden airplane crash at the height of a career? This seemed tragic for the fans and friends of Will Rogers and Carole Lombard. A long and private retirement? This seemed strange and uncomfortable for the fans and friends of Mary Pickford and Greta Garbo.

The arbitrary span of an hour and a half makes it possible for a movie story to arrange an ending with a scene of believable happiness. Human life is a lot less controllable. When the end comes, it is not "the end," fading out with some kind of dramatic satisfaction. It is usually accompanied not only by sorrows but by regrets.

For a movie star, no matter how brief the fame has been, there at least have been some remembered pinnacles of public adulation. And for some less tense, less tortured personalities the "final years"

---

1 *Dark Lady of the Silents,* (1973) p. 241.

after life in the spotlight can be relatively happy. The careers that seem to us to be unfinished or unfulfilled are those we may consider tragic.

The real lives of silent movie stars were as different from each other as any knowledgeable observer of the human scene might expect. They were not all copies of *Sunset Boulevard*, Billy Wilder's sardonic distortion of Mary Pickford as recluse. Nor were they the same as *A Star Is Born*, the story of a star whose rising crosses the falling career of her suicidal husband—a story pattern drawn in part from the life of Colleen Moore.

Although the most familiar beginning pattern was the struggle to move out of a background of privation and get ahead in the dazzling atmosphere of Hollywood, the end of the story was sometimes ugly or galling. For "country boy" Charles Ray, who put all his money in a costume picture that failed, it was return to the ranks of extras, taking what jobs he could find. For dignified Blanche Sweet, after a short but happy marriage, it was tending counter in a Los Angeles department store.   For beautiful Barbara LaMarr, after three disastrous marriages (one of them to a man revealed as a bigamist) it was alcoholism, tuberculosis, death at 29.   Like the unexpected knock of opportunity, sudden failure was unpredictable, and comebacks were rare.

Of the three longest-lasting silent stars, only Lillian Gish never yielded to the demands of marriage-seekers, although George Jean Nathan, the dramatic critic, tried hard to win her over. True to her preferred dream of success, she seemed content with the lonely life of hard work and self-expression: her spirit and her skills brought her many chances on stage and screen even as she neared the century mark.

Mary Pickford stopped work 46 years before her death at 86: wealthy and active in charities like the Motion Picture Country Home, she was at least blessed with the companionship of third husband Buddy Rogers all those declining, memory-haunted years at Pickfair.

Gloria Swanson, still experimenting with marriages late in life, worked at painting, fashions, sponsoring inventions, rescuing a group of Jews from wartime Austria—and occasional movies and plays. She had one grand comeback in *Sunset Boulevard* (1950), and was able to relish best-seller status for her memoirs before she died at 84.

It's curious that these three child-women of the screen, who became rich and famous crown princesses, all lived into their

80s—given long lives, if not happiness. The boy princes, on the other hand, died much sooner—Fairbanks at 56, Valentino at 31.

From 1912 to 1923, Mary Miles Minter was a popular actress, of demure demeanor and petite stature, competing for parts and publicity with Marguerite Clark and Mary Pickford. Like Clark, whose elder sister guided her career, and like Pickford, whose mother was present at all financial negotiations, Minter was in the beginning an impoverished, fatherless adolescent, steered by a protective mother.

Most of her 50 silent movies are lost, but there is a still photograph of Mary Miles Minter which reflects, with a special and poignant charm, the early spirit of that informal community of movie-makers that was Hollywood. She is in a very full skirt, her ankles almost showing, sitting in a swing on somebody's front lawn. The actor-director James Kirkwood is giving her a push. It is a lively, ingratiating picture. She seems the very embodiment of the movie star as the girl next door. What the photograph proposes to us, at the very least, is that Hollywood can be a happy place even for those who are rich and famous.

But if we look at this picture with a deeper historical perspective, we may find its charm somewhat shadowed. Of course it is posed, and we may wonder if this swing ever got swung. But then we remember, too, that Mary Minter in 1922 had a crush on another director who was mysteriously murdered. Many people thought Mary (or more likely her jealous mother) had caused the death of William Desmond Taylor. Her career, along with the career of her romantic rival, Mabel Normand, was ruined. Zukor paid off her contract and she went into real estate.

Yes, there were chances on the new Hollywood frontier for persistent and attractive people to reach and hold public favor. But there was also the threat of swift decline, of studio disfavor and unexpected public coolness. The stories of John Gilbert and Clara Bow, for example, were certainly in the rags-to-riches mode, but after a time of excited popular approval their lives turned into tragedy—into the kind of dramatic downbeat formula copied in later plots about Hollywood.

Gilbert was an extreme example of a child unwanted and uncared for. His mother was a compulsive actress who left her parents in Utah to join a minor traveling stock company, married the manager, and had a baby she regretted. She tried to place the child with relatives, divorced the father, dragged the boy around the theater circuits, dumped him at the age of six on a strange woman in New York City whose daughter was a prostitute, and took him back during another marriage only to put him in military school. She died when he was fourteen.

Jack had been adopted by his latest stepfather, a comedy player named Walter Gilbert, who extended favors after his mother's death only as far as putting the youngster on the train to San Francisco with ten dollars in his pocket. There the boy scrubbed floors, washed dishes, sold tires, and finally did some stage management.

He appealed again to his stepfather, who then was able to put him in touch with someone at Tom Ince's movie ranch near Santa Monica. He got a job as an extra for $15 a week. There he was helped along to better parts by Bill Hart, Rowland Lee, and Lee Garmes. After another bleak period of near starvation in 1918-19, when the whole industry was in a depression, he was approached by Maurice Tourneur and worked for him as actor, writer, and occasional director. In 1920-21, he started on the first of 20 pictures for William Fox for $1000 a week, and by 1925 he had reached super stardom in King Vidor's *The Big Parade* and Erich von Stroheim's *The Merry Widow* at M-G-M.[2]

Then John Gilbert became one of the prime examples of a fast falling star. His voice was supposed to have displeased the public in his first sound roles, but on-the-spot observers have disputed that accusation. It is more likely that tense mannerisms applied to inadequate lines, plus a somewhat marginal sex appeal, had something to do with public apathy. But there were other factors at work.

Louis B. Mayer (his sworn enemy, according to his daughter's biography) saw to it that the vehicles given Gilbert were bad for him, the staffs incompetent, the reviews shrugging. One director assigned to him was Lionel Barrymore, who was inexperienced and without talent in that function. Gilbert got the help of his friend Irving Thalberg, head of production, more than once, and he thought by signing his new $1,500,000 contract personally with Nicholas Schenck, president of M-G-M since Marcus Loew's passing, he had gained the upper hand. But Gilbert could not protect himself

2   Leatrice Gilbert Fountain and John R. Maxim, *Dark Star* (1985), pp. 10, 13, 16-27, 73, 89.

from the wrath of the head of the studio. He withdrew to his hillside mansion and more or less drank himself to death.[3]

Clara Bow certainly came into the Hollywood system from the bottom rungs of society. Living in a Brooklyn tenement with a mother who was intermittently insane and a father who wanted nothing to do with her, she told reporters in later years, "I have known hunger, believe me." Her father beat her frequently and her mother several times threatened her with a butcher knife. Her only good times were in the street playing stickball with the neighborhood boys. With the help of a cousin she managed to finish fifth grade, but her real temple of learning and her refuge was the movie house, where she worshiped Wallace Reid and yearned to be like Mary Pickford.

Clara was certain she was going to be a movie star. Somehow she collected fan magazines and kept up on the contests. When a Brooklyn publisher in 1921 proposed a "Fame and Fortune" contest, she got her father to buy two photographs of her for a dollar and took them in to the office herself. The judges kept calling her back for screen tests, impressed with her youth, vitality, and quickness to learn. They gave her the prize, which included a role in a picture. She was cut out of that film, but she kept getting small roles until B.P. Schulberg signed her for a trial period, brought her to Hollywood, and then proceeded to exhaust her by using her or loaning her out in fifteen pictures a year.

When she finally woke up to her value, her lawyer saw to it that from 1927 to 1931 her salary would increase from $1500 to $5000 a week and she would make fewer pictures with more time off. In 1929 she was getting 45,000 letters in one month, more than double

3   Fountain, pp. 122, 131, 165, 186 (for Mayer's hatred). See chapters 13-18 for years of decline. It appears, from Fountain's account and from Bosley Crowther's biography of M-G-M studio boss Louis B. Mayer, *Hollywood Rajah*, (1960) that John Gilbert at some point in a meeting with Mayer had defended a script reference to a prostitute by announcing that his own mother was a whore. He knew what he was talking about, but this automatically shocked the publicly puritanical Mayer and he lunged at Gilbert. To Mayer, mother love was supposed to be sacred. On the other hand, when Garbo did not turn up at her own wedding in 1926, Mayer had the brass to tell Gilbert to give up marrying her and just sleep with her. Witnesses say that Gilbert then hit Mayer and his head fell against the tiles of the men's room.

the fan mail of any star up to that time. But Clara Bow's contract bondage to Schulberg and Paramount, as David Stenn shows in his biography, never included a program to help her improve and shine. The theater men wanted her. The public came to see her no matter what kind of story she was in. So why try harder? Besides, she was constantly getting into scrapes around Hollywood—the crazy Brooklyn kid was unacceptable at Hollywood parties and known for love affairs with Gilbert Roland, Victor Fleming, Gary Cooper, and others in and out of the movie colony.

The Clara Bow saga reached public climax when her extracurricular life began to include Rex Bell, and her longtime secretary, Daisy DeVoe, got jealous. Lawsuits on both sides led to a wild trial and petty accusations, plus revelations of Clara's headlong lifestyle, some true and some untrue, which had a destructive effect on her fan popularity.

After 1931 it was all downhill. Her marriage to Rex Bell and their retirement to the desert was happy and successful for a time. There were two children, both boys, and two more films. But her strange reactions and accusations within the family when she was no longer working were a puzzle and a trial for her loyal husband, and she began to be in and out of sanitariums. The final diagnosis was schizophrenia. She outlived Bell, giving up at 60, in 1965.[4]

Luck was not enough for Clara Bow. Hard work was not enough for John Gilbert. Their early destitution and lack of family love drove them into motion picture careers, and they rose quickly to stardom. But they were also unloved by their studios and were brought down from their public pedestals in a very public and humiliating way.

Such prominent examples of tragic decline, on screen and in life, contrasted with the lives of other, lesser luminaries who suffered, worked, yearned for the heights of stardom, reached their goal, and retired in comfort and self-possession. The careers of Charles Farrell and Mary Brian, for example, followed a remarkable pattern of dream, work, success—and after all that, a reasonable degree of happiness.

Farrell's father ran a lunch counter and a movie house in a small town on Cape Cod. As soon as he got home from school, Charles

4   David Stenn, *Clara Bow: Runnin' Wild*, (1988), pp. 159, 263.

would head for the restaurant to wash dishes and peel potatoes, then rush over to the theater to sweep out. After a bite to eat, he would sell tickets to the show, and after that go home and do his school work. He got a job in a paper mill to pay for business school at Boston University.

All those years, he was sure he was going to be a movie actor. He saved enough to make it to the west coast. His instincts told him to "linger behind" in the mornings when the extras were sent home, and his fresh, easygoing personality got him small jobs that started him up the ladder.[5] After a series of brief contracts at several studios, he was cast in *Seventh Heaven* with Janet Gaynor in 1927 and their co-starring seven-year career at Fox made them both popular and wealthy. After 44 films, Farrell retired from the screen in the 1940s, started the Racquet Club at Palm Springs, was mayor there for seven years while working in TV, and was still around in his 80s.

Mary Brian's father died when she was one month old. Her mother tried to carry on with the jewelry store, but had to move to a larger store in a west Texas town where her brother owned the opera house and showed movies. They moved to Dallas, where Mary went to high school. For years she kept house and cooked meals for mother and brother, as well as three boarders, nursing all the while her longing to be a movie actress. In 1924, her mother finally agreed they could manage a trip to California.

Young Taurrence found work in Long Beach, and mother and daughter took a tiny room in Hollywood, doing the rounds of the studios, especially the little companies on Poverty Row. Sometimes they walked 75 blocks in one day. Their hoard of savings was down to five dollars, and they were preparing to seek other jobs, when they picked up pieces of a discarded newspaper with news of a beauty contest the next day in Ocean Park.

Mary's mother decided to risk all—to buy her daughter a swim suit with two of the five dollars, and a swatch of chiffon for two dollars more, to add glamor to her only good dress. When this was done, she prayed earnestly to know if it was right for Mary to be in motion pictures. She had her answer: Mary's sweet earnestness was awarded $100 and the title of "Miss Personality"—by a jury including Esther Ralston—and within a week she was cast as Wendy in Peter

5 Harry Brundidge, "Charles Farrell," *Twinkle, Twinkle, Movie Star!* (1930) pp. 149-155

Pan at Paramount (1924).[6] She had prominent—often starring—roles as "nice" girls in 53 films during the next thirteen years. She married a film editor in 1937, and later worked in a few low-budget films and in a TV series.

Bessie Love, whose heart-shaped cheerful face looked even more innocent than the other strong-willed characters who reached for success in silent films, wrote in her autobiography of Los Angeles High School days (up to 1915): "For years we had been exhaustingly, drably poor...Mother read about Mary Pickford spending the winter in Palm Beach. That did it!...People were always saying that I looked like the little film actress: I, too, would enter films...Mother, then working in Jantzen's Bathing Suit factory, and up for promotion to forelady, could not get away herself. So Mrs. Delano, the wife of the couple renting a room from us, would accompany me to the studio."

Being five feet tall and not quite 17, Bessie was just the type for D.W. Griffith, who asked her if she was rich, seemed glad to know she was not, then asked why she wanted to act. Because "Mama said I wasn't trained to do anything so there was nothing left for me but acting." She got the job, perhaps because she did resemble the spunky Pickford he had lost. He put her into the Judean episode of *Intolerance*, (1916). Her career was a succession of ups and downs (she played opposite Hart, Fairbanks, Gilbert, Barthelmess) but her good humor, her ukelele, and her capacity for friendship made her a survivor.[7] Only with the utmost brevity does she mention a "marriage."

Bessie Love claimed that every five years the bottom drops out of an actor's career, but "I was discovering that success will never desert you if you can find exciting parts, however small." She did keep getting those small parts, often through personal friends. She and Bebe Daniels, who had often strummed their ukeleles together at beach parties, both proved they could not only talk but sing for sound pictures. It turned out that Bessie's best known role was in the early sound picture *The Broadway Melody* (1929), which won her an Oscar nomination. In 1935 she moved to England and continued to work in radio, theater, and films all the way into the 1980s, meanwhile writing light-hearted bits of her reminiscences for magazines and newspapers.[8]

---

6   Brundidge, "Mary Brian," *op.cit.*, pp. 101-109.
7   Bessie Love, *From Hollywood With Love* (1977), pp. 24-26.
8   Love, pp. 76, 90.

Betty Compson, like Bessie Love, was not easily discouraged when career opportunities slowed down. She had lost her father twice. Shortly after she was born he disappeared into Alaska in search of gold. He brought some back a few years later, but spent it in the stock market, failed in business, and died of tuberculosis. His wife then went back to work as a maid in a hotel, and his daughter, who was 15 and had been playing in the orchestra at a Salt Lake City movie house, went on the road as "the Vagabond Violinist." An actor friend wired someone in Hollywood that she "ought to be in pictures," and before long she was working in comedies for Al Christie at Universal.

Chosen by George Loane Tucker for a starring role in *The Miracle Man*, Compson found she was famous—and up for a Paramount contract. Unlucky in some of her pictures and directors, she was back on her own within two years, and moved to London, where she was given two good roles. Returning to Paramount, she was working once more when she decided to bow out and enter into a somewhat combative marriage with the director James Cruze. Divorced, the trim blonde with the keen blue eyes tried a second comeback. It meant being willing to take three-day parts from Poverty Row studios. Soon she got better roles—one of them for Josef von Sternberg, *The Docks of New York*.

From then on it was top roles at RKO and brief appearances at Monogram, vaudeville tours with her trusty violin (also singing and doing star imitations), touring with plays, two more marriages, and management of a series of business firms—cosmetics, House of Suede on Wilshire Boulevard, Ashtrays Unlimited. "From childhood I've had the fear of poverty. But I've saved money," she told interviewers. "There will never be a benefit performance for Betty Compson."[9]

Marguerite Clark is perhaps the best example of success against great odds followed by a perfectly calm and satisfied departure from the scenes of her triumphs. Born in Cincinnati, she was left at 13 with $4000 at the death of her father, who had owned a clothing

9   Brundidge, "Betty Compson," *op.cit.*, pp. 65-70. DeWitt Bodeen, "Betty Compson," *From Hollywood*, (1976), pp. 23 to 247. As in a few other instances, Bodeen here trusts and uses material from the earlier Brundidge book ("no benefit performance").

store. Her mother had died when she was ten. Her older sister Cora, having determined from school plays that her little sister's voice and personality were pleasing to audiences, set out to manage Marguerite's career. First in Baltimore, then in New York and on a national tour (1900-1914) Marguerite found success in the theater. Adolph Zukor decided that her four-feet-ten was just right for movies and signed her up for three years at $1000 a week.

Clark starred first for Alan Dwan in *Wildflower* and soon became the brunette counterpart of Mary Pickford, vying with her for roles. Her best performance, on stage and screen, was in *Prunella*, a story of conflict between showbusiness and quiet home life. This Maurice Tourneur production in 1918 may have had some kind of influence on the popular Hollywood beauty. That same year she married a rich Louisiana lumberman. Never ambitious for stardom, she soon found the quieter Southern atmosphere much to her liking, and before long (after 37 films) settled happily in Louisiana, presiding gracefully over small town social life.[10]

Corinne Griffith, like Norma Shearer, had early advantages of middle class comforts and a supportive family. She was planning an extended musical education and possibly a career, when her father suffered "business reverses" and she moved from Texas to California to be with relatives, having no idea what direction to take.

> I was dancing one evening at a Santa Monica ballroom with some friends. I did not even know at the time that a Brunette Beauty Contest was being held; but presently I heard my name called out. During the process of elimination I won the contest—much to my surprise and somewhat to my amusement! I had no idea that it would lead to anything. But among the judges was Rollin Sturgeon, then a director for Vitagraph, and he offered me a small part.

One of the most notable beauties of the American screen (sometimes compared with Hedy Lamarr), Griffith became a contract star at Vitagraph (1916) just as Norma Talmadge was leaving. She followed Talmadge to First National and also followed her example by making highly profitable investments. On a dozen of her pictures (1924-1927) she was listed also as executive producer.

---

10 Bodeen, "Marguerite Clark," *op.cit.* (1976), pp. 31-43. Only two of Marguerite Clark's films still exist.

She retired in 1932 to manage her business affairs and write successful novels. Her third husband (1936-1958) was Preston Marshall, owner of the Washington Redskins, and thus the "Orchid Lady" of the movie capital became a popular ornament of the social scene in the nation's capital.[11]

Ramon Novarro, one of nine children of a prosperous dentist in Mexico City, slipped the bands of happy family life and ran away to Los Angeles in 1916. He and his brother had ten dollars when they got there. For four years he tried to gain a foothold in theater or film—as actor, singer, musician, or dancer. Meanwhile he taught voice and piano to beginners. He did find some work as an extra in films and among other things volunteered for an experimental pantomime at the Hollywood Community Theater, where Rex Ingram first saw him. Then a friend got him in to see Ingram. Make-up box in hand, he persuaded him he could be Rupert of Hentzau in *The Prisoner of Zenda.*

Novarro starred in four pictures (including *Scaramouche*) for Ingram, who then decided to set up a studio in Europe. He advised Ramon to stay in Hollywood and get the best deals he could. His pupil negotiated well: from $500 a week, he moved to $10,000 at M-G-M. When *Ben-Hur* went through a reorganization, he was given the lead. The next year, he starred for Lubitsch in *The Student Prince* (1927), the last of his notable pictures.

The diffident boyish good looks celebrated in the fan magazines did not carry him long after Ingram let him go. Never married, he tried to live and work on the periphery of films and theater, growing old and alcoholic, seeing mainly family members. Nearing 70, he was bludgeoned to death in his own house by two young drunks he picked up in a bar.[12]

Colleen Moore was one of the rare ones who grew up within a happy family (in Florida). Yet her youthful yearning to be a movie actress was so strong that she lighted candles in church on nine successive days. On the ninth evening (she says in her memoirs) her family got a phone call from an uncle, an editor in Chicago who had assisted D.W. Griffith in his bouts with the local censors. She was to have a six months trial at the Griffith California studio. Her

---

11 Hal C. Herman, *How I Broke Into the Movies: Signed Stories by Sixty Screen Stars.* "Corinne Griffith," pp. 76-77.
12 DeWitt Bodeen, "Ramon Novarro," *More From Hollywood,* pp. 193-211.

grandmother went west with her, since she was only 15 at the time. She was never in a Griffith film, but worked for Tom Mix and Marshall Neilan, and found fame only after she had her hair cut and played a "flapper" in *Flaming Youth* (1923). By 1926 she was topping the *Exhibitors Herald* boxoffice poll.

With success came harder times: she lived a personal tragedy that became a part of Hollywood lore. Colleen fell in love with a handsome publicity man at First National. He persuaded her to marry him and let him manage her career, an advantage which helped move him up to become head of production at the studio. John McCormick soon revealed himself to be an alcoholic. She was increasingly embarrassed by his escapades and threats of suicide. More than once she feared for her own life. Yet she was loyal to him and in one instance saved his job. She heard that his position was in danger, and she made a point of calling the head of First National in New York, announcing: "This is Mrs. John McCormick speaking! I just called to say hello."

But the studio's top star could not protect her husband from himself. After their separation, she heard that he had taken a house at Malibu. According to Colleen Moore's account, one day Adela Rogers St. Johns, staff writer for *Photoplay*, looked out her window to see McCormick swimming out much too far into the distance. She managed to hail John Gilbert to row out with her and pull him in.

Adela St. Johns had also been present when Colleen Moore made her call to the president of First National. When she was called upon to rewrite *What Price Hollywood* into the story for *A Star Is Born*, (1937) she made use of both events she had experienced. In the new story, drowning at Malibu is the way the drunken Norman Maine chooses to end his life. Later, at a premiere, the script has his now-famous wife speak the line originated by Colleen Moore. She steps up to the microphone, announcing: "This is Mrs. Norman Maine." Thus facts woven into fiction became another strand of Hollywood's tragic myths.[13]

13   Colleen Moore, *Silent Star*, (1968), pp. 20-27, 174-177, 247. Also Adela Rogers St. Johns, *Love, Laughter and Tears: My Hollywood Story*, (1978), p. 221. Mrs. St. Johns quotes some paragraphs directly from the Moore book. She does not, however, offer on her own that she was present when McCormick tried to walk out to sea. Inspiration for this episode has more recently been attributed to an actor named John Bowers, but his ocean suicide came three days after the scene was enacted in the 1936 version of *A Star Is Born*. See Ron Haver, *A Star Is Born* (N.Y., Knopf, 1988) p. 43.

Colleen made six sound films, but flappers were out of style, and she separated herself from Hollywood, too. She had begun a super-elaborate hobby, known as Colleen Moore's Doll House, which now became a touring event to benefit crippled children. She found this deeply satisfying and after two years her sincere motive for service led her directly to a happy marriage with a prosperous broker in Chicago. After that for 27 years she cared for her husband and his two children, and worked as board member at the Art Institute, two universities, and a hospital. She outlasted Homer Hargrave, and in her seventies she began to do some traveling around the world (once with her granddaughter) and built a ranch house near Paso Robles in California.[14]

Perhaps the happiest of all the marriages in the silent era, and the longest-lasting, was between Bebe Daniels and Ben Lyon. Both DeWitt Bodeen and Adela Rogers St. Johns agree that Bebe was one of the most popular people in Hollywood, and that Ben had been a leading man for many of the most prominent stars. When they found each other, outsiders doubted it would last. But they were both 29 in 1930, unmarried, ready to settle down. And another thing: they moved away.

Bebe's mother was predominantly Spanish and her father was Scottish, both of them in show business. From infancy she was either on stage or in pictures, and her inheritance perhaps endowed her with versatility. Convent-schooled, she left at 13 to be Harold Lloyd's leading lady in four years of comedy shorts, then switched to DeMille to play wicked ladies in both elaborate and miniscule costumes, and from 1922 to 1928 played all kinds of starring roles at Paramount.[15]

She had been more or less in love with Lloyd, but that was too soon. And she had been much taken with Jack Pickford, but he played bridge too obsessively, drank too much. Then, just as she was about to gamble successfully on a singing role in *Rio Rita*, (1929), she accepted a ring from Ben Lyon. Her cautious, Scottish self required a year's engagement. Adela St. Johns, who had known her since childhood, was a bridesmaid. Her tag line for the occasion: "Ben taught Bebe to fly. Bebe taught Ben to play bridge. And there they were at the altar."

---

14 St. Johns, *op.cit.*, pp. 223-228.
15 Bodeen, "Bebe Daniels," *op.cit.*, pp. 261-265.

Five years later, after a wave of threats in imitation of the Lindbergh child kidnaping—and after an actual attempt to capture the Lyons' baby Barbara—the parents decided to move to England. There they were received with calm kindness and their variety shows were a great success. When the war began, they decided to stay, offering on the BBC a morale-raising comedy series (with guests) and at the Palladium a big show with special seats reserved for servicemen.

After Ben joined the American 8th Air Force, Bebe started a radio series heard in the U.S. called Purple Heart Corner, interviewing the wounded and their doctors and nurses, implying that competence was at work, that faith and prayer were called for. She took that show to France on D-Day-plus-20, the first civilian woman in Normandy, and later to Italy as well. Such services and sacrifices were a natural outcome and a natural support for a strong and happy, loving home.[16]

There is a photograph of Ben and Bebe on the royal receiving line at the end of the war, in which Mrs. Lyon looks every bit as motherly as the Queen of England does. They were there because they had once been movie stars, but they don't look the part. They look like weary and hopeful fiftyish members of the human race, sharing subconsciously the long struggle of wartime and a desire for the blessings of peace.

16 St. Johns, *op.cit.,*, pp. 184, 188-194.

ALEXANDER WALKER
Elinor Glyn and Clara Bow

In a book titled The Celluloid Sacrifice, *(London, Michael Joseph, 1966)*
the film critic for the London Evening Standard *made a serious attempt to*
gauge the importance historically of feminine personalities offering intense
sexual attraction, from Theda Bara to Elizabeth Taylor. An American
paperback version was called Sex in the Movies *(Penguin, 1968). It might*
be looked upon today by beleaguered males as a counter-argument against
feminist studies which claim that the editing of movies has been
characterized by a dominant male "gaze." Walker takes the point of view to
some extent that these women, at least on the screen, were bent upon
victimizing the men.

From pages 33-41, we have a succinct report on the views and influence
of "Madame Glyn," who surely deserves as much attention as any star or
director if we are to examine the choice of screen stories during the silent era.
She expected her female protagonists, in her novels and her film scripts, to be
formidable in their attractiveness. She picked Clara Bow as the prime
example of the magnetism she labeled as "It." For Walker, Bow was more
notable as a personality in motion. (For more on her, see introduction to this
chapter.)

A good example of Glyn's claim that American male actors were dismally
unattractive is the very film Walker offers as exemplifying Clara Bow's
unique talents. Percy Marmont and Ernest Torrence are among the most
preposterous hangdog visages ever seen on the screen. Yet they were
supposed to compete, in Mantrap, *for the "It" girl.*

Nowadays Elinor Glyn is inadequately remembered as the
authoress of *Three Weeks*, an audacious love story when published in
1907, and for her choice of a tiger skin upon which to sin — unless,
as the verse had it, you prefer to err on some other fur. But the
masterly biography by her grandson, Sir Anthony Glyn, reveals a
much more psychologically complex person, a blend of Celtic
dreamer and Gallic cynic, a reader of Arthurian romance and ribald
French fiction, a genuine gentlewoman and a shrewd publicist
whose life-long glorification of romantic love and passionate
adventure may have been encouraged by her early and bitterly
disillusioning discovery that her own marriage was going to provide
her with neither. What Emily Post did for manners, Elinor Glyn did
for love. In her novels and in works of practical advice, like *This
Passion Called Love*, she explained and codified it. According to her
biographer, she believed that "a wife . . . should be elusive,
mysterious, unpredictable so that her husband's hunting instinct
would never be lulled to sleep, later to be reawakened by some new
quarry."[1] This was the de Mille ethic, but without the de Mille

hypocrisy attached to it. By the early 1920s, it was being carried to extremes in films that preached a woman's right not only to keep her husband from taking her for granted, but also to shake him off altogether and live a fully independent sex life.

Elinor Glyn, along with other famous writers, was brought to Hollywood in 1920 by Paramount — to write and advise on films, she thought. She soon found it was only her name that was wanted, "as a shield against the critics," and not till 1923, when she went to Metro-Goldwyn-Mayer, did she become a power in the studios. But she had already made her presence forcefully felt outside them: she used her talent to impinge directly on the American people's love-affair with love. She wrote *The Philosophy of Love* on how to make love last, which sold a quarter of a million copies in the first six months. She gave ten-minute talks on love for £500 a week. She used her celebrity in this sphere to establish herself as an authority on which film stars had what was needed to make them good screen lovers. And she was hard to please. "I had not been long in Hollywood before I discovered that what I had always suspected was true. American men in those days could not make love. Not even the leading actors had any idea how to do it then. One after another screen tests of handsome young American film stars were shown me for approval, but in every case I considered that the performance was lamentable."[2]

Madame Glyn, as she preferred to be known, made it her business to remedy these short-comings. Just as she had taught good deportment to Beverly Hills hostesses, she taught selected stars how to project themselves romantically. She is reputed to have supplied Valentino with his arch little trick of kissing the open palm of a lady's hand, instead of the back of it. She also began testing players for star quality, as her rules defined it. She first looked for the player's general "outline"; and if this was intriguing, she concentrated on some individual feature, generally the eyes. "The true test of a real film actor," she called them in an interview.[3] She made the artists cover up the rest of their faces and express their emotions through their eyes alone. "If they cannot do it, it means they are not thinking their parts and I have no further use for them." She wrote about this personal magnetism in a novella published in 1927 in the magazine *Cosmopolitan*. It was called "It." In that slangy, trend-conscious era, "It" was an idea of simple genius and beautiful generality. America was soon agog to know what "It" was, who had "It" and how to get "It." Madame Glyn readily obliged, and, in articles, talks, interviews and even short instructional films, she defined "It" as "a strange magnetism which attracts both sexes . . .

there must be physical attraction, but beauty is unnecessary." One thing that "It" was not, she insisted over and over again, was sex appeal. "To call 'It' that is nonsense — why even a priest could have 'It'."

But as frequently happens, the idea did not travel as well as the catch-phrase. Sex appeal was what "It" connoted to Hollywood and millions of Americans. "It" boomed with the financial independence of the young female wage-earner who wanted to acquire not social status, but sexual attractiveness to match her spending power. So when Paramount resolved to film "It," which in its original form had been a romantically sombre story of a dynamic businessman and a store girl both of whom had "It," the studio decided to change the mood into light comedy and to make the girl the only one possessing "It." But at least Elinor Glyn, by now well established as an exacting supervisor of the films made from her novels, could still authenticate which of the actresses considered for the part had the genuine "It." She gave her approval to Clara Bow who became, and has ever since remained, the "It" Girl.

Why was Clara Bow selected? To say that Elinor Glyn felt she had "It" is self-evident, but an insufficient explanation. And in the teasing absence of more precise reasons in the Glyn autobiography, *Romantic Adventure*, one must fall back on speculation. Between the romantic novelist of sixty-two and the flapper girl forty years younger there must certainly have been some affinity. Nearly all Elinor Glyn's heroines are projections of her own personality and fantasies; and she had taken great pains when M-G-M were filming *Three Weeks* (1924) to select an actress who resembled her closely in looks, allowing for their age differences, to play the passionate Lady of the book. There was at least one distinctive feature she shared with Clara Bow. Both of them had red hair. In Elinor's childhood, red hair had been considered rather vulgar for a girl and, according to her grandson's biography, had condemned her to play the comic roles in amateur theatricals. In compensation, it would seem, she bestowed red hair on several of her heroines, including the "It" girl. Red-heads in the 1920s, on the other hand, were in fashion and thought to be highly sexed girls: just as black had denoted the vamp of the previous decade, and the sex symbol of the 1930s was to be the platinum blonde.

Some heroines in the Glyn romances had other characteristics of the flapper girl as played by Clara Bow, in particular the eponymous heroine of *The Vicissitudes of Evangeline*, written in 1906, and described by a critic as "cat-like . . . amusing (with) a mixture of wisdom and cunning . . . innocence and precocity and calculated demureness." This novel was later published in America under the title *Red Hair* — though it has nothing to do with the Clara Bow film of the same name written by Elinor Glyn the year after *It* (1927) which justified its title by a scene in early Technicolor.

But there is an even stranger anticipation of Clara Bow, in looks if not temperament, in the frontispiece of *Three Weeks*, representing the strange Lady who, on the rebound from the disappointing marriage, enjoys a romantic interlude with a young English aristocrat. The frontispiece is actually a painting of Elinor's daughter, Margot, now Lady Davson, who recalls it was done from a photograph, perhaps *upon* a photograph, of herself as a "still rather chubby fourteen-year-old, posed and dressed in one of her mother's black chiffon frocks and decorated with emeralds — obedient, but, as one can rather gather, a little sulky!"[4] The painting illustrated one of Elinor Glyn's ideas about personal magnetism; and allowing for the differences in media and mood, the heart-shaped face, meticulously outlined mouth and especially the heavily accentuated eyes all prefigure the looks that Madame Glyn was to approve in Clara Bow twenty years later.

Moreover, Lady Davson states: "It was always part of my Mother's personality-teaching that people emphasised their character and its projection much more by keeping their heads low, and glancing up from under the eyebrows, than by 'sticking their noses in the air'." The pose is perceptible in the *Three Weeks* frontispiece. But it is also a characteristic attitude of Clara Bow's, so common with her as to be almost a tic, except that what she projects is not the long, mesmerizing look of romantic passion, but the enchanting *moue* of the flirtatious flapper.

Clara Bow was born in Brooklyn, in 1905, an only child whose parents were too poor to do more than dress her shabbily. "The worst looking kid on the street," she recalled,[5] and for this reason she avoided playing with the better-dressed little girls and, instead, joined in the boys' games — baseball, football, even boxing. It is possible that her boyish approach to life owes much to this early companionship. Her figure was boyish, too, slender and very flat-chested; and it is not surprising that the critics first noticed her when she was masquerading as a boy in boys' clothes in *Down to the Sea in Ships* (1923), a film in which she got a part because its miniscule budget meant it had to use relative unknowns. She also had a boy's restlessness. Even when she stood still she seemed to be in motion, as if the rhythm of the Jazz Age was galvanizing her bones. "She constantly dances and jiggles while waiting on customers," Adolph Zukor wrote about her in *It*. "There is seldom, if ever, a moment in the entire picture when she is in repose."[6] Her hair was piled capriciously high but came down low on her face emphasising the boyish roundness to which her eyes were in intensely feminine opposition. Flirts' eyes. They revealed large areas of white which were increased by her habit of roguishly looking up at a man from under her brows, or back at him from over her shoulder.

But her highly individual way of projecting sexiness was by touch: she was always touching her man lightly and fleetingly, seldom lingering, as if she found it stimulating to break contact and come again. Through all her flirting runs a hint of playful boxing. It is characteristic of the impatient age she represented that she never went in for the long, premeditated embrace, but would pat a guy on the cheek, chuck him under the chin, fix his tie, brush an invisible speck off his lapel, or ferry a kiss from her lips to his on her finger-tips. For the really big moments, she would leap bodily on to the fellow's lap as if playing leap-frog. She has only to spot an unattached male 100 yards away and she starts freshening her make-up, patting her hair and giving her dress half a dozen more nips and tucks that in the course of a film took on an almost fetishist feeling.

Millions of girls copied her and Clara's roles made identification easy and attractive. After *Black Oxen* (1924), which had the gimmick of her playing a woman of sixty rejuvenated by the current craze of animal glands to look aged twenty, she significantly kept to roles within the average American girl's experience (and pay packet). She was a manicurist, usherette, waitress, cigarette girl, taxi dancer, swimming instructress and salesgirl generally found round the lingerie department. All were roles in the range of promiscuous but legal employment where a girl can flirt with an ever changing male clientele. In these films Clara is lifted out of a milieu familiar to her flapper fans and shown the shopgirl's dream world of high life and wild parties. There she snaps her garters for a reel or two with the cry that embodies the peculiar urge of the 1920s — "So this is freedom!" — and having found it is nothing of the sort her natural goodness restores her to her sweetheart whom she recognizes with the glad cry, "Now I know what a real man is!" Except that she ends up making love to her boss on the giant anchor of his yacht, *It* is this sort of film. But it owes its fame, like *A Fool There Was*, largely to the publicity that heralded it — and "It." (Madame Glyn even appears in it, explaining her invention to Clara's boss at a table in the Ritz.) The film is a good showcase for Clara to display her flirt's repertory; but it was really the part that made her. Simply being designated the "It" Girl gave her a charmed reputation that put her out ahead of a large field of rival flapper types, including Colleen Moore of the Dutch

Boy bob who could claim to be the original screen flapper and who was making $12,500 a week at this date compared with Clara Bow's $2,500. Clara soared higher with the fame, but never did catch up on the pay.

For proof that Clara Bow had talent, as well as a highly publicized personality, one would not turn to *It. Mantrap*, directed by Victor Fleming in 1926, the year before *It*, shows her not only in the hands of a better director than Clarence Badger, but is a far less artificial film and reveals one astonishing aspect of her.

Mantrap is a log-hut community in the Canadian Rockies whose aging store-keeper takes off his apron and goes down to Minneapolis for the first time since 1903 on hearing that "ankles ain't the half of what the girls are showin' now." Finding Clara buffing the customers' nails in a barber's, he impulsively weds her and carries her back to Mantrap, whereupon she instantly begins making eyes at a smart divorce lawyer from New York who is on a hunting trip, and forces him to carry her back to civilization in his canoe. "Madam," he says, with the caginess of his calling, "you must look on me not as a man, but as a means of transportation." The story was by Sinclair Lewis; Percy Marmont and Ernest Torrence play the lawyer and the husband, and Fleming's humour is fresh-squeezed and slightly acid at Clara's expense where she starts prettifying herself on spotting her husband chugging over the lake in pursuit — with a shotgun. She imposes her little teasing tics on the great outdoors as successfully as in her city slicker pictures, even going one better than catching a guy's eye with a wink — she uses her powder-compact mirror to deflect a love-beam from the sun full in his face.

But what one is not prepared for is a love scene in the fir forest when the runaway couple are exhausted. It is an isolated patch of seriousness and for once Clara Bow is directed to act with surprising naturalism. Her hair blowing back softly from a tired face shows a mature, nearly carnal beauty and for a moment or two she resembles a warmly desirable 1920 version of Patricia Neal. For the first time one understands Elinor Glyn's cryptic reference in her autobiography to a tragic side to Clara Bow's talents as an actress. One bitterly regrets not seeing it more frequently employed: when the mood could be induced in her by a director like Fleming, who went on to make *Red Dust* (1932) with Jean Harlow and, of course, co-direct *Gone With The Wind* (1939), then she responded intuitively and with a sudden deepening of personality.

What ended Clara Bow's career was not simply the flat voice revealed by the Talkies. "The unrestrained vitality which had been her great asset was now a curious handicap," Adolph Zukor's memoirs record. "The technicians had not learned to use the microphones as skillfully as they do today, and the players had to manage to stay near one of them, which was likely to be concealed in a bouquet of flowers, without giving the impression that the voice was being aimed into it. Clara was too restless. She would be all over the set, and then, finding that the microphone was not picking up her voice she would sometimes stand and curse it."[7] Moreover the Depression quickly chased her flapper type off the screen; and when she tried a comeback in *Hoopla* (1933) it was as a hard-boiled Mae West type. But with the real Mae West around, anyone else was a two-minute egg at most.

What finished her off decisively was the immaturity of her own personality. Everything happened too quickly for her and she never really got on top of being the "It" Girl sex symbol, so that her words on finally quitting the screen in 1933 sound like those of a run-down clockwork doll: "I've had enough. It wasn't ever like I thought it was going to be. It was always a disappointment." ...

But not long before her death, in 1965, time and the sight of other sex symbols who had come to more tragic ends, had cheered her up sufficiently to look back on her career and offer a revised opinion. "We had individuality," she said. "We did as we pleased. We stayed up late. We dressed the way we wanted. Today, stars are sensible and end up with better health. But *we* had more fun." Even Elinor Glyn herself would hardly have put it more passionately.

Notes

1 Sir Anthony Glyn, *Elinor Glyn* (Hutchinson) p. 75.
2 *Romantic Adventure*, The Autobiography of Elinor Glyn (Ivor Nicholson & Watson), p. 299.
3 *Picturegoer*, April, 1930.
4 Margot, Lady Davson in a private letter.
5 Clara Bow, quoted by Rudy Behlmer, *Films in Review*, October, 1963.
6 *The Public Is Never Wrong*, by Adolph Zukor (G.P. Putnam's Sons), p. 248.
7 Adolph Zukor, *op. cit.*, p. 184.

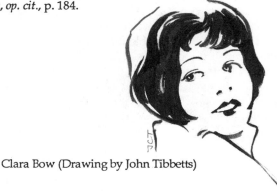

Clara Bow (Drawing by John Tibbetts)

LENNOX SANDERSON JR.
The Great K and A Train Robbery

A lot more presentable than Marmont or Torrence, Tom Mix was still a somewhat segregated star, working in westerns exclusively, first at Selig (1911-1917) and then at Fox (1917-1928). Like other westerns, his pictures tended to have their first runs at second-run houses. He stressed stunts and humor, thus separating himself from the solemnity of William S. Hart. Having learned about the west in the beginning only from working in "wild west" shows, he left movies for three years for a stint with the circus, then did some sound westerns at Universal. He was certainly the screen's archetypal daring American cowboy, with a long string of successes to his credit, when his life ended in an automobile crash.

This review appeared in Frank N. Magill, Magill's Survey of Cinema: Silent Films (1982) pages 505-507.

Released: 1926
Production: William Fox
Direction: Lewis Seiler
Screenplay: John Stone; based on the novel of the same name by Paul
          Leicester Ford
Cinematography: Dan Clark
Length: 5 reels/4,800 feet

Principal characters:	
Tom Gordon	*Tom Mix*
Madge Cullen	*Dorothy Dwan*
Eugene Cullen	*Will Walling*
DeLuxe Harry	*Harry Grippe*
Burton	*Carl Miller*
Bandit leader	*Edward Piel*

In the entire history of the motion picture, there are no other Western stars who have had the lasting appeal of Tom Mix. He made his film debut in 1910 and by the early 1920s, he had no rival as a cowboy star. In 1927, it was claimed that Mix was Hollywood's highest salaried player, and his parties and life-style became legendary. He had no problems starring in vaudeville, and he made an easy transition to talkies. In the 1930s, Mix toured with his Wild Animal Circus. From 1933 through 1950, *The Tom Mix Ralston Straightshooters* was a popular radio series, exploiting Mix, despite the cowboy star's having nothing whatsoever to do with the program. Even in the 1950s, more than ten years after the cowboy's death, Tom Mix gloves were still a popular item in department stores.

Born in 1880 in Clearfield County, Pennsylvania, Mix had a colorful early life if the reports of his publicists and biographers are to be believed. He may have been one of Teddy Roosevelt's Rough Riders, and also may have served in the Spanish-American War and fought in Peking during the Boxer Rebellion. The truth is probably that he never did any of those things, however, except in the imagination of his press agent and his adoring fans. More certainly, Mix did serve time as a real-life cowboy and, at one time, was sheriff of Dewey, Oklahoma, which now boasts a museum in his honor.

Mix made his screen debut in a short entitled *Ranch Life in the Great Southwest*, produced by the pioneering Selig Polyscope Company, and released on August 9, 1910. Shortly thereafter, Mix was put under contract with the Selig forces and remained with them through 1917, starring in dozens of fairly mediocre Western subjects, which are thankfully often relieved by a rough-and-ready humor aimed at the star himself. The Selig films were popular – they had to have been for Mix to remain so long with the company – but they did little to build a screen image for Mix, and certainly during this period, his importance was overshadowed by that of William S. Hart, whose screen *persona* had become very recognizable and pronounced.

In 1917, Mix joined the William Fox Company, and, at last, began to develop into a screen legend. The features boasted action-paced adventure, with touches of ingenious humor, and, in all of them, Mix was partnered by his horse, Tony. Many of the Selig cowboy films had been shot on location in Prescott, Arizona, and because of this experience, Mix preferred to shoot his Fox Westerns away from the confines of the studio, utilizing many of the National Parks of the Western United States.

Of his screen character, a 1927 writer noted,

> In no picture does Tom do the slightest thing to which the most exacting mother could object if copied by her own child. In no picture has he ever been known to take a drink; in no picture has he ever been seen to smoke; in no picture has he ever played a scene showing him gambling with cards or in any way taking unfair advantage of an adversary. In no Mix picture has he ever gained a monetary award. At no time has Mix even been pictured as a rich man in the final scenes. Usually his reward comes in the shape of a promotion to the foremanship of a ranch, a good job, or the hand of some nice girl.

Mix was starred in more than fifty Fox features, of which the most important are *Just Tony* (1922), *Sky High* (1922), *Dick Turpin* (1925), *The Rainbow Trail* (1925), *Riders of the Purple Sage* (1925), and *The Great K and A Train Robbery*. The last, apart from being a vastly entertaining film, is one of a handful of Tom Mix Westerns which has survived, and it has been preserved by the Museum of Modern Art.

In the film, Mix portrays a detective named Tom Gordon, who has been hired to investigate a series of robberies on the K and A Railroad. He boards the train disguised as a bandit, a disguise which does not totally fool Madge Cullen (Dorothy Dwan), the daughter of Eugene Cullen (Will Walling), the president of the railroad, who falls in love with Tom. Madge is loved by her father's secretary, Burton (Carl Miller), but it does not take Tom long to discover that Burton is one of the bandits, and it takes Tom even less time — in this surprisingly short feature — to round up the remainder of the bandits and win Madge's hand. Like so many of the Mix features, *The Great K and A Train Robbery* mixes a variety of elements: Western drama and a railroad mystery. It opens with a magnificent stunt in which Mix is discovered by the train robbers and slides down a rope from the top of a tall gorge right into Tony's saddle. It is as awe inspiring as Douglas Fairbanks' slide down the ship's sail in *The Black Pirate* and several times more daring.

The Great K and A Train Robbery was shot on location in Royal Gorge, Colorado, near the town of Glenwood Springs. As befitted his image, Mix arrived in fine style, in two special luxury Pullman coaches. While there, Mix staged a rodeo, including Roman chariot races and parachute jumps. He also staged a variety show with Dorothy Dwan, often his leading lady, although she is perhaps better known as Larry Semon's wife and leading lady.

It would be wrong to describe *The Great K and A Train Robbery* as a major production, for it most certainly was not. It was simply a typical Mix program picture, which was not even reviewed by *The New York Times*. Those reviewers, however, who did bother to catch it were more than enthusiastic. Sime Silverman, editor and founder of *Variety*, wrote in the October 27, 1926, edition of his paper,

This picture is perfect as a western. . . . Tom Mix, always the great looking guy in a picture, has set a high mark for the "western boys" in this one. They will have to go a lot to approach it in action; and, in fact, Tom will have to do the same to keep up with his record here. *The Great K and A Train Robbery* could safely be billed as the fastest-moving picture ever put on the screen.

Photoplay (December, 1926) commented,

Tom Mix shoots, rides, lassos and loves in a breezier manner than ever before in this ripping Western. Of course Tony helps Tom do all these things -- a Mix picture wouldn't be complete without Tony. The scenery alone in this picture is worth seeing. . . . There's a good evening's entertainment here.

Along with Mary Pickford and one or two others, Mix typified the film star living in high style. His Beverly Hills mansion was the scene of boisterous parties, many of which were perhaps a little rowdier than his screen image would suggest. He was probably the first cowboy star to dress exuberantly, adopting a style later to be copied by Will Rogers, and Mix was particularly proud of his silver saddle and his title "American Champion Cowboy."

As sound came to films, Mix left Fox, moving over to FBO (Film Booking Office) for a series of talkies. He briefly retired from the screen in 1929, but returned to the film industry in 1932 to star for Universal. Mix's screen career ended in 1935 with the Mascot serial *The Miracle Rider*, but the cowboy continued to entertain his fans in person with his circus and rodeo. Mix was killed in an automobile accident near Florence, Arizona, on October 12, 1940.

Of Mix and his contribution to the cinema, film historian William K. Everson has written,

If William S. Hart brought stature, poetry, and realism to the Western, Tom Mix unquestionably introduced showmanship, as well as the slick, polished format that was to serve Ken Maynard and Hoot Gibson in the Twenties and Gene Autry and Roy Rogers in the Thirties. His influence as such outlived that of Hart in the long run.

RICHARD GRIFFITH
The Coward

As type-cast as Mary Pickford or Theda Bara, Charles Ray was for a time almost as popular. Trying to break away, however, from his repeated role as the all-American country boy gaining confidence and overcoming great odds, he left Thomas Ince in 1920 to venture into independent productions. The fifth one was a costume picture, The Courtship of Miles Standish, and he sank all his resources in it. When it failed, he gave a lavish farewell party, auctioned his Beverly Hills house, and managed to make a couple of come-back pictures in his familiar role. But he found himself on the downward track, appearing in a two-reel comedy in 1932 and as a doorman in a 1934 talkie.

This review is from pages 19-20 in a volume called Film Notes, published as a guide to certain films in the collection of the Museum of Modern Art. Griffith (no relation to D.W.) was the first curator of films under Iris Barry, director of the Museum's film department. He was the author of the sections on American films in two histories by Paul Rotha (Documentary Film, The Film Till Now).

1915 *Produced by* Thomas H. Ince *for* Triangle Film Corporation
Directed by Reginald Barker
Cue sheets indicate a running speed of 62½ feet per minute, battle scenes faster 75 minutes
Cast: *Colonel Jefferson Beverly Winslow* Frank Keenan
Frank Winslow Charles Ray   *Mrs. Winslow* Gertrude Claire
Amy Margaret Gibson   *Negro Servant* Nick Cogley
Confederate Commander Charles K. French

Released in November, 1915, as Ince's contribution to the second Triangle program, *The Coward* was primarily designed to introduce to screen audiences the veteran stage star Frank Keenan, one of more than a score of theatrical celebrities whom Triangle had signed at large salaries in an effort to compete with Adolph Zukor's Famous Players. Too old in appearance to play romantic parts (which some of his contemporaries did attempt, with disastrous results), Keenan was fitted with the role of Colonel Jefferson Beverly Winslow, and provided with an effective foil in Charles Ray who, in spite of his youth, had been playing all kinds of parts at the Ince studio for three years. The old stager and the young actor made a popular pair, appearing together in several father-son dramas. Thereafter, Keenan remained a respected character actor while Ray went on to become one of the screen's great stars.

The Coward, like *The Birth of a Nation* earlier the same year, rode the crest of the wave of Civil War films that were produced in enormous numbers between 1911 and 1915. While Ince did not neglect the spectacular aspects of the conflict, he focused primarily on the intimate personal experiences of the people of the South.

At a time when many films subordinated all other elements to movement, *The Coward* makes conspicuous dramatic use of pause, even of immobility, to draw the spectator close to the emotional core of the action. That masterly holding of key scenes, accomplished on the stage by histrionic means, is here achieved by intercutting between multiple camera positions within the same scene.

Such is the genuineness of the characters and their relations to each other that the formula ending seems doubly shocking: contemporary critics, notably Julian Johnson in the December, 1915, *Photoplay*, expressed disbelief in the boy's last-minute heroism after such convincing cowardice. But he recognized the film as a whole for its excellence in the rendering of inner experience. The players seem to project with great intensity, but the rhythm of their performance is actually established by camera angle and by cutting, and it is these that really create the dramatic tension. The resulting seemingly involuntary revelation of unconscious passions is a form of acting unique to the film medium. "Soul-fights" was the period's phrase to describe this and other of Ince's films with Keenan and Ray.

It is of interest that for nearly a decade after this first success, Ray played, to great popularity, what was essentially the same role, that of a youth timidly shrinking from the major experiences of male adulthood, particularly aggression and sex. Two of the films featuring this character, *The Old Swimmin' Hole* (1921) and *The Girl I Loved* (1923), were considered masterpieces in their day; the second now appears to be lost. Like Mary Pickford, Ray found that his public refused to accept him in any other than his standard role. His attempts to change his type, as in the disastrous *The Courtship of Miles Standish* (1923), led a few years later to the end of his starring career.

ESTHER RALSTON
I Become a Star

In her 1985 autobiography, this former Paramount star reported: "At eighty-two I am still earning my own living"--from performance in TV commercials. Her earliest memories of acting were somewhat different: her family toured the northeast from 1911 on, often giving extracts from Shakespeare. And here is a rarity: Esther and her mother were not only provided for by a loving father but protected then and in later years by her four brawny brothers. The family determined to perform all the way across the U.S. in 1916: if they got to Hollywood, Esther's blonde beauty might support them all.

She played an angel in Charlie Chaplin's The Kid, *and after some westerns, she won a contract at Famous Players-Lasky and the part of Mrs. Darling in* Peter Pan. *She had many top roles, ranging in glamor from* The American Venus *(1926) to Josef von Sternberg's* The Case of Lena Smith *(1929). But like Colleen Moore, she married a man who wanted to manage her career. He was helpful to her training as an actress for a while, but he also lost a lot of her money in the stock market crash. All three of her husbands turned out to be dangerous alcoholics.*

The threatening sexual encounters she describes here are not the kind that are often told in print, even today. They are from pages 106-108, under the chapter title as given above, and pages 145-148, under the title "Heartbreak in Hollywood," in her book Some Day We'll Laugh *(Metuchen, N.J., Scarecrow Press, 1985). Note that L.B. Mayer literally sold her off to a second-rate slaveholder--Universal.*

In December, Dorothy Arzner, who had been the script girl on *Ironsides*, came to our apartment for a duck dinner and to discuss the plot of *Fashions for Women*. This film would be my first starring vehicle and Arzner's first directional effort. While we had always been friendly and courteous to each other on *Ironsides*, I didn't suspect the trouble I'd have when we were to work together on *Fashions* [1927].

Now that I was officially a star, I was given an elegant new dressing room and bath, with Clara Bow's dressing room on my right. I was so proud.

On Christmas Eve, George gave me a gorgeous diamond bracelet with a square-cut emerald in the center, and a new Lincoln town car which had just won first prize at the auto show in Chicago. Only two of these town cars were ever built, mine and the one Sue Carol bought. I reveled in at last reaching stardom and riding in the back of this elegant green car with its rabbit-fur lap robe, crystal rose vase, and phone to my chauffeur....

In January of 1927, we started work on *Fashions for Women*. I was to play two roles, the little cigarette girl from the cafe and a "look-alike" older woman, Madame DeGivray. I soon discovered that Dorothy Arzner (Paramount's first woman director) was way ahead of her times. Looking back now, I feel she would have made some sensational "Restricted" movies today, had she lived. But in those days of the Hays censorship, and being conscious of my public image as "Mrs. Darling," I began to resent some of the sexy scenes Arzner was asking me to do. The photographing of my backside and the display of my legs just wasn't me! One day, in rebellion, Arzner and I went to the front office to talk to our producer, Ben Schulberg. We each had our say and, thank goodness, Mr. Schulberg decided that I did not have to do any more suggestive scenes. Arzner never forgave me. . . .

In May, I started *Ten Modern Commandments*, with Neil Hamilton as leading man and again with Dorothy Arzner directing. I was determined to do each scene to the best of my ability but, with Arzner trying to get me to sit on her lap between takes and insisting on patting and fondling me, I began to freeze up and resent her attentions.

In this picture, I was playing a young slavey in a theatrical boarding house, in love with the handsome young composer (played by Neil) who has just written a musical. His opera was to be played on a certain night and the leading lady (played by Jocelyn Lee) suddenly refuses to go on stage to do his play.

I dash to the theater to try to persuade her to go on and when she refuses, I end up choking her, stealing her costume, and going on stage to sing my lover's songs. (It was a good thing this was a silent movie, for I can't carry a tune from here to the door.)

The day we were to shoot the choking scene, ten or twelve of the exhibitors who ran our pictures all over the country came on the set to watch us work. I could just see Arzner chuckling and saying to herself, "Okay, miss smarty pants, swell-headed new star, here's where we find out who's the boss on this set."

During my years at Paramount, I had earned the title of "One Take Ralston" because usually my first take was spontaneous and much the best. However, with those VIP exhibitors watching, Arzner made me do seventeen takes. Between each take, she would tell me (being sure the Exhibitors heard every word) that I wasn't getting the idea. "I want you to put more into this scene."

Finally, with tears of humiliation streaming down my face, I took her by the arms and, slowly and distinctly, said, "I want you to tell me, exactly, what you want me to do, and I will do it. But this will be the last take, period!"

I think Arzner finally realized she had pushed me too far, for she mumbled something about "putting more into it" and went back to the camera.

I almost killed poor Jocelyn, choking her, throwing her on the floor, grabbing her costume and dashing out the back door. Since by this time I was sobbing hysterically and did not relish going back on the set to meet our audience, I started for my dressing room and found myself on the next set, where Pola Negri was doing a dramatic scene in the snow. I crawled on my hands and knees through the fake snow, hoping to avoid being caught by Pola's camera, and raced for my dressing room. And which take do you think was picked for the picture? The first one!

After the picture was finished in June, I went back to New York and had a long talk with Jesse Lasky about Arzner, and I never had to do another film with her again. . . .

On August ninth, the day before Mary's second birthday, George had been sullen and mean to me. I had refused to go out on the road again and told him I was going to stay home and try to get what work I could here in Hollywood. He had been lying on the couch for hours when he suddenly got up and went outside. I was busy preparing for Mary's birthday party the next day and happened to look out the window to see where George had gone. To my horror, I saw him standing in the yard, just below the window, with a gun held against his temple.

I screamed for Nana and she came running in and looked out the window. As I turned to rush out of the room, she grabbed me and said, "Don't you dare go out there! He won't shoot himself. He's just waiting for you to come out and 'save' him again!"

She rocked me in her arms as I sobbed in terror. After about ten minutes with no sound of a shot, George came back in the house, went into the bathroom, and swallowed a whole bottle of aspirin. Again, Nana held me back, and then went into the bathroom and held George's head over the toilet bowl while he threw up all the aspirin.

When he finally emerged, pale and apologetic, I faced him furiously and said, "That's the ninth and LAST time you will commit 'suicide' to torture me. I'm leaving you tomorrow."

The next day, I waited until after Mary's party guests had left, then packed my things and, with Mary and Nana, was driven by my chauffeur, Johnny, in the Lincoln to the Chateau Marmont in Hollywood, where I engaged a suite. I then got in touch with my attorney, Ronald Button, and asked him to start divorce proceedings against George. . . .

While at the Chateau Marmont, Frank and Victor Orsatti, the Hollywood agents, contacted me and told me they could get me a long-term contract at M-G-M, although at the greatly reduced salary of $750.00 a week. Sick with worry over finances, I went with them to see Louis B. Mayer and signed the contract. Mr. Mayer seemed pleased with me and arranged for wonderful publicity, and told me he planned to cast me opposite Clark Gable. Suddenly, I was the "white-haired girl" at M-G-M.

I borrowed ahead on my salary to completely furnish a home for Mama, Papa, and Carleton on Bradbury Road in Cheviot Hills. I even bought a baby grand piano for Carleton. Mama told me later that Carly's face was a study in joyous amazement. Next, I moved Nana, Mary, Sing, Johnny, Blanchy, Marion, and their mother, Mrs. Blanche Frey, with me to a lovely home on Warner and Wentworth in Westwood.

Papa built for Mary's third birthday the most wonderful wooden "walk-in" doll house with windows and a front porch, which we set up in the back yard. What fun I had decorating my new home! *Liberty* Magazine sent photographers to photograph it and do an article about it. I was ecstatic to be "in the chips" again.

Although I hadn't yet been cast in a picture, my days were filled with portrait sittings, interviews, and personal appearances. I was invited to a party at Jean Harlow's lovely home, and one night William Powell invited two of his friends and me to dinner at his home. During the dinner, the Powell butler came over to me and said I was wanted on the phone. Puzzled as to who it could be, I went over to answer it. I was met by a burst of vilification from George. It seems he had followed me to the Powells, and said, "Don't you know Bill Powell is a WOLF. You aren't safe there in his house. Come out at once." I hung up on him and went back to the table.

After dinner, Mr. Powell took us over to the home of Richard Barthelmess to spend the evening. We were ushered into a large bedroom, and since I had never met the the Barthelmess family before, I was startled to see Mrs. Barthelmess calmly ensconced in bed with several large dogs lying beside her. Mr. Barthelmess sat us before a roaring fire and we chatted sociably with him and his wife until it was time to go home.

One night, Mr. Mayer invited me to go with him to attend a big M-G-M preview and, after the show, we went to the Colony Club for refreshments. We sat with Groucho Marx and other famous celebrities, and I also noticed Randy Scott and Claire Trevor at the bar. It seemed that everybody made a fuss over me, and I suppose I didn't have sense enough to realize that people were figuring I was the current "Mayer Favorite" and they'd better be nice to me.

Since I always had Johnny drive me in the Lincoln whenever I went out, we had picked up Mr. Mayer in my car. During the evening, Mr. Mayer kept patting me and trying to put his arm around me. I began to suspect that this kindly "Grandpa" had designs on me, so when he leaned close and whispered in my ear, "Let's leave now, Esther," I replied, "Of course, Mr. Mayer, I'll tell Johnny to bring the car around."

As I passed the bar, I stopped to speak to Randy Scott. "Please, Randy, can I take you home now? Mr. Mayer wants to leave, and . . . "

Randy smiled and said, "Trouble? You think the old man's got ideas?"

"I'm afraid so," I said. "Would you just go sit in my car? I'm going to call Johnny."

Mr. Mayer and I walked out to the car, Johnny opened the door, and when Mr. Mayer saw Randy and Claire sitting there, his face got livid and he climbed in after me without a word. We took him home first and then took Randy and Claire back to the club.

When I arrived at the studio the next morning, I was told to go at once to Mayer's office. He wanted to see me.

"Good morning," I said cheerfully as I entered his office.

Mr. Mayer glared at me and, shaking his finger at me furiously, he shouted, "Think you're pretty smart, eh? Think you fooled me? Let me tell you, I can have any woman on this lot – Joan Crawford and . . ."

I stood up indignantly and interrupted his tirade. "Perhaps you can – any woman but Esther Ralston."

"Just who do you think you are?" he sputtered.

"I thought, Mr. Mayer, I was hired as an actress, but evidently you had other plans for me."

Getting up from his chair, Mayer paced up and down the room, shouting, "You sing your psalms, young lady, and see where you get! I'll blackball you in every studio in Hollywood, and what's more, you'll get nothing here!"

I turned and went and sat in my dressing room and wept with the injustice of it all. From then on, all the "friends" who had made much of me while I was in favor passed me by without a word as though I was some kind of leper. No more lovely publicity, no role with Clark Gable, and so on. I called Frank Orsatti and asked if he had sold me to M-G-M, knowing what I'd be up against, and he said, "Sure, Esther, but I figured you'd be able to take care of yourself."

My six months option was coming up and I knew Mayer would never keep me on. Then I heard that Clarence Brown was going to direct Joan Crawford in *Sadie McKee* and that in the picture there was a wonderful part of a night club singer that was right down my alley. I went into Mr. Brown's office and told him all about Mayer. When I finished my sad tale, Mr. Brown stood up and slammed his fist down on his desk.

"God damn it," he said. "Nobody tells me whom to cast in my pictures. YOU are going to play the part of Dolly!"

Since my option came due in the middle of the picture, of course M-G-M had to keep me on for another six months. However, when I finished *Sadie McKee* [1934], M-G-M "sold" me to Universal for thirteen pictures.

BEN LYON
How I Broke Into the Movies

This is a characteristic page (15) from a fan book edited in 1928 by Hal Herman, in which each of 60 stars offered a full page photograph, a personal signature, and a facing page telling the "story" of the book's title (above). These were no doubt written by publicity people, working for either the star or a studio. But they would have been done in close consultation with the star in the attempt to reflect his or her personality, and some may have been corrected by the source.

The last paragraphs sound like the conscientious and cheerful man Lyon was reputed to be--although he uses the word "fatalist" for what is really a typical American get-ahead optimism. He was quite popular with audiences and in Hollywood and played an important role in Howard Hughes' Hell's Angels. He and Bebe Daniels were married in 1930, and they spent most of their 40 years together in England, before, during, and after the war, doing stage revues, radio programs, and occasional films. Ben reached the rank of lieutenant-colonel in the U.S. 8th Air Force during World War II. (For more on Bebe and Ben, see introduction to this chapter.)

I broke into the movies twice, so there shall be two answers to this apparently popular question.

First of all, I became a veritable "movie nut" from the very first time I saw a picture. I was just a little more than an infant but I kept my mother and dad in a frenzy — always wanting to go to the "pitchers." Even when they refused I cajoled my brother or two sisters into taking me.

This seeming mania for "seeing" the pictures slowly but surely developed into a desire to take part in them — and by the time most boys of my acquaintance were determined to become policemen, firemen or railroad engineers, my ambition, secretly nurtured when the family was around, was to become a movie actor.

When I was fifteen years old, it was decided to send me from our home in Baltimore to New York where my education was to be completed.

This decision on the part of the family met with my hearty approval and I guess the folks were a little surprised at my apparent thirst for knowledge. However it cheered them to know I was going to be a studious youth but they little suspected that deep down in my heart was a nefarious plan.

Quite a bit of the movie center was still in New York — that is, the studios — and I was leaving home with no desire whatever, except to "get in pictures."

Luck was with me for I had not been in New York two days when I saw my first opportunity in a sign outside the old Famous Players studio — "Extras Wanted." I walked in and went right to work.

A tough problem loomed on my financial horizon before long as a lot of opportunities were being missed because I had no tuxedo — and to write home for the necessary funds wherewith to purchase one would have resulted in a lot of conjecture as to how, when and why formal or semiformal dress was required at school.

I finally hired one for three dollars a day, but since my daily check was only five dollars and car fare and lunch money had to be considered it wasn't long before this procedure became a financial fizzle.

The customary hunt of the extra for work went on for two years with little or no progress so in something akin to disgust I went on the stage. I toured the United States in repertoire and stock, an experience which has furnished immeasurable aid in learning poise, expression and best of all — a background.

Then came the goal of all stock players — Broadway and a good part with Jeanne Eagles in *Three Live Ghosts* to be followed by *Mary, the Third* in which Fate took a hand.

Samuel Goldwyn, after attending a performance, sought an interview and in my dressing room said, "My boy, I think you would make a great success in the movies."

I told him I had thought so myself but hadn't had much luck.

He hustled me off to Hollywood where his company was making *Potash and Perlmutter* and I found myself once more before the camera — but not for five dollars a day. From the juvenile lead in that picture I went to an important role in *Flaming Youth* and then a five year contract with the First National company.

So my early childhood hunch wasn't so far from being right at that. It has made me somewhat of a fatalist, this experience; proving to me that even after you think the "breaks" have gone against you, it may only be that you have expected them too soon.

And with the "breaks" one always finds Hard Work waiting right around the corner to take you on the road to Success.

HARRY BRUNDIDGE
Charles Farrell

Totally lacking in acting experience and accompanied only by the disarming shy sweetness that would later win the hearts of moviegoers, Charles Farrell had a harder time getting an extra job in Los Angeles than the more accomplished Ben Lyon did in New York. But with a willingness to "linger behind" after the casting window closed, and later with the aid of a bugle and "a lot of macaroni and canned meat," Farrell got started up the ladder.

Brundidge was evidently a rather short, sobersided, balding fellow from Kansas City, who sold his Hollywood stories to Liberty *magazine. (In a photograph, Gary Cooper looks down on him with a superior smile.) The material he gathered may of course be less than exact, just as press agentry is, and Esther Ralston found she didn't care for some of his embellishments. But he seems to have worked hard in lengthy interviews to get the "real life stories." Jesse Lasky thought enough of him to write an introduction for the collection of pieces E.P. Dutton published in 1930 (Twinkle, Twinkle, Movie Star!, reprinted by Garland Publishing in 1977). Our selection is from pages 149-155.*

Charles Farrell, tall, dark and handsome, and one of the most popular of the screen's male stars, sat with the writer in the livingroom of his beautiful Cape Cod home, "Out of Bounds," on Toluca Lake, a suburb of Hollywood, and the telling of his tale began at 5 P.M. before a crackling log-fire and continued until after 11 o'clock. There had been only one interruption and that came from Alfred, his Malay boy, when dinner was announced. Much of Farrell's story – the real truth about him – has not previously been published.

"There wasn't so much laughter in my boyhood," said Farrell. "I was born in Walpole, Mass., August 9, 1990. My father is David H. Farrell, my mother Mrs. Estelle W. I went to the public school in Walpole where father had a little lunch room, 'The Tiot,' and as soon as I was big enough I began my career in the lunch counter business, as a dishwasher. I sold newspapers besides, and didn't have much time for play.

"We never had much money. When I was ten or eleven the family moved to Onset Bay, Cape Cod. Dad bought a lunch counter and a little motion picture theater there and called the theater 'The New Onset.' Onset, you know, is a suburb of Wareham. As I grew older there was plenty of work for me in the restaurant and at the theater.

"I would come home from high school, change my clothes and hurry down to the restaurant where I'd find a stack of dirty dishes and a note from the old man, 'Wash these dishes.' I'd look at that stack of dishes and think no human could wash them in a day, but somehow I did it.

"Then there would be a couple of water buckets full of potatoes and another note from the old man, 'peel these spuds.' When the vegetables had been prepared I would rush over to the theater, sweep it out, fix the seats, get the tickets ready and then rush back to the lunch counter, put on a white apron and be a waiter until show time. Then I'd grab a bite to eat, go home, change clothes and go to the theater, where I sold tickets. When the show was out I'd go back home and do my school work.

"We did a rushing business at the lunch counter on Saturday and Sunday, and on those days I spent many hours in the kitchen learning to cook and helping with odd jobs. I became an expert short order chef and held the job for several weeks while the old man was looking for a chef to take my place so I could return to school.

"Even in those surroundings I knew I was going to be a great motion picture actor. I never sold a ticket at the theater but what I looked the customer in the eye and said to myself, 'Some day that person will be going to a theater to see Charlie Farrell.'

"I finished high school in 1917 and after much deliberation the family agreed to send me to Boston University for a course in business administration. The old man thought that would be good for me and for him, too, for he never seemed to make any money out of his business enterprises. The money always got away from him. I enrolled in 1917 and remained there four months, but times were hard at home and I left school and went to work in the Hollingsworth and Vose paper mill. I was what is known as a third hand on a machine. It was dangerous business.

"There was scarcely a man in the shop who hadn't lost a finger or two in the paper rollers. I saved enough money to go back to school and returned for the 1918 class.

"As soon as I matriculated I got a job at Ginter's restaurant on Tremont Street, just across from the Boston Common. I was a sort of headwaiter. My job was to stand at the door and be nice to people. I had two assistants and when I would greet a patron, I'd snap a clicker in my hand and one of my assistants would show the hungry person to a seat. I had to be at Ginter's front door at exactly 12 o'clock noon. I finished a class each day at 11:58 and then, hatless, ran all the way down Boylston Street from Copley Square, where the college was located, to the restaurant on Tremont, a distance of about eight blocks. As the clock struck 12 I would be at the door with just enough breath to smile and gasp, 'good afternoon!' I had to work until 1:45 P.M., cram my lunch and dash back to the school for a 2 P.M. class. I was forever in trouble at the restaurant or the college, for I was always late at one or the other. I was paid $4 a week and allowed 75 cents for luncheon and $1.25 for dinner.

"I kept this up until 1922 when I realized that my C-minus total would prevent my graduation. It has always been said that I was graduated, but I wasn't. When I saw what was going to happen I looked about for a job and I got it with 'Little Billy,' the dancing and singing midget. I had not lost sight of my determination to be a motion picture actor and I saw in 'Little Billy' an opportunity to get to Hollywood. I was supposed to be a sort of business manager and secretary for him, but in reality I was nothing more than his valet, just as Alfred here is my 'man.' We moved westward over the Orpheum time, playing Chicago, Milwaukee, St. Paul, Minneapolis and St. Louis, and then, after some smaller towns, in Forth Worth, Tex., I quit cold.

"A girl named Adelaide whom I first met when I was eleven years old and she was thirteen and with whom I had been in love from that time on, was in New Orleans, employed in a hospital. I bought a ticket to New Orleans and saw her. We talked of getting married, but I didn't dare. I then bought a ticket to Los Angeles, rode a chair car and ate fruit for three days while studying a book on 'Facial Expressions.' I knew I was going to be a picture star.

"I arrived in Los Angeles, April 13, 1923, with $18.75, a blue suit, a sport suit of knickers, a pair of shoes, which I wore with the blue suit, a golf bag with some ancient sticks, a cornet, a battered suitcase containing a few shirts, and a paper bundle in which I had some soiled shirts and linens. I had met a couple of acrobats on the train who had been very kind to me and they led the way to a cheap hotel and showed me where I could buy rice for three cents a bowl and coffee for two cents a cup. I took a walk that night and noticed how men were dressed. I didn't think my clothes were so hot, so I invested $4.75 in a pair of two-tone shoes to go with my sport outfit.

"The next morning I started out to conquer screenland. I didn't dare spend carfare, so I walked to Hollywood.

"At a studio casting office I went up to the window, but became so frightened that I couldn't open my mouth, so I walked away. What a sap I was!

"I visited other studios, but just looked. Maybe I was going to have difficulty in getting into the pictures after all!

"I returned to my hotel, disconsolate, but set out on my walk back to Hollywood early the next morning.

"On the second day I met a boy who told me about extra players being needed at Famous-Players for *The Cheat*, in which Pola Negri was being starred. I was ordered away from the window of the casting director ten times that day, but on the eleventh trip the man looked at me and said: 'You win.' I worked for three days at $5 a day and that was the biggest thrill of my life.

"I was getting acquainted with a lot of the extra boys who were much excited over a report that a lot of the boys were to be hired at the Chaplin studio at $10 a day. A crowd went over there the next morning. Eddie Sutherland, the director, ordered them all home, but I lingered behind and was hired for three days at $10 a day. Then I got three weeks' work as an extra with Mary Pickford in *Rosita*. Then came *The Ten Commandments*. Someone heard me blow a bugle, and I was sent to Cecil de Mille, who hired me at $10 a day to ride a horse by his side and blow a bugle when he ordered it. That was the signal to start filming and to 'cut.' I worked thirty days and had $300. I rented a little shanty in Laurel Canyon, bought a lot of macaroni and canned meat and spent the rest of the money on clothing. I fed a lot of hungry extras in that shack, too. There was no work for the extras all summer.

"Sometimes I would live two or three weeks on $5 or $7.50. Then I worked in *The Thief of Bagdad*, and then, when things opened up, began to be in demand as an extra because of my $300 wardrobe. This was in 1925.

"Seven or eight months of high-class extra work followed. I turned down $7.50 a day jobs and took only $10 work. Then I began refusing $10 work and holding out for $15. Then I got a small part in *The Wings of Youth*, and when Fox executives saw the 'rushes' (executives look at the film scenes shot just as soon as the negative is developed on all important pictures and these are called 'rushes') I was offered a contract with an initial salary of $150. I said to myself, 'Charlie, you have arrived. You must be good, so hold out for more money,' I did — and lost that contract.

"I loafed until Mack Sennett hired me at $100 a week. He fired me after a couple of weeks. Warner Brothers gave me $75 and let me go after three months. Then I got a part in *A Trip to Chinatown*, after which Fox offered me a contract at $125 a week for the first six months. I accepted and soon after this we made *Seventh Heaven*, the picture that made Janet Gaynor and myself. *Street Angel* followed.

Then came some other fairly good pictures and now Janet and I are making the greatest pictures of our careers."

Charles Farrell is the fire chief of Toluca Lake. Richard (Dick) Arlen, who lives just a half-block away, is the mayor.

"Have you ever been back home?" the reporter asked.

"Yes. I went back to Onset Bay in August, 1927. Dad has three theaters now, and upon my arrival I found that all three were 'in the red.' We made arrangements to show some of my pictures and my personal appearance was advertised. I sold tickets and acted as usher and then made a little speech from the stage, at each of the three theaters. After show-time, I went behind the lunch counter in Dad's restaurant and in two weeks, the theaters and the lunch counter were showing a good profit."

POLA NEGRI
How I Saved the Lubitsch "Touch"

The tone of cheerful backstage hi-jinks in this anecdote reveals that not all the talents imported to Hollywood from Europe were gloomy. Whether this episode happened exactly as recalled in her Memoirs of a Star *(Garden City, N.Y. Doubleday, 1970, pages 243-248) may well be discounted. But what we know of Lubitsch and Negri from other sources makes it all seem likely--a good deal more likely at least than Pola's claim to have had affairs with Chaplin and Valentino.*

A prominent stage and screen star in Poland and Germany, Pola Negri had played Madame du Barry for Lubitsch. This resulted in an offer from Famous Players-Lasky, where her forthright personality became a continuing focus of publicity for years. Until Garbo, she was probably the best known foreign actress on the U.S. screen. Her role as Catherine the Great in Forbidden Paradise *was in 1925. (The title above has been proposed by the present author. See Appendix A.)*

Lubitsch bought the house next to mine on Beverly Drive, and it was natural that we should resume the old Berlin pattern of warmth and shared confidences. He had recently completed *The Marriage Circle* for Warner Brothers and was extremely disappointed by its reception. Although the highbrow critics had acclaimed it, with one of them actually making the first public reference to the celebrated "Lubitsch Touch," it was not doing well at the box office.

Ernie was enough of a pragmatist to know that all of the critical reception in the world counted for nothing in Hollywood if a film did not show a profit in theaters. His characteristic ebullience had been replaced by a depressed cheerless view of his prospects in America. I was very worried about him. A Lubitsch devoid of an antic spirit was something as pitiful to behold as an amputee.

He had helped me through so many difficult periods in the past, that I began desperately to search for some way to repay him. While in this mood, I first came across a copy of Melchior Lengyel's satire on the life of Catherine the Great, *The Czarina*. Before I was half through, I knew that I had found what I was looking for and bounded across the lawn to his house, waving the book in my hand like a victorious banner. "Ernie!" I cried, "Ernie, I've got it!"

He looked up quizzically, as I thrust the book upon him. "This is going to be our next picture. I've got to play Catherine. And you're going to direct me."

He chewed on his ever-present cigar, and the flicker of a smile appeared for the first time in months, but it quickly faded and he became morose again. "It's no use. Lasky will never trust his valuable property to a failure."

"You let me worry about that. They think Swanson has temperament, Valentino is difficult —" I smiled enigmatically. "Well, they haven't seen anything yet."

"What are you going to do?"

"Why, Ernie," I replied reasonably, "I'm going to take your advice and act like a star."

For the next few weeks, nothing that the studio did satisfied me. I returned scripts with the most caustic rejections: I vetoed every director on the lot: there was not a leading man for whom I expressed anything but disdain. They finally asked hopelessly what would make me happy. When I replied that I wanted them to buy *The Czarina* and borrow Lubitsch to direct me in it, their first reaction was that it was impossible. I replied, "You forget, gentlemen. If it were not for Lubitsch I would not be here today. No Lubitsch, no work. I sit out my contract and return to Europe."

My expression must have indicated how serious I was, and they were forced to capitulate. There were no further obstacles. Warners was only too happy to loan Ernie for a Pola Negri film in the hope that it would establish his American reputation, thereby increasing his value to them. As far as Famous Players was concerned, I became as docile as a lamb, fully cooperating with all departments working on the picture that was to be known as *Forbidden Paradise*.

Even before the casting was completed, I was toiling on costume and make-up tests. I had worked with Adolphe Menjou before and was delighted when he was chosen to play the crafty minister. He was an American of enormous savoir-faire who knew all the fine points of his craft and was impeccably professional in his approach to his work.

The only remaining problem was to find the right leading man. Aware that I did not need a big name to support me at the box office, the studio kept suggesting its new contract players who would cost very little money and might conceivably build a following through the screen exposure with me. We tested dozens, but they were all unacceptable. Alexis was a very difficult part that required an actor who could convincingly be ardent, romantic, and, most of all, capable of playing sophisticated comedy.

One evening, as I was getting into my car after an exhausting session of fittings and publicity pictures, Rod La Rocque came sauntering over to me. We had met casually at the studio and I had always found him a most agreeable young man. His dark continental good looks had earned him a place with American moviegoers as a Latin lover. To the more discerning European eye, his amusing combination of high spirits and a carefree manner suggested nothing so much as the typically American male. He said, "You look like you've had a hell of a day."

I smiled wearily. "I have."

"Then why not come for a drive with me? The fresh air will do you good."

"It's a splendid idea," I said, astonished that he would ask.

The time passed very rapidly, as we laughed and joked together, and I was reminded of how pleasant it was to be in the company of a man who was the right blend of nonchalance and attentiveness. As the drive lengthened to include dinner at a little restaurant on the beach, it occured to me that what was most impressive about Rod was that he never tried to be impressive. Boyish and manly, ardent, romantic, amusing – of course! Here was my Alexis.

I told Lubitsch about my casting inspiration, and he immediately agreed, wondering why we had not thought of it before. Everything was falling into place beautifully. We started production on *Forbidden Paradise* in a state of elation, convinced that we were about to add another to our string of successes.

Towards the middle of production, we were setting up for a scene in which I was to run through interminable corridors and down the winding stairway of the magnificent set reproducing the Winter Palace in St. Petersburg. My costume was a heavily brocaded negligee with a long sable-trimmed train. It was perfection in the wardrobe room, but in the context of set and action it was obvious that it would prove unwieldy and possibly dangerous. I turned to

Ernie and said, "If I run down those steps in this, I might fall and kill myself."

"Nonsense," he said in a no-nonsense tone. "You'll manage perfectly."

"Let me change into something without a train. If it catches on the railing, I'll break my neck."

"What's wrong with you? Remember the fall in *Eyes of the Mummy Ma*? We did much more dangerous stunts in Berlin."

"I was younger then."

"Three years younger."

"In those years, I've learned not to take chances." I added slyly, "Besides, my neck is more valuable now."

"Here. Give me that negligee. I'll show you how it's done." He snatched the garment off me and stepped into it. It was like old times. We were fighting on a set again and both enjoying it enormously.

Clad in my stunning creation, puffing on his inevitable cigar, Ernie dashed down the stairs, along the corridor and back again. Returning the costume to me, he remarked, "You see how easy it is?"

The entire company was in hysterics and, stifling my own laughter, I said, "Thank you. You've convinced me. And the cigar is a brilliant 'Lubitsch touch.' So right for Catherine."

During the course of production, Rod and I became very close. It was a relationship much more closely aligned to comradeship than passion. I was fond of him without loving him and, after my experiences with Chaplin, delighted in the unstrained ease with which a man and woman could enjoy each other's company.

I wanted to give Rod a particularly nice present for his birthday but, because we were working so hard, I had no time to shop. Looking through my jewel box, I came upon the loose diamond Charlie had given to me as an engagement present. It had been forgotten ever since that Christmas of our first big row. It would make an elegant present and I sent it to the jeweler where Charlie had originally purchased it, to have it set in a platinum man's ring.

At first, Rod was delighted, but a week later he came storming up in a frenzy, "Did Chaplin give you this stone?"

"It's rude to ask where your presents come from."

"Manners be damned! Charlie's saying that if he catches me wearing it, he's going to knock me down and tear it off my finger. Now, I'll have to beat it every time I see him."

I was amused. "What do you care? You are over six feet tall. You can't be afraid of him."

The implied slight to his manhood was too much and the discussion rapidly degenerated into a heated argument that continued through a big love scene we were filming. Only lip readers could tell what we were actually calling each other during that impassioned screen moment.

A few nights after the fight, I heard a strange noise at my window. At first I thought it was a burglar. It was a well-publicized fact that I wore my own jewels in pictures, and for a film about Catherine the Great there would naturally be a great quantity around the house. I groped in the drawer of my night table for the revolver, which, amusingly enough, I had actually learned to use expertly in the shooting galleries at Venice Amusement Park. I crept silently towards the window and, pointing the gun in the direction of the sounds, shouted, "Don't move, or I'll shoot!"

"For God's sake — don't! It's me — Rod!" He was on a ladder that he had propped against the building. I felt faint with relief and asked weakly, "What are you doing here? Is this a new joke — scaring the wits out of people?"

After calmly climbing into my room he sat on the window ledge and said, "I'm paying a visit."

"Did you ever hear of the front door?"

"Yes. It's the thing that slams shut in my face. This was the only way to make you talk to me again." He pushed the shaft of the gun aside. "Would you please stop waving that thing at me? It makes me nervous. I had to talk to you."

Replacing the revolver in the drawer, I stifled a smile and said sternly, "You took a chance on not talking to anyone again."

He strode over and, taking me in his arms, kissed me gently on the brow. "Am I forgiven?"

"Yes," I murmured.

The Negri-Lubitsch combination triumphed again. *Forbidden Paradise* was acclaimed a masterpiece of sophistication and my best American film to date. What was even more gratifying to me was that it did so much to establish Ernie's reputation as the cinema's most subtle delineator of adult romantic comedy and he went on to make such great films as *Lady Windermere's Fan, The Student Prince, The Love Parade,* and *Ninotchka.*

KEVIN BROWNLOW
Gilbert and Garbo

Brownlow's The Parade's Gone By *(1968), with its many interviews with survivors, is a landmark work for students of the silent era. From a later book,* Hollywood: The Pioneers *(1979), written to accompany a television history of the period, here is a chapter (pages 192-195) which attempts to describe the ups and downs of one of Hollywood's most exotic and puzzling love affairs. (For more on Gilbert see the author's introduction to this chapter.)*

As for the Garbo image--and the critical and popular response to it--there is a very extensive literature attempting to explore and explain it. But that story really belongs to the era of sound. (See Appendix A.)

John Gilbert began in pictures as an extra in Inceville, in April 1915. His career was steady but unspectacular until he joined MGM in 1924. Like Valentino, he soared to fame in a war classic — King Vidor's *The Big Parade* (1925). After the death of Valentino, he inherited his title of The Great Lover. Gilbert also died young, but first he had to endure a most humiliating plunge from popularity.

Gilbert was ambivalent about acting; he loved it, but felt directing was more creative. He worked as an assistant to the great French director Maurice Tourneur, together with a man who would have a decisive role in shaping his career, Clarence Brown. Tourneur wanted to leave his financial backer, Jules Brulatour, to direct independently; Brulatour agreed only on condition that he make one more picture before he went. The drawback was that the star had to be Brulatour's mistress, Hope Hampton, whose acting was even less impressive than her performance at the box-office. Tourneur agreed, but escaped the chore by ordering John Gilbert to direct it.

Brulatour was impressed by Gilbert's work, and sank in his claws; Gilbert was offered an ever increasing sum to make more films with Hope Hampton. Gilbert fought against it, but his every refusal seared Brulatour's pride. . . .

"I arrived at a decision. To hell with this town and to hell with this $1,000 a week. I tore the contract to pieces and scattered it all over Brulatour's office. Then I boarded the Twentieth Century Limited for California. At last I was free! He might sue me, but let him sue me. I discovered that, on that very afternoon, Brulatour had consulted his attorneys regarding the possibility of buying me off for $10,000."

Gilbert reluctantly accepted a role at the Fox studios. He played poor parts in cheap pictures and was miserable. He was rewarded with one or two outstanding productions, but he refused to be browbeaten into any more Fox films. He had heard from Irving Thalberg of the formation of a big new combine – Metro-Goldwyn. Fox released him from his contract, and he signed with Thalberg. At once his fortunes improved. *His Hour*, an Elinor Glyn film directed by King Vidor, brought him acclaim. Thalberg next cast him as Prince Danilo in *The Merry Widow*, against the wishes of the director, Erich von Stroheim. Said von Stroheim: "Gilbert, I am forced to use you in my picture. I do not want you, but the decision was not in my hands. I assure you I will do everything in my power to make you comfortable." Gilbert said he felt utterly humiliated, and at the first opportunity he walked out. "A furious session on the set resulted in my telling him where he could put the Merry Widow. I went into my dressing room and tore off my uniform. Von followed and apologised. Whereupon we had a drink. I apologised to Von and we had another little drink. That disagreement cemented a relationship which for my part will never end."

The Merry Widow made John Gilbert famous. "Everywhere I went I heard whispers and gasps in acknowledgment of my presence. 'There's John Gilbert!' 'Hello, Jack!' 'Oh – John!' The whole thing became too fantastic for me to comprehend. Acting, that very thing which I had been fighting and ridiculing for seven years, had brought me success, riches and renown. I was a great motion picture star. Well, I'll be damned!"

At MGM, Gilbert's greatest success was in *The Big Parade*. At first, director King Vidor opposed the idea of the immaculate leading man taking the part of a marine, but Gilbert entered completely into the spirit of the picture and gave a performance that ranks as one of the finest of the entire silent period. "The Big Parade!" wrote Gilbert. "A thrill when I wrote the words. As a preface to my remarks pertaining to this great film, permit me to become maudlin. No love has ever enthralled me as did the making of this picture. No achievement will ever excite me so much. No reward will ever be so great as having been a part of *The Big Parade*. It was the high point of my career. All that has followed is balderdash."

When MGM leased the Astor Theater in New York for the East Coast premier, Jack Gilbert accompanied the film on the train, keeping the transit cases under his obsessive gaze. He asked Leatrice Joy – they were now divorced – to go with him to the opening, but she was advised to go with Valentino instead.

"It so offended me, the thought that anyone would suggest anything like that," said Leatrice Joy, "that I immediately sent an overwhelming telegram to his hotel so he'd be reassured that all I wanted to do in life was go to that opening with him.

"We sat through *The Big Parade* and I cried and my handkerchief was torn to pieces — and his also. It was a very sad evening."

The reviews were unanimous raves. "No such adjectives had been used to describe a movie," wrote Gilbert. "I sat for hours crying and thrilling to the printed phrases. Then I staggered to bed and slept round the clock.

"I had sounded the depths and reached the peak of emotional excitement. I never expect such an experience to occur to me again. And so I say, and please understand, that I have concluded my career in pictures." Written in 1928, before he knew the reaction to his first sound film, the bravado behind those words strikes a chillingly ironic note.

Gilbert's fame reached legendary proportions when the name of another star was linked romantically with his. "I had already started a picture," said Clarence Brown, "and we were trying to get a woman to play opposite John Gilbert. We were up at Arrowhead on our first locations when the studio gave us the okay to go ahead with Greta Garbo. And it just happened that the scenes we started shooting when we got back were the scenes in which Garbo was introduced to Gilbert at the railroad station. From then on, that was the development of their love affair in the picture. I just had a real love affair going for me that you couldn't beat any way you tried."

"It was an explosion," said Adela Rogers St. Johns. "They looked at each other and said all those awful, trite things that we don't say any more. 'Where have you been all my life?' and 'You are everything.' I have never seen two people so violently, excitedly in love. I mean, when she walked through a door — if he was in the room — he went white and took a great long breath and then walked toward her as though he were being yanked by a magnet or something. She had always been rather aloof, but she just adored him, and when they made love scenes together for a movie they had sometimes to be censored a little bit. They were so violently in love they couldn't conceal it."

"She's hard to classify," said Eleanor Boardman. "Because, like Chaplin, she was man, women and child. You can't pigeon-hole Garbo. She was fascinating. Extremely selfish, beautiful, strange. She'd walk around Jack Gilbert's garden perfectly nude, with a dressing gown over her back. She was completely unconscious, being a Swede, and was quite used to it. She was an introvert, but adorable."

Gilbert proposed to Garbo, and she accepted. At the same time, Vidor planned to marry Eleanor Boardman, and they agreed to make it a double wedding. The ceremony was attended by Louis B. Mayer. Garbo failed to appear. "Gilbert was getting very nervous," said Eleanor Boardman, "he was getting rather violent. It seems that Mayer was in the men's room with Gilbert and Gilbert was crying about this situation, and Mayer said, 'Sleep with her, don't marry her.' Gilbert socked him, and knocked him down and he hit his head on a tile. And that was really the beginning of the end of Gilbert's career."

"After Jack had knocked him down," said his daughter Leatrice Gilbert Fountain, "and drawn blood, Mayer said, 'I'll destroy you.' From that point on you can see Jack's career going like this; he is pulling in one direction, and some absolute force is pulling him back."

In 1928, Jack Gilbert signed a contract which made him incredibly wealthy and, as he thought, kept him away from the vindictiveness of Mayer. It ensured that his pictures would be supervised by Thalberg, and the contract had the built-in protection of Nicholas Schenck. Schenck had succeeded Marcus Loew as the power-behind-the-throne at MGM, and he conducted his own private feud with Mayer. Gilbert's contract, at the staggering fee of $1,500,000, represented a severe blow to Mayer's prestige, and it was not an act he could forgive.

By this time, sound was a certainty and all the studios were going over to it, or going out of business. Gilbert's new contract made no provision for a voice test. He gave a public dress-rehearsal in *Hollywood Revue of 1929*, when he played the balcony scene from *Romeo and Juliet* opposite Norma Shearer. There were no complaints from the public, although one review referred to his speech being "too mincing and affected for words." Fortunately, the scene was also played in slang, and the burlesque wiped out the bad impression.

Gilbert had already finished his first sound film when he played this scene. His director was veteran actor Lionel Barrymore (who appeared in the same *Hollywood Revue* as the director). The film was given the risible title of *His Glorious Night*.

When audiences saw and heard Gilbert in a serious love scene, they killed his career with laughter. "It was the problem of an image," said King Vidor. "Valentino had the same image, and I think he would have suffered the same death had he lived. You couldn't put this image into words. If you do, it becomes funny. People are waiting; what was he saying all the time in silent films? They hear him speak and all he says is, 'I love you, I love you, I love you.' They hear these words and laugh."

The idea that Gilbert had a squeaky voice has persisted for years. One theory suggests he was sabotaged by bad recording. We ran *His Glorious Night* for the series, and Gilbert's voice sounded no different to the other talkies in which he appears. It was quite low. The television technicians who saw it with us said he could not have been incorrectly recorded without affecting the other players in the same scene.

The direction, however, was lamentable. Gilbert seemed tense and his eyes constantly stared at the girl during the love scenes. The script was appalling, and worse still was Gilbert's delivery. His enunciation of every line with the correct 'pear-shaped' tones was what aroused the laughter. If only he had been encouraged to relax, and to abandon that dreadful enunciation. . . !

Said *Variety*: "The dialogue is inane. Gilbert's prowess at love-making takes on a comedy aspect that gets them tittering at first, then laughing outright at the very first ring of the couple of dozen 'I love you' phrases designed to climax the thrill in the Gilbert lines."

Recalling his foolhardiness with the Brulatour contract, he refused to walk out of the MGM one. He sat it out, subjected to one poor picture after another, his box-office grosses falling as fast as shares on Wall Street, that desperate autumn of 1929.

Gilbert wanted to avoid any possibility of MGM dropping him for breach of contract, so he religiously attended the studio every day — even when there was no work. Some people were entrusted to make it difficult for him — the gateman sometimes failed to recognise him. There were other attempts at humiliation, aimed at forcing him to quit. But he wouldn't — even though he and Mayer were no longer on speaking terms. Not surprisingly, Gilbert began drinking very heavily. And at last, his contract expired.

Less than a year later, to their intense chagrin, MGM was forced to take Gilbert back again. Greta Garbo insisted on his playing the lead in the 1933 *Queen Christina*. Her motives can only be guessed at; they suggest a generosity rare in the film industry. At first she approved Laurence Olivier, but then she changed her mind. She evidently wanted to do something positive to help her old friend, who had once done so much to help her. It was an outstandingly brave decision, and thanks to director Rouben Mamoulian, it also proved a successful one.

Sadly, the success of *Queen Christina* did little to help Gilbert reconstruct his self-confidence. His last picture was a story in which he played a character the public now strongly suspected him to be — a dissipated, bitter, cynical drunk. In *The Captain Hates the Sea* (directed by Lewis Milestone for Columbia), Gilbert played an ex-Hollywood writer, pushing himself out on a cruise in the hopes of staying off the bottle and starting a new book.

"I think Gilbert was his own most destructive enemy," said Sam Marx. "He did not agree that his voice was wrong for his character. He took to drinking very heavily, and he sort of willed himself to die, in a beautiful place in Beverly Hills, surrounded by some rather attractive women and a lot of empty bottles."

The career of John Gilbert indicates that the star, and the person playing the star, were regarded by producers as separate entities, subject to totally different attitudes. Gilbert, as an ordinary human being, had no legal right to the stardom which was the sole property of the studio. When Gilbert, as an employee, tried to seize control of the future of Gilbert the star, the studio decided that to save their investment from falling into the hands of rivals, they had to wreck their property. Other properties — books, films, sets — were equally ephemeral, and although they had consumed vast amounts of effort, could be destroyed with impunity. But the destruction of a star carried with it the destruction of a person. Producers like Mayer behaved like scrap-yard proprietors, wrecking cars with the drivers still at the wheel. The star system undeniably brought pleasure to millions but it seems somehow abhorrent that it took such tragedies as that of John Gilbert to bring us our entertainment.

L.B. Mayer

DEWITT BODEEN
Flesh and the Devil

A former stage actor, a working screenwriter in the 1940s, and a conscientious chronicler of events and lives in the movie capital (From Hollywood, More From Hollywood) (1976, 1977), Bodeen here reviews the film which first brought Jack Gilbert and Greta Garbo together at Metro-Goldwyn-Mayer. The review appears in Frank N. Magill, Magill's Survey of Cinema: Silent Films, pp. 431-433.

Flesh and the Devil *represents a yearning for dramatic grandeur which was characteristic of the new M-G-M studio as it strove to pull ahead of Paramount in star power just before the sound era.*

Released: 1927
Production: Metro-Goldwyn-Mayer
Direction: Clarence Brown
Screenplay: Benjamin Glazer; based on the novel *The Undying Past* by Hermann Sudermann
Titles: Marian Ainslee
Cinematography: William Daniels
Editing: Lloyd Nosler
Art direction: Cedric Gibbons and Frederic Hope
Costume design: André-ani
Length: 9 reels/8.759 feet

Principal characters:

Leo	*John Gilbert*
Felicitas	*Greta Garbo*
Ulrich	*Lars Hanson*
Hertha	*Barbara Kent*
Pastor	*George Fawcett*
Leo's mother	*Eugenie Besserer*
Count von Rhaden	*Marc MacDermott*

If there had ever been any doubt in the minds of studio executives at M-G-M that Swedish actress Greta Garbo, whom Louis B. Mayer had imported, was a great star, that misgiving vanished after the release of *Flesh and the Devil*, her third film for them. She did not get star billing in the film, having been featured after John Gilbert and Lars Hanson, but she was indubitably the film's central attraction. She did not get star billing, in fact, until her fifth feature for M-G-M, *The Divine Woman* (1927), a picture now lamentably "lost."

Flesh and the Devil was an immediate box-office success, just as were Garbo's first two films in the United States, which had been released in 1926 and which were based upon Vicente Blasco Ibáñez's stories *Torrent* and *The Temptress*.

Flesh and the Devil has the gloss of a fine German classic. It is the story of two upper-class boys, born Leon von Sellenthin and Ulrich von Kletzingk. One day when they are in the company of a little girl with whom they have both grown up, Hertha Prochvitz, they row over to the Island of Friendship, where the boys go through a serious ritual, swearing a blood bond of eternal friendship. The boys continue to be the closest of friends throughout military school, and as the years pass they grow to be everyone's idols. The adult Leo is played by John Gilbert, and Ulrich is played by Lars Hanson.

After graduation, with the young men and their families meeting at the railway station, Leo gets his first glimpse of the woman known as "Felicitas" (Greta Garbo). She smiles when he returns a glove she has dropped, but the carriage drives on, and he believes her to be one of those beautiful out-of-towners invited to the military ball that evening. Leo sees Felicitas again at the ball, and ignores Hertha (Barbara Kent) to go over to Felicitas and ask her for a dance. She dances with him, the camera following them seductively as they turn on the floor. He asks her to go outside with him for a breath of air, and after she assents, the pair is seen in matchlight and the glowing tips of their cigarettes, the first of several entrancing love scenes.

The next time they are seen, they are in her boudoir, and it is obvious that their relationship has become a more intimate one. Her husband, Count von Rhaden (Marc MacDermott), enters unexpectedly, and it is the first time that the audience and Leo know that Felicitas is married. The two men quarrel, and Leo is challenged to a duel publicly because they have quarreled at cards, but actually because Felicitas' husband has caught her in a compromising situation with Leo. The count is killed in the duel, and because he was a man of public importance, Leo is advised to seek five years of military service abroad. At the railway station he begs his friend Ulrich to seek out Felicitas, now a widow of course, and console her in his own absence.

Three years later, Leo is pardoned by the emperor and cannot wait to get home to Felicitas and marry her. On his first visit to her, however, he realizes that Felicitas is now the wife of Ulrich, his friend. Felicitas will not make a decision between the two men; she would be happy if they could go on as a threesome; thus, between the two of them, she would enjoy Ulrich for his wealth and Leo for his love.

When she broaches such a scheme to Leo, he is horrified and is about to strike her when Ulrich enters the room. There are bitter words between the men, and they agree to meet the following morning on their beloved island, now shrouded in snow and ice, to fight a duel with pistols.

Hertha learns of the forthcoming duel and goes to Felicitas to persuade her to intervene. Felicitas suddenly realizes that she might lose both men, and grabbing up a fur coat, she makes her way across the frozen river to the island. As the men take up their positions with pistols and turn to aim and fire, the veil lifts in Ulrich's mind and, aghast, he lets the pistol fall into the snow. At the same time, Leo drops his weapon unfired, and the two men make their way toward each other through the snow, embracing in forgiveness and remembering the vow they had made of eternal friendship.

Felicitas hurries, but the ice breaks, and she falls into the cold water and drowns. After this, there is a brief epilogue, showing that Hertha, now very much a young lady, gets Leo as a lover and husband.

It is a curious triangle because one is captivated at once by the Garbo mystique, and although she is playing a selfish woman of the world, she becomes and remains sympathetic. Leo and Ulrich are only pawns in her game, and she plays them off, one against the other. The weekly *Variety* noted that in Garbo, M-G-M had everything and that "properly handled and given the right material, will be as great a money asset as Theda Bara was to Fox in years past." Garbo never made a film in America for any other studio but M-G-M. From 1926 to 1941, with twenty-five vehicles, she stood at the top, above and beyond all the other M-G-M stars; and she was such in spite of the fact that barely a half-dozen or so of her features were lustrous and worthy of her presence.

Garbo and Gilbert became an immediate "team." After *Flesh and the Devil*, they made three other pictures together: *Love* (1927), a silent version of *Anna Karenina*; *A Woman of Affairs* (1928), a sterilized version of *The Green Hat*; and eventually *Queen Christina* (1933), because Garbo realized that a youthful Laurence Oliver was wrong as a partner for her image and told M-G-M brusquely, "Get Gilbert." They got him, and in spite of Mayer, who loathed him, he had a chance to prove that not only was there nothing wrong with his vocal delivery, but that he also could still carry his part with a great female star. On the screen they were always ideally matched.

They had been lovers in reality too, however briefly. Clarence Brown, the director of *Flesh and the Devil*, once revealed that while making the picture, "they were in that blissful state of love which is so like a rosy cloud that they imagined themselves hidden behind it, as well as lost in it." "Sometimes," he added, "I felt I was intruding on the most private of emotions."

She called him "Yacky," and he called her "Flicka," but when she consented to marry him at a double ceremony, in which the other couple was Eleanor Boardman and King Vidor, Gilbert was on hand, but Garbo had changed her mind, and never showed up. It provoked a brutal physical fight between Mayer and Gilbert, when Mayer muttered a vulgar derogation of Garbo, and Gilbert sprang to her defense at once. Mayer threatened publicly to ruin Gilbert professionally, which he did. It was like a scene in an Adrian-dressed melodrama which M-G-M made so successfully, as written by Adela Rogers St. Johns, a scene about Garbo but without her.

Garbo lives every time one of her films is flashed upon the screen, even though in real life she has been retired since her final film, *Two-Faced Woman,* released in 1941. She was an international star, and when the world was in chaos, she withdrew. One hears of her now walking alone along the streets of Manhattan, sometimes visiting briefly in Hollywood, sometimes in her native Sweden, or taking the sun in some Mediterranean port, but she is usually contentedly alone, despite the intense interest of millions of fans who are still intrigued by her mystique.

She was age thirty-six when she left the screen, and now she has survived more than another thirty-six years as that one woman who lighted up the screens of the world with a living magic that has never shone again.

JOE FRANKLIN
Lon Chaney

From Franklin's illustrated Classics of the Silent Screen *(1959) we draw an account (pages 141-143) of the life and works of a man who was probably the most accomplished make-up artist and character player in U.S. film history.*

A few years ago, in *Man of a Thousand Faces,* Universal told the story of Lon Chaney, with James Cagney playing the famous silent star. It was the best biography of a star ever filmed (I still shudder when I recall the alleged "stories" of Buster Keaton and Pearl White) and apart from some minor errors and too-sweeping generalizations, it was for the most part accurate.

Chaney was a strange man personally — moody, intensely loyal to those he loved, unforgiving to those who had wronged him, and above all, dedicated to his art. His mastery of the art of makeup has never been equalled, let alone surpassed. It was Chaney who wrote the article on makeup in the *Encyclopedia Britannica.* But Chaney's genius — and I use that much-abused word deliberately — went much further than the skilled application of makeup. He was a master pantomimist and actor, much of his sensitivity and understanding deriving from his own childhood. His parents were deaf-mutes, and in order to converse with them and cheer them up, he not only became familiar with sign language, but was also adept at creating, via pantomime, pictures of his little escapades and adventures.

Between 1913 and 1918, Chaney appeared in at least a hundred minor roles, mainly in films for Universal release. During this period he also did some directing, and even wrote scenarios. Thus when he became a top screen name, he was always more than just an actor. He was often as much of a guiding factor behind his films as were the official producer and director. It is not commonly known that many sequences in his films — such as the trial of Esmerelda in *The Hunchback of Notre Dame* — were actually directed by him.

Although in later years, he tended to specialize in the grotesque, Chaney was never just a "horror player." Behind all the makeup, there was usually a tremendous amount of pathos. Without benefit of the spoken word, he would create characters who repelled with *physical* ugliness, yet attracted by the suffering or humanity of their souls.

Chaney's truly marvellous makeups (and the duplications of them in *Man of a Thousand Faces* were but pale shadows of the originals) often involved acute pain through their prolonged distortion of muscles and limbs, yet Chaney steadfastly refused to accept easier, and less convincing, substitutes for the devices he designed. Some of his feats were almost beyond belief; one of the most astounding was in *The Penalty*, in which he played a cripple whose legs had been amputated at the knees. Chaney's legs were bound tightly behind him,giving a completely convincing picture of a man so afflicted. But not content with walking in what must have been excruciating pain, Chaney even gave himself scenes in which he *jumped* from heights and landed on his knees! Chaney's performance as the heavy in a 1918 western, *Riddle Gawne*, was what really brought him to the attention of producers, and he remained forever grateful to director Lambert Hillyer and star William S. Hart for giving him that chance. *The Miracle Man* (in which Chaney played a cripple) followed, and made a star not only of him but also of Thomas Meighan and Betty Compson. *Treasure Island, The Penalty, Oliver Twist* (Chaney's performance as Fagin drew the praise of the critics) and *Victory* were other notable pictures before *The Hunchback of Notre Dame* (discussed at length elsewhere in this book) arrived in 1923 to establish Chaney as one of the half-dozen greats of the silent screen. His performance in that film is still intensely moving and poignant.

Thereafter, with the exception of *The Next Corner* for Paramount, and *The Phantom of the Opera* back at Universal, Chaney made all of his films for Metro. They were all strong, "gutsy" films, but not all were melodramas or thrillers. Films like *The Tower of Lies*, made by the Swedish director Victor Seastrom, and also featuring Norma Shearer, gave him a chance to show what a really fine straight actor he was. For seven of his M-G-M films, Chaney teamed with an old friend who had directed him earlier, Tod Browning. Browning was a master of atmospheric chillers that aimed at far more than the superficial goose-pimple, and he and Chaney made an unbeatable combination for such films as *The Blackbird, The Road to Mandalay, The Unknown, London After Midnight* and *The Unholy Three*. Despite his success in off-beat and somewhat gruesome roles, it was in a straight adventure film, minus any kind of makeup, that Chaney scored one of his biggest hits. This was as the tough sergeant in *Tell It to the Marines* — still one of the most subtle portrayals of its kind, with far more depth than the average current "tough-soldier- with-a-heart-of-gold" performance.

Chaney was dismayed when sound came in. He had a good voice, but he was afraid (and events have proved him right) that talkies would do away with the visual art of pantomime. However, he was persuaded to re-make, in sound, his great silent success *The Unholy Three*, which concerns a trio of weirdly assorted criminals, one of whom (Chaney) is a ventriloquist who masquerades as an old lady. Despite the modifying of some of the stronger elements of the original, and the introduction of added scenes to pacify the now more militant censors, the new *The Unholy Three* was a better film than the old. And it proved to Chaney that, in his case at least, pantomime need not necessarily be killed by the talkie. Audiences were fascinated by his great portrayal, in which he utilized four different voices. Sound, it seemed, would make Chaney a greater star than ever!

All sorts of vehicles were planned for him, including *Dracula*, which, of course, was ultimately done by Bela Lugosi. But a growth in his throat had begun to give him increasing trouble. As usual, he had not spared himself during the shooting of *The Unholy Three*, and undoubtedly the unusual strain on his vocal chords had only aggravated the condition. He entered a Los Angeles hospital, and cancer was diagnosed. He died on August 26, 1930 — in silence. Towards the end, he had been completely unable to speak, and had been forced to return to the sign language and pantomime of his youth.

Chapter 6

Sidelights on the System

I am one of the millions who follow Names from cinema to cinema....I enjoy sitting opposite him or her, the delights of intimacy without the onus, high points of possession without the strain... Directly I take my place, I am on terms with these Olympians; I am close to them with nothing at all at stake. Rapture lets me suppose that for me alone they display the range of their temperaments, their hesitations, their serious depths. They live for my eye.
— Elizabeth Bowen[1]

Admiration and the desire for it are intertwined in the history of the cinema. The fan loves the star, and the star needs love. And when popularity is bestowed on a star it is also shared with other givers, in fan clubs and in letters to the editors of fan magazines.

Soon after star names began to be exploited — that is, about 1910[2] — and feature-length movies began to be produced — about 1912[3] — there was a natural commercial desire to build more comprehensive bridges of loyalty between the movie business and its customers. In addition to paid advertising and publicity stories

1 Elizabeth Bowen was a popular British novelist. She wrote an essay on "Why I Go to the Cinema," for Charles Davy (ed.) *Footnotes to the Film*, (London, Lovat Dickson, 1937) reprinted in Richard Dyer MacCann, *Film: A Montage of Theories*, (1966) p. 241.
2 See introduction to Chapter 2.
3 See MacCann, *The First Tycoons*, (1986) especially pages 92-99, for discussion of the difficulty of establishing dates for the first appearance of feature films in America.

(offered as news) for the newspapers, plus celebrity interviews and trend stories in a few general weeklies, there also began to be a new kind of magazine devoted entirely to films, film making, and stars.

Motion Picture Magazine, Moving Picture World, Motion Picture News — all were contributors to this new apparatus of publicity. At first there were merely story synopses of the films. Then in 1914 James R. Quirk was hired by the creditors of a bankrupt "theater program" in Chicago called *Photoplay*. He built circulation from 13,000 to 500,000 by 1926, and in terms of editorial quality and influence, this monthly became the leading fan magazine of them all.

Quirk had been on newspaper staffs in Boston, Washington, and New York, and he had built new loyalty and circulation for *Popular Mechanics Magazine*. He was a man of strong convictions, unflagging energy, and wide-ranging enthusiasms. One of his innovations was a concern with the contributions of directors and production executives, in addition to star personalities. There were interviews, trend stories, brisk evaluative film reviews, lots of news, and emphatic editorials.[4]

"The motion picture is not a luxury. It is a necessity." So said an editorial in May, 1922, entitled "What Do You Want?" All of you are sharing the new visual culture offered by the screen. But you should "save time" by choosing which movies you really must see. Using the reviews in *Photoplay*, Quirk said, you need only go to the movies we recommend. That was his message, and it gave him power. He claimed two million readers, of whom 25,000 wrote letters every month.

The brief reviews — usually about three paragraphs long under a single still photo from the film — were often written by Quirk himself. Others were by Julian Johnson, later story editor at 20th Century-Fox, or Burns Mantle, future New York theater critic. The pictures chosen for review might also be cited for a "best"performance by leading actor or actress, and at the end of the year the personalities with the most such citations were given special notice on a page of portraits.

4   Terry Ramsaye, *A Million and One Nights*, (1926), p. 682. Also "first draft" chapters in *Photoplay*, October 1924, p. 132, where Ramsaye's history of the movies first appeared. There is more on Quirk by his nephew, Lawrence J. Quirk, and by Richard Griffith in *The Talkies*, (N.Y., Dover, 1971). He died in August 1932, and the magazine was sold to Bernarr Macfadden in 1934, retaining through several editors some of its original quality, but finally becoming a lesser product, along with a lot of other fan magazines, in 1941.

Starting in 1920, Quirk topped off his campaign as arbiter of quality in the industry by giving a *Photoplay* Gold Medal of Honor to the year's "best" motion picture. The first five were *Humoresque, Tol'able David, Robin Hood, The Covered Wagon, Abraham Lincoln.*

Such high-toned awards and comments were accompanied by more popular topics, tailored to appeal to people like Mr. and Mrs. Ed Mauer of Omaha, who were discovered in March 1926 to be the world's champion picture fans. They had gone to the movies every night for eight years. Their favorite stars were Charlie Chaplin, Harold Lloyd, Mary Pickford, Gloria Swanson, and Milton Sills.

A feature published in August 1925, intended to cause controversy, had staff member Herbert Howe choosing the ten most beautiful women on the screen: Pola Negri, Corinne Griffith, May Allison, Florence Vidor, Greta Nissen, Mary Astor, Alice Terry, May McAvoy, Barbara LaMarr, and Nita Naldi. By December 500 newspaper critics had been polled. They accepted seven on Howe's list, but rejected LaMarr, Naldi, and Nissen in favor of Gloria Swanson, Norma Shearer, and Marion Davies.

Then in January 1926, Adela Rogers St. Johns proposed "Ten Handsome Men of the Screen": Richard Barthelmess, John Barrymore, Jack Gilbert, Richard Dix, Ramon Novarro, Reginald Denny, Ben Lyon, George O'Brien, Lewis Stone, and Ronald Colman. She said she also wanted to find in her favorites "strength, cleanness, and intelligence, combined with artistic symmetry of features and body."

By June, Howe had approached Joseph Schenck, producer for his wife, Norma Talmadge. He was willing to propose a list of "real boxoffice stars." The test of a star, he advised, is the ability to bring people in to see bad pictures. His ten top people were: Douglas Fairbanks, Harold Lloyd, Charlie Chaplin, Tom Mix, Rudolph Valentino, Mary Pickford, Norma Talmadge, Gloria Swanson, and Thomas Meighan.

In February of 1926, there was a list of predictions by 100 publicity men (the Western Association of Motion Picture Advertisers) for "baby" WAMPAs stars of the future: Mary Astor, Joan Crawford, Janet Gaynor, Mary Brian, Fay Wray, Dolores del Rio, Dolores Costello.

Up front in the magazine there were usually several full page photos of leading performers, with a few lines about a recent film, or offering good wishes for the next one, observing signs of personal advancement ("Leatrice Joy is Gloria's successor as Cecil DeMille's leading lady," December 1922), or proposing a personality judgment (Thomas Meighan "stands for a certain substantial Americanism.")

Of course there were interviews or speculative stories about individual stars in every issue: "Re-Introducing Miss Davies" (April 1922), "The Mystery Girl of Pictures" (Carol Dempster, July 1925), "The Enigma of the Screen" (Lillian Gish: Is she a genius or a mechanic? March 1926), "Ronald Colman Talks at Last" (January 1926). Often there were strong personal advisories by the editor, commenting on stars' careers and public behavior and on industry policies.

There was always lighter material, including a page answering readers' questions ("Mary Pickford is five feet tall and weighs 100 pounds") and humorous commentary by Herbert Howe or gossipy material written by Cal York (a pseudonym for Quirk himself as writer and editor of contributed material, the by-line referring to both coasts).

One ambitious comic photo-story in April 1925 showed Estelle Taylor in "A Day With a Movie Star," which declared that she gets up before six, does exercises, has a light breakfast, and reads Nietzsche for a while before playing her guitar. A wider lens showed in each case the reality: the clock beside her bed reads 11:00 a.m., her press agent stands by to keep her from falling over on deep knee bends, the breakfast is very fattening indeed, and the press agent has had to deprive her of *Photoplay* to pose with the book, holding his ears soon after as she twangs the guitar.

In March 1923 there was an illustrated feature on bedrooms of the stars: Gloria Swanson, Marie Prevost, Bebe Daniels, Lois Wilson, Tom Mix. A more elaborate spread in the same issue pictured some of the 22 rooms in Gloria Swanson's new house. In April 1926, the set decorator for Paramount's eastern studio suggested ways moviegoers might use the movies to decide on furnishings for their own homes: "A Beautiful Bedroom Means a Beautiful Life."

Acting could be seen to have notable high-rise rewards: In October of 1924, Joseph Schenck celebrated the 8th anniversary of his engagement to Norma Talmadge by giving her the $1,500,000 Talmadge building in the Wilshire district, containing 46 apartments with 8-10 rooms each.

In March 1926, on the other hand, there was a calm article about "the girls who failed" to get ahead in the movies but found success in other film jobs — as scenarist, casting agent, script girl, designer, secretary to a star. April 1926 began the first of three articles on numerology: "Your Name! What Does It Mean to Your Destiny?"

Then there were the advertisements — revealing sidelights on American culture and the yearning for self-improvement. They would have been read and responded to by readers within the industry, as well as by moviegoers. The appeals are not very different from the exercise machines, cosmetics, and diet formulas of our day.

Earle E. Liederman, in January 1923, urged readers to send for a new 64-page book, *Muscular Development*, for ten cents. "I will make you physically perfect....a successful leader of men....a credit to your community." Benny Leonard, lightweight champion of the world, offered a more modest promise: "Why shouldn't you, too, have a glowing, healthy body?"

Besides antiperspirants like "Odorono" (ten cents for a sample) and Listerine's mouthwash prevention of "halitosis," more subtle helps to matchmaking were offered by Psychology Press in June 1925: "What Made Him Propose?" Send ten cents for a new book, *Fascinating Womanhood*. Also: "Do your eyes invite? Darken your lashes with WINX. Ten cents for sample." And finally, "Prove your right to popularity. Play this easiest-to-learn of all saxophones."[5]

Of course advertisements of this sort also appeared in magazines like *Cosmopolitan* and *Colliers* and *Boys Life*. The editors of movie magazines were not out of touch with American civilization. And the Hollywood community — although still on the periphery of what called itself Los Angeles society — was just about as representative of the people of the United States as any other hardworking town and just as protective against immorality and crime.

When Colleen Moore came to the west coast in 1917 for a six-month contract with D.W. Griffith, she and her grandmother had been met at the train by "a sort of studio chaperone."[6] Bessie Love had encountered the very same Mrs. Brown after she was hired by Griffith in 1916, and her autobiography tells of the ordinary kinds of evenings and weekends she and her family had — bicycling, driving around town, going to vaudeville shows, and enjoying ice creams.[7]

5   The author/editor of this book made it a project to try to absorb some of the atmosphere of the time by going through page by page on microfilm the monthly issues of *Photoplay* from 1921 to 1926.
6   Colleen Moore, *Silent Star*, (1968), p. 27.
7   Bessie Love, *From Hollywood With Love*, (1977) pp. 43-45. "The studio had their hands full making a lady of me...Our behavior was governed by the invisible reins of a charm school."

Party pictures survive primarily in private archives, or at least we find more of them in published memoirs than in fan magazines. But the life of Hollywood offscreen got written up from time to time in the gossip columns. Readers can find extensive evidence of Sunday afternoons to which a variety of people (usually within about the same salary range) were invited, and evening masquerade parties at which guests were asked to come as their favorite character. There was dancing midweek at the Hollywood Hotel on Hollywood Boulevard, and dancing after dinner on weekends at the Ambassador Hotel and at more intimate restaurants in Santa Monica, where there also might be contests with prizes for the best couple. There were bridge games at Louella Parsons' house and sometimes at Pickfair. And at private suppers everyone would adjourn to the living room to play the inevitable charades, followed often by the preview of a new film in the lavishly appointed projection room.[8]

Movies were the central excitement of their lives, and it was all new for quite a while. Ninety percent of it was like play practice in high school, with everyone known to everyone else. The main question was: who will be cast in upcoming productions at the studios?

That is why it was such a shock when beloved Wally Reid died trying to kick the drug habit. Similarly, it was hard for all who knew him to believe that Fatty Arbuckle had caused the death of a woman by rape, or that Mabel Normand and Mary Miles Minter had anything to do with the killing of William Desmond Taylor. We now know that Reid's habit was the result of his loyal effort to keep working while in pain. We know that Arbuckle was acquitted, with a special statement of exoneration from the jury. And that the obsessive and jealous mother of Mary Minter undoubtedly shot Taylor. But these unhappy events, together with the less troublesome matter of the Fairbanks-Pickford marriage after they divorced their spouses, convinced a lot of people in the early 1920s that Hollywood was a sink of iniquity.

The company bosses got together and hired Will Hays — a U.S. cabinet member, public relations man, and Presbyterian elder — to represent them and tell the public that things were no worse in Hollywood than in Pittsburgh. "The public never sees Morgan

8   See Kevin Brownlow, "Our Night to Howl," *Hollywood: The Pioneers*, (1979). See also Adela Rogers St. Johns, *Love, Laughter, and Tears*, *passim* especially a section beginning on page 125 with the words, "I am trying to paint for you a picture of the Neighborhood..."

making money or Ford making cars," as Leo Rosten later put it, "but it does see Robert Taylor making faces." When people got in trouble in the movie capital they were not only famous but familiar. That's what made their troubles seem so out of proportion. That's what Will Hays was hired to say, and it was mostly true.[9]

Of course it was true, too, that clowns and stunt men and women and leading ladies who were required to play seductive and emotional scenes over and over — and even upstanding well-groomed handsome men like W.D. Taylor — were likely to be surprisingly excitable, forgetful of propriety, and eager to take attractive risks. So it was not only because showpeople very often couldn't pay their bills that middle class owners of apartments and houses put up the protective sign: "No dogs or actors."[10]

By the end of the silent era, too, it was increasingly a question of numbers and timing. Thousands of aspiring actresses and actors were still swarming into Los Angeles, determined to be lucky, as some had been in the early days. Mary Pickford found this to be a tragic situation. She wrote an article for the monthly magazine, *Good Housekeeping,* in which she warned that "even the exceptionally talented girl of more than ordinary good looks" had little chance of finding a place on the screen. Things had changed. Once upon a time it was possible to become a star by being "at the right place at the right moment." But in the Hollywood of 1930 there was "work for just over 600 players each day" (apart from extras) and to supply that demand there were over 7000 experienced people available.

It was not the end of the moving picture frontier, as it was for the western lands in 1893 when Frederick Jackson Turner announced that the frontier, by definition, no longer existed. There was a great boom coming with sound pictures in the thirties, and another great expansion of production and employment in the 1950s when television spanned the continent. Cable and videotape were still in the future.

But Mary Pickford was right, as she was so often about her beloved movie business. It was the end of an era. The stakes were getting bigger and the complexities of production ever more

---

9   A concise characterization of Hollywood as a desirable "last frontier" — and on the other hand as a target in 1922 and afterward for moral recriminations — can be found in Leo Rosten, *Hollywood: The Movie Colony, the Movie Makers* (N.Y., Harcourt Brace, 1941),pp. 3-31.

10 Such signs were bitterly remembered by many performers — especially in later years when they were themselves wealthy and sought out by society people for contributions to charities.

challenging. So stay away: there was "not much more than one chance in fifty thousand" of getting a job and "not more than one in a quarter million of reaching the first ranks."

Furthermore, "admitting that the rewards at the top are magnificent, none of those who have reached the upper rungs of the ladder but will look back and wonder if they would have the courage to go through the long, hard climb to the top again."[11]

COLLEEN MOORE
Up From the Extra Ranks

Colleen Moore was one of those who rose to stardom by playing the great American game of "work-up." There were times when she wondered why it took so long. But her "extra" days were in Chicago. In Hollywood she started with an advantage: She was there because D.W. Griffith owed a favor to her uncle, a Chicago editor. After several years (1917-1923) of playing supporting roles with Tom Mix and others, she finally knew she had arrived because of one film, Flaming Youth.

Here she counsels extra players to be alert and work hard. But she doesn't say a word about the First National press agent who fell in love with her, helped guide her career, and then almost ruined it.

The selection is from Charles Reed Jones (ed.) Breaking Into the Movies *(N.Y., Unicorn Press, 1927), another interview-style book like the ones by Hal Herman and Harry Brundidge. This one sounds more smoothly impersonal, as if written by people in publicity departments, and is therefore somewhat less convincing. It states the case for something that happened rarely. Loretta Young, who became a top star, did work in extra roles from childhood, but it seems she got her first speaking part because her sister was not available.*

A recent poll of theatre owners throughout the country, conducted by the Exhibitors Herald, one of the leading trade journals of the motion picture industry, placed Colleen Moore first in "box office value." Her rise to this enviable position as the screen's most popular star was not sudden or easy. She served a long apprenticeship with D.W. Griffith and Marshall Neilan, working her way slowly and surely to the top.

Colleen has surmounted the obstacles that beset the path of every aspirant to a screen career. Coming "up from the extra

11 Mary Pickford, "Stay Away From Hollywood," *Good Housekeeping,*
    October 1930.

ranks," herself, her advice has the definite, incontrovertible authority of experience. Colleen is a First National star.

Breaking out of the extra line is more difficult than breaking into it.

I've been in Hollywood since I was fourteen and I've watched and talked with thousands of extra girls. I was an extra girl at the old Essanay studio in Chicago – although most of the time I sat on the bench for extras in the casting office, waiting for a call. . . .

We've just finished filming *Naughty But Nice*, which is a story with a girls' finishing school as its background. The scenes showing the annual prom brought a great many beautiful young extra girls and men on the set. I couldn't help wondering which of these girls would be one of the stars of two or three years from now.

Everyone in Hollywood is an unofficial self-appointed casting director, looking for the new faces that motion pictures must have from time to time. It's a thrilling sort of game, to look through a crowd of people on a set, not knowing which girl or man in the "mob" will have her or his name in electric lights over a thousand theatres a year hence. Later, you say to yourself:

"I knew that girl would make good." Or else someone you hadn't expected to rise above the crowd flashes to success and you wonder why you failed to recognize that person's ability in its cruder state. There are times, too, when someone you were sure had all the requisites remains in the extra line year after year. And you wonder again.

But to get back to the prom scene. Of all the girls gliding gracefully past the cameras I decided that two of them were material that could be developed. Millard Webb, who directed *Naughty But Nice*, was watching, too. It's an unconscious habit all directors have. We didn't compare notes and the chances are that he never even suspected my thoughts or the purpose of my watch.

Each was young with dark hair and blue eyes. Each was graceful and animated. Each possessed the quality, so important for screen success, screen personality.

The day wore on. One girl was all attention. The assistant-director never had to call her name twice to summon her onto the set. Earnestness shone in her eyes. She gave everything she had to the scene. She was as intensely interested as the director himself. The other girl did her work rather well, but indifferently. She had been careless in putting on her makeup and I knew it would be to her disadvantage on the screen. She was never near when the director wanted her – and as everyone in Hollywood knows, time is probably the most expensive element in the making of motion pictures.

You knew if that elusive person, Miss Opportunity, even so much as approached the first girl's neighborhood that she would have no chance to get away. The outcome? Yesterday, Loretta Young, sixteen, the girl who was ready, signed a long term contract with First National. Mr. Webb recommended her for a screen test and, as expected, it turned out well and the contract followed. The other girl? Everyone lost interest in her. There are too many like her knocking at the studio gates.

I don't think extra girls ever had better chances for getting ahead than now. The producers are always searching for starring material and it is only natural that the people who come before their daily scrutiny have an advantage. It is surprising how shortsighted some girls are sometimes.

When a director takes a girl out of a crowd of extras and gives her a piece of "business" to do in a closeup it is opportunity knocking at her door. It means that she will be seen on the screen in the projection room by the company's producer, not merely lost in the crowd. Again and again I have heard girls, thus singled out, first demand that they be assured of additional pay. The additional bit of work might have been worth two dollars and a half more or five dollars more but the opportunity presented to break out of the extra line was worth a thousand dollars.

Eternal vigilance and determination not to give in to discouragement are the greatest friends a girl can have in the struggle to get out of the extra ranks, and once out of them, to continue up the long, rough road. I don't think any girl ever was more determined to succeed in motion pictures than I was – and I'm still trying to climb – but there were a hundred times when I wanted to quit and go home.

Even after I had been playing featured parts, I was turned away by many studios in Hollywood. To use one of Hollywood's favorite phrases, I was "not the type." So you see, I understand discouragement. It is a great enemy and I don't think anybody in the walk of life is immune from its treacherous attacks.

Dan Kelly, who is casting director at the First National studio and who probably knows five thousand extras by sight, if not by name, says that a great many girls have difficulty in keeping out of the rut of extra work.

"At first they are enthusiastic and eager to succeed," he told me. "They are on the set promptly, they are very particular about the appearance of their clothes and their makeup, and they take advantage of every opportunity to further themselves.

"It is inevitable that some of them must wait a long time for opportunity to present itself and many of them become discouraged.

Finally, they are satisfied to obtain merely extra work. Their only worry is whether they are on the next day's call. Their thoughts of getting out of the extra line have practically vanished."

It is true that the very nearness of these girls to the studios sometimes prevents their ability from being seen. It is too close. Many of the best known stars on the screen today were extras a few or several years ago. Any studio could have had them; but fate decreed that they go from one to another until the right time and the right place presented themselves together.

I believe the chance of an extra girl who has real ability is good. It is much more difficult to obtain even extra work now than in the earlier days and as always, in the face of competition, the ability demanded of extra players is much higher. It is a first rate profession for skilled players, not just something that anyone can do. There is a night and day difference between trained and untrained extra players.

With the improved personnel the extra ranks become a better field from which to select those who have in them the qualities that will enable them to become popular favorites.

The chances of breaking out of the extra line are hard but they're there.

HARRY LEON WILSON
Merton of the Movies

Although Charlie Chaplin had adventures Behind the Screen *in 1916,
Wilson's novel (N.Y., Doubleday, 1922) was perhaps the earliest example of
a full-length satire of Hollywood. It was dramatized for Broadway in 1922
by George S. Kaufman and Marc Connelly. Its first film version, with
Glenn Hunter (from the stage production) in the lead and Viola Dana as his
helpful friend, was directed by James Cruze in 1924 for Paramount. (It was
remade in 1932 with Stuart Erwin and in 1947 with Red Skelton.)*

*After the hapless manifestations of fan-frenzy we read about below,
Merton Gill gives up his job in a small town general store and runs away to
Los Angeles, where he is blessed by the encouragement of a pretty girl.
Through her help, after several misfires as an extra player, he gets a role not
unlike that played by his idol, Harold Parmalee. He plays it quite seriously
but discovers at the preview the film is a burlesque. Still, he accepts a
contract--and the girl.*

*The moral is not so much that a kid from the sticks can "make it" in the
movie capital. It is rather that the traditions of comedy in the theater and in
Hollywood are worthy of just as much respect as the solemnities of drama.*
Show People, *with King Vidor directing Marion Davies, offered the same
message in 1928.*

On the boards of the partition in front of him were pasted many
presentments of his favourite screen actress, Beulah Baxter, as she
underwent the nerve-racking Hazards of Hortense. The intrepid girl
was seen leaping from the seat of her high-powered car to the cab of
a passing locomotive, her chagrined pursuers in the distant
background. She sprang from a high cliff into the chill waters of a
storm-tossed sea. Bound to the back of a spirited horse, she was
raced down the steep slope of a rocky ravine in the Far West. Alone
in a foul den of the underworld she held at bay a dozen villainous
Asiatics. Down the fire escape of a great New York hotel she made a
perilous way. From the shrouds of a tossing ship she was about to
plunge to a watery release from the persecutor who was almost
upon her. Upon the roof of the Fifth Avenue mansion of her
scoundrelly guardian in the great city of New York she was gaining
the friendly projection of a cornice from which she could leap and
again escape death — even a fate worse than death, for the girl was
pursued from all sorts of base motives. This time, friendless and
alone in profligate New York, she would leap from the cornice to the
branches of the great eucalyptus tree that grew hard by. Unnerving
performances like these were a constant inspiration to Merton Gill.
He knew that he was not yet fit to act in such scenes — to appear

opportunely in the last reel of each installment and save Hortense for the next one. But he was confident a day would come.

On the same wall he faced also a series of photographs of himself. These were stills to be one day shown to a director who would therupon perceive his screen merits. There was Merton in the natty belted coat, with his hair slicked back in the approved mode and a smile upon his face; a happy, careless college youth. There was Merton in tennis flannels, his hair nicely disarranged, jauntily holding a borrowed racquet. Here he was in a trench coat and the cap of a lieutenant, grim of face, the jaw set, holding a revolver upon someone unpictured; there in a wide-collared sport shirt lolling negligently upon a bench after a hard game of polo or something: Again he appeared in evening dress, two straightened fingers resting against his left temple. Underneath this was written in a running, angular, distinguished hand, "Very truly yours, Clifford Armytage." This, and prints of it similarly inscribed, would one day go to unknown admirers who besought him for likenesses of himself.

But Merton lost no time in scanning these pictorial triumphs. He was turning the pages of the magazines he had brought, his first hasty search being for new photographs of his heroine. He was quickly rewarded. *Silver Screenings* proffered some fresh views of Beulah Baxter, not in dangerous moments, but revealing certain quieter aspects of her wondrous life. In her kitchen, apron clad, she stirred something. In her lofty music room she was seated at her piano. In her charming library she was shown "Among Her Books." More charmingly she was portrayed with her beautiful arms about the shoulders of her dear old mother. And these accompanied an interview with the actress.

The writer, one Esther Schwarz, professed the liveliest trepidation at first meeting the screen idol, but was swiftly reassured by the unaffected cordiality of her reception. She found that success had not spoiled Miss Baxter. A sincere artist, she yet absolutely lacked the usual temperament and mannerisms. She seemed more determined than ever to give the public something better and finer. Her splendid dignity, reserve, humanness, high ideals, and patient study of her art had but mellowed, not hardened, a gracious personality. Merton Gill received these assurances without surprise. He knew Beulah Baxter would prove to be these delightful things. He read on for the more exciting bits.

"I'm so interested in my work," prettily observed Miss Baxter to the interviewer; "suppose we talk only of that. Leave out all the rest — my Beverly Hills home, my cars, my jewels, my Paris gowns, my dogs, my servants, my recreations. It is work alone that counts, don't you think? We must learn that success, all that is beautiful and fine, requires work, infinite work and struggle. The beautiful comes only through suffering and sacrifice. And of course dramatic work broadens a girl's viewpoint, helps her to get the real, the worthwile things out of life, enriching her nature with the emotional experience of her rôles. It is through such pressure that we grow, and we must grow, must we not? One must strive for the ideal, for the art which will be but the pictorial expression of that, and for the emotion which must be touched by the illuminating vision of a well-developed imagination if the vital message of the film is to be felt.

"But of course I have my leisure moments from the grinding stress. Then I turn to my books — I'm wild about history. And how I love the great free out-of-doors! I should prefer to be on a simple farm, were I a boy. The public would not have me a boy, you say" — she shrugged prettily — "oh, of course, my beauty, as they are pleased to call it. After all, why should one not speak of that? Beauty is just a stock in trade, you know. Why not acknowledge it frankly? But do come to my delightful kitchen, where I spend many a spare moment, and see the lovely custard I have made for dear mamma's luncheon."

Merton Gill was entranced by this exposition of the quieter side of his idol's life. Of course he had known she could not always be making narrow escapes, and it seemed that she was almost more delightful in this staid domestic life. Here, away from her professional perils, she was, it seemed, "a slim little girl with sad eyes and a wistful mouth."

The picture moved him strongly. More than ever he was persuaded that his day would come. Even might come the day when it would be his lot to lighten the sorrow of those eyes and appease the wistfulness of that tender mouth. He was less sure about this. He had been unable to learn if Beulah Baxter was still unwed. *Silver Screenings*, in reply to his question, had answered, "Perhaps." *Camera*, in its answers to correspondents, had said, "Not now." Then he had written to *Photo Land*: "Is Beulah Baxter unmarried?" The answer had come, "Twice." He had been able to make little of these replies, enigmatic, ambiguous, at best. But he felt that some day he would at least be chosen to act with this slim little girl with the sad eyes and wistful mouth. He, it might be, would rescue her from the branches of the great eucalyptus tree growing hard by the Fifth Avenue mansion of the scoundrelly guardian. This, if he remembered well her message about hard work.

He recalled now the wondrous occasion on which he had travelled the nearly hundred miles to Peoria to see his idol in the flesh. Her personal appearance had been advertised. It was on a Saturday night, but Merton had silenced old Gashwiler with the tale of a dying aunt in the distant city. Even so, the old grouch had been none too considerate. He had seemed to believe that Merton's aunt should have died nearer to Simsbury, or at least have chosen a dull Monday.

But Merton had held with dignity to the point; a dying aunt wasn't to be hustled about as to either time or place. She died when her time came — even on a Saturday night — and where she happened to be, though it were a hundred miles from some point more convenient to an utter stranger. He had gone and thrillingly had beheld for five minutes his idol in the flesh, the slim little girl of the sorrowful eyes and wistful mouth, as she told the vast audience — it seemed to Merton that she spoke solely to him — by what narrow chance she had been saved from disappointing it. She had missed the train, but had at once leaped into her high-powered roadster and made the journey at an average of sixty-five miles an hour, braving death a dozen times. For her public was dear to her, and she would not have it disappointed, and there she was before them in her trim driving suit, still breathless from the wild ride.

Then she told them — Merton especially — how her directors had again and again besought her not to persist in risking her life in her dangerous exploits, but to allow a double to take her place at the more critical moments. But she had never been able to bring herself to this deception, for deception, in a way, it would be. The directors had entreated in vain. She would keep faith with her public, though full well she knew that at any time one of her dare-devil acts might prove fatal.

Her public was very dear to her. She was delighted to meet it here, face to face, heart to heart. She clasped her own slender hands over her own heart as she said this, and there was a pathetic little catch in her voice as she waved farewell kisses to the throng. Many a heart besides Merton's beat more quickly at knowing that she must rush out to the high-powered roadster and be off at eighty miles an hour to St. Louis, where another vast audience would the next day be breathlessly awaiting her personal appearance.

Merton had felt abundantly repaid for his journey. There had been inspiration in this contact. Little he minded the acid greeting, on his return, of a mere Gashwiler, spawning in his low mind a monstrous suspicion that the dying aunt had never lived.

Now he read in his magazines other intimate interviews by other talented young women who had braved the presence of other screen idols of both sexes. The interviewers approached them with trepidation, and invariably found that success had not spoiled them. Fine artists though they were, applauded and richly rewarded, yet they remained simple, unaffected, and cordial to these daring reporters. They spoke with quiet dignity of their work, their earnest efforts to give the public something better and finer. They wished the countless readers of the interviews to comprehend that their triumphs had come only with infinite work and struggle, that the beautiful comes only through suffering and sacrifice.

At lighter moments they spoke gayly of their palatial homes, their domestic pets, their wives or husbands and their charming children. They all loved the great out-of-doors, but their chief solace from toil was in this unruffled domesticity where they could forget the worries of an exacting profession and lead a simple home life. All the husbands and wives were more than that – they were good pals; and of course they read and studied a great deal. Many of them were wild about books.

He was especially interested in the interview printed by *Camera* with that world favourite, Harold Parmalee. For this was the screen artist whom Merton most envied, and whom he conceived himself most to resemble in feature. The lady interviewer, Miss Augusta Blivens, had gone trembling into the presence of Harold Parmalee, to be instantly put at her case by the young artist's simple, unaffected manner. He chatted of his early struggles when he was only too glad to accept the few paltry hundreds of dollars a week that were offered him in minor parts; of his quick rise to eminence; of his unceasing effort to give the public something better and finer; of his love for the great out-of-doors; and of his daily flight to the little nest that sheltered his pal wife and the kiddies. Here he could be truly himself, a man's man, loving the simple things of life. Here, in his library, surrounded by his books, or in the music room playing over some little Chopin prelude, or on the lawn romping with the giant police dog, he could forget the public that would not let him rest.

Nor had he been spoiled in the least, said the interviewer, by the adulation poured out upon him by admiring women and girls in volume sufficient to turn the head of a less sane young man.

"There are many beautiful women in the world," pursued the writer, "and I dare say there is not one who meets Harold Parmalee who does not love him in one way or another. He has mental brilliancy for the intellectuals, good looks for the empty-headed, a strong vital appeal, a magnetism almost overwhelming to the susceptible, and an easy and supremely appealing courtesy for every woman he encounters."

Merton drew a long breath after reading these earnest words. Would an interviewer some day be writing as much about him? He studied the pictures of Harold Parmalee that abundantly spotted the article. The full face, the profile, the symmetrical shoulders, the jaunty bearing, the easy, masterful smile. From each of these he would raise his eyes to his own pictured face on the wall above him. Undoubtedly he was not unlike Harold Parmalee. He noted little similarities. He had the nose, perhaps a bit more jutting than Harold's, and the chin, even more prominent.

Possibly a director would have told him that his Harold Parmalee beauty was just a trifle overdone; that his face went just a bit past the line of pleasing resemblance and into something else. But at this moment the aspirant was reassured. His eyes were pale, under pale brows, yet they showed well in the prints. And he was slightly built, perhaps even thin, but a diet rich in fats would remedy that. And even if he were quite a little less comely than Parmalee, he would still be impressive. After all, a great deal depended upon the acting, and he was learning to act.

Months ago, the resolution big in his heart, he had answered the advertisement in *Silver Screenings*, urging him to "Learn Movie Acting, a fascinating profession that pays big. Would you like to know," it demanded, "if you are adapted to this work? If so, send ten cents for our Ten-Hour Talent-Prover, or Key to Movie-Acting Aptitude, and find whether you are suited to take it up."

Merton had earnestly wished to know this, and had sent ten cents to the Film Incorporation Bureau, Station N, Stebbinsville, Arkansas. The Talent-Prover, or Key to Movie-Acting Aptitude, had come; he had mailed his answers to the questions and waited an anguished ten days, fearing that he would prove to lack the required aptitude for this great art. But at last the cheering news had come. He had every aptitude in full measure, and all that remained was to subscribe to the correspondence course.

He had felt weak in the moment of his relief from this torturing anxiety. Suppose they had told him that he wouldn't do? And he had studied the lessons with unswerving determination. Night and day he had held to his ideal. He knew that when you did this your hour was bound to come.

He yawned now, thinking, instead of the anger expressions he should have been practising, of the sordid things he must do to-morrow. He must be up at five, sprinkle the floor, sweep it, take down the dust curtains from the shelves of dry goods, clean and fill the lamps, then station outside the dummies in their raiment. All day he would serve customers, snatching a hasty lunch of crackers and cheese behind the grocery counter. And at night, instead of twice watching The Hazards of Hortense, he must still unreasonably serve late customers until the second unwinding of those delectable reels.

He suddenly sickened of it all. Was he not sufficiently versed in the art he had chosen to practice? And old Gashwiler every day getting harder to bear! His resolve stiffened. He would not wait much longer — only until the savings hidden out under the grocery counter had grown a bit. He made ready for bed, taking, after he had undressed, some dumb-bell exercises that would make his shoulders a trifle more like Harold Parmalee's. This rite concluded, he knelt by his narrow cot and prayed briefly.

"Oh, God, make me a good movie actor! Make me one of the best! For Jesus' sake, amen!"

JOE FRANKLIN
Rin Tin Tin

This famous police dog was just about as important for the early fortunes of Warner Brothers as Theda Bara and Tom Mix were for Fox. On page 219 of Franklin's Classics of the Silent Screen *(N.Y., Citadel, 1959) the canine daredevil is given his due.*

In case you think I'm writing this page with my tongue in cheek, let me assure you that I'm *not*. Rin Tin Tin was one of the big box office names of the silent era; indeed, his pictures often saved the day for Warner Brothers, bringing home the bacon in sufficient quantity to pay off the losses on the costly prestige pictures with John Barrymore! And even if box office value weren't enough, Rinty was a good actor too. Moreover, he improved as he went along. In some of his early films, like *Where the North Begins*, you can see him looking to his trainer for direction. He'll go through some action, cock his head around for further signals, and obediently carry on. But in his later films, Rinty was much more sure of himself, going through long and complicated takes without a single fluff.

If you don't think that Rinty could really act, then you haven't seen films like *The Night Cry*, in which he is really put through an emotional wringer. Playing dead or listening at keyholes were elementary to Rinty; in *The Night Cry* he plays one whole scene in full closeup, literally registering hope and sorrow by a drooping of his ears and a moistening of his eyes. The heroine, in the same scene, has to express similar emotions, and Rinty acts her right off the screen. (The lady in question was June Marlowe — a very competent actress otherwise, but no match for her canine co-star!)

Rinty's films were often, admittedly, naive. In *Clash of the Wolves* for instance, he played a dog suspected of being a wolf. To "disguise" him, the hero cleverly fits him up with a false beard! Walking through the mining town, the bearded Rinty is taken for granted.

Nobody spots him, or even pays attention, but ultimately the beard drops off, and then immediately — recognition, and a lynch mob hot on his heels. And this, believe me, was written and played straight and not for laughs!

But for the most part the Rin Tin Tin films were exceedingly well done, full of sure-fire mixtures of action, comedy, and sentiment. Although cheaply made, they were often given production treatment of a high order, with exceedingly fine photographic quality and excellent handling of animal material. Chester Franklin, who worked on the famous *Sequoia* and *The Yearling,* staged many of the animal scenes, and directors included such top-liners as Mal St. Clair and Herman Raymaker. One of the writers most frequently employed was Darryl F. Zanuck! But no matter who the writer was, the basic idea was to give Rinty as many *human* dilemmas as possible. He has to make decisions — whether to rescue his doggie ladyfriend or the heroine was a typical one — and he had to think his way out of situations as well as be something of a canine acrobat!

Rinty was a beautiful animal and looked most docile, except to villains. Actually he wasn't docile, and was apt to take a bite at his co-star — whether it be husky John Harron or little Davey Lee — unless his owner and trainer, Lee Duncan, was around. Duncan, who rescued Rinty from an untimely end in World War I, raised him from a pup and had the dog's undying love and devotion. Nobody but Lee could handle Rinty. The canine star had no difficulty adjusting to the coming of sound, and barked far more dramatically than any of his many imitators. (Strongheart was Rinty's No. 1 rival. Other competitors, like Peter the Great, Napoleon Bonaparte, Dynamite and Lightning, weren't even in the running.)

However, Rinty was near the retirement age when sound came in, and he died, still in harness, shortly after finishing a serial for Mascot. Other Rin Tin Tins followed — all, like the current Rinty, trained by Lee Duncan — but not a one of them were a patch on their ancestor! Rinty never once let his audience down. He was a great star and a grand trouper.

ANTHONY SLIDE
The Fan Magazines

From one of the most prolific and knowledgeable commentators on the silent film era, we have an interview with Adele Whitely Fletcher, who was writing about those days when they were happening. She was editor of Motion Picture Magazine *from 1920.* She recalls her lunch interviews with Theda Bara, who knew the best restaurants, and her attempts to help Clara Bow, who had no social graces. We get a glimpse of the active interest writers like Adele Fletcher and Adela St. Johns must have had in stars who became special friends.

Slide's list of books is lengthy, including The Fan Magazines *(N.Y., A.S. Barnes, 1976), from which this is taken (pages 109-110, 112-113),* Early American Cinema *(1970), and* The Griffith Actresses *(1973). He has been a staff archivist for the American Film Institute and film historian for the Academy of Motion Picture Arts and Sciences.*

Photoplay began publication in 1911, under the managing editorship of Neil G. Caward. Caward was succeeded in 1913 by R.W. Hanford, and, then, with the January 1915, issue, James R. Quirk became vice-president of the Photoplay Publishing company.

James R. Quirk was to guide *Photoplay* until his death in Hollywood on August 1, 1932, at the age of forty seven. He built up *Photoplay* to be the finest film magazine of all time. Serious film criticism may be said to have begun with the introduction of Julian Johnson's "Department of Comment and Criticism on Current Photoplays" in the November 1915 issue. In 1920 the distinguished critic Burns Mantle began reviewing films for *Photoplay*. In the same year, Quirk introduced the Photoplay Gold Medals, the first award going to Frank Borzage's *Humoresque*. Adela Rogers St. Johns was possibly the most influential writer on the film industry, and she was a regular columnist for *Photoplay*.

Tailing just behind *Photoplay* in terms of both quality and popularity was *Motion Picture Magazine*, founded in February 1911 by J. Stuart Blackton and Eugene V. Brewster as *Motion Picture Story Magazine*. (The title was changed with the issue of March 1914.)

Motion Picture Story Magazine was established originally as a publicity organ for the companies comprising the Motion Picture Patents group; J. Stuart Blackton was vice-president of one of the member companies, Vitagraph. The magazine was to publish fictionalized versions of the film releases of the various companies, with each company being allotted equal space.

Gradually, the stock in the publishing company was bought up by Brewster until he eventually not only controlled the magazine, but was also able to launch further publications, notably *Motion Picture Classic, Shadowland,* and *Movie Weekly.* Eugene V. Brewster was quite a remarkable man. Born at Bay Shore, Long Island, on September 17, 1871, he attended Pennington Seminary and Princeton University. In 1906 he published *What To Do with Trusts,* and by the twenties, aside from his film magazines, was publishing biographies of Woodrow Wilson and Napoleon, together with books on art, the theater and finance. He estimated his wealth at three million dollars.

By the late twenties, Brewster had lost control of his empire and was in California, trying to promote his third wife, Corliss Palmer, into a star. He failed, and in August 1931 filed petition for bankruptcy, curiously enough within ten days of his one-time partner, J. Stuart Blackton's filing a similar petition. Eugene V. Brewster died in Brooklyn on January 1, 1939.

Motion Picture Magazine had its team of special writers, in particular Adele Whitely Fletcher, Gladys Hall, and Hazel Simpson Naylor. It must have been the only magazine to admit that many of its contributors also wrote for the periodical under pseudonyms. In the issue of December 1917, it announced that Lillian May was also Lillian Montanye, that Roberta Courtlandt was Pearl Gaddis, and that Peter Wade was really Edwin M. LaRoche.

The fan magazines, as they were once known and once so highly regarded, are gone. The majority of their writers have likewise disappeared, Frederick James Smith, Leonard Hall, Harry Carr, and Harriette Underhill are no more. Their work, however, like that of the filmmakers of whom they once wrote, lives on. As long as there are students and scholars researching the cinema's silent era, the early fan magazines and their writers will never be forgotten.

Adele Whitely Fletcher's first contact with the film industry came in 1916, when she went to work for Vitagraph's publicity department. Some of her first articles appeared in the long-forgotten *Photo-Play Journal,* which, interestingly, published the first writings of Edward Wagenknecht. Miss Fletcher became editor of *Motion Picture Magazine,* with the issue of February 1920, and for that periodical wrote the popular "We Interview" series with Gladys Hall. Since that time, Miss Fletcher has contributed pieces to, and edited, many film magazines, including *Movie Weekly* and *Photoplay.* She lives in New York, and still contributes articles to *Modern Screen* et al.

AS You started with Vitagraph around 1916, I believe?

AWF I did. I went down there. I had to leave school and go to work, and my family got me a job in the Metropolitan Life Insurance Company. Well, at the end of the first week I used to wish that the elevated structure that the subway went on to take me home would collapse, and it would be all over. Finally I was offered a job as secretary to the director of publicity at the old Vitagraph studios, which were not far from where we lived in Flatbush. My grandfather and great-grandfather were theatre people, and my mother had a horror of the theatre. It was feast or famine in her mind. It was incomprehensible to her that I would give up a nice, safe, decent job with a life insurance company, and go and work for the Vitagraph studio. I think she just thought the mark of Cain was on me, and there wasn't much that she could do about it.

Anyway, I loved it. Sam Spedon (Vitagraph's head of publicity) was a rough character, not rough in the sense of ill-bred, but tough, and he said this woman's magazine was very interested in a fashion story, and nobody in the department had been able to do it. These men were newspaper men. They didn't know anything about women's clothes. So, for two or three days, I would eat a sandwich at my desk for lunch, and I did fashion stories, rifling through all the fashion magazines that were available. I put them on Mr. Spedon's desk, and I don't think I've ever known such anxiety or nervousness as waiting for him to pick them up and read them. He said, 'Who wrote this?' I said, 'I did, Mr. Spedon,' and he said 'What the hell are you doing as a stenographer in this department? From now on, you're a writer.' And he raised me $15 a week. I couldn't wait to get home and tell my mother I had done right to go to the Vitagraph studio.

AS What were some of the first stories that you wrote?

AWF You've heard of Anita Stewart? I wrote her 'Talks to Girls.' When I think about it now, I die.

AS From Vitagraph, you went, I believe to Brewster Publications?

AWF I edited *Motion Picture Magazine*. Then I was made editorial director of all the Brewster Publications. When I first went to *Motion Picture Magazine*, Frederick James Smith was editor-in-chief. Then he got very interested in *Shadowland*, and Fred thought he was going to break away from *Motion Picture* with it.

AS Were you involved with the 'Fame and Fortune' contests that Eugene Brewster used to run?

AWF Clara Bow was one of our winners, and Mary Astor. I have always thought that was Mr. Brewster's ploy to bring a lot of attractive girls into the office. I must say he had something to do with the final choice, but you had to investigate these people. You couldn't let anyone win; you didn't know who they were.

Now, Clara Bow's background was horrendous. Her father used to come into the office, and he was practically illiterate. He would smoke the most foul-smelling cigars, and they were always down to nothing when he came in. He was determined that nothing was going to happen to his little rosebud, and that she was going to get all that was coming to her. And her mother was a really crazy woman. I understand she went for Clara once with a carving knife. Well, if you had any sensitivity at all, you were horrified at taking this girl, who was obviously going to win because she photographed like a dream, and throw her to the wolves. I did my best to let her see New York; let her see good places, take her to good plays. I never tried harder in my life to prepare Clara for what was ahead of her. I took her to the Waldorf – the old Waldorf on Fifth Avenue – for lunch, and Clara didn't know what to eat. Her Coney Island background dictated lobster salad as a very elegant thing. Well, she looked at the capers around the edge of the dish, and she must have thought it was some sort of vermin with which she was not yet familiar, because she said, 'Ugh,' and pushed them away with her fork. She was horrified. I can still see that vulnerable, ambitious and driven, and, in a way, sensitive, little figure sitting there.

AS Wasn't Madame Olga Petrova one of the judges of the contest?

AWF I wouldn't say she was involved. She was often there. Now there is a really great woman. She had such drive. I really love Madame; I really do. She and her late husband Lewis Willoughby, used to come and visit us. I had a daughter, who must have been then nine, and she has never forgotten Petrova. She says today she was the most beautiful woman she ever saw in her life.

I was always very fond of Gloria Swanson, and I must say Mary Pickford and Douglas Fairbanks were a highlight in my life. When they'd get to New York, after they'd been travelling, Mary would always get a cold, and what she did was to go to bed so she'd build up some energy. I'd go up and see her, and Douglas would be climbing up the door, showing me some new muscle flex or something. I think when Douglas left her, something very vital went out of her. I think she was never the same again.

AS Did any of the stars at that time resent your writing about them?

AWF No, stars at that time were very eager– not this breed of stars. Mae Murray was very difficult. I did a review of one of her films – I can't think which one it was – but she wrote to Eugene Brewster insisting that I be fired. I was not to be allowed to keep on this way! Corinne Griffith, I knew very well, still do.

AS Is it true that she now claims not to be Corinne Griffith, the star of silent films?

AWF She says her sister was Corinne Griffith, and she died, and that because she was a money-maker, Corinne stepped in. It could be true. I don't know that it isn't true, but I know the Corinne Griffith, who was a very young woman at the Vitagraph studios, and was married to Webster Campbell, is the same Corinne Griffith that I know today. She remembers Vitagraph. Webster Campbell was like so many men who married a star. It satisfies their egos to marry the star, and they can't take it. When Corinne wasn't at the studios, he used to entertain extra girls in Corinne's dressing room. We became close friends because I knew about it, and never told her. She always knew I knew it, and confronted me with it, and from that time on we were very good friends.

AS Which person most impressed you during the silent era?

AWF Theda Bara. She was one of the best informed women that I have ever known. She knew who she was. She was Theodosia Goodman. I think she started my interest in food. She would pick me up in her chauffeur-driven car, and we would go to a place in Jersey where they served beautiful Italian food, then we went to a place out on Long Island, where they did beautiful seafood. Always we'd stop along the road to wherever we were going, and the chauffeur would take out a silver cocktail shaker and we'd have a martini, or maybe one-and-a-half martinis, just enough to whet the appetite, and then we'd go and have our lunch.

AS Did you write for *Photoplay* while James Quirk was alive?

AWF I wrote for Quirk. I loved him. He was a real ripsnorting Irish whiskey-drinking Irishman. You could always tell if he liked what you came in with, because if he did, he'd bring this bottle out of the lower desk drawer, and you would have a snort with him before you left. I had an idea once for a series. 'Beauty, Brains or Luck?' I did it again for *Photoplay* not so long ago. If you can get a gimmick like that, it's amazing the material it evokes that you'll get no other way. Now, I'm doing this series for *Modern Screen* called 'The Tales Their Houses Tell,' and things come out that you'd never get in an interview. I've done Henry Fonda, Doris Day, Sandra Dee, Burt Reynolds, Joan Crawford and Mike Douglas. If you get an idea like that, then you can't fail. However dull the person is you can get something from them – and God knows today they're pretty dull, and deliberately antagonistic and difficult.

AS Tell me how you gave Joan Crawford her name?

AWF I was the editor of *Movie Weekly*, and there was a Winter Garden showgirl, Lucille LeSueur. Harry Rapf of Metro was very interested in her, and he offered a five hundred dollar prize for a name. He had very prestigious judges – oh my – but when it came time to judge they were all very busy, and some of them were not available, and they said to me, go ahead, any name you choose is all right with us. And Joan hated the name at first, hated it.

AS You mention being editor of *Movie Weekly*, which reminds me that much later, you were to become editor of *Photoplay*.

AWF I was editor of *Photoplay* for some years. I re-established the *Photoplay* Gold Medal Awards. We had to do something to remove us from all of the other magazines. I must say the Gold Medals were brought out of hiding on a very grand scale. Gallup Polls made the decisions. I left *Photoplay* to become woman's editor of *The American Weekly*, that must have been about nineteen years ago. That was probably the most enriching experience of my life. That's when I ghosted everything Elsa Maxwell did, first in *Photoplay*, and then in *The American Weekly*.

AS Does it depress you to see the way *Photoplay* has deteriorated through the years?

AWF I couldn't not get depressed. I think when I edited *Photoplay* — maybe this is wishful thinking — it was a young woman's magazine. We had fashion; we had Claudette Colbert doing an advice column; we had personalities; we had millions in circulation. I deplore what is said in motion picture magazines today, let me make that firm, but I can't conscientiously be critical of the editors, because I don't know what in hell they could do.

RUDOLPH MESSEL
Multiplying a Star

> *Here is a waggish version of the peculiar demands of the public on the star's image. It is from pages 169-172 of a little book,* The Film Business, *published by the Benn Company in London in 1928.*

Clara Kimball Young, a star possessed of enormous popularity, and therefore of tremendous S.A., was very cleverly exploited by her backers. There were quantities of Clara Kimball Young pictures, but still there were not enough, and still the public clamoured for more. A picture every two months was not enough, and by all calculations it should have been — but it just wasn't! And there was another drawback, besides that of insufficiency, to the picture-every-two-month programme, and it was this: however often the pictures appeared there was never enough of Miss Young in any of them; never enough to satisfy her admirers, who sat like so many voracious sponges absorbing and absorbing!

The situation was, to put it mildly, difficult. . . . Miss Young was popular; so popular was she, that there was not enough of her to go round. The supply was hopelessly inadequate to satisfy the demand. Now, by all the rules of economics, a demand should create a supply. This, of course, was precisely what had not happened: there had been a supply of Miss Young, wholly adequate at first, which had created the demand. . . .

The public, ever simple, ever trusting, had thought as they were intended to think, that Miss Young was a commodity capable of unlimited multiplication: for all they knew, she might have been a Ford car, or a best-selling novel. The situation was tense: Miss Young, a monopoly, was being demanded as though she were an ordinary everyday commodity! The public must somehow be satisfied; somehow the demand must be faced with an adequate supply. For a demand, if met with no supply at all, or even with an inadequate supply, is apt, after the way of all hungry things when left unsatisfied, to fall into a decline, to sicken, and finally to die. Such was the grim situation which confronted the Clara Kimball Young corporation: a case of *divide et impera* with a vengeance!

The solution to this problem was both simple and effective. . . . It was arranged for Miss Young to play no less than four different parts in the same picture! (It was still only *one* Clara Kimball Young, but there was also a very convincing illusion of multiplication!) Four different parts in the same picture meant, of course, four different stories: four different stories, all necessarily short, and all centering round Miss Young, mostly in close-up. Besides having the advantage of showing four times as much of Miss Young as any ordinary picture could possibly hope to show, this novel device had the advantage of showing Miss Young in at least sixteen different dresses, and in the throes of twice as many different phases of emotion (the average being two dresses per emotion). So the thing of monopoly value was given the appearance of a commodity; it was multiplied to meet the voracious demand for itself. The process was simple, and the film resulting from its application was "The Eyes of Youth." The film told the story of a girl, the daughter of rich parents, who suddenly finds that her father is bankrupt. She finds also four suitors for her hand; one rich, one an impresario desirous of exploiting her voice, a third fairly rich, but with prospects of far greater wealth, and the fourth a young engineer with no prospects apparent. Each of these four suitors is desirous of marrying the lady as soon as possible. The lady herself is in love with the young engineer and at the same time desirous of obtaining the wealth of one or all of the other three suitors. Into this gathering comes a Hindu mystic (note the oriental touch) who shows to the lady in question what will happen to her in the event of her marrying each of the rich suitors. The mystic, one sees, is a man of discrimination, or rather of prescience, for he does not show the life of the lady when married to the young engineer, for that, being a man of prescience, he knows that she will learn for herself! The three demonstrations are effected by means of a crystal. There is a great deal of thrill, a great deal more of Miss Young, and "all's well that ends well," even to the father's ruined business!

The new "Roxy" Theatre on Broadway was opened with a new version of the "Eyes of Youth," retitled "The Love of Sunya," and re-enacted by Gloria Swanson. This new version was in essentials the same as Miss Young's earlier effort. It may, however, be interesting to note that in "The Eyes of Youth" Clara Kimball Young played four parts, while in "The Love of Sunya" Gloria Swanson played five!

This little way of playing dual, triple, quadruple, or quintuple roles is now an established trick of the trade with all really popular stars. The greater the popularity of the star, the more he or she finds it necessary to multiply him or herself! Rudolph Valentino was his own father in "Sons of the Sheik," John Barrymore did the same in "Don Juan"; Conrad Veidt in "The Two Brothers" played both of them and in "The Coast of Folly" Gloria Swanson was her own daughter, and in "The Love of Sunya" she played, as we have seen, five characters almost simultaneously.

Miss Swanson's quintuple rôle holds the record to date with Clara Kimball Young a close second in "The Eyes of Youth!" So far Miss Swanson and Miss Young are the only stars that have found it necessary to do more than double themselves. Miss Swanson has multiplied herself by five, and seems, if anything, rather bettered by the process! Miss Young multiplied herself by four, and apparently the strain was too much for her, for she is no longer making pictures! How, one is tempted to ask, will all this end? Will Gloria continue to multiply, and will Miss Young take up the challenge and, with the aid of the megascope, swell as well as multiply? Will they, as time goes on, play, not five, but fifty-five parts? and is it not possible that the demand, once in danger of death from starvation, will meet an untimely end as a result of overfeeding?

NOTE

1   "The Eyes of Youth" is notable, among other things, as being the first picture in which Mr. Valentino appeared without a moustache.

HERBERT HOWE
Cheers for Deserving People

Having given the first word to Photoplay's *philosophic observer of the Hollywood star system, we might as well allow him the last word, too. Note that he begins his January 1926 holiday greeting (in his column, "Close-Ups and Long Shots") with Marcus Loew, founder and chairman of Metro-Goldwyn-Mayer, whose powerful position was uniquely tempered with humility.*

. . . The following, I feel, deserve a Merrie Christmas and a Happy New Year in the name of humanity, and accordingly I lift a glass to —

Marcus Loew because he's the most lavish patron of art since Pope Julius wrote checks for Michelangelo, for it was from Mr. Loew's pen that "The Four Horsemen" flowed, "Ben Hur," "The Big Parade" and all the glorious Ingram pictures, and because, for all this, he maintains simplicity, kindliness and an open door and is the only person connected with motion pictures whom I've ever heard say, "I don't know a great deal about pictures."

D.W. Griffith, because he's the little father of the motion picture and because his frayed fedora and open-faced watch testify to the fact that he's the only one who has practiced art for art's sake.

Rex Ingram because he discovered the finest actor, married the wittiest woman and made the most beautiful pictures.

Charlie Chaplin because he *is* the motion picture.

Joseph Schenck because he has done right by our Norma and by everyone else who ever had dealing with him, and because, therefore, he is becoming the greatest producing figure in Hollywood.

Adolph Zukor because from the first he has been able to keep his standard flying while all the rest went down to dust.

Harold Lloyd because as a comedian and producer he keeps the world's digestion fit and because as a man his character is ever great enough to meet his achievements.

James R. Quirk because he is the official dragoman to pictures, has all the eccentricities of genius, and pays me money.

Ernst Lubitsch because he illumined the genius of Pola and made two of our finest pictures, and because he's a genius even when throwing confetti for Warner Bros.

Mabel Normand because she is a genius with the greatest heart in the world.

Ramon Novarro because he has genius as an actor and musician, and with it the character of a shining knight, but especially because he supplies me with copy, is the best travelling companion since D'Artagnan and does Ed Wynn, Patricola, Fanny Brice, Harold Lloyd, Alice Terry, Rex Ingram and Ramon Novarro better than they do themselves.

Pola Negri because though she's playing good women in bad pictures she has the character and the genius to reform and become once more a bad woman in good pictures.

Marion Davies because for all the extolling of her talent and beauty, her shining quality is good sportsmanship.

Alice Terry because she glorifies Rex Ingram's pictures and, off screen, contributes wit and wisdom to their creation, and because she does the same for this page -- when she's on the job.

Corinne Griffith because she has been elected the most beautiful woman on earth by a just tribunal and because she's just as charming.

Vilma Banky because she is the most precious find since Pola.

Lillian Gish because she makes me weep with her and not for her and because therefore she is the greatest of tragediennes.

Antonio Moreno because he is a gentleman, a cavalier, and the first of the Latins, and because in "Mare Nostrum" he at last has a chance to prove the fine actor he is.

Douglas Fairbanks because he keeps making them bigger and better without shouting that he's going to.

Mary Pickford because her character, talent and wisdom have earned her the longest record of any star in pictures.

Jesse L. Lasky because he's leaving it up to the director to do his best or worst, and because though he's no more beautiful than other producers, he's easily the easiest to see.

Florence Vidor because as the grand duchess in "The Grand Duchess and the Waiter" she proves a contestant for the title of queen.

Bessie Love because there's no finer actress or sweeter character on the screen, and because she can do the Charleston and look like a madonna (simultaneously and without change of make-up).

Norma Talmadge because she's the wife of Joseph Schenck and vice versa, and will spend every dollar down to her last million to make a fine picture, and because my mother insists that I say she is the screen's most charming actress.

Richard Barthelmess because of *Tol'able David* and *Cheng Huan* and other fine characters and because as an actor and producer he radiates intelligence, breeding and sincerity.

Charles Ray because as a producer he sank on the Mayflower trying to stage a come-back for the pilgrim fathers, and because he's so great as an actor that he's coming to the top again.

King Vidor, because he has never made a bad picture and because, with "The Big Parade," he achieves the level of greatness....

Appendices

Appendix A
Performers in Silent Films

> *You have a Mary Pickford for one role, a Gloria Swanson for another, a Mae Murray for the vivacious girl, a Pola Negri for the intense one, a Barbara LaMarr for the supercivilized artificial beauty, a Nita Naldi for the play which requires a temptress. Each type becomes specialized, so standardized it is strengthened. It becomes an authentic example. . . . The foreign players themselves do it. They call themselves the French Jackie Coogan, the Italian Mary Pickford, the Danish Norma Talmadge. It is the dream of every European actress to come to Hollywood. — Vicente Blasco Ibanez in* Photoplay *July 1924*

The following list of leading performers for the silent screen is not intended to provide complete biographies or filmographies for all the personalities chosen. So far as possible birth and death dates, real names, place of birth, and beginning and ending dates for film careers are included, plus some characteristic films or events in their lives. Of course on these "facts" there may be doubts as to accuracy (especially on dates of birth) but the historian must make a judgment as to the sources available. In the case of major figures, the reader is referred to paragraphs on pages above, to reduce somewhat the inevitable duplications.

Of the 176 players listed below, 40 were born in 20 foreign countries (6 in Canada, 6 in England, 4 in Mexico) and 136 were born in the U.S. Of these 136, 21 were born in 8 southern states, 50 in 10 midwestern states, 53 in 8 northeastern states (including 25 in New York state), and 12 in 5 western states. Of the 176, 97 had had some kind of stage experience.

•

Adoree, Renee (1898-1933). Born Jeanne de la Fonte in France, she was a circus performer with her family from the age of six. Her father left them when she was ten, and mother, brother, and sister continued to tour Europe, escaping to England when the first world war began. She promoted herself as a specialty dancer in London and in Australia, and after her mother's death, in New York. Her first movie role (1920) was at Fox, and she played in three or four pictures every year of the 20s, working at MGM after 1924. Her best known starring part was with John Gilbert in King Vidor's *The Big Parade* in 1925. She died at 35 of tuberculosis. Last film 1930.

Allison, May (1895-). Born in Georgia of a well-to-do and well-known family, she attended schools in Birmingham, Cleveland, and Philadelphia. Her father died when she was 16, and her mother decided that her Southern beauty and lyric soprano voice might be valuable on Broadway. She was very quickly hired, and was at one point understudy to Ina Claire. She began in films as the ingenue in *A Fool There Was* (1915), and her next part was opposite Harold Lockwood, who soon after joined her in 14 films for American Flying "A" in Santa Barbara and eight more directed by Fred Balshofer for Metro release. The romantic pairing of Allison and Lockwood was one of the first in film history, outdistancing Francis X. Bushman and Beverly Bayne at the boxoffice, but by 1917 they began to be cast in separate films because they were too expensive. Her third marriage to James R. Quirk, editor of *Photoplay*, (1926) drew her away from acting and after he died in 1932 she did not return to films. Last films 1927.

Anderson, Gilbert M. (1882-1971). Born Max Aronson in Arkansas, best known as "Broncho Billy," the first screen cowboy hero, from series of 400 one- and two-reelers he directed and starred in, 1907-1914. Looking for a job on the New York stage, he got several roles in Edison's *The Great Train Robbery* and later worked for Vitagraph and Selig. Founded, with George K. Spoor, the Essanay production company in Chicago in 1907, selling out in 1916. Producer and director, 1920s. Special Academy Award, 1957.

Arlen, Richard (1899-1976). Born Richard van Mattimore in Virginia, he attended the University of Pennsylvania and worked as a sportswriter and pilot. His work in motion pictures began in 1920, but he is best known for *Wings* (1927), *Beggars of Life* (1928), and *The Virginian* (1929). He had many supporting roles and leads in sound pictures as a hearty friend or big brother. Last film 1976.

Astor, Mary (1906-1990). Born Lucille Langhanke in Illinois, she was pushed by her German-born father into beauty competitions and into films at 15. Her role opposite John Barrymore in *Beau Brummel* in 1924 made her an important star in five or six films a year for the rest of the decade and active thereafter for years as a worldly and somewhat dangerous type (e.g. *The Maltese Falcon* 1941). Last film 1965.

Ayres, Agnes (1896-1940). Born Agnes Hinkle in Illinois, at 19 she was already an extra in Essanay shorts, including Chaplin's *His New Job* (1915). Of her other starring silents, the most notable were two opposite Valentino, *The Sheik*, (1921) and *The Son of the Sheik* (1926). Her career effectively ended in 1929 except for a brief appearance in 1937.

Baggott, King (1874-1948). Born in St. Louis, he was a stage performer and one of the first film actors to be known by name. He was the escort at the time Carl Laemmle arranged Florence Lawrence's highly publicized "reappearance" as "Imp girl." Starring as early as 1911 in a version of *The Scarlet Letter*, and in 1913 in *Ivanhoe* (a print of which still exists) he was in hundreds of shorts and features. By 1921, when he was well into his 40s, he turned to directing, but in the 30s performed again in character roles. Last film 1941.

Bancroft, George (1882-1956). Born in Philadelphia, he was allowed to be in theatrical productions by his parents, who were not professionals, and in the navy (at 15 and big for his age) he organized a minstrel group. At 20 (after his parents' death) he went into vaudeville as a blackface comedian and for a number of years had important roles on Broadway. His first film was in 1921, and he starred in *Pony Express* (1925) at Paramount and for Josef von Sternberg as the gangster in *Underworld* (1927). Worked steadily in sound pictures (including *Stagecoach*), often as the villain. Retired 1942.

Banky, Vilma (1898-   ). Born Vilma Lonchit and educated in Hungary, acting in films there from 1920, she was brought to the U.S. by Samuel Goldwyn in 1925, then loaned out for roles opposite Valentino in *The Eagle* and *Son of the Sheik*. Her marriage to Rod LaRoque (1927) was handled as a Goldwyn publicity event, but it lasted happily till his death in 1969. Last film, Germany, 1932.

Bara, Theda (1890-1955). Born Theodosia Goodman in Cincinnati, she was the daughter of a prosperous tailor and a mother of Swiss and French descent. "Baranger" was the middle name of her maternal grandfather, and "Theda" was simply short for her real name. From about 18 to 25, she was in the cast of Broadway and touring companies. Looking for work, she was in the office of Frank Powell when he was trying to cast "the vampire" in Fox's *A Fool There Was* (1915). This was such a success that she was afterward in 38 melodramas, a good many of them featuring dominant females, seducing and "destroying" their men. Her first film is apparently the only one to survive, although she essayed also *Romeo and Juliet, Cleopatra, Camille, and Madame DuBarry*. Her career really lasted only through 1919; she undertook some stage work after that and two more films in 1925-26. Her marriage to one of her directors, Charles Brabin, in 1921, was happy and lasted till her death. (See Chapter 2, pages 58-65.)

Barrymore, John (1882-1942). Born John Blythe in Philadelphia, son of stage actors Maurice Barrymore (Herbert Blythe) and Georgiana Drew, younger brother of Lionel and Ethel. At first unwilling to be an actor, he went on as a replacement in support of his sister, and before long was well known on Broadway in his own right. In 1913, he signed with Famous Players-Lasky, playing *Dr. Jekyll and Mr. Hyde* for them in 1920. Known by then as "the Great Profile," he kept up his work on the stage, but moved to Hollywood and to Warners in 1922, where he played *Beau Brummell, The Sea Beast*, and *Don Juan* as the silent era closed. In spite of a growing problem of alcoholism, he was in many sound films through 1941.

Barrymore, Lionel (1878-1954). Born Lionel Blythe (older brother of Ethel and John) in Philadelphia, he was well known on Broadway by 1900, but also entered films at Biograph in 1909, writing and acting for D.W. Griffith. He chose films over theater in 1926, signing with the new MGM, where he stayed for the rest of his time in Hollywood. Known for character roles, he worked in some 250 movies, occasionally directing. Last film 1953.

Barthelmess, Richard (1895-1963). Born in New York City, he attended Trinity College (Conn.) and planned a business career, but was persuaded by Alla Nazimova, a friend of his mother, to take a role in her first movie, *War Brides* (1916). He worked steadily after that and *Broken Blossoms* (1919) and *Way Down East* gave him permanent fame. One other film, made on his own with Henry King directing, added to his stature: *Tol'able David* (1921). Active in a good many sound films, his last was in 1942, when he joined the wartime navy. (See Chapter 2, pages 73-76.)

Baxter, Warner (1891-1951). Born in Ohio, raised in San Francisco by his widowed mother, he dropped out of high school to work and found stage work rewarding. In films from 1917, he worked through the 20s but found fame with his role as Cisco Kid in his first sound film, *In Old Arizona*. Last film 1950.

Beery, Noah (1884-1946). Born in Kansas City, brother of Wallace, he was on the stage from about 1900, on the screen 1917. From *The Mark of Zorro* (1920) to *Beau Geste* (1926) he was perhaps the most serviceable villain of the silent era. He continued to work in less important sound films. Last film 1945.

Beery, Wallace (1885-1949). Born in Kansas City, at 16 he joined the Ringling circus as assistant elephant trainer. For ten years he worked in Kansas City stock and in Broadway musicals. In 1913 he joined the Essanay film company in Chicago, where he met Gloria Swanson; their marriage in 1916, when both were at Keystone, was brief. A heavy in both senses of the word, he also had comic, endearing roles and was a major star in important pictures at MGM in the early sound period. Last film 1949.

Bellamy, Madge (1900-   ). Born Margaret Philpott in Texas, she was the daughter of a professor of English at the University of Texas. On stage at five, she was in Hollywood from 1920, where she starred in thirty or more pictures, notably John Ford's *The Iron Horse* (1924). Last film 1935.

Bennett, Enid (1895-1969). Born in Australia, she came to the U.S. with a touring company and stayed to work in the movies with Thomas Ince in 1914. The most prominent of her roles was with Douglas Fairbanks in *Robin Hood* (1922). She married the director Fred Niblo and retired from the screen in 1926, returning for a few supporting appearances. Last film 1940.

Blue, Monte (1890-1963). Born in Indianapolis, his father was a Civil War veteran and railroad engineer who was killed on the job when his son was five. There were four boys and his mother could barely care for two as washerwoman and nurse. The younger ones went to a state soldiers' orphans home. After eleven years with 900 other boys, the youngest began job-hunting: messenger, railroad fireman, coal miner, cowboy, lumberjack, sailor, hobo, 1906-1912, finally a day-laborer in a movie studio, where D.W. Griffith soon used him as an actor as well as stuntman. Familiar as blunt outdoor actor at first, he was much in demand for a remarkable variety of roles. In 1924 he was in ten pictures, including Lubitsch's sophisticated *The Marriage Circle*, and worked steadily through the 30s and 40s, mainly as a character actor. Last film *Apache* 1954.

Blythe, Betty (1893-1972).   Born Elizabeth Blythe Slaughter in Los Angeles, she attended USC, worked in theater in Europe and New York, and entered films in 1918 with Vitagraph. Popular especially in exotic roles like *The Queen of Sheba* (1921) and *She* (1925), she continued to work in the sound period through the 40s in smaller parts. Last important role 1948.

Boardman, Eleanor (1898-   ). Born in Philadelphia, she worked as a model for Eastman Kodak publicity and after some stage work gravitated to Hollywood in 1922. She played leads in a number of silents and a few sound films, but she is best known for her work with King Vidor, especially in *The Crowd*. She was Vidor's second wife and in 1940 married Harry D'Arrast. Last film 1933.

Bosworth, Hobart (1867-1943). Born in Ohio, he ran away to sea at 12 and then to the stage at 18, starting in film in 1909 with the Selig company and working (often as screenwriter or director as well) mainly for his own company from 1913. In supporting roles during the 20s and 30s. Last film 1942.

Bow, Clara (1905-1965). Born in Brooklyn, her father a busboy and her mother subject to dangerous epileptic fits, she left school in the eighth grade to look for jobs that could help support her family. Movies were her refuge and her ambition, and to her amazement she won a personality contest sponsored by *Motion Picture Classic* (1921). Her small role in *Down to the Sea in Ships* (1923) got attention from the trade, and within a year she was under contract with Preferred Pictures. B.P. Schulberg sold her contract to Famous Players when he moved there as head of west coast production in 1925, and in that year she was in 15 pictures. By the time she starred in *It* (1927) she was one of a handful of top personalities in Hollywood. Her decline in popularity was almost as dizzy, after she sued her own secretary for embezzlement and the scandals offered in the trial testimony drove her out of town. She married western star Rex Bell in 1931 and went to live on his Nevada ranch, but was subject to nervous breakdowns and spent much time in sanitoriums. Last film 1933. (See Chapter 5, pages 189-190, 201-205.)

Boyd, William (1898-1972). Born in Ohio, he had to quit school when both of his parents died. As an oil field worker, he conceived of the idea of getting into the movies, and he worked his way west, taking what jobs he could find in California. In 1919 Cecil DeMille assigned him the first of many roles. He was in Griffith's *Lady of the Pavements* and star of Hopalong Cassidy series after 1935. Last film 1952.

Brady, Alice (1892-1939). Born in New York City, the daughter of the stage and film producer William A. Brady, she was busy from 1914 to 1923 in a wide variety of serious roles in both films and the legitimate theater. Turning from personal tragedies (an alcoholic husband, a son prematurely born and permanently injured) she committed herself to the theater for a decade. In 1933 she began a steady career in sound comedies, the brunette alternative to the flightiness of Billie Burke, notably as the screwball mother in *My Man Godfrey* (1936). Last film 1939.

Brian, Mary (1908-   ). Born Louise Byrdie Dantzler in Texas, she and her three-year-old brother were left fatherless when she was a month old. She and her mother moved to Los Angeles where she won a contest for "Miss Personality," which brought her $100, a brief "prologue" appearance, and a successful screen test for Wendy in *Peter Pan* (1924). Romantic leads followed in *Beau Geste* (1926), *The Virginian* (1929), and other sound films. Married and retired, 1937, she was in a few films afterward and in a 1953 TV series. Last film 1947. (See Chapter 5, pages 191-192.)

Bronson, Betty (1906-1971). From New Jersey, she had small roles in Hollywood at an early age and was chosen by Sir James Barrie to play Peter Pan in the film (1924) of his play. *A Kiss for Cinderella* was well received (1926), but it was too late in the 20s for her happy personality, so like Mary Pickford's. She was in five pictures in 1929, but after 1932 she retired to marry a wealthy Southerner. Character roles as late as 1968 and 1971.

Brooks, Louise (1906-1985). Born in Kansas, the daughter of a lawyer, she was a performing dancer from childhood and at 15 was with the

Denishawn Dancers. After experience with George White's Scandals and the Ziegfeld Follies, she signed with Famous Players in 1925. Her fame rests almost entirely on one film for G.W. Pabst in Germany, *Pandora's Box*, (1928) in the role of a charming, sexually insatiable vamp. With the same severe bobbed hair and flapper style as Colleen Moore, she found few chances on her return to the U.S. She spent nearly 50 years as a consort for rich men, as a sales girl for Saks, and as a recluse, sometimes writing acid essays about screen history, collected in her book *Lulu in Hollywood* (1982). Last films 1936, 1938.

Busch, Mae (1897-1946). Born in Australia, she was the daughter of the conductor of the Melbourne Symphony. Her mother was a singer who brought the family to America so she could work in light opera. At 15 the daughter was in musicals, then touring in vaudeville, and when she reached the west coast chose to enter Keystone comedies (1912). Busy through the 1920s, she was best known for her role as one of the "princesses" living with the "count" in Stroheim's *Foolish Wives* (1922). She was in *The Unholy Three* (1925) and after a slow period in 1930 was in many Laurel and Hardy movies. Last film 1942.

Bushman, Francis X. (1883-1966). Born in Baltimore, he took a bodybuilding course as a youth, and this led to work as a model and in stock companies. After 1911 at Essanay film company he appeared opposite Beverly Bayne in a popular series of short films and in 1915 moved with her to make features at Metro Pictures. He was the first male sex star, voted America's "most handsome man" and received heavy fan mail, but when it was revealed he had five children and had to be divorced to marry his costar (1918, divorced 1925), his popularity fell sharply and his studio almost stopped casting him. He is now best known for playing the villainous Messala in *Ben-Hur* (1926). He lost millions in the stock market crash, went into radio dramas, played a few notable roles in sound movies. Last film 1966.

Carey, Harry (1878-1947). Born Henry DeWitt Carey II in New York City, he studied at New York University and worked at various jobs and as a writer. At 31 he tried acting in films at Biograph (1909), appearing in Griffith productions. A favorite of John Ford, he was in many silent westerns and a character actor in early sound films, including the Vice President in *Mr. Smith Goes to Washington* (1939). Last film, *Red River* (1948).

Chaney, Lon (1883-1930). Born Alonso Chaney in Colorado, the son of deaf-mute parents, he worked at the local opera house as stagehand and went on the road at 17 as an actor. From 1913 he found work in Hollywood as a villain and with his skill in make-up earned the title of "The Man of a Thousand Faces." Last picture 1930. (See Chapter 5, pages 237-239.)

Clark, Marguerite (1883-1940). Born in Cincinnati, she and her sister were left with $4000 at the death of her father. Her mother had died when she was 10. First in Baltimore, then in New York, she found success on the stage (1900-1914) including a national tour in 1909 as Peter Pan. Adolph Zukor felt that her four-feet-ten was just right for movies and signed her up for three years at $1000 a week. She became the brunette counterpart of Mary Pickford at Famous Players-Lasky, vying with her for roles. After her marriage to a rich Louisiana lumberman, she moved south and lived happily there until her husband's death in 1936, when she moved to New York with her sister, who outlived her by ten years. Only two of her pictures are believed to exist. Last film 1921. (See Chapter 5, pages 193-194.)

Cody, Lew (1884-1934). Born Louis Joseph Cotée in New Hampshire, he gave up medical school for the stage, trying films in 1915. A popular leading man, often the subversive corner of a triangle, he made many silent pictures, seven in 1925. He was active in the early sound period until his last film in 1934.

Colman, Ronald (1891-1958). Born in England and an orphan at 16, he was in amateur theatricals while working as an office boy. Wounded in the first World War, he did stage work in 1916 and feature films by 1918. Coming to the U.S. in 1920, he found little to do until Lillian Gish chose him for her leading man in *The White Sister* in 1923. After that he was in constant demand for silent and sound films as the romantic, dignified hero with the modest mustache and calm demeanor. Famous for *Beau Geste* (1926), and for dramas costarring Vilma Banky. Last important feature role 1950, then in TV series "Halls of Ivy."

Compson, Betty (1897-1974). Born Eleanor Luicime Compson in Utah, her father died in 1912. She worked first in films at Al Christie's studio and then in various studios until George Loane Tucker chose her for *The Miracle Man* (1919), which made her a star. After two years and 15 pictures for Jesse Lasky, she worked in London, then again for Paramount, followed by a lot of Poverty Row pictures. She worked for Joseph von Sternberg in *The Docks of New York* and began a long list of talking pictures with *The Barker*, for which she got an Oscar nomination. Last film 1948. (See Chapter 5, page 193.)

Coogan, Jackie (1914-1984). Born Jack Leslie Coogan in Los Angeles, the son of vaudeville performers, he had appeared in a film called *Skinner's Baby* at the age of 18 months and was in an Annette Kellerman act when Charlie Chaplin saw him. Trying him out in the two-reel *A Day's Pleasure* (1919), Chaplin cast him as *The Kid* (1921), in an almost feature-length film. It was such a hit that the boy's price skyrocketed and he became a sudden international star. He was unlucky in his later roles, although he did such obvious ones as *Peck's Bad Boy, Oliver Twist, A Boy of Flanders,* and in 1930, *Tom Sawyer.* He was also unlucky in his parents: his father died in a car accident (1935), and his mother and new stepfather kept and spent most of his earnings until he had to sue them. His image in later years was ugly: he played villains in movies through the 70s and Uncle Fenster on TV's "The Addams Family."

Cooper, Gary (1901-1961). Born Frank James Cooper in Montana, son of a state supreme court judge, educated in England and Iowa (Grinnell), he wanted to be a cartoonist but once in Southern California was introduced to casting directors for western movies. By 1926 he won a second lead in Goldwyn's *The Winning of Barbara Worth,* and the next year a memorable bit in *Wings.* Strong, silent, awkward man of action: star in many sound films till his death.

Cooper, Miriam (1891-1976). Born in Maryland, she was in a few early Griffith films, especially *The Birth of a Nation* and *Intolerance*. Star of several films directed by Raoul Walsh, who was her husband from 1916 to 1926. Last film 1924.

Cortez, Ricardo (1899-1977). Born Jacob Krantz in Vienna, he was brought to New York City in 1902 by his parents. He sold papers, worked as a messenger boy and on the stage. Signed by Paramount, he was cast in such pictures as *Argentine Love* (1924) in the hope that his dark good looks could compete with Valentino. His earliest important role was at MGM opposite Greta Garbo in her first film *The Torrent* (1926). His very active career, sometimes as a villain, extended through the 40s, including two years as a director. Last film 1958.

Costello, Dolores (1905-1979). Born in Pittsburgh, she and her sister began acting as children at Vitagraph in 1911, where their father Maurice was active after a prominent stage career. A successful model for magazine illustrators when she was signed by Warners, she linked up with another famous theater family when John Barrymore chose her as leading lady in 1926 for *The Sea Beast* and asked her to marry him in 1928. He declared with some justice that she was "the most beautiful woman in the world," but they were divorced in 1935 after she provided him with a son and daughter. Next to last film, *The Magnificent Ambersons* (1942). Last film 1943.

Costello, Maurice (1877-1950). Born in Pittsburgh, he was in vaudeville comedy before he was twenty. After he reached stardom on Broadway, he was an early convert to films, working at Edison as early as 1906, acting and later directing at Vitagraph, but never permitting himself to help with scenery or props, as others were customarily expected to do. After a 3-reel version of *A Tale of Two Cities* he was voted most popular star by readers of *Motion Picture Magazine* in 1912. Appearing in many silents even in the 20s, his star paled during that decade. Last film 1941.

Crawford, Joan (1904-1977). Born Lucille Fay LeSueur in Texas, she had worked as laundress and waitress before winning a dance contest. She was in night clubs and a Broadway chorus line, then was singled out by MGM for a contract (1925). Her flapper roles in the 20s competed with Clara Bow (Paramount) and Colleen Moore (First National), as in *Our Dancing Daughters* (1928). Her ambition and determination in two consecutive starring careers in the sound period (MGM, Warners) are legendary. Last film 1970.

Crisp, Donald (1880-1974). Born in Scotland, he came to the U.S. in 1906, working on the stage and in 1908 at Biograph. His most notable Griffith role was in *Broken Blossoms* (1919) as the brutal father of Lillian Gish, and he was in many important supporting parts in the sound era. He also worked as director during the silent years (1914-30). Last film 1963.

Cunard, Grace (1894-1967). Born Harriet Mildred Jeffries in Ohio and active on the stage as a teen-ager, she joined Biograph in 1910. Moving to Lubin, then Kay Bee, she met Francis Ford, who persuaded her to marry him (1913-18) and go with him to Universal. They wrote, directed, and performed together a series of films, including a serial called *Lucille Love, Girl of Mystery* (1914) which made them famous and popular and was followed by three others. Forced to rest from her multiple tasks (1921-1924), she married a stuntman and went back to work in serials and features, with character parts as late as 1945.

Dalton, Dorothy (1894-1972). Born in Chicago, she was in a stage touring company in Los Angeles when Thomas Ince signed her for films in 1915. She was in nine of his films in 1918 alone, and in 1922 played opposite Valentino in his seagoing film, *Moran of the Lady Letty*. Last film 1924.

Dana, Viola (1897-). Born Virginia Flugrath in Brooklyn, she was on stage as a child and worked in Edison films at 13. A steady star at the Metro company during the early twenties, she was in *Merton of the Movies* (1924) and other light comedies. Last film (1929).

Daniels, Bebe (1901-1971). Born Phyllis Daniels in Dallas of theatrical parents, she was carried on stage at the age of ten weeks and was in early short films from the age of nine. At 14 she began with Hal Roach and Harold Lloyd what was to be a series of 172 shorts. She stayed to be a top star at Famous Players-Lasky during the 1920s, averaging six or seven silent pictures a year, including *Monsieur Beaucaire* (1924) with Rudolph Valentino. Then when Paramount was ignoring silent stars in favor of Broadway talent, she went to RKO to sing in *Rio Rita* (1929), following up with 15 more movies. In 1930 she embarked on her first marriage (which lasted happily until her death) with Ben Lyon, and after 1936 worked with him on stage and radio in England. Last U.S. film 1935. (See Chapter 5, pages 197-198.)

Davies, Marion (1897-1961). Born Marion Cecilia Douras in Brooklyn, she studied ballet and acting and appeared in musicals, in the Ziegfeld Follies (1916), and on the screen (1917). Thereafter she was the mistress of the newspaper magnate William Randolph Hearst, and she undertook a long series of films through his Cosmopolitan Pictures, a company which moved from Paramount to MGM and at last to Warners. *When Knighthood Was in Flower* (1922) was a success, but her comedic roles were more characteristic: *The Patsy, Show People* (1928). The praise lavished on her by the Hearst press warped her career, which might otherwise have been accepted as a contribution to light comedy. Last film 1937.

Dean, Priscilla (1896-). Born in New York City, she was one of those who learned acting with her parents on tour. This prepared her for films at 14 at Biograph and elsewhere. At Universal the following year (1911) she was in comedies and in 1917 was the heroic and popular star of a serial, *The Gray Ghost*. After that she had leading roles at Universal, but worked later in the 20s at smaller studios. Last film 1932.

De La Motte, Marguerite (1902-1950). Born in Minnesota, she was trained as a dancer. She entered films in 1918, and had many roles in the 20s, but her main claim to fame was playing opposite Douglas Fairbanks in *The Mark of Zorro* (1920) and *The Three Musketeers* (1921). Last films 1934, 1942.

Del Rio, Dolores (1905-1983). Born Lolita Dolores Martinez Asunsolo Lopez Negrette in Mexico, she was the daughter of a banker. The director Edwin Carewe met her at a Mexico City party and asked her to come to Hollywood (1925) where she starred in films for him and others (notably, in the sound period, Orson Welles and John Ford). She returned to Mexico in 1943 to become a prominent and wealthy performer-participant in film making as late as 1978.

Dempster, Carol (1902-   ). A dancer from Duluth, introduced to D.W. Griffith by photographer Henrik Sartov, she took part in stage presentations before screenings and later was in several films, first as co-star (*True-Heart Susie*, 1919) and then taking the place of Lillian Gish. She left Griffith and films in 1926.

Denny, Reginald (1891-1967).   Born Reginald Leigh Daymore in England, he was a child performer in London and became a star in American silent comedy and adventure pictures, starting in 1919. He became a familiar English-accented supporting character in sound films, including the Bulldog Drummond series.   Final appearance in *Batman* (1966).

Dexter, Elliott (1870-1941). Born in Texas, he spent his early acting years in vaudeville and on stage. At 45, he went to work for Cecil DeMille and was in many of his morality plays in the teens along with Gloria Swanson, (*The Affairs of Anatol*, 1921), and with Mary Pickford in *Stella Maris* (1925), his last picture.

Dix, Richard (1894-1949). Born Ernest Carlton Brimmer in St. Paul, he found campus theatricals at the University of Minnesota more attractive than medical study. After two years in Broadway roles he entered pictures in 1921 where his square-jawed directness won him popularity. *Cimarron* was his biggest sound success (1931). Last picture 1947.

Doro, Marie (1882-1956). Born Marie K. Stewart in Pennsylvania, a diminutive brunette, she was one of those enticed from Broadway success to work at Famous Players, mostly in the period 1915-19. Last film 1924.

Dove, Billie (1900-   ). Born Lillian Bohney in New York City, she was a model and a Ziegfeld performer before entering films in 1921. Popularly known from publicity as "The American Beauty," she starred with Douglas Fairbanks in *The Black Pirate* in 1926. Retired and married in 1932, she came back for a brief appearance in 1962.

Fairbanks, Douglas (1883-1939). Born Douglas Elton Ulman in Denver, Colorado, he was involved in stage plays from the age of twelve. Film career, starting with Triangle, 1915 to 1934. (See Introduction, pages 4-5, and Chapter 3.

Farnum, Dustin (1874-1929). Born in New Hampshire, two years older than his brother William and associated with him in stage roles, *The Squaw Man* (1914) is his main claim to fame as a leading character. It was Cecil DeMille's first film (codirected by Oscar Apfel) for the Lasky company. He continued as a cowboy star through 1926.

Farnum, William (1876-1953). Born in Boston, he was a performer at 12, touring with his older brother Dustin, and later with the *Ben-Hur* company. In 1914 he signed with Selig and starred in *The Spoilers*. The following year he began a long career as one of the top attractions at Fox, until an injury in 1925 led to smaller roles on stage and screen. Last film 1952.

Farrar, Geraldine (1882-1967). Born in Boston, she was the daughter of a small businessman who also played first base for the Philadelphia National Baseball Club. She made her debut in Berlin as Marguerite in *Faust*. Five years later she began a stellar career (1906-1922) at the Metropolitan in New York, often singing opposite Caruso. Recovering from a throat operation in 1915, she responded favorably to the idea that she try the movies. She was invited to Hollywood by Jesse Lasky and worked silently for DeMille in *Carmen* (1915) and *Joan the Woman* (1916) and 12 other films, the last in 1921. (See Chapter 2, pages 55-58.)

Farrell, Charles (1901-   ). Born in Massachusetts, he wanted above all to be a screen actor and finally earned enough to get him to California. He first acted as a film extra in a remake of *The Cheat* (1923). Best known for series of pictures with Janet Gaynor at Fox. Married to actress Virginia Valli. Star of two TV shows in 1950s. Last film 1941. (See Chapter 5, pages 190-191, 217-219.)

Fazenda, Louise (1895-1962). Born in Indiana, she was a comedian at Universal as early as 1913, moving to Keystone in 1915. Her offbeat style was seen in many features in the 20s and also in the sound period. Last film 1939.

Ferguson, Elsie (1883-1961). The daughter of a prosperous New York City lawyer, she was persuaded to try out for the chorus and then worked up through various roles to Portia in *The Merchant of Venice* (1916). The next year Adolph Zukor offered her $5000 a week to be one of his Famous Players and after four pictures by Maurice Tourneur, she became known as "the aristocrat of the screen." Her films are lost, including her only sound picture in 1930.

Ford, Francis (1882-1953). Born Francis O'Feeney (or O'Fearna) in Maine, he was the older brother of John Ford and son of an Irish immigrant saloonkeeper. After stock company experience he joined Edison as an actor (1907), then Vitagraph, and at Universal was also a director of shorts and serials. When John became the more successful director, Francis worked in his pictures and others as a character actor. Last film, *The Sun Shines Bright* 1953.

Frederick, Pauline (1883-1938). Born Beatrice Pauline Libbey in Boston, she agreed on a dare to try out for a vaudeville spot at the Boston Music Hall and won a singing contract, for which her disapproving father, a railroad conductor, later disinherited her. She went on to great success in musicals and dramas and an offer in 1914 from Zukor, for whom she starred in 28 features. For Goldwyn release she played *Madame X*, her most famous role. Last film, 1937.

Garbo, Greta (1905-1990). Born Greta Louisa Gustafsson in Stockholm, the daughter of an unskilled laborer who died when she was 13, she had to go to work as a barber's assistant and department store salesgirl, where she was chosen to be in publicity films. She won a scholarship to the Royal Dramatic Theater training school, where the prominent Swedish director, Mauritz Stiller, found her and gave her the second lead in *The Story of Gosta Berling* (1924). Louis B. Mayer, on a trip to Europe, hired Stiller, who is supposed to have insisted that he take Garbo as well. After delays and doubts, it was clear from her first U.S. film, *The Torrent* (1926) that she had a magnetic quality which could only lead to a unique starring career. Remote and mysterious on screen, simple and down to earth in actuality, she seemed to respond passionately to John Gilbert, her co-star in *Flesh and the Devil* (1927) but it did not last. The ultimate symbol of stardom, she was never given a truly outstanding story, never awarded an Oscar, and never married. After a number of extraordinary appearances in sound films (*Anna Christie, Grand Hotel, Queen Christina, Camille, Ninotchka*), she retired to a New York apartment in 1941.

Gaynor, Janet (1906-1984).   Born Laura Gainor in Philadelphia, graduated from San Francisco Polytechnic High School, she preferred to be in a business office, but her stepfather persuaded her to try the movies. After work in Hal Roach comedies, she won a Fox contract and was chosen at once for the lead roles in *Seventh Heaven* (1927) and *Sunrise* (1928), for which, taken together, she won the first Academy Award for acting. By 1934, after a series of films costarring Charles Farrell, she was the top boxoffice attraction in the U.S. She continued in sound films, notably in the first version of *A Star Is Born* (1937), after which she made two more pictures, then retired to a Brazilian ranch with her second husband, the designer Gilbert Adrian. Twenty years after her retirement, she returned for *Bernardine*, in 1957.

Gibson, Hoot (1892-1962). Born Edmund Richard Gibson in Nebraska, he was nicknamed as a youngster because of his owl hunting, which involved frequent imitations. As a teenager he worked in a circus and later as a cowboy, winning prizes at rodeos. In Hollywood (1912), he became a stuntman and supporting player, and after service in World War I starred in his first features for John Ford (1921). His westerns were especially popular in the early 20s, offering him as a humorous character who seldom used a gun. He retired twice (1936, 1944) but was seen in *The Horse Soldiers* in 1959.

Gilbert, John (1895-1936). Born John Pringle, in Utah, his parents were divorced soon afterward. In Hart westerns from 1916. Writer and assistant director for Maurice Tourneur, then working at Fox and M-G-M, where he managed to star for both Stroheim (*The Merry Widow*) and Vidor (*The Big Parade*) in 1925-26. Last film 1934. (See Chapter 5, pages 187-189, 228-233.)

Gish, Dorothy (1895-1968).   Born in Ohio two years after her more famous sister, Lillian, she entered film with her in D.W. Griffith's *An Unseen Enemy* (1912). They were together more notably in *Orphans of the Storm* (1922) but she was a popular star in her own right, especially in a series of comedies supervised by Griffith (1918-1921). She was in a handful of sound pictures. Last U.S. silent film 1925. Last film, *The Cardinal* (1963).

Gish, Lillian (1893-   ). Born in Ohio, she was first on the stage at age five. Her mother, who had vainly followed her wandering husband to New York, found that she and her two daughters could turn to the theater for a living. Soon Lillian and Dorothy were traveling in the care of other women in separate plays.   Visiting a friend (now named Mary Pickford) at Biograph, the two sisters were hired by D.W. Griffith in 1912. After many short films, she became Griffith's favorite actress and collaborator, starring in features from *The Birth of a Nation* (1915) to *Broken Blossoms* (1919), *Way Down East (1920)*, and *Orphans of the Storm* (1922). At MGM she confirmed her eminence as a star in *The Scarlet Letter* and *The Wind* (1928). She then elected to return to the stage and to play in sound films from time to time through 1988. (See Chapter 2, pages 76-86.)

Godowski, Dagmar (1897-1975). Born in Lithuania, the daughter of a well-known concert pianist, she was more convincingly foreign as a "vamp" than Theda Bara in the early 20s. Film career 1922-1926, including a starring role opposite Rudolph Valentino in *The Sainted Devil* (1924).

Goudal, Jetta (1898-1985). Born in France, she worked on the stage in Europe and the U.S., entering films in 1923, with *The Green Goddess* and playing sophisticated women in about three pictures a year. She was in D.W. Griffith's *Lady of the Pavements* (1929). Last picture 1933.

Griffith, Corinne (1896-1979). Texas-born, working first at Vitagraph (1916), then First National in Hollywood, she was noted for her beauty and was a popular star of many silents. Retired in 1932 to manage her real estate and write novels. (See Chapter 5, pages 194-195.)

Haines, William (1900-1973). Born in Virginia, he came to the screen (1922) as the beneficiary of a Goldwyn "new faces" contest and soon was typed as a happy-go-lucky youngster in such titles as *Tell It to the Marines* (1926) and *Free and Easy,* (1930). Perhaps his most memorable role was in King Vidor's *Show People* (1928) as the slapstick performer who persuades Marion Davies not to look down on what people love best--comedy. Last film 1934.

Hale, Creighton (1882-1965). Born Patrick Fitzgerald in Ireland, he took part in his father's touring company from infancy. He came to the States in his thirties, entering films in 1914, first in serials and then in a variety of polished roles in the 1920s, six in 1925. He worked less often in the 30s. Last film 1949.

Hamilton, Neil (1899-1984). Born in Massachusetts, a sometime player in stock and model for shirts, he was in films from 1918 and was chosen by D.W. Griffith to star in *The White Rose,* (1923) and *Isn't Life Wonderful,* becoming after that a popular star at Paramount. Active in sound pictures as late as 1970 and on TV as the police commissioner in *Batman*.

Hanson, Lars (1886-1965). Born in Sweden, he entered films there in 1913 but was first known abroad as costar with Greta Garbo in *The Story of Gosta Berling* (1924). He was brought to MGM, where he appeared opposite Garbo in *Flesh and the Devil* (1927) and Lillian Gish in *The Scarlet Letter* (1926) and *The Wind* (1928), his last film in the U.S. He made pictures thereafter in Germany, England and Sweden.

Harron, Bobby (1894-1920). From an Irish immigrant family in New York City, he was an errand boy for Biograph, playing bit roles and before long youthful leads for Griffith in *Intolerance, True Heart Susie,* and six other films in 1918-19. Depressed and unsure of himself, he died of what was believed to be an accidental bullet wound.

Hart, William S. (1870-1946). Born in upstate New York, he was the son of an itinerant laborer who took many trips to the west. Undertaking to study acting, he gained success in Shakespeare plays on Broadway, then as

Messala in *Ben-Hur* (1919) and in *The Squaw Man*. He determined to improve the westerns he saw in the movie houses and persuaded Thomas Ince (also a former Broadway actor) to put him to work, starting as an actor with *The Bargain* (1914) and later as director of his own pictures. As the "bad man" won over to civilization, often by a good woman, he established a special tradition in western films. Last film, *Tumbleweeds,* 1925.

Hatton, Raymond (1887-1971). Born in Iowa, active in vaudeville since the age of 12, he found jobs after 1912 in many Cecil DeMille pictures and worked with Wallace Beery in two-reel comedies.   A regular as a supporting actor in many sound movies, especially westerns.   Last film 1967.

Haver, Phyllis (1899-1960). Born Phyllis O'Haver in Kansas, she played piano for silent movies and soon afterward turned up in Hollywood as a Sennett bathing beauty (1917).   She starred as a sex object in many features of the 20s–ten of them in 1924 — and was in Griffith's *The Battle of the Sexes* in 1928. Marriage (1929-1945) took her away from Hollywood. Last film 1929.

Hayakawa, Sessue (1889-1973). Japanese-born, stage-trained, educated at the University of Chicago, he toured the western U.S. with his own company in 1913.   The following year he and his wife starred in *The Typhoon*, and Cecil DeMille cast him in a memorable villain's role in *The Cheat*. He remained an active performer in Europe, America, and Japan for years, his last prominent role in *The Bridge on the River Kwai* (1957).

Hersholt, Jean (1886-1956). Born in Copenhagen, he was the son of a well known acting family and was an accomplished performer when he arrived in the U.S. at 28. In 1915, he became a member of Thomas Ince's studio, and throughout the 20s worked at various companies in character parts. As the country Doctor Christian, he was in a series of sound pictures in the 30s. He was the founder of the Motion Picture Relief Fund. Last film 1955.

Holt, Jack (1888-1951).   Born in Virginia, he dropped out of Virginia Military Institute and knocked around the world a while before turning up in the movies in 1914-15. Mustached and pugnacious, he played villains at first in outdoor dramas, but drew leading roles as time went on, doing an average of six films a year 1918 to 1928 and similarly busy during the sound period. Last picture 1951.

Jannings, Emil (1884-1950). Born Theodor Emil Janenz in Switzerland but naturalized as an Austrian, his father was American-born. At 18 he was touring with German theatrical companies and four years later joined the Reinhardt theater. He was an important stage actor when he chose to enter films in 1914. After the war, in historical dramas like *Madame DuBarry (Passion)*, adaptations like *Tartuffe*, and Murnau's *The Last Laugh*, he became Germany's top star. Paramount signed him in 1927 and his brief American career included *The Last Command* and *The Way of All Flesh*, which together won him the first actor's Academy Award. The coming of sound drove him (and his heavy accent) back to Germany, where he played his most famous self-destructive role as the professor in *The Blue Angel* (1930). He was a strong supporter of the Nazi party, made films for them, and received a medal. He did not finish his last film project in 1945.

Johnson, Arthur (1876-1916). Born in Iowa, son of an Episcopal minister, he ran away to join a touring stage company and later had leading roles on Broadway. D.W. Griffith saw him on the street when he needed a father figure for his first directing experience, *The Adventures of Dollie* (1908). Anonymous during those early years, he yet became famous and was perhaps the first male star of the screen. Last film 1914.

Jones, Buck (1889-1942). Born Charles Frederick Gebhart in Indiana, he was an expert horseman from an early age and saw service in Mexico and the Philippines with the U.S. Cavalry. From 1913, he was in circuses and Wild West performances, and from 1917 was a stuntman in movies. One of the most prolific makers of westerns (including serials), his popularity lasted through the 30s. Last film 1942.

Joy, Leatrice (1896-1985). Born Leatrice Joy Zeidler in New Orleans, she worked as an extra starting in 1915, had leads in Oliver Hardy comedies, then became Cecil DeMille's frequent star in the early twenties, often as a sophisticated career woman. John Gilbert was her husband 1922-24. She retired with the coming of sound but had four later roles. Last film 1951.

Joyce, Alice (1890-1955). From Kansas City, she was a youthful telephone operator but started early in the movie business (Kalem in 1910), became a star at Vitagraph (1916), and had her most memorable role as the mother who walks out on her philandering husband and daughter in *Dancing Mothers* (1926). Wife of director Clarence Brown 1933-1945. Last film 1930.

Kellerman, Annette (1887-1975). Born in Australia, she was a champion swimmer and became the aquatic star of stage productions and a few highly profitable silent films from *Neptune's Daughter* (1914) to *Venus of the South Seas* (1924).

Kelly, Paul (1899-1956). Born in Brooklyn, he was a child actor at Vitagraph (1908), but as a trim blond youth he was mostly in crime pictures in the 20s, 30s, and 40s. Last film 1956.

Kennedy, Madge (1892-1987). Born in Chicago, she found a place on the New York stage, where she encountered Samuel Goldwyn in 1917. She was in six pictures in 1918, one of them reflecting the type of role she often played: *A Perfect Lady*. She quit the screen in 1926, but came back in several important sound films as character actress. Last film 1975.

Kerrigan, J. Warren (1889-1947). Born in Louisville, he was one of the very earliest, handsomest, and tallest movie stars, working primarily in the period 1910-1920. After three years caring for his mother until her death, he returned to play leads in *The Covered Wagon* and *Captain Blood* and three other pictures (1923-24) and then retired from the screen.

Kerry, Norman (1889-1956). Born Arnold Kaiser in Rochester N.Y., he first worked in films as a minor character in *Manhattan Madness* (1916) with Douglas Fairbanks. Often a swashbuckling mustached villain, he also played straight roles, as in *The Hunchback of Notre Dame*, *The Phantom of the Opera*, and other Universal pictures. Earlier, he played his part in film history by encouraging Rudolph Valentino and introducing him to people who gave him small roles. Last film 1941.

Kirkwood, James (1883-1963). Born in Michigan, he worked first on the stage, then in Griffith's early short pictures from 1909. From 1912 to 1919 he turned to directing, especially a number of Mary Pickford films, often acting in them as well. He returned to an active career as actor until about 1934. Last film 1956.

LaMarr, Barbara (1896-1926). Born Rheatha Watson in Richmond, Virginia, she began as a dancer on screen in 1920 in a film called *Flame of Youth*. So overpowering was her beauty that she was starred in roles as a vamp (or in costume pictures like *The Three Musketeers*) and in private life was beset by lovers, one of whom turned out to be a bigamist after they were married. She died of TB at 29. Last film 1926.

Landis, Cullen (1895-1975). Born in Nashville, he had stage experience when he came to films in 1917. At five feet six, he planned to be a director, but was cast in about a hundred films of all kinds till 1930, then went into the industrial film business in Detroit.

LaPlante, Laura (1904-   ). Born in St. Louis, she was in Christie comedies in Hollywood at 15 and became a top star at Universal, often in westerns. Effectively retired in 1931, she married a producer. Last roles in 1946 and 1957.

LaRoque, Rod (1896-1969). Born Roderick la Rocque de la Rour in Chicago, he was a popular romantic player in social comedies, making four or five pictures a year in the 1920s. His marriage to Vilma Banky in 1927 was a Samuel Goldwyn publicity performance yet it lasted till his death. He retired from the screen about 1940 to be a real estate broker. First film 1915; last film 1941.

Lawrence, Florence (1886-1938). Born in Ontario, she was on stage at three in her mother's theater company and took up acting full time when she finished school in Buffalo. The two ladies entered film in 1907 at Edison and 1908 at Biograph, where the versatile daughter appeared in so many Griffith one-reelers (including the Jones comedies) that she became known as "the Biograph girl." Carl Laemmle enticed her to IMP in 1910. In 1914 a stunt accident took her out of circulation. She had only some bit parts in the twenties, and died a suicide. Last film 1933.

Lee, Lila (1901-1973). Born Augusta Appel in New York, she was in vaudeville from the age of five, entering films at 17 and stardom opposite Valentino in *Blood and Sand* (1922). She worked steadily through the 20s, making eight films in 1929. Last film 1937, followed by a return to the stage.

Lincoln, Elmo (1899-1952). Born Otto Elmo Linkenhelter in New York state, he was a huge, muscle-bound man who first found his place in movie history in the racist barroom brawl of *The Birth of a Nation* (1915) and in several other bit roles and as "the mighty man" in *Intolerance*. He was the first actor to play the title role in *Tarzan of the Apes* (1918) and was also in two sequels and a serial (1921). He retired from the screen in 1926 but came back for bit parts, the last in 1952.

Lockwood, Harold (1887-1918). Born in New Jersey, he was active in school sports, attended a business college, and started out as a dry goods salesman. Then he told his father (a horse breeder and trainer) he wanted to be an actor. His father didn't object, only urging him to "aim high." After seven years trying to make it in theater, he was persuaded by a friend on the *Moving Picture World* to see Edwin Porter, who hired him for the Rex Company right away for lead roles (1911). As the extroverted, romantic, good-looking American image, he worked steadily from then on, for Al Christie at Nestor, Thomas Ince, Selig, Famous Players, and American, where he began his series of films with May Allison for which they are both remembered. His early death from wartime influenza was a shock to moviegoers. Last film 1918.

Love, Bessie (1898-1986). Born Juanita Horton in Midland, Texas, her father a bartender and her mother a restaurant manager, she was in high school in Los Angeles when she determined to try the movies. D.W. Griffith put her into the Judean episode of *Intolerance* (1916). Her career and parts were extremely varied, her lively sweetness hard to type. In 1925 she introduced the dance called the Charleston to the screen (*The King of Main Street*). Her best known role was in the early sound picture *The Broadway Melody* (1929), which won her an Oscar nomination. In 1935 she moved to England and continued to work in theater, radio, and films into the 1980s. (See Chapter 5, page 192.)

Lowe, Edmund (1892-1971). Born in California, he was the son of a judge, attended Santa Clara and taught school before finding his place with a Los Angeles stock company and on Broadway. Entering films in 1917, he was the mustached romantic lead in a number of silent features before winning attention as Sergeant Quirt in *What Price Glory?* (1926). He and Victor McLaglen were costarred in similar roles after that, but he branched out in more varied stories in the 40s and 50s. Last film 1960.

Lyon, Ben (1901-1979). Born in Atlanta, Georgia, raised in Baltimore, and sent to New York for further education, he tried hard to get into the movies. Luckier getting stage roles, he had a visit one day backstage from Samuel Goldwyn, who evidently liked his smile and sent him to Hollywood to be juvenile lead in one of his pictures and later in First National's *Flaming Youth*. In the late 1930s he and his wife, Bebe Daniels, moved to England, where he joined the 8th U.S. Air Force during World War II and afterward headed a London talent agency. Last U.S. film 1938. (See Chapter 5, pages 197-198, 217-219.)

Mackaill, Dorothy (1903-). Born in England, she was in London shows and Ziegfeld follies and from 1921 in Hollywood, acting in four or five pictures a year (1925-30) at First National, chiefly light comedies and romances. Last film 1937.

Marmont, Percy (1883-1977). Born in London, he was on the stage there from 1900, on Broadway in 1917, then went to Hollywood, where his tall blond distinction won him romantic leads. By the time he played *Lord Jim* (1925) for Paramount he was 42, and the following year he played opposite Clara Bow in *Mantrap*. He went back to London in 1928, where he was cast in upper class roles on stage and screen. Last film 1956.

Marsh, Mae (1895-1968). Born Mary Wayne Marsh in New Mexico and educated in a Los Angeles convent, her older sister was a D.W. Griffith player and she appeared in a Griffith west coast production in 1911. She is now best known for her work in three Griffith films: as the little sister in *The Birth of a Nation*, the wife in the modern story of *Intolerance*, and (after several years with the Goldwyn company) *The White Rose* in 1923. She left film work in 1925 but returned to do character parts throughout the sound period, notably in three John Ford films, 1960-63.

Marshall, Tully (1864-1943). Born William Phillips in California, a graduate of the University of Santa Clara, he was on the stage from 1890 but entered films at the age of 50. His many character roles extended from *Joan the Woman* (1917) through *The Covered Wagon* (1923) to Stroheim's *The Merry Widow* (1925). Active through the 30s and his 60s. Last film 1943.

Mason, Shirley (1901-1979). Born Leonie Flugrath in Brooklyn, she was Viola Dana's sister. She was on the stage as a child and entered films in 1914, continuing to play innocent romantic roles in many Fox pictures of the 20s. Last film 1929.

Maynard, Ken (1895-1973). Born in Indiana, he performed first with wild west shows and rodeos, entering films in 1923 and quickly becoming a popular star, along with his horse Tarzan. He made four westerns in 1927 and in the early 1930s was both acting and producing, but his stunting and occasional singing did not appeal to western fans beyond about 1938. Last films 1945, 1970.

McAvoy, May (1901-1984). Born in New York City in comfortable circumstances, she dropped out of high school to work as a model and an extra in New York feature films (1916), playing leading roles by 1919. *Sentimental Tommy* (1921) won her a Famous Players contract, but two years later a conflict with Cecil DeMille over provocative costuming led to a freelance period in which she prospered, playing varied star parts: *Lady Windermere's Fan, Ben Hur*, and *The Jazz Singer*. Last starring film 1929. Bit parts at MGM in 40s.

McCoy, Tim (1891-1978). Born Timothy John Fitzgerald McCoy in Michigan, he attended college in Chicago, but moved to a Wyoming ranch, where he became, after service in World War I, a U.S. Agent for a nearby Indian territory. His work as technical adviser for *The Covered Wagon* (1923) led him to move into acting (*The Thundering Herd*, 1925) and a contract the same year with MGM lasting to the early 30s. After that he made pictures at other studios, toured with the Ringling circus, and did a series at Monogram with Buck Jones. Last film (except for brief bits through 1965) 1942.

McLaglen, Victor (1886-1959). Born in England, he was one of nine surviving children of a minister--all of them six feet or taller. His adventures in Canada included farming, quarrying, silver prospecting, professional wrestling, and boxing, after which he took in Australia, India, and Africa, returning to England to join the army and go to the Near East for World War I. After an army boxing exhibition in England, he was offered parts in British films (starting 1920) and came to the U.S. for *The Beloved Brute* (1924). After *Beau Geste* and *What Price Glory* (1926) his career as the lean, tough, soft-hearted bruiser lasted through the 50s. He often worked for John Ford and won an Academy Award for *The Informer*. Last film 1958.

Meighan, Thomas (1879-1936). Born in Pittsburgh and active on the New York stage, he turned to films in 1913 where he easily found stardom in husky heroic roles (*The Miracle Man, Male and Female*, 1919) and continued to be popular throughout the 20s. Last film 1934.

Menjou, Adolphe (1890-1963). Pittsburgh-born, educated in part at Culver Military Academy, and trained as an engineer, he was attracted to the stage, and after a number of lesser films (1916-17, 1921-22) became famous as the wealthy, suave, and unscrupulous bachelor of *A Woman of Paris*, the Chaplin "art film" (1923) which set his style for years to come. Busy in many supporting roles in sound films, his last one was 1960.

Minter, Mary Miles (1902-1984). Born Juliet Reilly in Louisiana, her mother put her on stage at six and in the movies at ten. Popular as an innocent romantic player similar to Mary Pickford, she did not survive the scandal of the long-unsolved murder of her supposed lover, the director William Desmond Taylor. Retired into real estate business 1923. (See Chapter 5, page 187.)

Mix, Tom (1880-1940). Born in Pennsylvania, son of a log hauler and stableman, he quit school in the fourth grade, working at odd jobs, dreaming of the wild west he learned about from Buffalo Bill Cody's traveling show, riding horses, practicing stunts, sharpshooting, and playing freelance football for the local high school. During the Spanish-American war he joined the army but by 1902, a deserter, he moved to Oklahoma, where he found a showbusiness role as host for vacationers at the Miller Brothers' Wild West Ranch. The Selig company hired him for a movie and from 1911 to 1917 he was in a hundred of them. At Fox thereafter he became the smiling stuntman of western movies (most of them lost now) and the studio's chief moneymaker till 1928. He made sound features at Universal, retired in 1934. A radio show under his name ran till ten years after his death in an auto accident.

Moore, Colleen (1900-1988). Born Kathleen Morrison in Michigan, she won an invitation from D.W. Griffith to come west in 1917, finding her fame eventually in *Flaming Youth* (1923). She was a top star after that, but did not pursue her early sound film success. Last film 1934. (See Chapter 5, pages 195-197.)

Moore, Owen (1886-1939). Born in Ireland, he was one of three brothers who had romantic leads in many American movies in the 1920s. Owen tried it first, at 21 at Biograph, where Griffith used him frequently, especially in Mary Pickford's pictures. He and Mary were secretly married in 1910 (divorced 1920). Matt Moore, the youngest (1888-1960) was in films from 1913 to 1957. Tom, the oldest (1885-1955) worked from 1912 to 1950. Owen's last film, *A Star Is Born*, 1937.

Moreno, Antonio (1887-1967). Born Antonio Monteagudo in Madrid, he came to the U.S. at 14, did some stage work and began his film career in D.W. Griffith's 1912 short, *The Musketeers of Pig Alley*. Along with Ramon Novarro, he provided many of the Latin lovers the audience wanted after the early success of Rudolph Valentino. His strong accent limited him to lesser roles in sound films. Last picture *The Searchers* in 1956.

Mulhall, Jack (1887-1979). Born in New York state, he toured as a boy singer and in vaudeville and while he was in art school a book illustrator introduced him to Rex Ingram, then at Edison. He worked there and at Biograph and later played opposite Norma Talmadge, Colleen Moore, and Corinne Griffith. Rarely in important films, his appeal to audiences and to producers perhaps was epitomized by such a title as *Smile Brother Smile* (c.1926). From 1913 to 1959 he made hundreds of movies.

Murray, Mae (1885-1965). Born Marie Koening in Virginia of European parents, she studied dancing and at 22 was a star of the Ziegfeld Follies. On screen from 1916, typically a high-fashion blonde, she was the "girl with the bee-stung lips." Erich von Stroheim quarreled with her on *The Merry Widow*, (1925) but it was a triumph for both of them. Her very public marriage to Prince David Mdivani marked her decline as star. Last film 1931.

Nagel, Conrad (1897-1970). Born in Iowa, he was stage-struck when he played Scrooge at the age of 15, and after experience in a midwestern stock company, his dignity and good looks won him roles on Broadway. World Film Company cast him in *Little Women* (1919) and this took him to Hollywood, where he worked for both Cecil and William deMille. Averaging six or seven films a year in the 1920s, he was also a founder and president of the Academy of Motion Picture Arts and Sciences and president of the Motion Picture Relief Fund. He worked frequently during the 1930s. Last film 1959.

Naldi, Nita (1899-1961). Born Anita Donna Dooley in New York City, she was in the Ziegfeld Follies before entering films in 1920. She was the possessive "other woman" in *Blood and Sand*, (1922) and was in two other Valentino pictures. Last film 1928

Nazimova, Alla (1879-1945). Born in Russia, her parents gave her the advantages of study at a Swiss convent followed by training as a violinist and as an actress at Stanislavsky's Moscow Art Theater. During a tour abroad she chose to stay in New York (1905), where she performed in Russian and in English as an interpreter of Ibsen, and entered film with *War Brides* (1916), which she had done on the stage. As producer of her own starring pictures, such as *Camille, A Doll's House, Salome* (1921-23) she chose stylized, experimental forms. Retiring in 1925, she came back in a few sound films and again on the stage. Last films 1940-44.

Negri, Pola (1894-   ). Born Barbara Chalupiec in Poland, trained for ballet in St. Petersburg and drama in Warsaw, her successes on the stage led her into film work (1914) with Alexandr Hertz. Invited to Berlin by Max Reinhardt, she met Ernst Lubitsch, who put her in short films and historical features, especially *Madame DuBarry* (1919), which reached the U.S. as *Passion* and brought her an offer from Famous Players-Lasky (1923). Reputed to be earthy and passionate, she seldom found American screenwriters and directors in touch with her needs. For Lubitsch she was Catherine the Great in *Forbidden Paradise* (1924) and Mauritz Stiller cast her in *Hotel Imperial* (1927). She had a lively time of it in the public prints as a competitive movie star (vs. Swanson at Paramount) and claimed to have had affairs with Chaplin and Valentino. Sound revealed her difficult accent and she went back to Germany in the 1930s, returning to the U.S. when the war started. She had character parts in two films, in 1943 and 1964.

Nilsson, Anna Q. (1890-1974). Born in Sweden, she came to the U.S. for modeling work, then entered films in 1911 at Kalem. She was in seven films at First National in each of two years, 1923-24. An injury and the coming of sound kept her off the screen after 1928. Later there were only brief appearances, her last in *Sunset Boulevard* (1950).

Novarro, Ramon (1899-1968). Born Ramon Samaniegos in Mexico, he came to Los Angeles at 15. He gave singing lessons, danced in vaudeville, and found extra parts in movies from 1917. At M-G-M he was thought of as a successor to Valentino, who had moved to Paramount, and was cast as the hero of *Ben-Hur* and as *The Student Prince* (1927). Last film 1960. (See Chapter 5, page 195.)

O'Brien, George (1900-1985). Son of San Francisco's chief of police, a college athlete, boxer, and in 1922 a movie stuntman, he was chosen by John Ford as star of *The Iron Horse* (1924). By 1927 a popular leading man (tagged by the studio "The Chest") he was cast by F.W. Murnau in Fox's prestige art film, *Sunrise*. Sound pictures mostly westerns. Last role in *Cheyenne Autumn*, 1964.

Owen, Seena (1894-1966). Born Signe Auen in Spokane, Washington, she is best known for work with D.W. Griffith, as the princess in *Intolerance*, (1916) and other rather statuesque roles, including a stint for Stroheim in *Queen Kelly*. From 1918 she averaged three films a year, but after 1928 she retired as actress and became a screenwriter in the 1930s and 40s.

Pallette, Eugene (1889-1954). Born in Kansas, he was on the stage for six years and in early films from 1910, often as a leading man. He was in the French episode of *Intolerance* (1916). After service in World War I, he had an extensive career in movies needing a portly, genial character. Last film 1946.

Philbin, Mary (1903-   ). Born in Chicago, she was a beauty prize winner who went to Hollywood (1921) and had perhaps 20 leading roles in silent pictures, notably *The Phantom of the Opera, Stella Maris* (both 1925). Last film 1929.

Pickford, Mary (1893-1979). Born Gladys Smith in Toronto, Canada, she was already a recognized stage performer when she presented herself at 16 to D.W. Griffith (1909), who used her in 20 or more pictures a year. Progressing steadily in salary and control till she was one of the owners of United Artists, she retired in 1933. (See Introduction, pages 3-4, and Chapter 3.)

Pitts, ZaSu (1898-1963). Born in Kansas, raised in California, her peculiar gestures and tone of voice won her comedy roles in two films by a beginning director, King Vidor (who observed her on a streetcar). She had already done a small bit in Mary Pickford's *Rebecca of Sunnybrook Farm* (1917). But it was Erich von Stroheim, who had faith in her dramatic skills, who gave her a lead in *Greed* (1924) and a major role in *The Wedding March*.

In sound pictures she became typed (and worked steadily) as a weird but lovable comedian. Last film 1963.

Powell, William (1892-1984).   Born in Pittsburgh, he attended the American Academy of Dramatic Arts and was on Broadway at 20. His first film role was as adversary (Professor Moriarty) to John Barrymore's Sherlock Holmes in 1922, and he continued to play unpleasant people in about eight films a year (1926-28) until sound brought him more agreeable suave detective roles (*The Thin Man* 1934 and sequels) and a long career in Hollywood. Last film 1955.

Prevost, Marie (1898-1937). Born Mary Bickford Dunn in Ontario, she was educated in Montreal and Los Angeles, afterward switching from a legal stenographer's job to the Keystone studio as bathing beauty (1917). There she soon had leading roles and in 1921 she went to Universal as a star. In *The Marriage Circle* (1924) and two other films directed by Ernst Lubitsch at Warners she found her best achievement as light comedy actress, and she continued such roles into the sound period. Excessive dieting caused her death at 38. Last film 1936.

Pringle, Aileen (1895-   ). Born Aileen Bisbee in San Francisco, she was educated in Europe, appeared on Broadway, and not long after her first film role in *Redhead* (1919) she was chosen to represent the erotic notions of Elinor Glyn in films based on her *Three Weeks* and *His Hour* (1924). She was married first to Lord Pringle, governor of the Bahamas. Last film 1939.

Ralston, Esther (1902-   ). Born in Maine, she was part of a family of vaudeville performers who made their way across the country to try to place her in Hollywood movies. She started at 14 (1916) and in 1925 she was in nine films, playing Mrs. Darling in *Peter Pan* and the fairy godmother in *A Kiss for Cinderella*. Last film 1941. (See Chapter 5, pages 212-217.)

Ray, Charles (1891-1943). Born in Illinois, brought from stage to film by Thomas Ince (1913), he was usually cast as a country boy struggling to find himself and overcome limitations. His earliest success was *The Coward* (1915). Extremely popular and well thought of by his peers as an actor, he tried to go independent and also shift his image in *The Courtship of Miles Standish* (1923) and other pictures, but he eventually went into bankruptcy. Last film 1942.

Reid, Wallace (1891-1923). Born in St. Louis, his parents were theater people. His mother, separated early in his life from his father, sent him to a Pennsylvania prep school, and he developed wide interests--in reading, music, drawing, swimming, boxing, and auto racing. But before his mother could get him into Princeton, his father's influence drew him back to the stage. In 1910 he began playing parts at the Selig Company, where his father was writing scripts. At Vitagraph both of them wrote, directed, and acted, and occasionally the son would fill in as cameraman. At Universal, often working in two films a week, he married his costar, Dorothy Davenport. D.W. Griffith used him for the showy role of the vengeful blacksmith in *The Birth of a Nation*. Jesse Lasky, who signed him up after that, found him "charming, personable, handsome...and cooperative," and he became the most popular male star of the immediate postwar years. Yet he is primarily known in American film history as a drug addict: he was given morphine after an injury in a train wreck so that he could continue his role on location in a film. He died at 32 trying to break his addiction. Last film 1922.

Rich, Irene (1891-1988). Born Irene Luther in Buffalo, she was a successful real estate agent before she was a star. An extra in a Mary Pickford film (1918), she worked up to major roles as experienced or world-weary women in the silent period. After that she was in radio, theater and a few films. Last film 1948.

Rin Tin Tin (1916-1932). German shepherd dog brought back from a German trench in World War I by Captain Lee Duncan. He became a popular star (1922) and a leading source of revenue for Warner Brothers in the 1920s. Many of his scripts were written by Darryl Zanuck. Last adventure, *Lightning Warrior,* a serial, 1931.

Rogers, (Charles) Buddy (1904-   ). Born in Kansas, he attended the state university but was attracted by show business and became an orchestra leader and juvenile leading man in Hollywood, notably in *Wings* and *My Best Girl* (both 1927), the latter starring Mary Pickford. He married her in 1936 and was loyal till her death in 1979. Last film 1957.

Roland, Gilbert (1905-   ). Born Luis Antonio Damaso de Alonso in Mexico, he was trained by his father for bullfighting but turned to movies as a teenager when his family moved to California. Busy film career 1925-1979, often in "Latin lover" roles.

Santschi, Tom (1878-1931). Born in Indiana, he entered films in 1909 and worked steadily, occasionally directing his own performance as a rugged, ruthless hero or villain until 1931, when his last picture was called *The Last Ride.*

Shearer, Norma (1900-1983). Born in Montreal, the daughter of a successful businessman who paid for music and dance lessons, she had to go to work when her father went bankrupt. Her mother took her to New York, where she managed to get jobs modeling for billboards and appearing in small film roles (from 1920). Irving Thalberg remembered one of these when he was departing as executive producer from Universal to the L.B. Mayer company and he signed her to a contract. She worked in six pictures in 1923 and nine in 1924, and her particular combination of patrician poise and desire to get ahead brought her more prestigious stories, including the Lubitsch production of *The Student Prince* (1927). Thalberg married her in 1927 and provided for her some of the most prestigious pictures of the early sound period (*The Barretts of Wimpole Street, Romeo and Juliet*). After his death in 1936, she was less successful in choice of roles and her last film was 1942.

Shipman, Nell (1892-1970). Born Helen Barham in British Columbia, she persuaded her proper British parents, after they moved to Seattle, to let her try out (at 13) for a traveling theatrical group. One of the managers she encountered in later years married her and they went to Hollywood, where she made a living at first writing scripts, then found fame as an actress in a story about the north: *God's Country and the Woman* (1915). Three sequels followed (through 1923), which she produced, wrote, and co-directed. She became known not only as "The Girl from God's Country," but also an apostle of women's independence and the humane treatment of animals. She moved her company to northern Idaho, attempting to get financing to make movies there, but this was not successful, and she turned to writing novels and short stories, some of them published. Last film 1946.

Sills, Milton (1882-1930). Born in Chicago, he was sent by his parents to the University of Chicago, where he was active in the theater. He joined a stock company and later acted in New York, entering films in 1914. Tall, dignified, and compassionate as the schoolteacher friend of *Miss Lulu Bett* (1921) he was also versatile enough to play in westerns and comedies. Died of a heart attack at 48. Last film *The Sea Wolf* 1930.

Stewart, Anita (1895-1961). Born Anna Stewart in Brooklyn, in 1911 she followed the example of her brother-in-law, Ralph Ince, who was an actor-director at Vitagraph. There she met and became a friend of the Talmadge sisters. In 1917 she became the chief contractual "property" of Louis B. Mayer and later had her own company under his management. Last film 1928.

Stone, Lewis (1879-1953). Born in Massachusetts, he was a star on Broadway before trying films in 1915, then after World War I he found success as distinguished-looking heroes and gentlemen. He played the dual roles in Rex Ingram's version of *The Prisoner of Zenda* (1922) and after sound worked steadily at MGM in mature parts, some opposite Garbo, some opposite Mickey Rooney in the Andy Hardy series. Last film 1953.

Swanson, Gloria (1897-1983). Born Gloria Josephine Mae Swenson in Chicago, she was the daughter of an army captain who had to move from one station to another. She visited the Essanay studios in Chicago in 1913 and performed her first scenes there. She worked for Mack Sennett, Cecil DeMille, and Allan Dwan, and became the epitome of Hollywood fashion and glamor. Last film 1975. (See Introduction, pages 5-6, and Chapter 4.)

Sweet, Blanche (1895-1986). Born in Chicago, she was on stage as a child, cared for by her grandmother, and at 14 began working in film with D.W. Griffith in his second year at Biograph. He used her constantly, --*A Corner in Wheat* (1909), *The Lonedale Operator* and *The Battle* (1911)--and in 1914 in 19 films including *Judith of Bethulia*, a four-reeler which was his greatest effort up to that time. Moving to the Lasky company, she worked for DeMille and Marshall Neilan, whom she married (1922-1929). She continued to have roles in the 20s. Last film 1930.

Talmadge, Constance (1900-1973). Born in Brooklyn, she followed in her elder sister's footsteps at Vitagraph in 1914, playing in comedies primarily. D.W. Griffith cast her as the mountain girl in the Babylonian story in *Intolerance*. Through the influence of her brother-in-law, Joseph Schenck, she produced her own films, often written by Anita Loos. Last picture 1929.

Talmadge, Norma (1897-1957). Born in Niagara Falls, she grew up in Brooklyn, where her mother encouraged her to go after extra roles at Vitagraph. At 14 she was a leading woman, and her long list of performances from 1910 through the 20s reflected her great popularity. From *Smilin' Through* (1922) to *Camille* (1927) she represented the beautiful suffering heroine who was in need of emancipation. Her marriage to

Joseph Schenck (1916-1927) seems to have been relatively happy: he was 19 years older and managed her independent company and career, with releases through First National and United Artists, even after the divorce. Her often regal and charming image was not enhanced by a Brooklyn accent in two sound pictures. Last film 1930. (See Introduction, page 9, and Chapter 2, pages 48-54.)

Taylor, Estelle (1899-1958). Born Estelle Boylan in Delaware, she was first a typist, then studied acting and modeling, and was in Broadway musicals. Her first film work was in 1920 and she was in the Theda Bara debut vamp performance, *A Fool There Was* (1922), afterward doing the vamp herself from time to time. She had major roles in *The Ten Commandments* (1923) and *Don Juan* (1926). She costarred with Jack Dempsey, the heavyweight boxing champion, in a 1925 film and they were married (1925-1931). Last films 1932, 1945

Tearle, Conway (1878-1938). Born Frederick Levy in New York City, he went to school and worked on the stage in England. From 1905 to 1914, when he made his first film, he was an important Broadway actor. As a sophisticated, substantial husband and father, he averaged five pictures a year during the 20s, including *Stella Maris, Bella Donna, Black Oxen, Dancing Mothers*. Last film 1936.

Tellegen, Lou (1881-1934). Born Isidor van Dameler in Holland, he was on the stage in his native country and in 1909 was chosen as Sarah Bernhardt's leading man, including her three films, culminating in *Queen Elizabeth* (1912). He was a striking and attractive figure in a number of silent films, especially 1924-25, but was evidently too temperamental for his directors and not well thought of as an actor. He married the opera and film star Geraldine Farrar in 1916 but she divorced him after her last film in 1921. Last film 1931, his death a suicide.

Terry, Alice (1899-   ). Born in Indiana, she joined Triangle in 1916, and in the 1920s her career was mostly shaped by her husband and director, Rex Ingram at MGM. In *The Four Horsemen of the Apocalypse* she danced with Valentino and in *Mare Nostrum* (1926) she was a spy who faced a firing squad. The Ingrams separated themselves from Louis B. Mayer by departing for Nice, in southern France, and making a few pictures there for MGM release. She moved back to California after Ingram's death in 1950. Last U.S. film, 1929; one Spanish film 1935.

Torrence, Ernest (1878-1933). Born in Edinburgh, he graduated from music schools there and in London and performed in opera as a baritone. His lugubrious appearance and voice won him in Hollywood such parts as the criminal in *Tol'able David* (1921), Captain Hook in *Peter Pan* (1924), and Keaton's father in *Steamboat Bill Jr* (1928). Last film 1933.

Valentino, Rudolph (1895-1926). Born Rodolpho Alfonzo Raffaelo Pierre Filibert Guglielmi di Valentina d'Antonguolla in Italy, he was the son of an army veterinarian who died when he was 11. Coming to the U.S. in 1913, he failed at various jobs but finally began to get bit parts in movies with *Alimony* in 1918. After *The Four Horsemen of the Apocalypse* (1921) he became probably the most notable example of a male screen idol until his death, the year of his last film, 1926. (See Introduction, pages 6-7, and Chapter 4.)

Velez, Lupe (1908-1944). Born Maria Guadalupe Velez de Villalobos in Mexico and educated in a San Antonio convent, she was a dancer in a Hollywood nightclub and worked in Hal Roach comedies (1926) before winning the lead in *The Gaucho* (1927) with Douglas Fairbanks. Roles in Griffith's *Lady of the Pavements* and a series of "Mexican Spitfire" comedies drew on the volatility of her personal life. A very public affair with Gary Cooper was followed by a noisy marriage with Johnny Weissmuller, and eventually suicide. Last film 1944.

Vidor, Florence (1895-1977). Born Florence Cobb (changed to Arto when her mother remarried) in Houston, Texas, where she married King Vidor in 1915 and joined him in a hazardous auto trip to Hollywood. She found work at Vitagraph (1916), while his rise to directing was slower. At Famous Players, especially under Lubitsch and St.Clair, her gracious and sophisticated air won acclaim and popularity, but she and Vidor separated in 1923. After divorce, her marriage to the violinist Jascha Heifetz lasted till 1945. Her first sound film, 1929, was her last.

Walthall, Henry B. (1878-1936). Born in Alabama, he studied law but found success on Broadway, turning to films in 1909, when he became at once a regular performer for D.W. Griffith, culminating in the leading role as the southern colonel in *The Birth of a Nation*. He worked continuously after that but the films and/or the roles were not of major importance. Last film 1936.

Warner, H.B. (1876-1958). Born Henry Byron Warner in London, the son of a prominent actor, he was on the stage himself at seven and undertook a theatrical career. Entering U.S. films in 1914, he worked steadily playing dignified character leads, notably Jesus in DeMille's *The King of Kings* (1927) and Chang in Capra's *Lost Horizon* (1937). Last film 1956.

Washburn, Bryant (1889-1963). Born in Chicago, he worked on the stage there, joining Essanay in 1910, where he became a popular star. He worked steadily in three or four films a year during the 20s, mostly in serials in the 30s (a small role in *Stagecoach* 1939), and on into the 40s. Last film 1947.

White, Pearl (1889-1938). Born in Missouri, a farmer's daughter, she played child leads in amateur theatricals, joined a circus as a rider at 13, tried for jobs on Broadway, but settled for a job as secretary for the Powers film company. It was then she was "discovered" (1910) and given roles in westerns and comedies, followed by selection as star of the Pathe serial, *The Perils of Pauline* (1914). This was followed by *The Exploits of Elaine* and ten other tales of suspense. The notion of a continued story became enormously popular and her own boxoffice value was said to exceed that of Mary Pickford during several years. Last series 1924.

Wilbur, Crane (1889-1973). Born in New York state, he was in stock and repertory, entering films in 1910. Noted for his good looks, he nevertheless did most of his acting as Pearl White's co-star in features and in *The Perils of Pauline* serial (1914), and his time was occupied after about 1921 acting on Broadway, writing plays and scenarios, and directing. Last film as director 1962.

Williams, Kathlyn (1888-1960). Born in Montana, she joined up with a stock company and later went to drama school in New York. Her first film role in *All Is Not Gold* (1910) with Biograph led to steady work at the Selig studio, where she became their most familiar star ("the Selig girl"). Statuesque and yet amazingly versatile, she was quite at ease with the performing animals so important to the plots of many Selig productions, and it was as the star of the first U.S. serial, *The Adventures of Kathlyn* (1913) that she became internationally famous. She did not continue in serials, but moved to Famous Players-Lasky after 1918, working eventually in supporting roles in the 30s. Last film 1947.

Wilson, Lois (1896-1983). Born in Pittsburgh, she quit teaching school in Alabama to try films in 1916. Most of her roles were not exciting or glamorous, but she worked continuously at Famous Players-Lasky. She played the lead in *The Covered Wagon* (1923). In 1921, she was the unhappy slavey who did the dishes for her sister's family in *Miss Lulu Bett*, one of the few surviving works directed by William deMille. Last film 1949.

Wray, Fay (1907-   ). Born in Canada, she was raised in Los Angeles and yearned to be in movies. As early as 16, she began to get parts, but not till Erich von Stroheim cast her in *The Wedding March* (1928) was she thought of as a star. With the arrival of sound, she worked in horror movies, notably *King Kong*. The same year (1933) she made ten other pictures. She retired in 1942 for her second marriage, to Robert Riskin, and after his death came back for character roles. Last film 1958.

Young, Clara Kimball (1890-1960). Born Clara Kimball in Chicago, she was brought on stage at the age of three by her performing parents and went on to do vaudeville and stock. At Vitagraph from 1909, often directed by her husband, James Young, she was voted "most popular" by a movie magazine in 1914. She played mature women more often than ingenues. Lewis Selznick formed a company under her name during his brief time as a producer, but by the mid-20s she was working again in vaudeville, with occasional appearances in films in the 30s. Last film 1941.

These career sketches of 176 leading performers of the silent era would not have been possible without *The Film Encyclopedia,* compiled, researched, and written by Ephraim Katz. Information has also been drawn from relevant biographies, autobiographies, and shorter career essays, as listed in the introduction to the bibliography, below.

Note that comedy players are not included. Note also that many of the more important players are treated more fully in earlier chapters; in most of these cases page numbers are given.

The list above, which was originally intended to be limited to 100, began with the 71 silent film stars included in the *International Dictionary of Films and Film Makers, Volume III: Actors and Actresses,* then was augmented by the list of 75 in Joe Franklin, *Classics of the Silent Screen,* and was expanded further by cross-checking the books by Hal Herman, Brundidge, Deems Taylor, and especially Daniel Blum, *A Pictorial History of the Silent Screen.*

In general, by working through all the books available on the silent era and also the 1921-1926 issues of *Photoplay,* the author has made an effort to include the most often reappearing names.

The following, however, are written here as an indication of how many more might have been included and indeed, with better research and more access to films (many of them forever lost) such names as these might be considered more important by other observers. It appears — although this was not intended — that these 24 names bring the list to a round 200.

(Parentheses here are an attempt to indicate the years of film acting.)

George Arliss (1921-1937).
Bessie Barriscale (1913-1921; 1928-1935).
Belle Bennett (1916-1931).
Olive Borden (1925-1933).
John Bowers (1916-1931).
Harrison Ford (1917-1932).
Hedda Hopper (1916-1966).
Doris Kenyon (1915-1939).
Florence LaBadie (1909-1917).
Montagu Love (1915-1946).
Douglas MacLean (1914-1929).
Carmel Myers (1916-1934; 1946)
Greta Nissen (1925-1935).
Mary Nolan (1925-1932).
Olga Petrova (1914-1918).
Dorothy Phillips (1911-1927; 1962).
Vera Reynolds (1923-1932).
Alma Rubens (1916-1929).
Dorothy Sebastian (1925-1942).
C. Aubrey Smith (1915-1948).
Olive Thomas (1916-1920).
Victor Varconi (1924-1959).
Alice White (1927-1959).
Claire Windsor (1920-1929; 1933-1945

Appendix B
Chronology of Film Careers

1906: Maurice Costello 1906/41.

1907: G.M.Anderson 1907/14. Francis Ford 1907/53. Bobby Harron 1907/20. Florence Lawrence 1907/33. Owen Moore 1907/37.

1908: Donald Crisp 1908/63. Arthur Johnson 1908/14.   Paul Kelly 1908/56

1909: Lionel Barrymore 1909/53. Hobart Bosworth 1909/42. Harry Carey 1909/48. James Kirkwood 1909/34. MARY PICKFORD 1909/33. Tom Santschi 1909/31. Blanche Sweet 1909/30. Henry Walthall 1909/36. Clara Kimball Young 1909/41.

1910: Grace Cunard 1910/45.   Viola Dana 1910/29.   Bebe Daniels 1910/35. Priscilla Dean 1910/32. Alice Joyce 1910/30. J.Warren Kerrigan

1910/24. Eugene Pallette 1910/46. Wallace Reid 1910/22. Norma Talmadge 1910/30. Bryant Washburn 1910/47. Pearl White 1910/24. Crane Wilbur 1910/21. Kathlyn Williams 1910/47.

1911: King Baggott 1911/41. Francis X. Bushman 1911/66. Dolores Costello 1911/43. Harold Lockwood 1911/18. Mae Marsh 1911/25, 28/63. Tom Mix 1911/34. Anna Q. Nilssen 1911/28,50. Anita Stewart 1911/28.

1912: Mae Busch 1912/42. Hoot Gibson 1912/17,21/36,59. Dorothy Gish 1912/25,63. LILLIAN GISH 1912/28/88. Raymond Hatton 1912/67. Mary Miles Minter 1912/23. Antonio Moreno 1912/56. Lou Tellegen 1912/31.

1913: John Barrymore 1913/42. Wallace Beery 1913/49. Lon Chaney 1913/30. Lars Hanson 1913,26/28,65. Thomas Meighan 1913/34. Charles Ray 1913/28. Jack Mulhall 1913/59. GLORIA SWANSON 1913/28/75.

1914: Enid Bennett 1914/26,40. Alice Brady 1914/23, 33/39. Marguerite Clark 1914/1921. Miriam Cooper 1914/24. Dustin Farnum 1914/26. William Farnum 1914/52. Pauline Frederick 1914/37. Creighton Hale 1914/49. WILLIAM S. HART 1914/25. Sessue Hayakawa 1914/57. Jack Holt 1914/51. Emil Jannings 1914,27/29,45. Annette Kellerman 1914/24. Tully Marshall 1914/43. Shirley Mason 1914/29. Pola Negri 1914,23/30,64. Seena Owen 1914/28. Milton Sills 1914/30. Constance Talmadge 1914/29. Conway Tearle 1914/36. H.B. Warner 1914/56.

1915. May Allison 1915/27. Agnes Ayres 1915/29. Theda Bara 1915/19,25. Wallace Beery 1915/49. Monte Blue 1915/54. Lew Cody 1915/34. Betty Compson 1915/48. Dorothy Dalton 1915/24. Elliott Dexter 1915/25. Marie Doro 1915/24. DOUGLAS FAIRBANKS 1915/34. Geraldine Farrar 1915/1921. Jean Hersholt 1915/55. Rod LaRoque 1915/41. Elmo Lincoln 1915/26,52. Nell Shipman 1915/23. Lewis Stone 1915/53.

1916. Richard Barthelmess 1916/42. Jackie Coogan 1916,19/31,79. John Gilbert 1916/34. Corinne Griffith 1916/32. Leatrice Joy 1916/29,51. Norman Kerry 1916/41. Bessie Love 1916/31,83. May McAvoy 1916/29. Adolphe Menjou 1916/60. Mae Murray 1916/31. Alla Nazimova 1916/25. Esther Ralston 1916/41. Alice Terry 1916/29. Florence Vidor 1916/29. Lois Wilson 1916/49.

1917. Warner Baxter 1917/50. Noah Beery 1917/45. Marion Davies 1917/37. Elsie Ferguson 1917/30. Phyllis Haver 1917/29. Buck Jones 1917/42. Cullen Landis 1917/30. Edmund Lowe 1917/60. Colleen Moore 1917/34. Ramon Novarro 1917/34,60. ZaSu Pitts 1917/63. Marie Prevost 1917/36.

1918. Betty Blythe 1918/48. Ronald Colman 1918/50. Marguerite DeLaMotte 1918/34,42. Neil Hamilton 1918/70. Madge Kennedy 1918/26,75. Lila Lee 1918/37. Percy Marmont 1918/28,56. Irene Rich 1918/32,48. RUDOLPH VALENTINO 1918/26.

1919: William Boyd 1919/52. Carol Dempster 1919/26. Reginald Denny 1919/66. Laura LaPlante 1919/31,57. Ben Lyon 1919/38. Conrad Nagel 1919/59. Aileen Pringle 1919/39

1920. Renee Adoree 1920/30. Richard Arlen 1920/76. George Bancroft 1920/42. Madge Bellamy 1920/35. Barbara LaMarr 1920/28. Victor McLaglen 1920/58. Nita Naldi 1920/28. Norma Shearer 1920/42. Estelle Taylor 1920/32,45.

1921. Mary Astor 1921/65. Richard Dix 1921/47. Billie Dove 1921/32. Dorothy Mackaill 1921/37. Mary Philbin 1921/29. Ernest Torrence 1921/33.

1922. Eleanor Boardman 1922/33. Dagmar Godowski 1922/26. William Haines 1922/34. George O'Brien 1922/64. William Powell 1922/55. Rin-Tin-Tin 1922/31.

1923. Clara Bow 1923/33. Charles Farrell 1923/41. Jetta Goudal 1923/33. Ken Maynard 1923/38,45. Fay Wray 1923/42,58.

1924. Mary Brian 1924/37. Betty Bronson 1924/32,71. Ricardo Cortez 1924/58.

1925. Vilma Banky 1925/32. Louise Brooks 1925/31,38. Joan Crawford 1925/70. Dolores Del Rio 1925/78. Tim McCoy 1925/42. Gilbert Roland 1925/79.

1926. Gary Cooper 1926/61. Greta Garbo 1926/41. Janet Gaynor 1926/37,57. Buddy Rogers 1926/57. Lupe Velez 1926/44.

Appendix C
Bibliography

We are fortunate that DeWitt Bodeen, before he died, was able to research and write the lives of 30 early Hollywood stars, most of them based on his own articles in *Films in Review* or *Focus on Film*. His two books, *From Hollywood,* and *More From Hollywood,* are examples of professional and loving care, revealing along the way many thoughtful insights into a way of life now past.

Equally valuable are the more personal reminiscences of the prolific writer for *Photoplay,* Adela Rogers St. Johns. *Love, Laughter, and Tears: My Hollywood Story,* offers key scenes in the lives of 21 silent stars as she shared or observed them. Her emotional attachments and rejections are here made plain for us all to see, and her reporting therefore carries a special kind of authenticity as well as drama.

More comprehensive works of shorter biographies are the one-volume compilation by Ephraim Katz, *The Film Encyclopedia,* which is indispensable for the film scholar today, and *The International Dictionary of Films and Film Makers,* with its incomparable bibliographies. Volume III is on *Actors and Actresses,* including 71 from the silent period. Longer, more idiosyncratic essays may be found in David Thomson's *Biographical Dictionary of Film.*

Of particular interest and value for readers of this volume is Joe Franklin's *Classics of the Silent Screen,* (1959), an early contribution at a time when serious books about film, and especially about the earliest days, were few. Based on devoted show business research plus radio (starting 1948) and TV (1953) shows in New York City, he has given us his own responses to fifty movies and 75 stars. His collaborator was William K. Everson.

Again we must pay tribute, also, to Frank Magill, whose three-volume *Magill's Survey of Cinema: Silent Films*, gives us extensive recent descriptions and evaluations of the content of individual films together with much historical data.

Books of permanent value and pictorial interest for students of silent films, of course, are Richard Griffith, Arthur Mayer,and Eileen Bowser, *The Movies*, and Kevin Brownlow, *The Parade's Gone By.*

Notable attempts to deal with the phenomenon of the movie star, either as a concept or through a selective list are books by Charles Affron, Richard Dyer, Richard Griffith, Edgar Morin, Richard Schickel, David Shipman, Marc Wanamaker,Alexander Walker, Elisabeth Weis, Ken Wlaschin.

The 1970s and 80s brought us a number of valuable books about individual stars of the silent drama:

Miriam Cooper (with Bonnie Herndon). *Dark Lady of the Silents* (1973). Autobiography.

Marion Davies. *The Times We Had* (1977).

Leatrice Gilbert Fountain (with John R. Maxim). *Dark Star* (1985). Biography of her father, John Gilbert.

Booton Herndon. *Mary Pickford and Douglas Fairbanks* (1977).

Diane Koszarski. *The Complete Films of William S. Hart: A Pictorial Record* (1980).

Bessie Love. *From Hollywood With Love* (1977).

Paul E. Mix. *The Life and Legend of Tom Mix* (1972).

Pola Negri. *Memoirs of a Star* (1970).

Curtis Nunn. *Marguerite Clark* (1981).

Esther Ralston. *Some Day We'll Laugh* (1985). Autobiography.

David Stenn. *Clara Bow: Runnin' Wild* (1988).

Gloria Swanson. *Swanson on Swanson* (1980). Collaborator, Bill Dufty

Larry Swindell. *The Last Hero* (1980). Gary Cooper.

From earlier years we have these important contributions:

Bebe Daniels and Ben Lyon. *Life With the Lyons (1953).*

Lillian Gish. *The Movies, Mr. Griffith, and Me* (1969).

Adolphe Menjou and M.M. Musselman. *It Took Nine Tailors* (1948).

Colleen Moore. *Silent Star* (1968).

Mary Pickford. *Sunshine and Shadow* (1955).

Scholars and fans alike may wish to consult the files and indexes of the monthly *Films in Review* for numerous filmographies and biographies. Access to these and other magazine articles can also be assisted by consulting the "Biography" chapter of Richard Dyer MacCann and Edward S. Perry, *The New Film Index: A Bibliography of Magazine Articles in English, 1930-1970* (N.Y., E.P. Dutton, 1975).

Books from which extracts are reprinted in this volume:

Bowser, Eileen, ed. *Film Notes.* New York, Museum of Modern Art, 1969. Reviews of films in Museum collection.

Brownlow, Kevin, and John Kobal. *Hollywood: The Pioneers.* New York, Knopf, 1979.

Brundidge, Harry. *Twinkle, Twinkle, Movie Star!* New York, E.P.Dutton, 1930; reprinted Garland, 1977. 31 interviews.

Cooke, Alistair. *Douglas Fairbanks: The Making of a Screen Character.* New York, Museum of Modern Art, 1940.

Fairbanks, Douglas. *Laugh and Live.* New York, Britton Publishing Co., 1917.

Franklin, Joe. *Classics of the Silent Screen.* New York, Citadel, 1959. Many photographs.

Herman, Hal C. (with Jack Hoins). *How I Broke Into the Movies.* Hollywood, H.C.Herman, 1929. "Signed stories by 60 screen stars." Photos, autographed, on facing pages.

Jones, Charles Reed (ed.). *Breaking Into the Movies.* New York, Unicorn Press, 1927.

Koszarski, Diane. *The Complete Films of William S. Hart: A Pictorial Record.* New York, Dover, 1980.

Lasky, Jesse. *I Blow My Own Horn.* New York, Doubleday, 1957.

Lennig, Arthur. *The Silent Voice.* Lennig, 1969.

Katz, Ephraim. *The Film Encyclopedia.* New York, Harper & Row, 1979; Perigee Books, 1982.

Lejeune, C.A. *Cinema.* London, Alexander Maclehose, 1931.

Magill, Frank. *Magill's Survey of Cinema: Silent Films.* Pasadena, CA, Salem Press, 1982. New, content-oriented reviews.

Marsh, Mae. *Screen Acting.* Photo-Star Publishing, 1921.

Mencken, H.L. *Prejudices: Sixth Series.* New York, Knopf, 1927.

Messel, Rudolph. *This Film Business.* London, Benn, 1928.

Negri, Pola (with Alfred Allan Lewis). *Memoirs of a Star.* New York, Doubleday, 1970.

O'Dell, Scott. *Representative Photoplays Analyzed.* Hollywood, Palmer Institute of Authorship, 1924.

Pickford, Mary. *Sunshine and Shadow.* New York, Doubleday, 1955.

Ralston, Esther. *Some Day We'll Laugh.* Metuchen NJ, Scarecrow Press, 1985.

Slide, Anthony. *The Idols of Silence.* New York, A.S. Barnes, 1976.

Slide, Anthony and Edward Wagenknecht. *Fifty Great American Silent Films 1912-1920.* New York, Dover, 1980.

Swanson, Gloria. *Swanson on Swanson.* New York, Random House, 1980.

Tibbetts, John (ed.). *Introduction to the Photoplay.* Shawnee Mission, KS, National Film Society, 1977. Revised reprint of *Introduction to the Photoplay,* Los Angeles, Academy of Motion Picture Arts and Sciences and University of Southern California, 1929. Talks by Hollywood people to first USC motion picture class.

Wagenknecht, Edward. *Movies in the Age of Innocence.* Norman, University of Oklahoma Press, 1962.

Walker, Alexander. *Stardom.* New York, Stein & Day, 1970.

_____. *The Celluloid Sacrifice.* New York, Penguin, 1968.

Wilson, Harry Leon. *Merton of the Movies.* New York, Doubleday, 1922. A novel about a movie fan.

Zierold, Norman. *Sex Goddesses of the Silent Screen.* Chicago, Henry Regnery, 1973.

Zukor, Adolph (with Dale Kramer). *The Public Is Never Wrong.* New York, G.P. Putnam's Sons, 1953. His autobiography.

Articles reprinted in this volume:

Bodeen, DeWitt. *"Panthea."* In Frank Magill, *Magill's Survey of Cinema: Silent Films.* See above.

_____. *"Flesh and the Devil."* In Frank Magill, *Magill's Survey of Cinema: Silent Films.* See above.

Bowers, Ronald. *"Manhandled."* In Frank Magill, *Magill's Survey of Cinema: Silent Films.* See above.

Brownlow, Kevin. "Lillian Gish," *American Film* March 1984.

Edelman, Rob. *Stella Maris.* In Frank Magill, *Magill's Survey of Cinema: Silent Films.* See above.

Griffith, Richard. *"The Coward."* In Eileen Bowser (ed.), *Film Notes.* See above.

Howe, Herbert. "They Can't Fool the Public." *Photoplay,* June 1922. Stars on and off screen.

_____. "Close-Ups and Long Shots." *Photoplay* Jan 1926.

Lucas, Blake. "Acting Style in Silent Films." In Frank Magill, *Magill's Survey of Cinema: Silent Films.* See above.

Lyon, Ben. "How I Broke Into the Movies." In Hal Herman, *How I Broke Into the Movies.* See above.

Moore, Colleen. "Up From the Extra Ranks." In Charles Reed Jones (ed.), *Breaking Into the Movies.* See above.

Nagel, Conrad. "An Actor's Art." In John Tibbetts (ed.), *Introduction to the Photoplay.* See above.

Naremore, James. *"True Heart Susie* and the Art of Lillian Gish." *Quarterly Review of Film Studies,* Winter 1981.

Sanderson Jr., Lennox. *The Great K and A Train Robbery.* In Frank Magill, *Magill's Survey of Cinema: Silent Films.* See above.

Sherwood, Robert. *"The Thief of Bagdad." Life,* 1924. Reprinted page 137 in Douglas Fairbanks, Jr. and Richard   Schickel, *The Fairbanks Album.* See below.

Talmadge, Norma. "Close-Ups." *Saturday Evening Post,*   March 12, 1927. Her autobiography continued on alternate   weeks.   Longer extract reprinted in first edition, Tino Balio,   (ed.) *The American Film Industry.* Madison, WI,   University of Wisconsin Press, 1976.

Other useful books:

Affron, Charles. *Star Acting: Gish, Garbo, Davis.* N.Y., E.P.   Dutton, 1977.

⚓ Appelbaum, Stanley. *Silent Movies: A Picture Quiz Book.* NY,   Dover, 1974. With 212 stills from Culver Pictures.

⚑ Blum, Daniel. *A Pictorial History of the Silent Screen.* N.Y.,   Grosset & Dunlap, 1953.

Bodeen, DeWitt. *From Hollywood.* New York, A.S. Barnes, 1976.   "The Careers of 15 Great American Stars."

_____. *More From Hollywood.* New York, A.S. Barnes, 1977.

Bordwell, David, Janet Staiger, and Kristin Thompson.   *The Classical Hollywood Cinema.* N.Y., Columbia University Press, 1985.

⚐ Brooks, Louise. *Lulu in Hollywood.* New York, Knopf, 1982.   Observations on other stars.

Crowther, Bosley. *Hollywood Rajah.* N.Y., Holt, Rinehart, and   Winston, 1960. "The Life and Times of Louis B. Mayer."

Davies, Marion (1951 audio tapes edited by Pamela Pfau and Kenneth S. Marx). *The Times We Had.* N.Y., Bobbs-Merrill 1975/Ballantine   1977. Foreword by Orson Welles. Hearst,San Simeon and her movies.

Dyer, Richard. *Stars.* London, British Film Institute, 1982. ⚑

Everson, William K. *American Silent Film.* N.Y., Oxford, 1978.

Griffith, Richard, Arthur Mayer, Eileen Bowser. *The Movies.* New   York, Simon & Schuster, 1957/1984. More than half on silent era.

Griffith, Richard. *The Movie Stars.* Garden City, NY, Doubleday,   1970.

Guiles, Fred Lawrence. *Marion Davies.* New York, McGraw-Hill,   1972.

Haskell, Molly. *From Reverence to Rape: The Treatment of   Women in the Movies.*   New York, Holt, Rinehart & Winston,   1974 (Penguin paperback).

Higashi, Sumiko. *Virgins, Vamps, and Flappers: The American   Silent Movie Heroine.* Montreal, Eden Press Women's   Publications, 1978.

Hughes, Elinor. *Famous Stars of Filmdom (Women).* Freeport NY,   Books for Libraries Press, 1970. Original, 1931.

_____. *Famous Stars of Filmdom (Men).* Freeport NY, Books   for Libraries Press, 1970. Original, 1932.

Jorifin (John Richard Finch). *Close-Ups.* New York,   A.S. Barnes, 1978. "From the Golden Age of the Silent   Cinema." Full page photos of players;paragraphs about them.

Kobal, John. *People Will Talk*. London, Aurum Press, 1986. Taped interviews with stars, 8 from the silent era.

Lahue, Kalton C. *Gentlemen to the Rescue: The Heroes of the Silent Screen*. Cranbury N.J., A.S. Barnes, 1972.

_____. *Ladies in Distress*. New York, A.S. Barnes, 1971. Forty biographies of silent stars.

_____. *Winners of the West*. New York, A.S. Barnes, 1970. "The Sagebrush Heroes of the Silent Screen."

MacCann, Richard Dyer. *Film: A Montage of Theories*. N.Y., E.P. Dutton, 1966.

_____. *The First Tycoons*. Metuchen, NJ, Scarecrow Press, 1987. Laemmle, Zukor, Lasky, Fox, and others.

_____. *The First Film Makers*. Metuchen, NJ, Scarecrow Press, 1989. Emphasizes Griffith, Ince, and Stroheim.

Marion, Frances. *Off With Their Heads!* New York, Macmillan, 1972. Screenwriter's autobiography.

Menjou, Adolphe (and M.M. Musselman). *It Took Nine Tailors*. New York, Whittlesey/McGraw, 1948. One of the rare autobiographies by a male actor.

Morin, Edgar. *The Stars*. N.Y., Grove Press, 1960.

Paris, Barry. *Louise Brooks*. N.Y., Knopf, 1989.

Rosen, Marjorie. *Popcorn Venus: Women, Movies, and the American Dream*. N.Y., Coward, McCann & Geoghagan, 1973.

St. Johns, Adela Rogers. *Love, Laughter, and Tears: My Hollywood Story*. Garden City, NY, Doubleday, 1978. 21 silent stars.

Schickel, Richard. *The Stars*. N.Y., Dial Press, 1962.

Shipman, David. *The Great Stars: The Golden Years*. London, Hamlyn/N.Y., Crown, 1970. Revised 1979.

Shipman, Nell. *The Silent Screen and My Talking Heart*. Boise ID, Boise State University, 1987. The Canadian-born Hollywood actress who tried to set up a studio in Priest Lake, Idaho.

Swindell, Larry. *The Last Hero: A Biography of Gary Cooper*. N.Y., Doubleday, 1980.

Taylor, Deems, Marcelene Peterson, and Bryant Hale. *A Pictorial History of the Movies*. N.Y., Simon & Schuster, 1943 (revised 1950). Two-thirds on the silent era.

Thomson, David. *A Biographical Dictionary of Film*. New York, William Morrow, 1976.

Wanamaker, Marc (ed.) *Star Profiles*. N.Y., Gallery Books, 1984.

Weis, Elisabeth (ed.). *The Movie Star*. New York, Viking 1981; Penguin, 1981. Essays and star critiques (6 from the silent screen) by the National Society of Film Critics.

Wlaschin, Ken. *The Illustrated Encyclopedia of the World's Great Movie Stars and Their Films*. New York, Harmony Books (Crown Publishers) 1979; London, Salamander Books, 1979. "The Silent Movie Stars" pages 8-35.

Other useful articles:

Anon. "What Do They Earn Today?" *Photoplay* September 1923.

Anon. "Who Is the Greatest Beauty?" *Photoplay*, January 1924.   Out of 60, readers chose eight (April 1924): Mary Pickford, Norma   Talmadge, Corinne Griffith, Madge Bellamy, Pola Negri, Gloria   Swanson, Marion Davies, Alice Terry.

Berger, Spencer M. "The Film Career of John Barrymore." *Image*,   January 1957.

Biddle Jr., Craig. "The Millionaire Extra Man's Story."   *Photoplay*, June 1923. Wealthy heir tries to get attention of   casting office.

Bird, Carol. "A Man of Talents." *Photoplay* June 1926.   About Milton Sills.

Braudy, Leo.   "Film Acting: Some Critical Problems and Proposals." *Quarterly Review of Film Studies*, February 1976.

Card, James. "Winners of the Second Festival of Film Artists."   *Image*, October 1957. Eastman House medal for survivors of   1926-1930.

DeCordova, Richard. "The Emergence of the Star System in   America," *Wide Angle*, Vol. 6, No. 4, 1985. Awareness of   actors' names in earliest trade and fan magazines.

Dietz, Howard. "Album 1923: Motion Pictures." *Theatre Arts*,   August 1948. Comments on personalities.

Dougherty, Jack. "Why I Quit Being Mr. Barbara LaMarr."   *Photoplay*, October 1924.

Druesne, Maeve.   "Nazimova." *Films in   Review*. June/July   and August/September 1985.

Dyer, Peter John. "When the Stars Grew Up," *Films and   Filming* January 1958. Actors of 1920s.

Everson, William.   "Remembering Louise Brooks." *Films in   Review*, November 1985.

Ferguson, Elsie. "The Penalties of Being a Star." *Photoplay*,   December 1922.

"Favorite Sweethearts of the Screen." *Photoplay*, June 1924.   Novarro on Alice Terry, Dix on Betty Compson, O'Brien on Talmadge.

"Festival of Film Artists." *Image*, November 1955. Honors for   surviving personalities from 1921-1925. See James Card, above.

Goodman, Ezra. "The Movies' First Chaps and Spurs Hero." *New York   Times*, October 10, 1948. Gilbert M. (Bronco Billy) Anderson.

Graham, Charles. "Acting for the Films in 1912." *Sight and   Sound*, Autumn 1935. Vitagraph.

"Great Lovers of the Screen." *Photoplay* June 1924. Alice Terry   on Ramon Novarro, Nita Naldi on Valentino, etc.

Holland, Larry Lee. "Agnes Ayres." *Films in Review*.   April 1986.

Howe, Herbert. "What Are Matinee Idols Made Of?" *Photoplay*,   April 1923. Answers by Novarro and others.

Hughes, Elinor. "Janet Gaynor." In *Famous Stars of Filmdom*.   See above.

Knight, Arthur. "Dawn Over Hollywood (1919)." *Theatre Arts,* September 1950. Stars, directors, companies.

Lyon, Ben. "Vampires I Have Known." *Photoplay,* February 1925. Swanson, Negri, LaMarr.

McCormick, Elsie. "Emil Jannings." *New Yorker,* January 28, 1928.

McDonald, Gerald D. "Origin of the Star System."*Films in Review,* November 1953.

_____. "From Stage to Screen." *Films in Review,* January 1955. Survey 1903-1912 of futile attempts to attract stage stars.

Robinson, David, Tom Milne, and John Russell Taylor. "Twenties Show People." *Sight and Sound,* Autumn 1968. Tribute to Clara Bow, Marion Davies, Gloria Swanson.

Sills, Milton. "The Actor's Part." In Joseph P. Kennedy, *The Story of the Films.* N.Y., A.W. Shaw, 1927. One of a series of lectures to Harvard Business School students.

St. Johns, Ivan. "The Foreign Legion in Hollywood." *Photoplay,* July 1926. Europeans on the sets.

Spensley, Dorothy. "Bold But Not Brazen." *Photoplay,* August 1926. William Powell.

Staiger, Janet. "Seeing Stars." *Velvet Light Trap,* No. 20, 1983.

_____. "The Eyes Are Really the Focus: Photoplay Acting and Film Form and Style." *Wide Angle,* Vol. 6, No. 4, 1985. Connections with changing theater acting.

"Where Are They Now?" *Newsweek,* April 26, 1970. Now 70, living in San Antonio, Pola Negri emerges to comment on today's "shocking" films and call attention to her memoirs.

Winship, Mary. "The Tiger Queen." *Photoplay,* January 1924. About Aileen Pringle, chosen by Elinor Glyn to play in her story, *Three Weeks.*

Additional bibliography related to Chapters 1 and 2

Arvidson, Linda (Mrs. D.W. Griffith). *When the Movies Were Young.* New York, Dutton, 1925. Comments, sometimes acid, on actresses who succeeded her in major roles at Biograph.

Cooper, Miriam (with Bonnie Herndon). *Dark Lady of the Silents.* New York, Bobbs-Merrill, 1973. Autobiography of a Griffith actress.

DeCordova, Richard. *Picture Personalities: The Emergence of the Star System in America.* Urbana, University of Illinois, 1990. Based on 1986 dissertation.

Gish, Lillian. *The Movies, Mr. Griffith, and Me.* Englewood Cliffs, NJ, Prentice-Hall, 1969.

Kindem, Gorham (ed). *The Business of Motion Pictures.* Southern Illinois University, 1982. Chapter by Kindem on "Hollywood's Movie Star System: A Historical Overview."

Nunn, Curtis. *Marguerite Clark.* Fort Worth, Texas Christian University Press, 1981.

Paine, Albert Bigelow. *Life and Lillian Gish*. New York, Macmillan, 1932.

Pinchot, Ann. *Vanessa*. New York, Arbor House, 1978. A novel about a film director and his star, similar to Griffith and Gish; Pinchot assisted Gish with her 1969 autobiography.

Slide, Anthony. *The Griffith Actresses*. Cranbury, NJ, Barnes, 1973.

Bara, Theda. "How I Became a Film Vampire," and "The Curse on the Moving Picture Actress." *Forum*, June and July, 1919.

Brownlow, Kevin. "Glimpses of a Legend." *Sight and Sound*, Spring 1984. Lillian Gish at the December 1983   showings in London of *Broken Blossoms* and *The Wind*.

Cushman, Robert D. "Interview with Mae Marsh." *Silent Picture*, No. 17, Spring 1973.

Dunham, Harold. "Mae Marsh." *Films in Review*, June/July 1958. With filmography.

_____. "Robert Harron and D.W. Griffith." *Silent Picture*, Autumn 1969. Filmography.

Gish, Lillian. "Life and Living." *Films and Filming*, January 1970.

Jacobs, Jack. "Richard Barthelmess." *Films in Review*, January 1958. Career and 75 films.

Lewis, Kevin. "Happy Birthday, Blanche Sweet." *Films in Review*, March 1986.

McCormick, Elsie. "Emil Jannings." *New Yorker*, January 28, 1928.

McGaffey, Kenneth. "Jerry on the Job." *Photoplay*, January   1917. Admiration of crew for Geraldine Farrar.

O'Dell, Paul. "Miriam Cooper: Forgotten Star." *Silent Picture* Autumn 1969.

Reid, Dorothy Davenport. "The Real Wally." *Photoplay*, March 1925. Her late husband.

St. Johns, Adela Rogers. "The Lady of the Vase." *Photoplay*, August 1923. Norma Talmadge.

Spears, Jack. "Norma Talmadge." *Films in Review*, January 1967. Career and films.

Additional bibliography related to Chapter 3

[Mary and Doug]

Abdullah, Achmed. *The Thief of Bagdad*. New York, A.L. Burt Co., 1924. Based on Douglas Fairbanks' film, script by   "Elton Thomas" (Fairbanks).

Carey, Gary. *Doug and Mary*. New York, Dutton, 1977.

Fairbanks, Douglas. *Taking Stock of Ourselves*. New York, Britton Publishing Co., 1918.

_____. *Making Life Worthwhile*. New York, Britton Publishing Co., 1918.

Fairbanks, Douglas and Edward Knoblock. *The Three Musketeers*. New York, Prospect Press, 1921.

Fairbanks Jr., Douglas and Richard Schickel. *The Fairbanks Album*. Boston, N.Y. Graphic Society, 1975. Biography in pictures of father and son.

Hancock, Ralph and Letitia Fairbanks. *The Fourth Musketeer*. N.Y., Henry Holt, 1953. Letitia Fairbanks Smoot is the daughter of Douglas' brother Robert.

Herndon, Booton. *Mary Pickford and Douglas Fairbanks*. New York, Norton, 1977. "The Most Popular Couple the World Has Ever Known."

Marion, Frances. *Off With Their Heads!* New York, Macmillan, 1972.

Pickford, Mary. *Why Not Try God*. New York, H.C. Kinsey, 1934.

Schickel, Richard. *His Picture in the Papers*. Charterhouse, 1973. "A Speculation on Celebrity in America. Based on the life of Douglas Fairbanks Sr."

Talmey, Allene. *Doug and Mary and Others*. N.Y., Macy-Masius,1927.

Welsh, James M. and John C. Tibbetts. *His Majesty the American: The Cinema of Douglas Fairbanks Sr.*. N.Y., A.S. Barnes, 1977.

Windeler, Robert. *Sweetheart:The Story of Mary Pickford*. London, W.H.Allen, 1973; New York, Praeger, 1974.

Bowser, Eileen. *"The Three Musketeers."* *Film Notes,* Museum of Modern Art, 1969.

Card, James. "The Films of Mary Pickford." *Image,* December 1959. Selected shorts and all the features.

Fairbanks, Douglas. "One Reel of Autobiography." *Colliers,* June 18, 1921. Fantasy-report on how he reached a point where he could not stop smiling.

Fairbanks Jr., Douglas. "Douglas Fairbanks." *Vanity Fair* , May 1930.

_____. "Mary Pickford." *Vanity Fair,* June 1930.

Harriman, Margaret Case. "Mary Pickford." *New Yorker,* April 7, 1934.

Lindsay, Vachel. "The Great Douglas Fairbanks." *Ladies Home Journal,* August 1926.

Pickford, Mary. "Mary Is Looking for Pictures." *Photoplay,* May 1925. Why she chose certain roles; what should she do next? Letter contest for readers.

_____. "My Whole Life." *McCall's,* March through June, 1954. A portion of her autobiography, *Sunshine and Shadow*.

_____. "Stay Away From Hollywood."*Good Housekeeping,* October 1930.

Quirk, James R. "The Public Just Won't Let Mary Pickford Grow Up." *Photoplay,* September 1925. Readers reply to Mary Pickford article: 99 percent of 20,000 say "Be Mary Pickford!"

Robinson, David. "The Hero." *Sight and Sound,* Spring 1973. About Douglas Fairbanks.

Schickel, Richard. "Douglas Fairbanks: Superstar of the Silents." *American Heritage*, December 1971.

"Shrewd." *Time*, May 11, 1931. Mary Pickford plans to buy up and destroy her old pictures.

Silke, James R. "Douglas Fairbanks' Production of *Robin Hood*." *Cinema* (California) Vol. 1, No. 3, 1962-63.

Skig. "The Black Pirate." *Variety*, March 10, 1926.

Spears, Jack. "Mary Pickford's Directors." *Films in Review*, February 1966.

Taylor, Deems. "The Rise of Gladys Smith." *New York Times Book Review*, May 22, 1955. Review of Mary Pickford, *Sunshine and Shadow*.

Tibbetts, John. "Remembering the Glad Girl: An Appraisal of Five Mary Pickford Films." *American Classic Screen*, Vol. 1, No. 1-2, September/October and November 1976. Especially *Rebecca of Sunnybrook Farm*.

Additional bibliography related to Chapter 4
[Gloria and Rudy]

Hudson, Richard M. and Raymond Lee. *Gloria Swanson*. New York, A.S. Barnes, 1970. Descriptions of films.

Mackenzie, Norman A. *The Magic of Rudolph Valentino*. London, Research Publishing Co., 1974. Foreword by S. George Ullman.

Miller, Robert Milton. *Star Myths: Show-Business Biographies on Film*. Metuchen, N.J., Scarecrow Press, 1983. The 1975 and 1977 films about Valentino, pp. 240-244.

Oberfirst, Robert. *Rudolph Valentino:The Man Behind the Myth*. New York, Citadel, 1962.

O'Leary, Liam. *Rex Ingram: Master of the Silent Cinema*. Dublin, Academy Press, 1980. Detailed chapter on the making of *The Four Horsemen of the Apocalypse*.

Scagnetti, Jack. *The Intimate Life of Rudolph Valentino*. Middle Village, NY, Jonathan David Publishers, 1975.

Shulman, Irving. *Valentino*. New York, Trident Press, 1967. Emphasis on events after his death.

Steiger, Brad, and Chaw Mank. *Valentino*. N.Y., Macfadden Bartell, 1966. Speculations on his sex life by a fan club leader.

Talmey, Allene. *Doug and Mary and Others*. N.Y., Macy-Masius, 1927. On Swanson: "Her dignity is paralyzing."

Walker, Alexander. *Rudolph Valentino*. New York, Stein & Day, 1976.

Anon. "*The Four Horsemen of the Apocalypse*." In *Opportunities in the Motion Picture Industry*. Photoplay Research Society, 1922. Fictionized in 5000 words.

Anon. "The Sheik of Film-Araby." *Theatre Magazine*, October 1926. Valentino's last magazine interview.

Anon. "*The Son of the Sheik*." *New York Times* July 26, 1926.

Anon. *"The Son of the Sheik."* *Variety*, July 14, 1926.

Badger, Clarence G. "Reminiscences of the Early Days of Movie Comedies." *Image*, 6/No. 5, May 1957. Director recalls Sennett's enthusiastic first impression of Swanson at Keystone studio.

Card, James. "Rudolph Valentino." *Image*, May 1958.

Hansen, Miriam. "Pleasure, Ambivalence, Identification: Valentino and Female Spectatorship." *Cinema Journal*, Summer 1986.

Huff, Theodore. "The Career of Rudolph Valentino." *Films in Review*, April 1952.

Marberry, M.M. "The Overloved One." *American Heritage*, August 1965. The funeral and after.

Quirk, James R. "Everybody Calls Him Henry." *Photoplay*, June 1925. "What sort of a chap is this Marquis that Gloria married?"

St. Johns, Adela Rogers. "The Confessions of a Modern Woman." *Photoplay*, February 1922. Gloria Swanson's "startling views on the relations of man and woman."

_____. "Gloria: An Impression." *Photoplay*, September 1923.

Sheridan, Gene. *"Moran of the Lady Letty."* *Photoplay* April 1922. Story of the Valentino movie.

Smith, Helena Huntington. "Ugly Duckling." *New Yorker*, January 18, 1930. Profile of Gloria Swanson.

Swanson, Gloria. "There Is No Formula for Success." *Photoplay*, April 1926. Just hard work and lucky breaks.

Tully, Jim. "Rudolph Valentino." *Vanity Fair*, October 1926.

Valentino, Rudolph. "Woman and Love." *Photoplay*, March 1922. A man is attracted by the emotion he arouses in a woman.

_____. "An Open Letter From Valentino to the American Public." *Photoplay*, January 1923. Advertising for "My Life Story."

_____. "My Life Story." *Photoplay*, February, March, April, 1923. Probably written by Herbert Howe, magazine staff member, in collaboration with Valentino.

Waterbury, Ruth. "Wedded and Parted or in Other Words the Story of Natacha Rambova Valentino." *Photoplay*, December 1922.

Additional bibliography related to Chapter 5
[Some Sad and Happy Endings]

Bainbridge, John. *Garbo*. Garden City, NY, Doubleday, 1955.

Daniels, Bebe and Ben Lyon. *Life With the Lyons*. London, Odhams Press, 1953.

Durgnat, Raymond and John Kobal. *Greta Garbo*. N.Y., E.P. Dutton, 1965. Small "pictureback" book.

Fountain, Leatrice Gilbert (with John R. Maxim). *Dark Star*. N.Y., St. Martin's Press, 1985. Biography of John Gilbert by his daughter.

Love, Bessie. *From Hollywood With Love*. London, Hamish Hamilton, 1977.

⚘ Mix, Paul E. *The Life and Legend of Tom Mix.* New York, A.S. Barnes, 1972.

Moore, Colleen. *Silent Star.* New York, Doubleday, 1968.

Morella, Joe and Edward Z. Epstein. *The "It" Girl: The Incredible Story of Clara Bow.* New York, Delacorte, 1976.

Nunn, Curtis. *Marguerite Clark.* Fort Worth, Texas Christian University Press, 1981.

Stenn, David. *Clara Bow: Runnin' Wild.* N.Y., Doubleday, 1988.

Behlmer, Rudy. "Clara Bow." *Films in Review,* October 1963. Career study and filmography.

Corliss, Richard. "Greta Garbo." In Elisabeth Weis, *The Movie Star,* 1981.

Daniels, Bebe. "Why I Have Never Married." *Photoplay,* January 1924. Expectations of professional jealousy.

Fairbanks Jr., Douglas. "Greta Garbo." *Vanity Fair,* October 1930.

Fred. *"Mantrap," Variety,* July 14, 1926.

Gilbert, John. "Jack Gilbert Writes His Own Story." *Photoplay,* June to September 1928.

Mitchell, George. "Lon Chaney." *Films in Review,* December 1953.

Mix, Tom. "My Life Story," *Photoplay,* February, March, April 1945.

Pitkin, W.B. "Stars of Yesterday," *Woman's Home Companion,* November 1937. Francis X. Bushman now runs a hot dog stand.

Quirk, Lawrence J. "John Gilbert." *Films in Review,* March 1956. Biography and survey of films.

St. Johns, Adela Rogers. "Hail and Farewell." *Photoplay,* April 1926. Tribute to Barbara LaMarr.

Spears, Jack. "Colleen Moore." *Films in Review,* August/September 1963. Career and films.

Washburn, Beatrice. "Marguerite Clark Today." *Photoplay,* April 1925. Married to lumberman Harry Williams, living in Patterson, La.

York, Cal. "Gossip East and West." *Photoplay,* November 1923. Estrangement of Mary Minter and mother (Mrs. Shelby) after Taylor murder.

_____. "Gossip East and West." *Photoplay,* January 1926. Item: guest list for Charles Ray's farewell party.

Filmography

Available from the Museum of Modern Art on 16mm film:

The Lonedale Operator, 1911, 14 min. Blanche Sweet.
The New York Hat, 1912, 15 min. Mary Pickford.
The Mothering Heart, 1913, 30 min. Lillian Gish.
The Battle at Elderbush Gulch, 1914, 27 min. Lillian Gish, Robert Harron, Mae Marsh.
Judith of Bethulia, 1914, 68 min. Blanche Sweet, Henry Walthall, Mae Marsh, Robert Harron, Lillian and Dorothy Gish.
The Birth of a Nation, 1915, 180 min. Lillian Gish, Mae Marsh, Henry Walthall, Miriam Cooper, Robert Harron.
Intolerance, 1916, 170 min. Mae Marsh, Robert Harron.
The Mother and the Law, 1914/1919, 104 min. Mae Marsh, Robert Harron.
Broken Blossoms, 1919, 92 min. Lillian Gish, Richard Barthelmess, Donald Crisp.
True Heart Susie, 1919, 86 min. Lillian Gish, Robert Harron.
The White Rose, 1923, 136 min. Mae Marsh, Carol Dempster.

A Fool There Was, 1914, 82 min. Theda Bara.
The Coward, 1915, 74 min. Charles Ray, Frank Keenan.
The Taking of Luke McVane, 1915, 29 min. William S. Hart.
Excuse My Dust, 1920, 68 min. Wallace Reid.
Tol'able David, 1921, 109 min. Richard Barthelmess.
Sky High, 1922, 66 min. Tom Mix.
The Marriage Circle, 1924, 118 min. Adolphe Menjou, Marie Prevost, Florence Vidor, Monte Blue.
Lady Windermere's Fan, 1925, 85 min. Ronald Colman, May McAvoy.
Hotel Imperial, 1927, 78 min. Pola Negri.
Seventh Heaven, 1927, 120 min. Charles Farrell, Janet Gaynor.

Wild and Woolly, 1917, 67 min. Douglas Fairbanks.
His Majesty the American, 1919, 114 min. Douglas Fairbanks.
When the Clouds Roll By, 1919, 93 min. Douglas Fairbanks.
The Mollycoddle, 1920, 94 min. Douglas Fairbanks.
The Mark of Zorro, 1920, 90 min. Douglas Fairbanks, Marguerite de la Motte.
The Nut, 1921, 86 min. Douglas Fairbanks.
Robin Hood, 1922, 121 min. Douglas Fairbanks, Enid Bennett.
The Thief of Bagdad, 1924, 135 min. Douglas Fairbanks.
Don Q, Son of Zorro, 1925, 113 min. Douglas Fairbanks, Mary Astor.
The Gaucho, 1928, 100 min. Douglas Fairbanks, Lupe Velez.

The Iron Mask, 1929, 98 min. Douglas Fairbanks, Marguerite de la Motte.

Teddy at the Throttle, 1917, 22 min. Gloria Swanson, Wallace Beery, Bobby Vernon.

Male and Female, 1919, 133 min. Gloria Swanson, Thomas Meighan, Lila Lee, Bebe Daniels.

Blood and Sand, 1922, 113 min. Rudolph Valentino, Lila Lee, Nita Naldi.

Monsieur Beaucaire, 1924, 106 min. Rudolph Valentino, Bebe Daniels, Lois Wilson.

Blackhawk Films (a subsidiary of Republic Pictures) have had in recent years a valuable few of the Mary Pickford films:

A Poor Little Rich Girl, 1917, 64 min.
Rebecca of Sunnybrook Farm, 1917, 77 min.
Pollyana, 1920, 60 min.
Little Annie Rooney, 1925, 60 min.
Sparrows, 1926, 75 min.
My Best Girl,, 1927, 78 min.
The Taming of the Shrew, 1929, 66 min.

According to the 1990 *Bowker Home Video Directory* (1989 title, *Variety's Complete Home Video Directory)* the following were available from various sources, notably *Video Yesteryear:*

Richard Barthelmess: *Broken Blossoms, Tol'able David, Way Down East.*

Clara Bow: *Down to the Sea in Ships, Wings.*

Betty Compson: *The Great Gabbo, Inside the Lines, These Girls Won't Talk, The Invisible Ghost.*

Bebe Daniels: *Dangerous Female, Feel My Pulse, 42d Street.*

Douglas Fairbanks: *His Picture in the Papers, The Matrimaniac, Reaching for the Moon, Wild and Woolly, The Mark of Zorro, Don Q--Son of Zorro, The Iron Mask, The Thief of Bagdad, The Taming of the Shrew, The Private Life of Don Juan.*

Charles Farrell: *Sunny Side Up, Old Ironsides.*

William S. Hart: *The Disciple, The Taking of Luke McVane, Hell's Hinges, The Narrow Trail, The Return of Draw Egan, Three Word Brand, Tumbleweeds.*

Bessie Love: *Broadway Melody, The Lost World.*

Colleen Moore: *Ella Cinders, The Scarlet Letter, These Girls Won't Talk.*

Esther Ralston: *Lonely Wives, The Marriage Circle, Old Ironsides, Shadows of the Orient.*

Gloria Swanson: *Airport 1975, Queen Kelly, Indiscreet, Sadie Thompson, Sunset Boulevard.*

Rudolph Valentino: *Blood and Sand, The Eagle, The Eyes of Youth, Son of the Sheik.*

This is manifestly an unsatisfactory situation—some of these pictures are listed only in case someone wants to see what the performer looked like. The seeker for videocassettes of silent movies has a hard time of it, and until some dedicated group brings together all the news on the existence of archive films and helps to make them available to a wider public, the silent cinema buff cannot even know what he can see sometime in the future.

Many other titles exist and are available through various channels, including exchange lists in fan papers like *Classic Images*. One can see Clara Bow in *It*, *Dancing Mothers*, and perhaps other films. John Gilbert can be seen in the sound film, *Queen Christina* and M-G-M's films under Ted Turner's ownership include *The Big Parade, Flesh and the Devil*, and others. Gloria Swanson in *Manhandled* is out there somewhere, and *Fine Manners*, along with a good many other films of interest are "viewing prints" available for scholars in the Library of Congress collection. The lesser people have been poorly served.

Meanwhile there are such compilations as *Mr. Super Athletic Charm*, a 56 minute part of a History of Motion Picture series from Blackhawk, including Fairbanks footage from *The Black Pirate*. Another such Blackhawk contribution is *The Birth of a Legend* (1984, 24 min) about Pickford and Fairbanks "when they reigned as king and queen of the movies in 1926." A nonfiction short, *Abroad With Doug and Mary*, (1921) may be seen at the Museum of Modern Art.

Available from HBO Home Video for sale by individual 52-minute program is the series of thirteen by David Gill and Kevin Brownlow called *Hollywood*. Number 6 is on Swanson and Valentino, and number 12 is called "The Star Treatment."

Index

[This index does not cover footnotes, cast lists, filmographies, lists of names, picture captions, the preface, or the appendices.]

Film Titles